ADORNO'S NIETZSCHEAN NARRATIVES

D1614450

ADORNO'S NIETZSCHEAN NARRATIVES

CRITIQUES OF IDEOLOGY, READINGS OF WAGNER

———

Karin Bauer

State University of New York Press

Published by
State University of New York Press, Albany

© 1999 State University of New York

Printed in the United States of America

For information, address
State University of New York Press, State
University Plaza, Albany, N.Y., 12246

Production by Dale Cotton
Marketing by Anne M. Valentine

Library of Congress Cataloging-in-Publication Data

Bauer, Karin, 1958–
    Adorno's Nietzschean narratives : critiques of ideology, readings
of Wagner / Karin Bauer.
        p.   cm.
    Includes bibliographical references (p.   ) and index.
    ISBN 0-7914-4279-9 (hc. : alk. paper). — ISBN 0-7914-4280-2 (pbk.
: alk. paper)
    1. Adorno, Theodor W., 1903–1969. 2. Nietzsche, Friedrich
Wilhelm, 1844–1900. I. Title.
B3199.A34B378 1999
193—dc21   98-17953
                                                                           CIP

10 9 8 7 6 5 4 3 2 1

For Elena Friederike Kennedy,
and in memory of
Erika Bauer and Ernst Behler

CONTENTS

ACKNOWLEDGMENTS

It is impossible to express the depth of my gratitude for the intellectual endowment, encouragement, generosity, professionalism, friendship, and laughter of Professor Ernst Behler, who inspired and supervised the dissertation out of which this book has arisen. His recent death has left a void in my life.

For their generous assistance I thank my father and his wife.

I am indebted to the following scholars for sharing their knowledge and expertise and/or providing support and encouragement: Diana Behler, Peter Daly, Leslie Eliason, Bruno Hillebrand, Andrea Gogröf-Voorhees, Richard Gray, Jacques Le Rider, Imke Meyer, Jeffrey Peck, George Peters, Brigitte Prutti, Jens Rieckmann, Sabine Wilke, and Karin Wurst. Many others cannot be named here. I thank them collectively.

A special thanks goes to the witty, funny, strong, and outrageous "free spirits" Martina, Marie Anna, Tiphaine, and Andi, who enriched my life immeasurably, and to Karin, Monika, Shirley, and Minky for their loyalty and friendship.

I thank Matthew Pollard and Cathrin Winkelmann for their good humor, dedication, and help in preparing this manuscript. I am grateful for the financial support from McGill University and the University of Washington and for the kindness and support of my colleagues and the graduate students at the Department of German Studies at McGill University.

Finally, I would like to thank Jim and Elena for their love.

I am grateful to the following publishers for granting permission to use the following materials:

From *On the Genealogy of Morals* by Friedrich Nietzsche, translated by Walter Kaufmann and R. J. Hollingdale. Copyright 1967 by Random House. Inc. Reprinted by permission of Random House, Inc.

From *Beyond Good and Evil* by Friedrich Nietzsche, translated by Walter Kaufmann. Copyright 1966 by Random House, Inc. Reprinted by permission of Random House, Inc.

From *The Birth of Tragedy and the Case of Wagner* by Friedrich Nietzsche, translated by Walter Kaufmann. Copyright 1967 by Random House, Inc. Reprinted by permission of Random House, Inc.

From *The Gay Science* by Friedrich Nietzsche, translated by Walter Kaufmann. Copyright 1974 by Random House, Inc. Reprinted by permission of Random House, Inc.

From *Human, All Too Human* by Friedrich Nietzsche, translated by R. J. Hollingdale. Copyright by Cambridge University Press. Reprinted by permission of Cambridge University Press.

From "Twilight of the Idols" by Friedrich Nietzsche, "Nietzsche Contra Wagner" by Friedrich Nietzsche, edited by Walter Kaufmann, "On Truth and Lie in an Extra-Moral Sense" by Friedrich Nietzsche, from *The Portable Nietzsche* by Walter Kaufmann, editor, translated by Walter Kaufmann. Translation copyright 1954 by Viking Press, renewed © 1982 by Viking Penguin Inc. Reprinted by permission of Viking Penguin, a division of Penguin Putnam Inc.

From *Dialectics of Enlightenment* by Max Horkheimer and Theodor Adorno. English translation copyright 1972 by Herder and Herder, Inc. Reprinted by permission of the Continuum Publishing Company.

From *Negative Dialectics*, by Theodor Adorno. English translation copyright 1973 by the Continuum Publishing Company. Reprinted by permission of the Continuum Publishing Company.

From *Notes to Literature*, Vols. 1 and 2, by Theodor W. Adorno. Copyright 1991, 1992 by Columbia University Press. Reprinted by permission of the Columbia University Press.

From "Adorno in Reverse: From Hollywood to Richard Wagner" by Andreas Huyssen in *New German Critique* 29 (Spring/Summer 1983). Copyright by Telo Press. Reprinted by permission of Telos Press.

From *The Philosophical Discourse of Modernity* by Jürgen Habermas, translated by Frederick Lawrence. English translation copyright 1987 by MIT Press and Suhrkamp Verlag. Reprinted by permission of MIT Press and Suhrkamp Verlag.

From *Minima Moralia: Reflections on Damaged Life* by Theodor W. Adorno, translated by E. F. N. Jephcott. English translation copyright 1974 by New Left Books, 1978 by Verso. Reprinted by permission of Verso.

From *In Search of Wagner* by Theodor W. Adorno, translated Rodney Livingstone. English Translation Copyright 1981 by NLB. Reprinted by permission of Verso.

INTRODUCTION

Adorno's Nietzsche

No figure in the German history of ideas has been received with such critical and creative vigor as Friedrich Nietzsche. The range of interpretation is as diverse and contradictory as Nietzsche's philosophy, and the reception of Nietzsche by the Frankfurt School is no exception. As part of the Frankfurt School's formulation of a critical theory of society, Nietzsche was often brought forward as a witness to the multidimensional critiques of the ideological aspects of cultural phenomena. Critical theory was conceived as an interdisciplinary approach toward the analysis and immanent critique of societal processes. As a combination of philosophy and social science, it sought to integrate historical materialism, elements of psychoanalysis, and themes of the critiques of rationality and ideology. In the works of some Frankfurt theorists, Nietzsche's philosophy reappears as a counterweight to the Enlightenment tradition, creating a productive tension with the works of Kant, Hegel, Marx, Weber, and Freud. The incorporation of these various intellectual traditions has increased critical theory's visibility within various disciplines while simultaneously exposing it to both constructive criticism and misinterpretation. Critical theory's appropriation of Nietzsche is a case in point. His influence can not only be felt in the theses, themes, and motifs of critical theory, but also in the structures of thought, dynamics of argumentation, fragmentary presentation, and styles of articulation. While contributing to critical theory's complexity and breadth, Nietzsche's legacy has hindered the work of the Frankfurt School from gaining wider recognition within the social sciences. Gillian Rose argues that this inheritance from non-Marxist critical traditions has itself never been widely understood even within Germany. While increasing the Frankfurt School's appeal, this inheritance prevented "the work of the School from having a more cogent and continual impact on sociology."[1] More concretely, it has provoked attacks on critical theory from all parts of the political and academic spectrum; however, in the wake of postmodernism and the revival of Nietzsche, the combination of various traditions of thought has also contributed to the renewed interest in critical theory in many areas of the humanities. The Frankfurt School's Nietzsche reception has become an issue in the various contemporary debates about modernity and postmodernity and such related issues as, for example, the contested oppositions between hermeneutics and deconstruction, between normative standards and relativism, between communicative rationality and poststructuralism, and finally between popular culture and high art. Jürgen Habermas's *The Philosophical Discourse of Modernity* (1988) is but one of the most prominent examples of this contentious discourse.

Theodor W. Adorno's lifelong occupation with Nietzsche's thought attests to its impact upon critical theory. Adorno was one of the most philosophically and artistically minded theoreticians of the Frankfurt School, and his reception of Nietzsche is marked by an acute sensitivity toward the critical potential of Nietzsche's thought. Adorno conceives Nietzsche as one of the most radical enlighteners and critics of enlightenment and sympathizes with Nietzsche's interest in the reevaluation of all values. Both Adorno's and Nietzsche's examinations and reevaluations of the history of rationality and of the tradition of enlightenment share a common emphasis on the realm of the aesthetic. Their critiques of values and postulated truths consistently refer back to art, which functions as an integral and integrating element in all of Nietzsche's and Adorno's criticism. Their mode of criticism stands in opposition to the modern emphasis on rationality, which culminates in the antiphilosophical and anti-aesthetic obsession with facts and positivistic data. Both see the state of art and culture as symptomatic for the larger ills of society, and both analyze art and the various artistic trends in view of their implications for society as a whole. Their criticism reaffirms the twofold importance of the aesthetic experience: firstly, it offers an alternative mode of perception and manner of gaining knowledge and experience, and secondly, it also counters the marginalization of art not only in philosophy but also in everyday life. Adorno and Nietzsche resist the promotion of the rational order of things at the expense of art and are also unwilling to exclude art from social criticism as the Other of reason. Beyond the reaffirmation of art and their shared affinity for music, Nietzsche's and Adorno's philosophical projects are firmly situated within the realm of aesthetics, and their critiques of aesthetics function simultaneously as critiques of ideology and society. Adorno not only uses Nietzsche's texts as testimony for his own conceptualizations for a critique of rationality, morality, and art, but also appreciates Nietzsche's stylistic and formal efforts to overcome the limits of his own thought.

In the *Dialectic of Enlightenment*, Max Horkheimer and Adorno note that Nietzsche's thought, along with Kant's and de Sade's, is the "merciless" culmination of enlightenment.[2] Nietzsche, according to Horkheimer and Adorno, "was one of the few after Hegel who recognized the dialectic of enlightenment."[3] Although Horkheimer's position toward Nietzsche is much more ambivalent than Adorno's, he shares his colleague's respect for Nietzsche as one of the great philosophers in history. Horkheimer saw in Nietzsche the only great mind who gained insight and freedom from illusions in the thick bourgeois fog setting in at the middle of the last century.[4] The second "Excursus" of the *Dialectic*, "Juliette or Enlightenment and Morality," which, according to Gretel Adorno, was mainly written by Horkheimer, contains the *Dialectic*'s most ambiguous portrait of Nietzsche. Here Nietzsche appears in connection with the justification of violence and sadism. While Nietzsche's thought is celebrated as the completion of enlightenment, the judgments about his claims to amorality and the evaluation of his critique of enlightenment ideals, presented as being entwined with the fictional texts of Sade, exhibit an ambiguity toward Nietzsche not normally present in Adorno's work. Norbert Rath points out that the *Dialectic* does indeed contain two competing Nietzsche interpretations, eventually arriving at the conclusion that the authorship of the various chapters of the *Dialectic* was not as communal as Adorno and Horkheimer had claimed. To be sure, Adorno is not uncritical toward Nietzsche's philosophy. While he admires Nietzsche for his uncompromising critique of society, he also criticizes him for remaining trapped in theological and metaphysical prejudices characteristic of the nineteenth century. Adorno's ties to Nietzsche cannot be assessed merely on the basis of his agreement with Nietzsche's thought, but must be further considered within the context of the categories, attitudes, and performative features which he shares with him.[5]

To present Nietzsche's thought in the context of Adorno's critical theory is an ambitious enterprise. Such an enterprise can be neither a systematic influence study nor an exploration of all the possible angles from which the relationship between Nietzsche and Adorno could be viewed. The task of the present study is not to compare the two thinkers, but to map out some shared terrain and to point out how the philosopher Adorno idiosyncratically and uniquely molds Nietzsche's thought. Nietzsche himself warns his readers about the risks of comparing two thinkers; if mediation is the goal of the comparison, a quest for similarities often becomes the imposition of a forced identity, which subsequently leads to a neglect of important differences. Adorno cites Nietzsche's aphorism 228 from the third book of *The Gay Science* in *Minima Moralia*:

> "He who seeks to mediate between two bold thinkers . . . stamps himself as mediocre: he has not the eye to see uniqueness: to perceive resemblances everywhere, making everything alike, is a sign of weak eyesight."[6]

Adorno could not agree more with Nietzsche's assessment that the desire to level differences is an expression of mediocrity. Moreover, for Adorno it is an issue of integrity, the morality of thought, which urges the thinker to use a "procedure that is neither entrenched nor detached, neither blind nor empty, neither atomistic nor consequential."[7] Throughout his entire oeuvre Adorno advocates the non-identical and opposes false reconciliations that seek to cover up differences. His criticism engages in subtle differentiations, often at the expense of stylistic clarity. His unresolved contradictions demonstrate how he attempts to do justice to the object under examination, while simultaneously reflecting upon the position of the subject's consciousness. In the simultaneous process of "'pure looking-on'" and consideration for the phenomena's relation to consciousness, reflection "expresses this morality most directly and in all its depth of contradiction."[8] While stylistic and argumentative clarity must remain the goal of the present study, it will keep in mind the risks involved in comparisons and will try to avoid the establishment of forced identities and the leveling of differences.

Thus, in attempting to escape as much as possible the symptoms of weak eyesight, this study takes Adorno's morality of thinking into account and avoids a totalizing comparison. It delineates themes and motifs common to both thinkers and makes visible the productive tensions between their works. Nietzsche's and Adorno's preoccupation with the critique of rationality, metaphysics, morality, and modern culture brings forth pressing issues of importance to contemporary thinkers and testifies to the continual relevance of their work. Similar to the way in which he challenges some philosophers of postmodernism, Nietzsche represents an intellectual challenge to Adorno. Adorno incorporates elements of Nietzsche's thought into his own theories without being concerned with smoothing out the discrepancies and incongruities within Nietzsche's work or minimizing those complications arising from the constellation of Nietzsche, Marx, Freud, Hegel, and the other elements contributing to critical theory. Adorno's texts show that his critique aims neither to pacify differences nor to harmoniously integrate various critical traditions and theories, but rather to operate within the contradictions and paradoxes of various disparate elements and to transform the resulting tensions into a productive form of criticism.

Nietzsche's and Adorno's radicalized critiques of modernity strive to lay bare the ideologies underlying human existence. They reject dogmas and absolutes and question moral values and categories and explanations, such as identity, origin, telos, substance, and appearance, as institutionalized narratives created to establish a rational order of things. Constructed to legitimize claims to power, these concepts perpetuate notions of continuity, progress, and absolute truth. By acknowledging the limits of thought and the potential for error and both the repressive-regressive and progressive-emancipatory dimensions of values and norms, Nietzsche's perspectivism turns, like Adorno's negative-dialectical thought, to the undogmatic reevaluation of all values. Both contend that the traditional concept of rationality is bankrupt and has been reduced to forms of instrumental reason: a reason utilized for the purpose of self-preservation and the legitimation of claims to power. Modern rationality is dominated by logic and numbers, while the reductionist approaches of positivism operate in the name of science and technology. Nietzsche argues against theoretical men and Socratism, Adorno against commodification and instrumental reason.

Nietzsche's thought represents for Adorno a model for a materialist critique of society that includes art as an essential element of criticism. Their critiques of enlightenment rely upon an analysis of culture and hold out the hope of art as a source of knowledge and understanding. Tied to their materialist critiques are the rejection of metaphysics and the refusal to ground their philosophies upon first or final principles. They reject teleological thought and refuse to construct a concrete and positive utopian model. The utopian dimension of their thought can be located only in their negativity, and in their radical and self-reflexive renunciation of metaphysical principles and social ideologies. Adorno admires Nietzsche, whose "imperious tone" others have tried to imitate, for refusing to sanction the world as it is.[9] This is indeed no small compliment from a thinker who persistently pointed out the dialectics of negation and affirmation and labored hard to outwit the spirit of "heinous affirmation."[10] Nietzsche's and Adorno's critiques are not based on a systematic explication of the wrongs in society; the importance of Nietzsche for Adorno resides as much in his fluid form as in the varied subjects of Nietzsche's criticism. In the writings of both Nietzsche and Adorno, the rejection of systematization finds its parallel in the stylistic refusal of totality. Adorno's stylistic considerations come to the foreground especially in *Minima Moralia* and "The Essay as Form," in which matters of style play an explicit role and his stylistic "engagement with Nietzsche is most evident."[11] Adorno places as much emphasis on the style and method of his criticism as on its content. The potential for criticism lies as much in what is said as in how it is presented. Method and style define the "relation between ideas and the composition of texts"; they present seminal ideas and "are not devices imposed on material in order to organize and explain it."[12] In other words, both Adorno and Nietzsche recognize and emphasize the performative dimension of their critiques. They not only argumentatively advocate an expanded concept of rationality, but also demonstrate it in their writings, and their antisystematic impulses reach beyond the mere conceptual criticism of metaphysics. They enact their criticism by resorting to an aphoristic, essayistic, and ironic style of writing. This concern with the aesthetics of criticism and philosophy is shared by many contemporary thinkers who struggle to find modes of expression appropriate to their thought—often, as in Adorno's case, at the risk of lapses in communication.

Adorno's preoccupation with Nietzsche is evident in his early as well as his later work. In the forties, he refers to him more explicitly than in his later works. *Minima Moralia* and *Dialectic of Enlightenment*, for example, contain more direct references to Nietzsche than any of his other works. Not including "Excursus II" of the *Dialectic*, for which Max Horkheimer is mainly responsible, *Min-*

ima Moralia is also the text most influenced by and most critical of Nietzsche. In the course of his works, Adorno makes many remarks about misinterpretations and misrepresentations of Nietzsche by fascists, anti-intellectuals, vitalists, and existentialists. As was the case with many of his contemporaries, Adorno's interest in Nietzsche is enhanced by the tragedy of the latter's personal life, which is seen by many as exemplifying the contradictory and self-destructive nature of modernity. The critical assessment of his work is mixed with the fascination toward a philosopher who apparently philosophized himself into madness, oscillating between the virulent negation of all existing values and norms and the stubborn affirmation of life. Walter Benjamin, Thomas Mann, Herbert Marcuse, and Adorno were among those readers of Nietzsche who undertook pilgrimages to Sils Maria, where Nietzsche spent several summers. Benjamin appreciates Nietzsche's critique of Wagner, but is not equally enthusiastic about his other works. In a letter to friends he remains noncommittal about Nietzsche, and withholds his as yet undetermined judgment.[13] Nietzsche's impact upon the works of Thomas Mann, who wrote about and referred to him extensively, has been thoroughly documented.[14] Mann suggested that in his case it would be up to those of his critics who feel up to such a task to examine the inclusion and transformation of Nietzsche's thought, ethos, and artistry in his own work.[15] Not only was Nietzsche's life exemplary for the portrayal of the modern artist and musician Adrian Leverkühn in *Dr. Faustus*, but also his essayistic style, irony, and critique of art and decadence were of singular importance to him. As a contemporary critic of Nietzsche and Wagner, Adorno was also not without influence on Mann's *Faustus* project. In his book on the writing of *Dr. Faustus*, Mann acknowledges Adorno's invaluable contributions to his novel and especially to the central chapter, the meeting between Leverkühn and the devil. According to Mann, Adorno was the "strange mind" that provided the artistic-sociological perspective and the theoretical background for the excursus on music; coupling an extensive knowledge of music with a style of "doom" evocative of Nietzsche and Karl Kraus, Adorno's writings convinced Mann that he must recruit Adorno's expert advice.[16]

Adorno shared with Mann a fascination with Nietzsche's life, and, like many scholars of his generation, was drawn to the place where Nietzsche spent the last years of his life before his breakdown. His brief essay, entitled "Aus Sils Maria," concerns a trip Adorno undertook to Sils Maria accompanied by Herbert Marcuse.[17] Written in an essayistic style, but nonetheless divided into twelve short, interrelated paragraphs evoking aphorisms, Adorno's piece pays tribute to both Nietzsche and his own *Dialectic of Enlightenment*. Poetically and metaphorically, he paints a melancholy portrait of the landscape, the town, and the tragic figure of Nietzsche. The mountainous heights of the Engardin bring to the spectator a different spatial and temporal experience. When he describes the ever-shifting view of and from the mountains and connects the landscape to Nietzsche's thought processes, Adorno alludes to Nietzsche's perspectivism and his notion of the pathos of distance. As evidenced by Nietzsche's insistence upon a physiology of art and thought, Adorno's connection between thought and the environment moves along Nietzschean grounds, for Nietzsche saw himself in constant interaction with nature and postulated an interdependence between physical conditions and thought processes. Artistic and philosophical creations are, in Nietzsche's view, influenced and even determined by the conditions of their production and are dependent upon such factors as climate and diet. As a physiological function, thinking stands in direct relation to the state of mind, the condition of the body, and the physical surroundings of the thinker. Considered in light of Nietzsche's state of ill-health, his physiology of art and thought might well be connected to his own experience of suffering and its impact upon his work.

Adorno contends in his essay that standing high above the village empowers the spectator; seen from the top of the mountains, the villages of the Alps resemble toys, whose apparently diminutive size hold out to the viewer's imagination the pleasure and possibility of doing with them what one pleases. The landscape is one of extremes, allowing no middle ground for humanity. It exhibits the scars of men's domination of nature and serves as the model, witness, and victim of the dialectic of enlightenment. The piles of industrial waste lie next to scenes of untainted nature, conceived as a reconciling force destroyed by civilization. The unpaved road through these opposing images represents the philosophy of culture.[18] The whistles of the gophers are frightening, mechanical sounds of terror that are no longer expressions of life but of death. Terrorized by the intrusion by civilization in the form of campgrounds, the animals flee deeper into the mountains. The expressionless landscape, which exhibits a transcendental sadness, parallels the animals' lack of expression. Adorno describes the cows wandering contentedly on the path made by human beings, who created the path without consideration for the animals. These paths are a model for the possibility of a civilization that comes to the "aid" of nature.[19] Civilization also intrudes upon the sky, and Adorno "must" watch the Sputnik from the roof of a house in Sils Maria. Had it not staggered in its course, Adorno states, one would be unable to distinguish the Sputnik from a star or from the planet Venus. This is the stuff of humanity's victories: what is used for the domination of the cosmos and the realization of dreams, appears dreamlike, crooked, powerless, and as if it were inclined to fall.[20]

Testimony to the domination of nature, Sils Maria's landscape and sky thus become Adorno's metaphors for Nietzsche's struggles with the world and with himself. The village marks and is marked by the passage of time: in Sils Maria Nietzsche becomes a historical figure largely forgotten by its inhabitants. The house in which Nietzsche lived is marked by a tacky inscription, but shows nonetheless how one could live honorably with little money in Nietzsche's times. He could still buy his intellectual independence by living very modestly.[21] What was then possible for Nietzsche is no longer possible for intellectuals now, because in our times it would be seen as degrading to live in relative poverty.[22]

Adorno ends his essay with an anecdote about the local children, who apparently put rocks into Nietzsche's ubiquitous red umbrella, which he even used in good weather, presumably as protection against the sun and his recurring headaches. Upon opening the umbrella, the rocks supposedly fell on his head, and he pursued the children. This was the sole detail Adorno could elicit from the only person in Sils Maria who could still remember Nietzsche. The old man was one of the children who put the rocks in the red umbrella, and he could not remember anything else about Nietzsche. The man was disappointed when his guests were not interested in his recounting of a visit to Sils Maria by Queen Victoria. Adorno's story adds yet another dimension to Jacques Derrida's speculations about the significance of Nietzsche's note stating "I have forgotten my umbrella."[23] Beyond the Freudian symbolism and the Heideggerian metaphor for *Seinsvergessenheit*, the forgetfulness of being, might linger the struggle for self-preservation, which he ultimately lost. By forgetting his umbrella, Nietzsche risks a headache caused by exposure to the sun; however, by remembering to take his umbrella, he exposes himself to headaches caused by falling rocks.

Adorno feels compassion for the difficult situation of the suffering philosopher, who might, in the end, have to endorse the actions of the children because they represent the struggle of life against the spirit of the intellect, the confrontation between *Leben* and *Geist*. Alluding to Nietzsche's denunciation of pity, Adorno speculates that the experience of a very real lack of compassion from the children might have resulted in Nietzsche's irritation with some of his own philosophical theorems.[24] Adorno's remarks evoke Thomas Mann's critique of Nietzsche, which postulates two great and interconnected errors in Nietzsche's thought: asserting the privileging of instinct over the intellect and the opposition of life to morality. Adorno shares Mann's view that these features of Nietzsche's thought are part of a historically outdated reaction to the primacy of rationality and rationalism.

In Adorno's essay, "life," as represented by the children, attacks *Geist* in the figure of Nietzsche and confronts him with a practical application of his own teachings, namely his plea for amorality. Adorno's ironic mention of the apparent gap between theory and real life brings to mind Adorno's own conflict-ridden relationship to praxis. The relationship between theory and practice became an issue in Adorno's confrontations with political activists and their Marxist call for action. He had been personally and professionally confronted with the question of praxis not only during the Nazi period in Germany, but also toward the end of his life during the student revolts of the sixties. Many student activists no longer accepted the division between theory and practice and demanded that theory provide strategies of action. Adorno was accused of fleeing from the political arena into aesthetics and pure thought. In his defense, Adorno enlists the help of Nietzsche, who, according to Adorno, had recognized the failure of a mandate for total *praxis*. Nietzsche thus serves as Adorno's predecessor for a critique of a concept of praxis turning into a form of domination. As Horkheimer explains it,

Nietzsche withdrew from the call for action, as conceptualized by many of his contemporaries, and instead expanded the established categories of praxis. Nietzsche realized that the term *praxis* could not adequately delineate the actual difference between a barbaric and civilized world. The moment of truth in Nietzsche's philosophy occurs precisely at the point at which he does not issue instructions, because the forms of domination tend to reproduce themselves when *praxis* takes on a defining and comprehensive role.[25]

On the 153rd anniversary of the French Revolution, a group of exiled German intellectuals, including Adorno, Horkheimer, and Herbert and Ludwig Marcuse, gathered in Los Angeles to discuss the failure of enlightenment and socialism in light of the rise of fascism. Adorno mobilizes Nietzsche for a radicalized critique and exposure of the ideological elements of socialism. Horkheimer recognized that specific elements of Nietzsche's theory were true, in that he saw not only how democracy, but also how socialism had become an ideology. For Horkheimer, the challenge was to reformulate socialism without its ideological character, and in certain critical issues Nietzsche can be seen as having gone further than Marx.[26]

While some Marxist critics view Nietzsche as a protofascist, as an irrationalist, and a philosopher of the ruling class, others see him as the most rigorous antimetaphysical thinker to expose structures of power and domination. Adorno belongs to the latter group, while Herbert Marcuse in the anniversary discussion echoes the view of many Marxists when he insists that Nietzsche could not be reconciled with Marxism: if Marx was right, he argues, then Nietzsche was wrong.[27] Of course, between these two extremes there exist as many shades of interpretation as there are critics. Although Nietzsche asserted repeatedly that his philosophy was apolitical in its content and intentions, calling himself the last antipolitical German,[28] many Nietzsche interpretations nonetheless evaluate the political content and implications of his thought. The framework for such analyses usually examines the protofascist or antifascist and the regressive or emancipatory potential in Nietzsche's works. Karol Sauerland argues that Adorno does not share Bertolt Brecht's view that scientists and artists are responsible for the consequences of their experiments, discoveries, and theories. In Sauerland's opinion, Adorno is accordingly unwilling to accuse extraordinary minds, such as Nietzsche, Schönberg, and Oppenheimer, of having contributed to the dehumanization of modern civilization.[29] On the contrary, Adorno comes to their defense.

Interestingly enough, the political orientation of the critics seems to have little bearing upon the evaluation of Nietzsche's political views and his relationship to fascist thought. Critics from both the political right and left see Nietzsche as a fascist visionary who provided the philosophical basis and justification for the total breakdown of humanism. Many Marxist critics continue the tradition of Georg Lukács's interpretation of Nietzsche, which claims that Nietzsche is a modern irrationalist who destroyed reason and morality. There are many similarities, for instance, between Lukács's and Jürgen Habermas's critical strategies in their critique of Nietzsche, although the latter's critique is more perceptive and differentiated than Lukács's. Adorno's estimation of Nietzsche belongs clearly to the antifascist tradition of critics, a configuration that includes Thomas Mann as well as Nietzsche translator Walter Kaufmann and the editors Mazzino Montinari and Giorgio Colli, who see Nietzsche as a diagnostician and potential opponent of the developments and tendencies leading to fascism. Their investigations of Nietzsche's thought are in line with Max Scheler's and Karl Jaspers's early-twentieth-century receptions. Scheler's interpretation of the Nietzschean concept of *ressentiment* as a creative force in modern labor relates not only to Adorno's interest in utilizing Nietzsche for a critique of capitalism, but also to the investigations of postmodern philosophers, such as Gilles Deleuze and Michel Foucault.[30] Despite the controversy surrounding Heidegger's relationship to fascism, his lectures continue to influence the interpretations of the New Nietzsche. Heidegger perceives Nietzsche as the summit and end of philosophy and by entwining and thinking together the eternal recurrence and the will to power, Heidegger wants to bring Nietzsche's thought to its self-realization.[31] Although he conceives of Nietzsche's thought as the reversal of Platonism and the end of metaphysics, he nevertheless attempts to ground Nietzsche's thought. In Heidegger's work the will to power becomes the doctrine and foundation upon which Nietzsche's entire philosophy rests.

Adorno sharply questions the ontotheological foundationalism in the thought of Heidegger and contends that this motif is also present in Jaspers's work on Nietzsche. Adorno's *Jargon of Authenticity* contains his most pointed critique of Heidegger and existentialist ontology. Nietzsche, Adorno contends, did not live long enough to experience the disgust with this jargon, which seeks to reconstruct an original meaning. As a *ressentiment* phenomenon *par excellence*, the jargon of authenticity gives, by Adorno's account, a new meaning to Nietzsche's "it does not smell good."[32] Like Adorno, Jaspers finds the work of Kierkegaard pivotal for the unfolding of modernity. For Jaspers, Nietzsche represented modernity in a somersaulting fashion. Nietzsche and Kierkegaard ran modernity into the ground, and "overcame it by living it through to the end."[33] Jaspers identified Nietzsche's break with metaphysics as the end of modernity. The latter's antisystematic questioning of reason recognizes Being only as infinite interpretation and engages, according to Jaspers's understanding, in unlimited and infinite reflection, which can neither exhaust nor stop itself. Kierkegaard and Nietzsche did not oppose reflection in order to annihilate it, but rather in order to overcome it by limitlessly engaging in it and mastering it.[34] This mode of thought is an "endlessly active dialectic, the condition of freedom. It breaks out of every prison of the finite."[35]

Although Adorno is also thoroughly impressed by Kierkegaard's and Nietzsche's antisystematic and antimetaphysical efforts, he does not share Jaspers's view that they mark a definitive end to metaphysics or modernity. While he sees

Nietzsche's thought as completing enlightenment and in some respects as a turning point in the Western philosophical tradition, Adorno also criticizes Nietzsche for remaining caught within that same tradition. On the one hand, Adorno maintains that Nietzsche expresses the strongest argument against theology and metaphysics, while he claims on the other that Nietzsche's critique never reached the last stage of appeal. Nietzsche's concepts of *amor fati*, the *Übermensch*, and his view of women are but some examples of his unsuccessful escape from conventionality and tradition. Adorno makes the further claim that Nietzsche reverts to myth when he advocates, for instance, the concept of master-slave morality.

For Adorno, Jaspers's belief that Kierkegaard marks the overcoming of modernity overestimates the latter's impact. Whereas Nietzsche, despite his setbacks, is a turning point in the history of ideas, Kierkegaard remains trapped in idealism. Although Kierkegaard's works make the first steps out of metaphysics, he does not escape them. In his habilitation thesis, which was published under the title *Kierkegaard: Construction of the Aesthetic*, Adorno approaches Kierkegaard through a mode of criticism that simultaneously attempts to de(con)struct Kierkegaard's work and to rescue it. Adorno characterizes Kierkegaard's philosophy as a form of late idealism and contends that Kierkegaard's concept of objectless interiority or inwardness expresses yet another yearning for an absolute and transcendent truth. Kierkegaard turns Hegel inward, and while Hegel focuses on world history, Kierkegaard concerns himself with the individual. In contrast to Nietzsche, Kierkegaard advocates a philosophy of subjectivity and inwardness. For Adorno, this retreat into interiority is unacceptable, because "the whole philosophy of inwardness, with its professed contempt for the world, is the last sublimation of the brutal, barbaric lore whereby he who was there first has the greatest rights; the priority of the self is as untrue as that of all who feel at home where they live."[36] By rejecting the historical world, Kierkegaard became an accomplice to the reification he had frequently denounced; his dialectics were objectless and were thus "a return to the idealism he claimed to have left behind."[37] However, Adorno found in the aesthetic realm a possibility of reclaiming Kierkegaard from existentialism and theology by reconstructing his thought against its own intentions. Adorno's advisor, Paul Tillich, remarked that Adorno's salvaging of the aesthetic in Kierkegaard indicates the path of Adorno's future philosophy, whose truth lies in the interpretation of a historic moment's smallest detail.[38] His rescue mission is the first demonstration of the mode of criticism that expresses itself most distinctly in Adorno's critical approach to Wagner. Despite strong reservations, he finds in Wagner's work a point at which Wagner can be rescued from the complete submergence into an ideology of modernism.

Adorno's interest in the smallest phenomena of a historical moment illustrates his struggle against all forms of domination and his attempt to expose the prevailing views of history, philosophy, and culture as ideological prejudices. As

Nietzsche indicates in his critique of morality, values are set and perpetuated in an effort to maintain or overturn power relationships. During the power struggle, the questions of when, where, how, and why certain values are created and privileged over others become forgotten. Their origins are related to the principles of exchange rather than to the purpose for which they are later used, or to the meaning later attached to them. Adorno follows Nietzsche's interest in reconsidering the functions of values and interpretations in search of that which is repressed in the struggle for meaning and power. Nietzsche and Adorno postulate that the perception of a definite purpose, value, meaning, and identity is misleading. For them, one way of looking beyond the immediate is to explore the multiple functions and exchange values of phenomena.

Nietzsche's critique of dialectics and logic and Adorno's project of establishing a negative dialectic, the latter of which entailing a critique of identity thinking, attempt to overcome the limits of rationality and reductive thinking in terms of opposition, dualities, and cause and effect. Both Nietzsche and Adorno sought to free their thought from the subjugation of reductive concepts and categories. Nietzsche's perspectivism and Adorno's negative dialectics aim to expose structures of domination and hierarchies by performing their anti-systematic and antitotalitarian tenets. Through their common refusal to ground their thought, by which they resisted traditional patterns and metaphysical and social hierarchies, Nietzsche and Adorno strove to avoid ideological traps and to uncover the forgotten, overlooked, and repressed Other. Combined with a radical skepticism, their mode of criticism leads to a fundamental crisis of legitimation. The radical critique of rationality, as performed by Nietzsche and Adorno, questions the very foundation of criticism and rational thought, and therefore presents what Habermas calls a performative contradiction. If what is considered reality or being is only a matter of interpretation with no grounding upon first principles, and if, furthermore, these interpretations are connected to the prevailing power relations, then how can philosophies, theories, and arguments be legitimized and privileged over and against one another without falling into relativism? The need for legitimization relates, according to Nietzsche and Adorno, directly to the desire for rational order and normativity. However, this desire is not rooted in reason, but rather in the will to self-preservation and the will to power. By attacking rationality as the foundation for human action and historical developments, Nietzsche's and Adorno's criticism turns against itself. As Adorno remarks, a thinker must at all times be "inside and outside" of things.[39] Consequently, the thinker must stand inside and outside of rationality as well, and criticism must be both immanent and transcendent. As a rational activity, criticism operates from the inside, while the self-reflective critique of criticism and rationality must transcend the limits imposed upon itself by reason. Criticism thus performs a peculiar gesture similar to that of Baron Münchhausen, who hoists himself out of the swamp by his own pigtail.[40]

HABERMAS'S NIETZSCHE

The self-contradictory critique of rationality leads Habermas to establish a connection between Adorno, Horkheimer, Nietzsche, and postmodernism. Nietzsche, who embodies in Habermas's view the turning point in the history of Western metaphysics, also provides the entry point of postmodernism. Habermas claims that the critique of reason executed by Nietzsche and the *Dialectic of Enlightenment* becomes totalized. Aside from the performative contradiction of their critique, Habermas argues that Nietzsche and Adorno and Horkheimer confuse claims to truth and legitimization with claims to power. By rejecting reason as a grounding principle and declaring the Enlightenment bankrupt, Nietzsche, Adorno, and Horkheimer dispense with the emancipatory content of philosophy.[41] The dialectic of enlightenment and myth cancels out any progression: enlightenment reverts to myth. Neither Nietzsche nor Adorno and Horkheimer attempt to reconcile the contradiction of their critiques, for this contradiction is unavoidable if one wants to twist out of metaphysics and avoid forced reconciliations. Habermas, however, condemns the crisis of legitimation as a loss of normative standards. It is precisely this drive and desire for normativity that Nietzsche criticizes as the debilitating dependence upon Christianity, first principles, and ordering categories. Adorno agrees in his remark that the desire for truth, already sufficiently suspect in its need for stability and order, guarantees neither the truth-value nor the objectivity of the desired object. Nietzsche's insight is as valid today as it was in his time: that a value's justification, which stems from the need to have such values, presents an argument against such a value rather than for it.[42]

The totalized critique of reason, the interdependence of truth and power, and the lack of emancipatory potential are thus the features through which Habermas establishes a connection between Nietzsche, Adorno, and postmodernism. The relationship between them certainly deserves further inquiry, especially when they are freed from Habermas's unfavorable judgments. Habermas laments Adorno's and Horkheimer's affinity to Nietzsche and dismisses postmodernism as irreconcilable antimodernism. Ironically, in his acceptance speech of the Theodor W. Adorno Prize awarded by the city of Frankfurt, he indirectly "defames" Adorno— whose connection to postmodernism, despite Habermas's explicit denials, he establishes implicitly via Nietzsche in "The Entwinement of Myth and Reason"— by accusing the postmoderns, among other things, of being apolitical and ahistorical anarchists, conservatives, and antimodernists allied with premodernists. Although he recognizes Adorno's affinity to Nietzsche and Nietzsche's affinity to postmodernism, he never fully investigates this intellectual triangle. By attempting to disassociate Adorno from Nietzsche, he rescues Adorno for his own project of modernity and also avoids questioning his own judgments regarding the alleged conservativism of Nietzsche and postmodernism. To associate the father of critical theory with the imputed antimodernism and conservativism would have certainly raised eyebrows, especially in a speech accepting the Adorno Prize. Although Habermas names Adorno "the very image of emulation for the intellectual,"[43] he nonetheless attempts to cleanse Adorno and critical theory from its Nietzschean elements and refuses to acknowledge any significant affinity between Adorno's work and postmodern thought. Presumably, the "image of emulation" must exclude Adorno's affinity to Nietzsche. However, it is the contention of this study that it is precisely these Nietzschean elements that carry Adorno's work beyond traditional theory and philosophy and rescue him from falling prey to philosophical dogmatism. Adorno utilizes the potential in Nietzsche's thought for the critique of ideology, domination, and the Marxist concepts of praxis and the belief in a progressive utopia. Norbert Rath concedes that uncovering this critical potential is as pressing today as it was during Adorno's lifetime.[44]

Adorno shares with the poststructuralists and the exponents of the "New Nietzsche" an interest in the antisystematic dimensions of Nietzsche's work. Like the French critics, such as François Lyotard, Gilles Deleuze, Michel Foucault, George Bataille, and Jacques Derrida, he does not approach Nietzsche's work as a hermeneutic interpreter, but rather as a fellow philosopher whose thought is to be examined, criticized, expanded, and continued. His reception of Nietzsche centers on many issues of contemporary concern that link Nietzsche to critical theory and poststructuralism: the end of the subject, the rejection of systems and absolute truth, and the critique of domination, rationality, and culture are a few thematic examples. The postmoderns, moving in a similar direction as Nietzsche and Adorno, are redefining the relationship between aesthetics and philosophy, and in many ways Nietzsche's perspectivism and Adorno's negative dialectics anticipate deconstruction. Deconstruction is the radicalized consequence of a critique of modernity that leads back to Adorno's no less radical negativity and the continuation of Nietzsche's genealogical examination of culture. Michel Foucault, like Adorno and Horkheimer in the *Dialectic*, recognizes the validity of Nietzsche's demand for the genealogical study of values and morality, and approaches the so-called truth of humanity as "a continuous sign-chain of ever new interpretations and adaptations,"[45] which is to be deciphered and reinterpreted. It is clear that such critical undertakings must dispense with the notion of a stable and irrevocable truth. Foucault, in an interview, states that a timelier acquaintance with the Frankfurt School would have saved him a lot of work, in that he would have avoided making detours and uttering nonsense during his attempt to maintain his sense of direction, while the Frankfurt School had already in fact opened these routes.[46]

NIETZSCHE AND ADORNO:
SECONDARY LITERATURE SURVEY

While there are many similarities between Adorno and poststructuralism, there are also many differences—as many opponents of postmodern thought are quick to point out. Nietzsche presents a challenge to both Adorno and the post-modern thinkers, and an investigation of Adorno's interest in Nietzsche will demonstrate that postmodernist thought does not represent the Other of modernity, but rather continues, expands, and reconceptualizes Nietzsche's and Adorno's project of radical self-reflection and self-criticism. Although the present study is among the first book-length accounts of particular intersections of thought between Adorno and Nietzsche, the Nietzschean elements of Adorno's philosophy have received in the past varying attention: some critics of critical theory ignore them entirely, some mention them and then ignore them, while the remaining others who do discuss them also exhibit a pronounced bias against either Nietzsche or Adorno. There are, of course, a few who draw connections between Nietzsche and Adorno without prejudice. Helpful from this point of view are the articles by Peter Pütz and Norbert Rath, both of which provide important philological evidence of Nietzsche's influence. Pütz's article examines Nietzsche in the light of critical theory and draws attention to the importance of Nietzsche for the *Dialectic*, in that he embodies the climax of the Enlightenment and posits the will to power as the primary force of civilization following the abdication of reason. Pütz also emphasizes the stylistic similarities between Nietzsche's and Adorno's mode of criticism, noting, for instance, the similarity between the aphorism and essay form as a mode of resistance against system-atized and homogenized philosophy.

In his contribution, Norbert Rath speculates that Habermas's expulsion of Nietzsche from critical theory may result in the loss of critical impulses and philo-sophical self-criticism. Rath identifies Habermas's project as an attempt to convert Adorno and Horkheimer's self-referential and self-contradictory critique of reason and ideology into a normative theory of communicative rationality, upon which a consensus can be built. Describing Adorno's attitude toward Nietzsche as relatively stable, Rath follows mainly Horkheimer's changing and often contra-dictory reception of Nietzsche. The *Dialectic*, by Rath's account, represents the fulfillment of Nietzsche's demand for further genealogical studies of morality. In *The Melancholy Science*, Gillian Rose connects Nietzsche and Adorno in terms of their "search for style." Rose discusses several aspects of Adorno's reception of Nietzsche, including the critique of identity thinking and of morality, and presents examples of Adorno's ironic inversions of Nietzschean terms, such as Adorno's "melancholy science" as an inversion of Nietzsche's *Gay Science*. In his article on Nietzsche and critical theory, Reinhart Maurer, in contrast to the majority of critics, reveals himself as pro-Nietzsche and argues that the Frankfurt School missed its mark by attempting to reconcile Nietzsche and Marx. He emphasizes that he does not attempt to present historic-philological evidence of Nietzsche's influence upon the critical theory of the Frankfurt School, nor does he explore direct connections between Adorno and Nietzsche. He deals with critical theory as a collective theory of the Frankfurt School, which he sees as a type of neo-Marxism inspired by Nietzschean perspectives.[47] Critical theory aims, in Maurer's view, at establishing an *Übergesellschaft* and misinterpreted Nietzsche's concept of *Übermensch* by extending it from the individual to the collective. Maurer comes to the conclusion that critical theory is a social ideology with less critical potential than Nietzsche's thought. In Habermas, the contemporary inheritor of critical theory, Maurer diagnoses a fashionably opportunistic shift toward a theory even further removed from a rigorous Nietzschean criticism.

Rüdiger Sünner's study focuses on the presentation of Nietzsche's and Adorno's plea for art as a necessary corrective to a scientific society.[48] Unfortunately, Sünner presents Nietzsche's and Adorno's critique of science and scientific thinking in connection with anthropological tales and myths of nature, thereby adding a nostalgic flavor to his analysis that is entirely foreign to the work of Nietzsche and Adorno. Sünner repeatedly connects Nietzsche's and Adorno's critiques of reason to religious and mythical worldviews, such as Indian and Eastern traditions. Sünner muses, for example, about North American Indians who apologize to plants before picking them, and he registers with a sense of sadness and loss that the modes of perception in Greek mythology are lost today. Sünner believes that this postulated mythological and holistic mode of perception was capable of seeing through the data of the senses to the forces behind them.[49] Although the emphasis of Sünner's chapters on art lies in music, his examination of Adorno's thought on music and his analysis of Wagner remain unconnected and appear without consideration of Nietzsche's Wagner critique.

Both Norbert W. Bolz and Bernd Bräutigam establish connections between Nietzsche's and Adorno's theory of aesthetics. Bräutigam analyzes Hamann's, Nietzsche's, and Adorno's concepts of art in order to reject them. By presenting them in opposition to Hegel, Bräutigam attempts to prove their "regressive tendencies" and their inferiority to Hegel's aesthetic theory.[50] Bolz traces Nietzsche's influence upon Adorno's *Aesthetic Theory* in the context of the construction of modernity. In Bolz's view, Nietzsche anticipated Adorno's critique of culture and the philosophy of history. In his dense study, conducted in a stenographic manner, Bolz illustrates how Nietzsche's notions of truth, myth, genius, and the historicity of art are reflected in *Aesthetic Theory*. He also elicits parallels between Nietzsche's critique of decadence and Adorno's logic of decay, which express Nietzsche's and Adorno's perception of modernity, a modernity that is in their view a historical accumulation of symptoms of deterioration. In comparing Adorno's position with the poststructuralist reception of Nietzsche, Bolz concludes that Adorno's negative dialectics actualizes Nietzsche from a point of view that stands in opposition to the poststructural thinkers. While Foucault celebrates the beginning of language in the demise of the individual, Adorno constructs his sadness around the transient nature of humanity. Adorno, in Bolz's opinion, extracts Nietzsche's spirit, while poststructuralism extracts the body.[51] Bolz claims that Nietzsche's thought is rendered impotent by poststructuralism, because it reproduces his refusal to establish a connection between thought and the socioeconomic context.

Among the scholars and philosophers who consider Nietzsche and Adorno in the context of modernity and postmodernity, Habermas remains one of the most outspoken opponents of postmodern thought. Habermas's analysis, largely contained in *The Philosophical Discourse of Modernity*, is paradigmatic of the contemporary debates on rationality. He sets out by denouncing Nietzsche's influence on Adorno, and by trying to forestall the confusion of Adorno's thought with postmodernism. However, his project ultimately turns against its intention. Habermas ends up, in fact, establishing convincing connections between Nietzsche, Adorno, and postmodernity. In the course of his discussion, the differences between these thinkers appear increasingly less substantial than Habermas claims. For example, Habermas argues that Nietzsche's thought presents the entry into postmodernism, but he is less convincing in his denial of a relationship between Adorno and postmodernism. Although Habermas establishes Nietzsche as the father of postmodernism and a model for Adorno's critique, he refuses to accept the profound impact of Nietzsche upon the entirety of Adorno's work. Habermas argues against the conceptualization of enlightenment as a process of self-destruction and attempts to rescue reason in form of the theory of communicative rationality.

Other scholars of both Nietzsche and Adorno make valuable contributions to the recognition of a genial connection between the two thinkers. Rudolf Reuber, who examines the inseparable bond between Nietzsche's conception of life and the realm of the aesthetic, recognizes Adorno's thought as an important continuation of Nietzsche's philosophy,[52] while Adorno scholars, such as Rose and Lambert Zuidervaart, consider Nietzsche an integral part of Adorno's intellectual heritage. An examination of Nietzsche's and Adorno's critique of enlightenment and reason in light of the contemporary and contentious discussions surrounding the project of modernity will provide insights into the unresolved contradiction between enlightenment and the enlightenment of enlightenment. Nietzsche's and Adorno's entwinement of the critiques of reason and modernity exhibits formal and structural characteristics that attest to the continuing need to rethink the relationship between criticism and other elements of culture, including ideology, philosophy, and art. Adorno's insistence upon the aesthetics of criticism and his advancement of such concepts as non-identity and negativity place his work much closer to the postmodern discourse and the Nietzschean-based interpretations of poststructuralism than Bolz and others are willing to admit and, at the very least, lead toward the destabilization of popular dichotomies in anti-postmodernist discourses, such as rationalism-irrationalism, modernism-postmodernism. Adorno shows that these dichotomies form integral parts of an entwinement that cannot be grasped by setting up oppositions, but rather by thinking of them in terms of constellations of thought that inform both criticism and self-criticism. Adorno's reception of Nietzsche provides productive alternatives to one-dimensional political labeling and the adamant rejection of Nietzsche and the postmodern critique of modernity.

The first three chapters of this study explore Nietzsche's and Adorno's critiques of rationality, history, and metaphysics as a basis for their critique of modernity in order to gain a clearer understanding of their search for style and the significance of art for their thought. The first chapter considers Nietzsche's and Adorno's radicalized critique of rationality to be the key component of their critique of ideology and confronts Nietzsche's and Adorno's questioning of reason with Habermas's critique of their refusal to accept rationality as humanity's foundational activity leading toward the betterment of society. Read against the grain, Habermas provides a productive framework for an exploration of the tensions and similarities between Nietzsche's and Adorno's relentless critique of ideology and enlightenment. Against Habermas, this first chapter argues that Nietzsche's and Adorno's brilliant demonstration of the self-destruction of enlightenment does not lead them outside of the Western tradition of philosophy, as Habermas claims with regard to Nietzsche, but radicalizes modern self-reflection and self-consciousness and attempts to enlighten enlightenment about its own ideological pitfalls.

The second chapter discusses the genealogical approach to writing history within the framework of Foucault's interpretation of genealogy, Nietzsche's *Genealogy*, and Adorno and Horkheimer's *Dialectic*. No attempt is made to present Foucault's interpretation of Nietzsche's use of genealogy as a "correct" interpretation. The same is valid for Adorno and Horkheimer's *Dialectic*, which is not presented as an interpretation of Nietzsche, but as a project informed by Nietzschean figures of thought. It is argued that viewing the *Dialectic* as a genealogical project provides a critical perspective from which it is possible to conceptualize the regressive moments of the history of civilization. The *Dialectic* clearly shows a Nietzschean shift from a claim to historical truth to an examination of the functions of values and concepts. The *Dialectic* presents a narrative construction of history rather than a so-called objective reconstruction, and it does so without pretending to present historical truth. It shows and performs its own entanglement with myth without, however, completely giving up the claim to enlightenment. As enlightenment of enlightenment, the *Dialectic* undermines traditional approaches to the interpretation and writing of history in a manner reflecting Foucault's determination of genealogy as parodic (aimed against historical reminiscence and the illusion of the recognition of historical events), dissociative (aimed against the constructions of fictitious identities and continuities), and sacrificial (aimed against claims to truth).

Nietzsche's and Adorno's critiques of the ideological presuppositions ruling rational and metaphysical thought, including their critique of concepts and logic, are discussed in more detail in the third chapter. In connection with the previous discussions of Nietzsche's and Adorno's critique of rationality and history, the critiques of metaphysical concepts lay the groundwork for an understanding of Adorno's disagreements with Nietzsche. Adorno's critique of the Nietzschean call for amorality, of the love of fate, of the affirmation of life, and of Nietzsche's view of women are central to the self-definition of Adorno's thought. Adorno's relentlessly paradoxical negativity directly opposes Nietzsche's affirmations and makes visible the gulf dividing their approach to criticism, philosophy, and life. These differences in mood and attitude are partly explainable through their different positions in history. More than that, these differences lead to the very core of Adorno's and Nietzsche's thought.

The fourth chapter explicates Nietzsche's and Adorno's critiques of Richard Wagner, which serve as models for their critiques of modernity. For both Nietzsche's and Adorno's critiques, Wagner—representing the modern artist *par excellence*—and his music dramas provide a foil, substitute, and typology that enables them to formulate their theories of the aesthetic. Wagner exemplifies the condition of modern art and culture, and with his critique of Wagner as an actor and man of the theater, Nietzsche lays the groundwork for Adorno's critique of the culture industry. Both see Wagner at the beginning of the commercialization of art and reproach him for bowing not only to the Christian cross but also the taste of his time. They find Wagner's works to be totalitarian, calculated, and fatalistic commodities that embody the ideologies of modernity; for Adorno, an analysis of Wagner functions additionally as an exploration of the roots of fascism. However, Adorno's Wagner criticism also undermines his own rigid division between genuine art and the products of the culture industry; it also shows not only the birth of totalitarianism from the spirit of the *Gesamtkunstwerk*, but also the birth of the culture industry from the spirit of high culture. Furthermore, in contrast to Nietzsche, Adorno does not find in decadence a suitable critical framework for the critique of Wagner. Nietzsche argues that decadence is the most honest expression of and for Wagner, and he reproaches Wagner for deceiving the public and denying his decadence. Adorno thinks that the elements of decadence actually rescue Wagner from becoming totally immersed in bourgeois ideology. In this way, Adorno and Nietzsche agree that decadence constitutes a moment of sincerity—and in Adorno's mind a moment of resistance—in Wagner's work. Despite other similarities in their appreciation of decadence, they differ, however, in their foci and evaluations of decadence.

The excursus on *Bildung* indicates the parallel between the view of *Bildung*—in terms of a "higher" education—and Nietzsche's and Adorno's view of high art as an autonomous realm functioning as a pocket of resistance against the pressures of conformity. Both retain a critical notion of *Bildung* while decrying the fact that the ideal of *Bildung* has, under present conditions, no chance of becoming reality. The broadening and popularization of *Bildung* caused it to degenerate into *Halbbildung*. Adorno concludes that, since *Bildung* and consequently citizens possessing true *Bildung* no longer exist, only critical reflection upon this pseudo-education from the position of pseudo-education—that is, critical reflection about pseudo-education by the pseudo-educated—can keep alive the ideal of *Bildung*.

Contrasting Nietzsche's and Adorno's styles, the fifth chapter focuses upon their respective use of aphorisms and essays. This form of writing represents one aspect of their resistance and protest against traditional philosophy and functions simultaneously as an embodiment of their thought. Both insist upon the use of open structures that permit experimental thought, while undermining the claims to systems, strict logic, and absolute truth. Reflecting the differences of mood and attitude outlined in Adorno's critique of Nietzsche, their style of writing and their use of irony differs considerably. While Nietzsche's styles reflect his oscillation between his unswerving critique of society and the affirmation of life—between philosophizing with a hammer or with laughter—Adorno's styles reflect his conscious labor of negativity, which never allows itself to forget, in a Nietzschean sense, the sufferings of humanity.

1

The *Bildungsroman* of Reason
and the Rational Project of Modernity

True thoughts are those alone which do not understand themselves.

—Adorno, *Minima Moralia*

The evaluation and reevaluation of reason represents one of the most significant features of discussions on modernity. The various critics debating issues of modernity and postmodernity invariably focus on the position taken toward reason and its connection to modes of understanding. Whether the controversy involves hermeneutics versus deconstruction, communicative rationality versus postmodern play, or the promotion of pragmatism and contingency versus universal standards of judgments, the definition, role, and function of reason never fails to ignite controversy. The debates between Gadamer and Derrida, Habermas and Lyotard, and the North American contributions to the French-German discussions by Richard Rorty and Charles Taylor testify to the centrality of the defense or contestation of the rational foundation of modernity. Habermas devoted his life's work to convincing his readers to take heed of rational argumentation, to retain rationality and to continue the project of modernity. *The Philosophical Discourse of Modernity*, a response to his French colleagues, tries to rescue rationality from the attack of supposed irrationalists and to reveal the failures and flaws of a totalized critique of reason that attacks its own foundations. Habermas locates the performative contradiction in critics of rationality such as Nietzsche, Adorno and Horkheimer, and the contemporary philosophers of postmodernity, such as Lyotard, Derrida, and Foucault. Habermas complains that the totalized critique of reason and enlightenment leads these thinkers to dispense with the idea and ideal of emancipation. The exponents of the project of a rational enlightenment, such as Habermas or Georg Lukács in his work *The Destruction of Reason*, devise a *Bildungsroman* of reason whose major figures are Kant, Hegel, and Marx.

The literary term *Bildungsroman*, which is usually applied to novels of "education" or development, refers in this usage not to the formation of an integrated individual who finds his or her place in society, but to the metanarrative of a progressive march of enlightenment spearheaded by the rational subjects of a rational society. Kant is the Enlightenment thinker who brought this narrative to its high point by not only confirming reason as the supreme faculty of judgment, but also by categorizing rationality, knowledge, and understanding. Kant maintains that genuine knowledge is universal and necessary. While reason can never comprehend the thing-in-itself, the mind has a priori categories at its disposal by which it becomes capable of synthesizing, understanding, and judging. Kant's theory of knowledge differentiates between that which is given in reality and the a priori categories of reason that process the perceived reality. Reasoning, in Kant's view, is a creative activity centered in the individual. The individual realizes freedom in morality and religion, and history is time's movement toward the realization of this freedom. Reasoning is thus not an abstract privilege, but a human responsibility and duty. Morality is the final purpose of reason, and as rational beings we are compelled to accept the moral order. As a variation of Hegel's claim that the rational is the real and the real is the rational, Kant's dictum might be: What is rational is moral, and what is moral is rational. Determined by reason, human action must be justified and legitimized by the categorical imperative: Always act so that the determining principles of your action could become moral law. Kant emphasizes the responsibility of the individual to act according to rational and moral principles, and enlightenment is the realization of freedom through the acceptance of duty.

> Enlightenment is man's release from his self-incurred tutelage. Tutelage is man's inability to make use of his understanding without direction from another. Self-incurred is this tutelage when its cause lies not in lack of reason but in lack of resolution and courage to use it without direction from another. *Sapere aude!* "Have courage to use your own reason!"—that is the motto of enlightenment.[1]

Enlightenment is thus the emancipatory process by which reason unfolds and develops toward self-determination. Kant's thought laid the foundation for German idealism and Hegel's concept of subjectivity. For Hegel, however, the individual subject no longer acts autonomously, but is rather a necessary agent of history. The individual realizes freedom, because freedom realizes itself through the individual. History is not the realization of individual freedom, but the movement toward the self-realization of the objective spirit. World-historical reason controls history and determines the reasoning of the individual. Hegel can therefore equate the real and the rational, and it is only the cunning of reason that might disturb and subvert the rational course of history. When Marx takes up Hegel's dialectical philosophy of history, he converts it into a materialistic critique of society. Economic antagonisms, which form the basis for the struggle between the classes, propel history toward its final goal and self-fulfillment. Like Kant and Hegel, Marx retains the teleological notion of a progressive development: Kant's individual realization of freedom and Hegel's realization of the absolute spirit manifest themselves as Marx's concrete utopian ideal of the classless society. The historical process remains in Marx the progressive and continuous development toward revolution and emancipation. Reason is the emancipatory force, and history is the realization of its highest potential, namely economic and social equality. These linked notions of rationality and history testify, according to the proponents of reason, to the need for continuity and normativity. Reason is the foundation and ordering principle behind the construction of the view of reality; it grounds human activities and discursive practices.

Those supporting the rational project of modernity as a movement toward the realization of enlightenment ideals, such as Marxists and Hegelians, have a problematic and often hostile relationship to Nietzsche's work. Nietzsche is perceived as the moment at which philosophy turned in the direction of irrationality and antimodernism. Habermas acknowledges the Nietzschean heritage of the so-called postmodern thinkers and adds them to his list of those who detract Enlightenment ideals. He criticizes Adorno's and Horkheimer's *Dialectic*—whose two main theses are *in nuce* that myth is already enlightenment and that enlightenment reverts to myth—for its failure to salvage the rational pursuit of the Enlightenment's emancipatory potential. Habermas finds Nietzsche's influence upon Adorno disturbing and dismisses it as an unfortunate, historically motivated misstep. Since he requires Adorno for his project of Enlightenment, Habermas minimizes Nietzsche's influence by thematizing it in his critique of the *Dialectic*, while barely acknowledging it in the rest of Adorno's ouevre. However, to cleanse Adorno's work from its Nietzschean elements not only suspends a crucial critical perspective found in Adorno's thought, but also distorts the reception of critical theory as such.

The *Bildungsroman* of reason does not, of course, begin with Kant, Hegel, or Habermas. The belief in reason as the center of human potentiality is as old as the questioning of the concept, and the drive toward enlightenment has always provoked criticism. Traditionally, those who challenged the absolute power of reason were labeled irrationalists and were portrayed as opposing reason and emancipation. The discussions about rationality, irrationality, and antirationality pervade the history of ideas and are generally conceptualized as enlightenment and counterenlightenment. However, these discussions escalate in their intensity when they become part of the debates concerning modernity. On the one hand, modernity is tied to a belief in progress, science, and technology and to the optimism that rationality will instigate, realize, and criticize its own project. On the other hand, modernity radicalizes the critiques of these hopes. The bourgeois ideal of modernity continues the tradition of the Enlightenment:

> The doctrine of progress, the confidence in the beneficial possibilities of science and technology, the concern with time (a measurable time, a time that can be bought and sold and therefore has, like any other commodity, a calculable equivalent in money), the cult of reason, and the ideal of freedom defined within the framework of an abstract humanism, but also the orientation toward pragmatism and the cult of action and success—all have been associated in various degrees with the battle for the modern.[2]

Within this tradition of enlightenment and rationality, the perception of the cause of the crisis of modernity varies: pointing toward the ills of modern society and the scars of civilization, the critics of the Enlightenment contend that these crises originate in the untenability of the ideals of progress; according to the proponents of Enlightenment, such societal problems are caused by the radical questioning of the foundations of Enlightenment. In the tradition of Kant, for whom a rational being cannot will a contradiction, the rational project of modernity disallows contradictions and thus limits criticism to the confines of a rationality that cannot, logically, question its own foundation. By questioning its own truth-claims, such a critique turns against itself, oversteps the boundaries of acceptable critical activity, and thus falls outside of the rational project of modernity. Criticism as a rational activity may reflect upon itself; however, should critical discourse undermine its own presuppositions, it would become, in the eyes of rational traditionalists, the Other of reason and a threat to it. In opposition to the paradoxical and self-contradictory play of forces of a totalized critique of reason, a critical method based on rational foundations is an activity grounded by traditional concepts of rationality, a logical enterprise obeying the dictates of utility, the common good, relations of cause and effect, and includes, as in Habermas's case, the negotiation of a consensus. The affirmation of the Enlightenment and the project of modernity thus correlate to rationality's assigned role of a liberating and emancipatory force. The problems of the rationalist appropriation of reason becomes apparent in Habermas's stubborn insistence on universality in his critiques of Nietzsche, Adorno and Horkheimer, and his crusade against postmodernism. Measuring the legitimacy of thought in terms of a priori categories of rationality, Habermas is repelled by the performative contradiction he finds in a totalized critique of reason and the foreclosure of the hope for an emancipatory potential. One of his main objections concerning the "irrationalist" critique is against the respective attempts by Nietzsche, Adorno and Horkheimer, and the postmodernists to establish a relationship between claims to truth and power. While insisting upon communicative rationality as a means of building a consensus among negotiating parties, the results and consequences of the entwine-

ment of truth and power appear to escape Habermas's criticism. However, before
turning to Habermas's critique in more detail, Nietzsche's and the *Dialectic*'s
portrayal of the impoverished project of enlightenment and the truncated *Bildungsroman* of reason shall be considered first.

RATIONALITY, MODERNITY, AND THE
DIALECTIC OF ENLIGHTENMENT

The Enlightenment cast reason as the supreme faculty of judgment and as
the instrument of gaining knowledge. Reason held out the promise of challenging myth, debunking superstition, and eliminating ignorance, while scientific
investigations of the laws of nature would not only control the forces of nature,
but would also lead to a permanent and universal foundation for morality.
Enlightenment thinkers hoped that justice, liberty, and the pursuit of happiness
for all would result from the establishment of a rational order. The utopian
moment for the project of the Enlightenment rests in its desire for a just society
based upon rational principles. For Adorno and Nietzsche, however, the hope for
a better future is no longer tied to enlightenment, since in their view the process
of enlightenment prevents the realization of its own ideals and is engaged in a
process of self-destruction. Enlightenment sets reason as an absolute and allows
rationality to spin out of control. Rationality has been instrumentalized for the
domination of nature and the self, and has displaced more complex notions of
reason. Through its deterioration into positivistic, scientific, and utilitarian
thought, rationality has reduced itself to a mode of finding practical applications
for ideas. In the scientific field, the search for solutions promotes an obsession
with advanced technology, while religion and philosophy are expected to offer
solutions to the moral dilemmas accompanying the increasing domination over
nature and human beings. Nietzsche and Adorno dispose of the notion that the
ideals of progress, autonomy, and justice are solely grounded in rationality and
expose the ideological nature of the faith in these ideals. Furthermore, they deny
that these humanist ideals are realized in history through the progressive march
of reason and enlightenment. For them, reconciliation, morality, and freedom are
no longer synonymous with rationality and enlightenment. As in many of Nietzsche's writings, the *Dialectic* affirms the dissolution of the Kantian bond
between morality and rationality. Referring to Nietzsche, the *Dialectic* asserts the
abdication of absolute standards and "the impossibility of deriving from reason
any fundamental argument against murder."[3] However, neither Nietzsche nor
Adorno and Horkheimer can dispense entirely with the idea of enlightenment, for
they recognize that even the critique and enlightenment of enlightenment remain
caught within the philosophical tradition of the Enlightenment. Nietzsche speaks
of the ideal of a New Enlightenment, while Adorno and Horkheimer insist that
the critique of enlightenment must remain part of the enlightenment:

The dilemma that faced us in our work proved to be the first phenomenon for investigation: the self-destruction of the Enlightenment. We are wholly convinced—and
therein lies our *petitio principii*—that social freedom is inseparable from enlightened
thought. Nevertheless, we believe that we have just as clearly recognized that the
notion of this very way of thinking, no less than the actual historic forms—the social
institutions—with which it is interwoven, already contains the seed of the reversal
universally apparent today. If enlightenment does not accommodate reflection on this
recidivist element, then it seals its own fate.[4]

In arguing that their critique should not be separated from the tradition of
enlightenment, Adorno and Horkheimer formulate a project of modernity which
promotes radicalized forms of self-criticism and self-reflection. Adorno's and
Horkheimer's critique does not wish to destroy enlightenment, nor does it constitute a slip into irrationality, but is "intended to prepare the way for a positive
notion of enlightenment which will release it from entanglement in blind domination."[5] Behind the image of enlightenment's self-destruction lurks the utopian
vision of an enlightenment freed from the destructive mechanisms of so-called
progress. However, this utopian vision can only be articulated in negative terms.
It does not develop a positive vision of the future, but rather voices a hope for an
absence, namely, the absence of enlightenment's entanglement in domination.
This process of emancipation or liberation from domination can only be accom-
plished when the prime cause of the "retreat of enlightenment into mythology"
is not sought outside but "in the Enlightenment itself."[6]

In the footsteps of Nietzsche's *Genealogy of Morals*, Adorno and Horkheimer
affirm that moral values and ideals are not founded on rational and universally
normative principles, but are rather historical formations instituted to fulfill various purposes catering to various interests. Values and ideals direct and control the
dynamics of domination and self-preservation. They are also instrumental in
maintaining the hierarchical structure, a structure that provides the playground for
power struggles. Religious dogmas, philosophical thought, and cultural values
function foremost to legitimate the drive to domination and the desire for self-
preservation. Instead of a theodicy, the Enlightenment erects the ideal of a rationality, which in turn provides the normative standards for a supposedly
enlightened society of rational human beings. The *Dialectic* begins by explaining
the concept of enlightenment in terms of a dialectic of autonomy and domination:
"In the most general sense of progressive thought, the Enlightenment has always
aimed at liberating men from fear and establishing their sovereignty."[7] However,
in the process of demythologizing reality, enlightenment mythologizes its own
operations, such as scientific investigations, technology, and quantitative analyses. Having overcome superstition, the human mind is to exert control over disenchanted nature, other human beings, and the self: "knowledge, which is power,
knows no obstacles: neither in the enslavement of men nor in compliance with the
world's rulers."[8] At the root of the need for order and normativity lies the fear of
the transitory and discontinuous. The tools of metaphysics, enlightenment

thought, and the dogmas of religion construct and legitimize orders and hierarchies, which serve to pacify the fear of rupture, the unknown, and the world without a center. Adorno speculates that a more humane existence would be one devoid of foundations, a condition with nothing left to hold on to would be "the only condition worthy of men, the condition that would at last allow human thought to behave as autonomously as philosophy had always merely asked it to, only to prevent it in the same breath from so behaving."[9] Like Nietzsche, Adorno envisions a world liberated from the shadows of God, metaphysics, and the myths of enlightenment, and in his typically negative fashion, he does not—unlike Nietzsche's idealizations, such as the *Übermensch*—project an alternative. It is the absence of foundations and groundings which must suffice as an *ex negativo* utopian ideal.

Adorno thematizes the possibility, that is, the impossibility, of autonomous thought in a society in which thought has been firmly institutionalized. Within its institutional context, philosophy paralyzes itself in two ways: by establishing ordering principles and by hindering thought from moving beyond these self-imposed limitations. Enlightenment thought reproduces these failures of philosophical systems, because it thinks in terms of identity and excludes that which does not fit into the systematic preconceptions: "the Enlightenment recognizes as being and occurrence only what can be apprehended in unity: its ideal is the system from which all and everything follows. . . . The multiplicity of forms is reduced to position and arrangement, history to fact, things to matter."[10] In complicity with philosophy, the Enlightenment relies on formal logic, which schematizes calculability and connects first principles and observational judgments.

Enlightenment, by Adorno's and Horkheimer's account, falls back into these systematization and mythologizes them. Enlightenment shares with myth its basic principle of anthropomorphism, defined as "the projection onto nature of the subjective."[11] Nietzsche also decries the reduction of multiplicity to a false unity, and criticizes Enlightenment philosophy for creating a view of the world supposedly in harmony with the laws of nature, but which actually concurs with people's self-interest. For Nietzsche, values and judgments are projected onto nature in an effort to establish or maintain power; living entails "estimating, preferring, being unjust, being limited, wanting to be different,"[12] and must thus be seen in opposition to philosophy's drive for order, justice, infinitude, and identity. It is the philosopher's pride that wants to impose morality and ideals upon nature, and philosophy begins to err once it believes in itself: "It always creates the world in its own image; it cannot do otherwise. Philosophy is this tyrannical drive itself, the most spiritual will to power, to the 'creation of the world,' to the *causa prima*."[13] Philosophy expresses the drive for ordering principles and the will to create a worldview based on its self-imposed rules of thought. Subsequently, the creation of a so-called rational order and the instrumentalization of thought have led to an enlightenment that has turned against its own intentions. Although the project of enlightenment presumably demythologizes the world by dispelling myths and replacing them with knowledge, Nietzsche and the *Dialectic* contend that this process has reverted to myth by concentrating on knowledge gained by instrumentalized rationality. The result is a glorification of empirical facts and conceptual categories. Nietzsche maintains that this overestimation produces the myth of enlightenment, and that one should use notions, such as cause and effect, only as pure concepts or "as conventional fictions for the purpose of designation and communication—*not* for explanation."[14] Nietzsche affirms that the "in-itself" knows no causal connections, necessity, or law: "It is *we* alone who have devised cause, sequence, for-each-other, relativity, constraint, number, law, freedom, motive, and purpose; and when we project and mix this symbol world into things as if it existed 'in itself,' we act once more as we have always acted—*mythologically*."[15] Serving as a model for Adorno and Horkheimer's examination of enlightenment's reversion into myth, Nietzsche's affirmation of the dialectic of enlightenment shows how the system building of the Enlightenment and the instrumentalization of reason turn the Enlightenment into a self-destructive process.

Philosophical and metaphysical categories regress to mythological thought because they maintain the fictions surrounding the terms origin, telos, and first principles. Metaphysical speculation represents the earlier form of scientific and positivistic modes of thought, in which myth plays the role accorded to the logos. According to the *Dialectic*, thought thus renounces the claim to construct meaning and substitutes creative thought with formulas, rules, and probabilities. It is dominated by categories such as utility and measurability: "For the Enlightenment, whatever does not conform to the rule of computation and utility is suspect."[16] Enlightenment and bourgeois society are obsessed with numbers and equivalents, to the extent that the number became the canon of the Enlightenment: "Bourgeois society is ruled by equivalence. It makes the dissimilar comparable by reducing it to abstract quantities. To the Enlightenment, that which does not reduce to numbers, and ultimately to the one, becomes illusion; modern positivism writes it off as literature."[17] Enlightenment excludes that which is incommensurable by declaring it fiction, while scientific and positivistic thought reproduces metaphysical thought by replacing God, qualities, and substances with quantifiable entities.

The patriarchal gods were absorbed by the "philosophical *logos*,"[18] and reason itself has become a mere instrument of the economic apparatus in the capitalist system. It is a tool firmly directed toward the achievement of economically motivated ambitions. Enlightenment has become an instrument of capitalism, and the actions of instrumental reason are as calculated as the processes of material production.[19] Technology, the buttress of the bourgeois economy in the factories and on the battlefields, has become the essence of knowledge and is controlled by "kings" and "businessmen" alike; it is as "democratic" as the economic system it supports. Technology does not work by concepts and images, but "refers to method, the exploitation of others' work, and capital."[20] The object of knowledge is to find ways to dominate nature and other men: "That is the only aim. Ruthlessly, in despite of itself, the Enlightenment has extinguished any trace of its own self-consciousness."[21] The search for knowledge is at the same time the search for power. Through its pandering to instrumental rationality, enlightenment engenders and falls prey to the claims to power. According to Nietzsche, the search for the so-called facts of nature aims at "the tyrannically inconsiderate and relentless enforcement of claims of power."[22] Thus demythologization does not liberate thought, but merely reverts into another form of repression. Instead of God, the Enlightenment sets up reason as the absolute. Although the object of absolutization is replaced, the structures of thought producing and legitimizing it remain unaltered. The shadow of God lurks in the form of enlightenment, indicating the close relationship between the Enlightenment and metaphysics. In a fashion similar to Adorno and Horkheimer, who claim that man strives to dominate nature and other men, Nietzsche maintains that man seeks to institute himself as the supreme being, who bears "the entire and ultimate responsibility for . . . actions" himself, and wishes "to absolve God, the world, ancestors, chance, and society."[23] Nietzsche, using the same analogy found in Adorno's *Minima Moralia*, compares the paradoxical situation of the modern thinker with "Münchhausen's audacity, to pull oneself up into existence by the hair, out of the swamps of nothingness."[24]

By tracing the regressive movements of enlightenment, Nietzsche and the *Dialectic* undermine conventionalized notions of progress. The so-called advances of modern society are, however, also inherently regressive and eventually reveal themselves as backward steps toward the increased domination of nature and of people. The deductive form of science reflects the hierarchy, coercion, and repression of the non-identical in society. Deductive thought desires power over the individual element, and "the whole logical order, dependency, connection, progression, and union of concepts is grounded in the corresponding conditions of social reality—that is the division of labor."[25] The division of labor goes hand in hand with the separation of science and art and the relocation of language in the realm of utility. As a system of signs, language is allocated to the transmission of facts and figures and assigned the function of calculation in order to know nature; as sound or image, language is ascribed to art and assigned the task of imitating nature. This twofold appropriation of the functions of language helps to sustain the separation of art and science, which facilitates their smooth integration into the administered world, and makes "them both manageable as areas of culture."[26] However, the result is that art and science, though postulated oppositions, blend with one another, and their separation is, in fact, an ideological fiction. Similarly, Nietzsche argues in his examination of Socrates that science must in the end rely on art and the myth-making power of language in order to justify itself. Rationality must thus revert to myth in order to legitimize its claims. Enlightenment, in the view of Adorno and Horkheimer, does not admit opposition, because it can identify itself with myth, which has always previously existed as enlightenment. Whatever myths one might invoke in order to offer resistance to enlightenment thought, the very fact that myths become "arguments in the process of opposition" acknowledges "the principle of dissolvent rationality" and testifies to the entanglement of myth and rationality; enlightenment, Adorno and Horkheimer conclude, is totalitarian, and "every spiritual resistance it encounters serves merely to increase its strength."[27]

While enlightenment seeks on the one hand to liberate the individual from superstitions and outdated beliefs, it enacts on the other a violent and totalitarian process of regression. By attempting to shatter myth, enlightenment thought is "ultimately self-destructive."[28] The *Dialectic* demonstrates through the exemplary adventures of Odysseus how individuals must pay for their liberation from the powers of nature, superstition, and magic with self-alienation, self-renunciation, and sacrifice. In order to attain their goal of self-preservation and the expansion of power, individuals must make sacrifices, such as the repression of feelings and instincts and the deferral of gratification. In the *Genealogy of Morals*, Nietzsche describes self-denial and self-sacrifice as a masochistic drive to power. Nietzsche maintains that virtues, such as selflessness, goodness, beauty, and nobility, have no universal validity in themselves, but are constructed in connection with the endless struggle for self-preservation and power which underlies all events. "Good" and "evil" are values assigned by an instrumentalized rationality in accordance with relations of power. Describing instrumental reason in terms of *ressentiment* and the cunning of the ascetic priest, Nietzsche asserts the volatile nature of both power structures and values. The strong master morality is eventually overturned by the weak slave morality when the *ressentiment* of the powerless changes from a purely reactive to a creative force. The emphasis upon instrumental rationality brings with it the devaluation of the instincts; human drives are repressed and "reduced to thinking, inferring, reckoning, co-ordinating cause and effect."[29] However, repressed instincts that "do not discharge themselves outwardly *turn inward*."[30] This internalization becomes visible in Adorno's interpretation of Odysseus as the prototype of the cunning bourgeois, who engages in a series of exchanges in order to attain his goals. His instrumentalized reason and internalized principle of exchange leads him to subordinate his desires in order to attain these goals. The result is the repression of his drives and the sacrifice of pleasure. Satisfaction is deferred in the hope for a future reward greater than the one attainable at the moment. For Nietzsche, internalization, marked by the origin of bad conscience, causes the instincts to turn "backward *against man himself*."[31] A bad conscience arises not from the failure to adhere to moral values, but rather derives from an internalized mechanism of power and control. In this way, so-called civilized society breeds an individual with a memory who does not forget to repay his debt. The outward barbarism of physical violence as a reminder to pay up is thus superseded by the more subtle mechanism of cruelty of the self against the self.

While the *Dialectic* describes the process of internalization in connection to the totalization of enlightenment and in terms of the regressive movements of instrumental rationality, Nietzsche recognizes it not only as the beginning of "man's suffering *of man, of himself,*" but also as "something so new, profound, unheard of, enigmatic, contradictory, *and pregnant with a future* . . . a spectacle too subtle, too marvelous, too paradoxical to be played senselessly unobserved on some ludicrous planet."[32] In art, the cruelty against the self, the "secret self-ravishment" and contempt for life serves as a womb for imaginative phenomena and brings about "an abundance of strange new beauty and affirmation, and perhaps beauty itself."[33] It could be argued that Nietzsche, by pointing toward the emergence of the new and profound in the process of enlightenment, thinks more dialectically than the *Dialectic*, for its pessimistic analysis and its claim of a totalization of enlightenment makes the *Dialectic* appear, as many critics have pointed out, to abandon dialectical thought itself. The *Dialectic's* critique of enlightenment as a process of complete regression and repression would seem to indicate an undialectical negativism. However, Adorno also recognized in art a pocket of resistance against the totalization of enlightenment and domination, and even the *Dialectic* itself affirms a vision of enlightenment freed from domination. Adorno and Horkheimer explicitly state their allegiance to enlightenment by way of an enlightenment of enlightenment, and the *Dialectic* positions itself between the continuation and revocation of enlightenment. Although the *Dialectic's* anamnestic critique of enlightenment runs the risk of totalizing its conclusions, it does situate itself within and not outside of the enlightenment project. It finds its interest in Nietzsche in his radical critique and relentless analysis of structures of power and domination and clearly not in his affirmations of the dialectical formation of the new. The *Dialectic* attempts to explicate enlightenment's process of self-destruction and asserts "how hard it is to take the self-destruction of truth, splendidly anticipated by Nietzsche, through a process of enlightenment set in motion without reflection."[34] The *Dialectic's* interpretation of the concept of enlightenment and the reading of Homer's epic illustrate and elaborate upon the Nietzschean cycles of self-destruction, thus proving them to be *überhistorisch*, that is, a historical phenomenon not only operating continuously within history, but also changing constantly according to historical circumstances.

The dehistorization of the Enlightenment into a continuous process of enlightenment is not without its problems. It can lead to the conspicuous leveling lamented by Habermas and to the homogenization of history as a repressive and regressive mechanism. Almost all critics of the *Dialectic* notice its totalizing view of history, enlightenment, and notion of identity, that is, the loss of identity.[35] Albrecht Wellmer criticizes the *Dialectic* as a "phenomenology of instrumental rationality,"[36] while Axel Honneth sees in the totalization of the critique of ideology an inability to formulate a critique of society. Honneth diagnoses, especially in Adorno's later works, a final repression of social dimensions.[37] Others argue that the totalizing tendencies can be explained by the *Dialectic's* critical impetus. Herbert Schnädelbach contends that Adorno and Horkheimer's dehistorized concept of enlightenment must be understood within the context of a structural critique of society rather than an attempt to understand real historical events. If enlightenment wants to enlighten without taking a counterenlightenment position, it must be dehistorized and can only function as a structural concept.[38] An open concept of enlightenment allows the *Dialectic* to make visible the various enlightenment phenomena and the dynamics of its processes.[39] Schnädelbach sees the origin of misunderstandings and misinterpretations of the *Dialectic* in the singularity of the terms used by Adorno and Horkheimer, such as *the* Enlightenment, *the* rational, and *the* modern. According to Schnädelbach, these singular terms describe a wide variety of phenomena, and their usage leads many readers, among them Habermas, to criticize the *Dialectic of Enlightenment* for underestimating the complexity and rational potential of modernity.

Habermas's critique represents the main critical objections leveled against Adorno and Horkheimer's work and can therefore serve to illustrate those tendencies of their work that have been perceived as problematic. Generally viewed as the inheritor of critical theory, Habermas is the most widely cited, respected, and controversial critic of the *Dialectic*. The roots of this controversy are intimately related to Habermas's position on Nietzsche and postmodernism, for Habermas argues that Nietzsche is the turning point and entry into postmodernism. Modernity, as Habermas sees it, stands "above all under the sign of subjective freedom."[40] Secured by civil rights, society guarantees the right to pursue rationally one's own interest; the state guarantees equal rights, and in the private realm the realization of subjective freedom allows ethical autonomy and self-realization. The emancipation of the subjective spirit also effects the alienation and emancipation from religion. In contrast to Nietzsche's and Adorno's devaluation of rationality, Hegel's philosophy validated reason as an equivalent for the "unifying power of religion."[41] According to Habermas, Nietzsche's entry into the discourse of modernity relocates the conception of reason from the ground up. Nietzsche submits subject-centered reason to an immanent critique and abandons the perceptions of reason as "a reconciling self-knowledge," "liberating appropriation," and "compensatory remembrance."[42] For Habermas, Nietzsche relinquishes the program of an intristic dialectic of enlightenment: "He renounces a renewed revision of the concept of reason and *bids farewell* to the dialectic of enlightenment." Additionally, he explodes "modernity's husk of reason as such."[43] Although Romanticism also questioned the privileging of reason, this questioning was not complete. Only with Nietzsche did "the criticism of modernity dispense . . . for the first time with its retention of an emancipatory content."[44]

For Nietzsche, as for Adorno, progress is always tied to regression and enlightenment is inextricably bound to myth. For them, the emancipation from religious and metaphysical views of the world is not synonymous with a progressive expansion of reason, nor does it liberate the individual. On the contrary: the supposedly emancipatory process restores the individual's dependency by other means. Nietzsche and Adorno maintain that enlightenment itself has become a myth that functions as a substitute for religion and metaphysics. For Habermas, Nietzsche cast away reason to gain "a foothold in myth as the other of reason."[45] Like all thinkers who step outside of the dialectic of enlightenment, Nietzsche undertakes a "conspicuous leveling" of modernity, which loses its singular status and "constitutes only a last epoch in the far-reaching history of a rationalization initiated by the dissolution of archaic life and the collapse of myth."[46] Habermas's interpretation of Nietzsche relies heavily upon the *Birth of Tragedy* and the concept of the Dionysian, which he sees as an unoriginal attempt to establish a new mythology. The difference between Nietzsche's and the Romantics' new mythology is that the latter equated Dionysus with God: "This identification of the frenzied wine-god with the Christian savior-god is only possible because Romantic messianism aimed at a *rejuvenation* of, but not a departure from, the West."[47] In contrast to Nietzsche, the new mythology of the Romantics "was supposed to restore a lost solidarity but not reject the emancipation."[48] In other words, Habermas seems to be claiming that Romantic messianism, the belief in God, and the Romantics' sympathies toward the Catholic church hold more emancipatory potential than the rejection of Christianity. Habermas finds Nietzsche's shift from religious to aesthetic perspectives problematic, asserting that Nietzsche continues the Romantic purification of aesthetic phenomena from all theoretical and practical associations.[49] Nietzsche is on an escape route from modernity, and confronts subject-centered reason with reason's absolute Other: "As a counterauthority to reason, Nietzsche appeals to experiences that are displaced back into the archaic realm—experiences of self-disclosure of a decentered subjectivity, liberated from all constraints of cognition and purposive activity, all imperatives of utility and morality."[50] Habermas's claim is only valid within the confines of the Dionysian experience, which Nietzsche clearly relegates to the realm of art, for nowhere in the *Genealogy*, for instance, can one speak of a subjectivity liberated from the constraints of cognition, purpose, and utility.

As an optimist, Habermas believes that things can only get better if they are given a chance. Insights "can only be repressed or corrected by better insights."[51] Habermas criticizes the *Birth of Tragedy*'s view that the world is only justifiable as an aesthetic phenomenon and contends that such an aesthetic understanding of the world has led Nietzsche to see all things as illusory appearances. The world appears in Nietzsche as "a network of distortions and interpretations for which no intention and no text provides the basis."[52] More importantly, Nietzsche's ungrounded critique refuses to distinguish between claims to truth and claims to power, and Habermas reproaches Nietzsche for reducing everything that is and should be to the aesthetic dimension:

> Together with a sensibility that allows itself to be affected in as many different ways as possible, the power to create meaning constitutes the authentic core of the will to

power. This is at the same time a will to illusion, a will to simplification, to masks, to the superficial; art counts as man's genuine metaphysical activity, because life itself is based on illusion, deception, optics, the necessity of the perspectival and of error.[53]

While Habermas grants that the arguments for the will to power and the power to create meaning are not objectionable in themselves, he does object to Nietzsche's refusal to ground judgement in rationality. Nietzsche "does not recognize as a moment of reason the critical capacity for assessing value," and becomes thus caught up in the "dilemma of a self-enclosed critique of reason that has become total."[54] Nietzsche replaces ethical values with aesthetic criteria. Errors, accidents, and perspectives become the pillars of his epistemology and view of history. Habermas, in turn, does not recognize the positing of value judgments as an activity of instrumental reason, whose underlying motivations do not rest necessarily in an objectively subjective rationality that seeks the better argument. In Nietzsche, Adorno, and Horkheimer rationality functions not as the universalized ground for subjective agency, but rather as a tool for the subject's objectivizing will toward self-preservation and self-affirmation.

A further weakness of Habermas's critique of Nietzsche is his focus on his early work. He projects the aesthetic justification of the world, which Nietzsche had already renounced beginning with *Human, All too Human*, and the Dionysian as the overriding principles of Nietzsche's thought. This move allows him to relegate Nietzsche's thought to the realm of art, thereby disqualifying it from other spheres of influence. At times, it appears as if Habermas deliberately makes use of the postmodern interpretations of Nietzsche, which stress Nietzsche's critique of reason, metaphysics, and ideology, in order to turn those interpretations against him. By emphasizing that Nietzsche sees the world as a network of distortions with no intention and no text, Habermas accentuates the postmodern Nietzsche, who activates the elements of myth and play and whose work seemingly exemplifies the arbitrariness of signs and values. Unlike Adorno, who sees Nietzsche as the major figure in the enlightenment of enlightenment, Habermas disregards the implications of Nietzsche's critique of ideology for the formulation of a self-reflexive critique of modernity and modern society.

In his essay "The Entwinement of Myth and Enlightenment: Max Horkheimer and Theodor Adorno," Habermas attempts to forestall a confusion of postmodern moods and attitudes with the thought of Adorno and Horkheimer. Their "blackest" book, the *Dialectic*, is a work influenced by the "dark" and the "black" writers of the bourgeoisie. The "dark" writers, such as Machiavelli and Hobbes, still thought in a constructive way, and their lines of thought lead to Marxist social theory.[55] However, the "black" writers, such as the Marquis de Sade and Nietzsche, broke the ties to the rational tradition of thought, and Adorno and Horkheimer join these writers in conceptualizing the Enlightenment's process of self-destruction. They no longer place their hope in the liber-

ating force of Enlightenment.[56] As a consequence of the poststructuralist revital-
ization of Nietzsche, "moods and attitudes are spreading that are confusingly like
those of Horkheimer and Adorno."[57] However, Adorno and Horkheimer differ
from Nietzsche and postmodern thought, according to Habermas, by retaining
the Benjaminian hope of the hopeless and by continuing the paradoxical labor of
conceptualization.[58] In contrast to Nietzsche, who gives the critique of reason
such "an affirmative twist," Adorno and Horkheimer hold on to "determinate
negation on an ad hoc basis."[59] Although Habermas sees Nietzsche as "the great
model for the critique of ideology's totalizing self-overcoming," he nevertheless
insists that the "two sides," Adorno and Horkheimer on one side and Nietzsche
on the other, pursue their critiques of culture from "contrary orientations."[60]
However, because Habermas draws such convincing parallels between Nietzsche
and the *Dialectic* and presents strong evidence of their similarities, the reader
might question how substantial the differences and how contrary the orientations
of the two sides really are. In comparison with the many similarities Habermas
establishes, the *Dialectic*'s Benjaminian hope and ad hoc negation fail to provide
a definitive boundary between departing from and remaining within the Western
tradition. Habermas claims that despite their totalized critique of enlightenment,
Adorno and Horkheimer, unlike Nietzsche, never entirely stepped out of the
rational tradition of enlightenment. Whether Habermas's interpretations of Nietzsche's work and the *Dialectic* do justice to the authors themselves remains debat-
able. What is clear, however, is Habermas's important contribution to the study
of those patterns of thought shared by Nietzsche and Adorno.

Adorno and Horkheimer challenge the opposition between myth and
enlightenment, as well as enlightened thinking's implicit status as a counterforce
to myth, through their thesis of the secret complicity between myth and enlightenment. Habermas criticizes the *Dialectic*'s and Nietzsche's mutilation of reason
and claims that Adorno, Horkheimer, and Nietzsche have driven reason out of
morality, law, and science. They falsely equate claims to truth with claims to
power: "In cultural modernity, reason gets definitively stripped of its validity
claim and assimilated to sheer power. The critical capacity to take up a 'Yes' or
'No' stance and to distinguish between valid and invalid propositions is *undermined* as power and validity claims enter into a turbid fusion."[61] The *Dialectic*
oversimplifies modernity by disregarding the Weberian differentiation between
three autonomous value spheres: art, science, and law work out respectively
questions of taste, truth, and justice and therefore "unfold in accord to their own
proper logics," while the formation of expert cultures assist the "claims of propo-
sitional truth, normative rightness, and authenticity [to] attain *their own logic*."[62]
The development of the separate spheres competes with the "assimilation of
validity claims to power claims and the destruction of our critical capacities."[63]
The *Dialectic*, according to Habermas, does not do justice to the rational content
of modernity, because it fails to take into account that rationality and the dynamics of theory push the sciences beyond merely engendering technically useful

knowledge. A second weakness is the *Dialectic*'s failure to acknowledge that rationality functions as the universal foundation of law and morality. Thirdly, Adorno and Horkheimer do not properly account for the rationality of the aesthetic experience with its "innovatively enriched range of values proper to self-realization."[64] With Nietzsche, Adorno, and Horkheimer, the drama of the enlightenment arrives at its climax, because the critique of ideology itself comes under the suspicion of being incapable of producing truths. According to Habermas, the uninhibited skepticism of Nietzsche, Adorno, and Horkheimer toward reason renders them blind to the emancipatory potential of communicative rationality. Their perspective is tainted by aesthetic judgments that interfere with their ability to arrive at rational judgments. Nietzsche emphasizes

> the aesthetic horizon of experience . . . and stylizes aesthetic judgment, on the model of a 'value appraisal' exiled to irrationality, into a capacity for discrimination beyond good and evil, truth and falsehood. In this way, Nietzsche gains criteria for a critique of culture that unmasks science and morality as being in similar ways ideological expressions of a perverted will to power, just as *Dialectic of Enlightenment* denounces these structures as embodiments of instrumental reason. This confirms our suspicion that Horkheimer and Adorno perceive cultural modernity from a similar experiential horizon, with the same heightened sensibility, and even with the same cramped optics that render one insensible to the traces and the existing forms of communicative rationality.[65]

Adorno and Horkheimer regarded the foundations of an ideological critique as shattered and advocated a radicalization and self-overcoming of such a critique of ideology. Reason assimilated itself to power and thereby "relinquished its critical force."[66] Habermas assumes that "*we*" no longer share Adorno and Horkheimer's skeptical attitude toward reason and Enlightenment, and classifies Adorno and Horkheimer's perception of enlightenment as historically motivated, pessimistic, and unsuitable for describing present conditions. Presumably "*we*" do not share this "mood" because we do have hope: the hope for a life world reconciled by communicative rationality. Habermas envisions a life world in which the Weberian spheres of art, morality, and science each operate within and according to their own criteria. Communicative rationality is the model for the discursive negotiation of a consensus between the various expert cultures and value spheres, and communicative rationality can rescue the *Dialectic* from completely falling into Nietzsche's trap. Habermas argues that Adorno and Horkheimer's aim to lift the veil "covering the confusion between power and reason" reveals a purist intent; what is needed is a "mediating kind of thinking" that procedurally separates the spheres of reason and power and recognizes at the same time that convictions "are formed and confirmed in a medium that is not 'pure' and removed from the world of appearances."[67] If, according to Habermas, one could relinquish the "purist" attitude, one could find a way out of the aporetic situation of a totalized critique of reason. Horkheimer and Adorno should have weighed the grounds that would have cast doubt on their skepticism itself, and "in this way, perhaps, they could have set the normative foundations of critical theory."[68] When one considers their radical skepticism and their anti-systematic impetus, it is doubtful whether Adorno and Horkheimer wanted to formulate normative foundations. For this reason, Habermas's suggestion that they could and should have done so seems, at the least, irrelevant.

In his critique of Nietzsche and postmodernism, Habermas consistently ascribes to both an antimodernism. Rather than criticizing modernist and post-modernist positions for their inherent shortcomings, Habermas attempts to define, criticize, and disqualify these positions by placing them in opposition to the rational tradition of thought, mainly in opposition to Kant, Hegel, and Marx. Habermas decries the loss of normative standards and the flight into irrationality, apolitical ineffectuality, and conservativism. In criticizing Habermas's interpretation of Nietzsche as a reversion to myth, Ernst Behler summarizes the difference between postmodernism and the thought of Adorno and Horkheimer:

> They [Adorno and Horkheimer] realized only too well the injuries caused by "instru-mentalized" reason, the coercion of systematized conceptual thought, and the pre-tensions of utopian reconciliations. Yet they maintained Hegelian wholeness and integrity in the structural patterns of their thought by lamenting its absence and unre-alizability as a lack, a loss, a deficiency and not, as in poststructuralist and postmod-ern thought, as the appropriate human condition. They suffered from this situation and increased their suffering by insisting on a critique of reason through reason, and by not giving in to a prerational, suprarational, or transsubjective, but in any event irrational, lapse into myth as Nietzsche and his French followers have done accord-ing to Habermas.[69]

Habermas's speech "Modernity—An Incomplete Project," given on the occasion of his receiving the Theodor W. Adorno Prize of the city of Frankfurt, gives a condensed version of his critique of postmodern positions. Habermas criticizes the postmoderns, including Derrida, Lyotard, and Foucault, for disposing of "the normalizing functions of tradition," and for the "anarchistic intention of blowing up the continuum of history."[70] He categorizes postmodern thinkers with the labels "young conservatives" and "neoconservatives." Habermas draws a line of irrational thought from the Romantics and Nietzsche to Bataille, Foucault, and Derrida. Behler points out that this image of irrationalism is as problematic as the equation of postmodernism with conservatism, and maintains that "it is Haber-mas's critique of postmodernism and its foundationalist drive that shows a spon-taneous alliance with a traditionalist, conservative fundamentalism of basic values and basic norms."[71]

Habermas firstly conceives of postmodern thought as exhibiting a preoccu-pation with the moment and as purveying a static view of history. Secondly, since traditional standards are neutralized by overemphasizing the present, the transi-tory, and the discontinuity of everyday life at the expense of a consciousness of the past, postmodern philosophers, in his view, thus reproduce the basic failure of the artistic avant-garde. In the tradition of Nietzsche, philosophers such as Foucault, Derrida, and Lyotard step outside of modernity and "justify an irreconcilable antimodernism" by putting in place of reason the "powers of imagination, self-experience and emotion."[72] Behler asserts that Habermas's reception of the "irrational" thinkers is marked by gross misinterpretations, including his allegation of conservatism and the invention of a religious dimension in the thought of Nietzsche and the postmoderns. Behler further suspects that Habermas's construction of an irrational tradition of thought from Schlegel and Nietzsche to Derrida is the result of Habermas's failure to read them carefully and recognize their uniqueness.[73]

Habermas's project of modernity, which hopes for the reconciliation of the mutually exclusive expert cultures, the Weberian value spheres of science, morality, and art, relies upon communicative rationality as the salvation of modernity. Based on the assumption that a consensus is desirable and achievable, communicative rationality is, for Habermas, the reasonable activity that will continue the Enlightenment project. It grounds his thought and justifies his identification of the "better" argument. However, communicative rationality can also be read against Habermas's intentions as a subtext of instrumental reason. As is the case with instrumental reason, communicative rationality acts in the light of utility and necessity. Negotiating a consensus and convincing someone of the "better" argument can be envisioned, as Habermas does, as domination-free dialogue, *herrschaftsfreies Gespräch*, but whether conversations freed from domination and power interests can and do occur in reality is indeed questionable. As an ideal speech situation and utopian vision, the negotiation of a consensus and the conviction that the "better" argument will prevail are not without merit. However, when these discursive practices are bound to social, political, and economic interests, the boundaries between the "better" argument and claims to power become fluid and are not necessarily distinguishable.

When unencumbered by its foundationalist drive and the hostility toward Nietzsche, Habermas's perceptive analysis of the connections between the works of Nietzsche, Adorno and Horkheimer provides a productive basis for further investigations, and his criticism offers itself for a reevaluation of its inherent prejudices. Nietzsche's and Adorno and Horkheimer's critique of rationality points not toward the departure or the danger of a departure from Western tradition, but rather toward a mode of criticism that must operate within Münchhausen's paradox. In the spirit of Nietzsche the question would have to be: What is the value of these Habermasian values? By turning Nietzsche against Habermas's claim to truth—in good humor, of course—it can be affirmed that judgments and value judgments "can in the last resort never be true: they possess values only as symptoms, they come into consideration only as symptoms—in themselves such judgments are stupidities."[74] It would lead beyond the scope of this study to venture into an examination of Habermas's judgments as symptoms.

It is sufficient to suggest that Habermas's critical stance toward Nietzsche is not atypical for his generation of thinkers, whose experience of Nietzsche was influenced by the entanglement of antihumanism, antirationalism, and the Third Reich. In holding on to reason as the grounding force of human interaction, Habermas remains a voice of conscience and political morality in Germany.

THE OLD AND THE NEW ENLIGHTENMENT

In the *Dialectic*'s first excursus, "Odysseus or Myth and Enlightenment," Adorno acknowledges Nietzsche's ambiguous relationship to the Enlightenment and maintains that his thought is simultaneously an unrelenting critique and a consistent completion of it.[75] Nietzsche thinks the ideas and ideals of the Enlightenment through to their radical conclusion. Adorno distinguishes between two major attitudes prevalent in Nietzsche's work: on the one hand, Nietzsche remains critical toward the nihilistic forces of enlightenment, but on the other, he also saw himself as part of the process of enlightenment, understood as the thought of sovereign minds. Both as a participant in and a critic of enlightenment, Nietzsche sheds light on it and formulates its relationship to domination and power. According to Adorno, Nietzsche turns the double nature of enlightenment into a basic motif of history. For Nietzsche, enlightenment is both "the universal movement of sovereign Spirit (whose executor he felt himself to be)" and a "'nihilistic' anti-life force."[76] The latter view of enlightenment is the one that Nietzsche's "pre-Fascist followers retained" and perverted into an ideology, which becomes "blind praise of a blind life subject to the same nexus of action by which everything living is suppressed."[77] But even as a movement of sovereign Spirit, enlightenment should not be seen as an unambiguously positive term. Enlightenment illuminates the actions and motives of those in positions of power while it serves, at the same time, to perpetuate the structures of power. Enlightenment is a tool of oppression that creates the illusion of liberation and progress. Nietzsche was "one of the few after Hegel who recognized the dialectic of enlightenment" and it was he "who expressed its antipathy to domination."[78] It is this antipathy to domination that attracts Adorno's attention. In the following passage Adorno cites Nietzsche:

> "The Enlightenment" should be "taken into the people, so that the priests all become priests with a bad conscience—and the same must be done with regard to the State. That is the task of the Enlightenment: to make princes and statesmen unmistakably aware that everything they do is sheer falsehood. . . . On the other hand, Enlightenment has always been a tool for the 'great manipulators of government' [. . .] . . . The way in which the masses are fooled in this respect, for instance in all democracies, is very useful: the reduction and malleability of men are worked for as *progress!*"[79]

Revealing as historical principles these two aspects of enlightenment, Nietzsche traces the notion of enlightenment as progressive thought back to the beginning of traditional history. Suggesting its complicity with power, Nietzsche simultaneously calls into question the so-called "progressiveness" of enlightened thought. It is thus not, as some critics claim, some form of aristocratic conservativism that constitutes the basis for Nietzsche's antidemocratic position; it is rather his antipathy toward and acute analysis of structures of domination, which expose such notions as equality and progress as ideological tools for power, and which buttress his critique of modernity and the modern state.

In his exploration of Nietzsche's position toward enlightenment, Henning Ottmann agrees with Adorno's assessment, which contradicts Habermas's position, that Nietzsche is part of the enlightenment process. Ottmann maintains that the *Dialectic* has proven beyond a doubt that Nietzsche's philosophy cannot be turned into an irrational and anti-enlightened myth, but must be perceived as having moved through the Enlightenment. Nietzsche's thought is not counterenlightenment fighting enlightenment, Ottmann argues, but rather part of a process of enlightenment arriving at a stance of radical opposition. Reason, which does not accept that which is incommensurable and Other to it, becomes itself particular and irrational. When thought through to its conclusions, the freedom of enlightenment unveils itself as the will to domination over nature and human beings.[80] Ottmann argues that Nietzsche's relationship toward the Enlightenment underwent three major stages: firstly, the speculations of the free spirit; secondly, the recognition of the dialectic of enlightenment; and thirdly, the renewal of enlightenment, which seeks a reconciliation between myth and enlightenment. Ottmann sees Nietzsche's first concept of enlightenment in the notion of *Freigeisterei* (free-spiritedness), which was of special importance to his works in the years between 1876 and 1882. Ottmann claims that Nietzsche became an enlightened thinker when his hopes for a rebirth of tragedy were disappointed. This disappointment and his turn toward thinking as a free spirit are connected to the personal break with Wagner, all of which was part of a general process of liberation: liberation from religion, metaphysics, morality, and politics.[81] During this period, the emphasis of Nietzsche's thought shifts from art and the *Artistenmetaphysik* in the *Birth of Tragedy* to the theoretical retraction of the mistakes and failures of metaphysics, religion, and morality. Nietzsche identifies the human, all-too-human sources of these errors and contends that the intellect should recognize its own failures and limitations. However, the destruction of errors comes into conflict with the life-affirming quality *(Lebensdienlichkeit)* of errors and illusions, and Nietzsche's awareness of this conflict leads him, according to Ottmann, to his recognition of the dialectic of enlightenment. Beyond being an unavoidable part of life, errors and illusions are simultaneously unacceptable prejudices and yet necessary for the correction of other errors.

> The falseness of a judgment is for us not necessarily an objection to a judgment; in this respect our new language may sound strangest. The question is to what extent it is life-promoting, life-preserving, species-preserving, perhaps even species-cultivating. And

we are fundamentally inclined to claim that the falsest judgments . . . are the most indispensable for us; that without accepting the fictions of logic, without measuring reality against the purely inverted world of the unconditional and self-identical, without a constant falsification of the world by means of numbers, man could not live—that renouncing false judgments would mean renouncing life and a denial of life.[82]

Untruth is a condition of life, and recognizing this condition means resisting accustomed value judgments; a philosophy that goes beyond conventional values places itself "beyond good and evil."[83] Nietzsche proposes the entwinement of truth and error, myth and reason, and argues that one cannot function without the other, because myths and fictions provide the basis for judgments that are conducive to life. Ottmann locates a tragic moment in Nietzsche's recognition of the dialectic of enlightenment, because it leads to a contradiction between knowledge and life, and thus even the life-affirming quality of enlightenment turns out to be an illusion.[84]

Realizing that the opposition of life and knowledge leads to an impasse, Nietzsche, following Ottmann's scheme, turns to the ideal of a *New Enlightenment*. In two aphorisms written in 1884, Nietzsche explains his idea of *The New Enlightenment*, to which he accords several tasks: the first task involves uncovering the basic errors and misconceptions about life, such as causality, the freedom of the will, evil, the will to truth, and God; Nietzsche wants to replace the idea of sin with the general miscarriage of the idea of humanity.[85] The second task of the New Enlightenment is the discovery of the creative drive, and the third is self-overcoming as a step toward overcoming man, *die Überwindung des Menschen*. Similar to the *Dialectic*, Nietzsche remains within the precincts of enlightenment by projecting the possibility of its renewal. Nietzsche's New Enlightenment aims at a differentiation rather than a homogenization of the "old" enlightenment, which thought in terms of the "democratic herd" and "equality for all."[86] The "old" enlightenment is an unfailing instrument of power and domination, deployed to control and govern the masses and to render people more insecure, weaker-willed, dependent, and needy. In short, the "old" enlightenment develops the instinct of the herd animal in human beings. Because of this link between enlightened thought and power, "the great manipulators of government"[87] utilized enlightenment as an instrument of power. In the end, the masses only deceive themselves about enlightenment and the freedom it promises, which is in turn useful for those in power, because it diminishes the demands of the masses and makes them pliable. Through enlightenment thought the ruling class deceives the masses and realizes its own goals, while the masses believe that enlightenment contributes to their emancipation. In citing Nietzsche's aphorism in the *Dialectic*, Adorno calls forth Nietzsche as a witness for his contention that enlightenment is an ideological fiction with a double-edged relationship to power, and that the masses, immersed in the bourgeois context of delusion *(bürgerliche Verblendungszusammenhang)*, participate willingly in their own repression. Adorno and Horkheimer avoid Nietzsche's antidemocratic stance, which identifies the masses as an assembly of weak-willed herd animals, by pointing out how the deliberately impenetrable context of delusion controls and deceives them, and eventually turns the masses into gullible objects of economic and political forces. The masses are drilled to form "yet another battalion" serving the "present and future great plans of the system."[88] They are fed and quartered, and every rise in the standard of living reinforces their powerlessness and dependence. In the eyes of the masses, "their reduction to mere objects of the administered life, which preforms every sector of modern existence including language and perception, represents objective necessity, against which they believe there is nothing they can do."[89]

While Nietzsche projects concrete steps, such as the unveiling of errors, the discovery of creative forces, and the self-overcoming of man, toward a positive vision of his *New Enlightenment*, the *Dialectic*'s "positive notion" of enlightenment is in fact a negative model: namely an enlightenment freed from "entanglement in blind domination."[90] The *Dialectic* never specifies what a positive notion of enlightenment could be, and this refusal to provide an utopian vision, the *Bilderverbot* noted by many critics, must be seen in the context of Adorno's emphasis on negativity and his later project of a negative dialectics. For Adorno, dialectical thought functions as criticism and negativity, while utopian visions offer affirmations. These affirmations posit not only a better future, but also falsify present reality and past injustices. Adorno refrains from projecting utopian goals or issuing instructions for a political praxis, because it would imply an attempt by thought to restrict reality: "The utopian impulse in thinking is all the stronger, the less it objectifies itself as utopia—a further form of regression—whereby it sabotages its own realization. Open thinking points beyond itself."[91] Utopian speculations pretend to have a superior understanding of reality and the potential for the future. Perpetuating enlightenment's myth of progress, they come close to its totalitarian claims to truth. Since Adorno rejects claims to absolute truth, he can offer nothing more or less than critical negativity and experimental analysis. Like Nietzsche, who maintains that philosophy often replaces one error with another, Adorno and Horkheimer want to avoid dogmatism and systematization: "Explanations of the world as all or nothing are mythologies."[92] Transfiguring negativity into a promise of redemption represents an untrue form of resistance against deception. Determinate negation, however, rejects idols and ideas of the absolute, and the dialectical mode of thought makes visible the illusionary and fictional quality of philosophical investigations; it "interprets every image as writing. It shows how the admission of its falsity is to be read in the lines of its features."[93] Although Adorno's attempt to refuse all affirmations concurs with Nietzsche's view of the falsity of absolute claims, it also leads him to criticize Nietzsche's insistence on the affirmation of life.

Of course, one must see this lack of a positive vision and the pessimistic tone of the *Dialectic* in the historical context of the forties, when the hope for historical progress and a better future appeared remote enough to be abandoned altogether. The experience of fascism, Stalinism, and the capitalist consumer society and culture industry in the United States seemed to have left little hope for anything more than a radical negation of the course of Western civilization. Gunzelin Schmid Noerr argues that as a regression to barbarism, fascism is not just the historical background of critical theory, but the defining moment of the very questions the *Dialectic* poses.[94] The *Dialectic*, argues Schmid Noerr, represents the search for the fascist structures underlying civilization. In Horkheimer and Adorno's view, fascism is neither explainable as a singular accident of history, nor is it by any means classifiable as an occurrence integrated entirely into the history and development of European totalitarian systems, as claimed by some historians such as Ernst Nolte, to name one example.[95] For Horkheimer and Adorno, the historical development of rationality and power culminates in fascism, but it does not do so by teleological necessity. Consequently, by historicizing the horrors of the fascist present, the *Dialectic* portrayed the history of rationality as a history of inhumanity. It identifies those moments and structures that tendentially lead toward fascism without, however, claiming that they necessarily or inherently lead to it.

SOCRATISM

Both the *Dialectic* and Nietzsche share the view that enlightenment is not a historical period with a beginning and an end, but rather a process extending back to the beginning of the historical tradition. Horkheimer and Adorno locate the roots of enlightenment, and therefore the beginning of the development toward fascism, in myth, which has always previously existed as enlightenment, and exemplify their claim with Odysseus and the Homerian epic. For Nietzsche, Socrates embodies the traits of enlightenment's logocentrism and stands at the beginning of the civilized decay toward modernity. Nietzsche uses Socrates as an example to show the limits of rationality and the dialectic of enlightenment and to support his—and the *Dialectic*'s—argument that enlightenment inevitably reverts to myth.

Nietzsche locates this rationalist turn in the decay of Greek culture. The rise of the logos, the devaluation of art, and the demise of tragedy are simultaneous processes that lead to the rationalization of life and to a culture dominated by rationality. Scientific and positivistic thought reduce rationality to a tool for numbering and categorization, ontological thought reduces the diversity of phenomena and multiplicity of meaning to a unifying first principle, and teleological thought directs itself toward achieving finality and completion. Trapped in its own fictions, enlightenment's expansive reason of emancipation becomes the repressive reason of limitation and destruction. As the philosopher of enlightenment who simultaneously caters to the masses and deceives them, Socrates is the representative *par excellence* of logocentric thought. In contrast to the artist, who values and admires the surface, Socrates is the archetype of the *theoretical man*, who wishes to see through appearance, reveal the hidden, and uncover the veiled.

Whenever the truth is uncovered, "the artist will always cling with rapt gaze to what still remains covering even after such uncovering; but the theoretical man enjoys and finds satisfaction in the discarded covering and finds the highest object of his pleasure in the process of an ever-happy uncovering that succeeds through his own efforts."[96] Unlike the artist and the Greeks, who knew how "to stop courageously at the surface, the fold, the skin, to adore appearances, to believe in forms, tones, words, in the whole Olympus of appearance," who were "superficial—out of profundity,"[97] the theoretical type is more interested in the self-satisfaction derived from the act of unveiling rather than in the remaining, ever-new mystery and hidden qualities of the unveiled. However, the theoretical desire for truth is connected to a narcissistic pleasure derived from the act of unveiling, and the will to truth is thus not as rational as it had initially appeared. The Enlightenment thinker Gottfried Ephraim Lessing, whom Nietzsche characterizes as the honest theoretical type, dared to voice the theorist's most fundamental secret, by admitting that the search for truth is more important than truth itself:

> Beside this isolated insight, born of an excess of honesty if not of exuberance, there is, to be sure, a profound *illusion* that first saw the light of the world in the person of Socrates: the unshakable faith that thought, using the thread of causality, can penetrate the deepest abysses of being, and that thought is capable not only of knowing being but even of *correcting* it. This sublime metaphysical illusion accompanies science as an instinct and leads science again and again to its limits at which it must turn into *art*.[98]

Resting on the belief that reason can not only uncover the secrets of being but also correct it, Socrates institutes its tyranny. Beyond satisfying the desire for the discovery of facts and ordering principles, Socrates is possessed by the desire for thought to legitimate and change being. Socrates does not accept and affirm existence but rather feels the need to explain and correct nature. Here Socrates, the theoretical type, reaches the limits of rationality and becomes entangled in the dialectic of enlightenment: science must turn to art, fiction, and myth in order to justify its claims. Enlightenment turns to and into myth. Socrates devises a myth of the enlightenment by suggesting that thought can change being. Faced with the necessity of justifying his "illusion" about rationality, Socrates must also lay claim to art as a creative force, for to change the interpretations and perceptions of being, the theorist has no choice but to become an active creator and to revert to art. The instincts and desire for discovery lead theoretical men to leave behind rationality. The mission "to make existence appear comprehensible and thus justified" goes to great lengths to justify its claim, for "if reasons do not suffice, myth has to come to their aid in the end—myth which I have just called the necessary consequence, indeed the purpose, of science."[99] The construction of myth is therefore not only an indispensable result of scientific thought, but also its undeclared rationale. Spurred by its illusions, science "speeds irresistibly toward its limits where its optimism, concealed in the essence of logic, suffers shipwreck."[100]

Socrates, the prototype of the theoretical optimist and "the one turning point and vortex of so-called world-history," has limitless faith in reason and the ability to grasp the nature of being.[101] Knowledge and insight have the power of a universal panacea, while errors are understood as the ultimate evil. Socrates believes in the human capacity to know nature and believes that knowledge and rational thought can eradicate errors and superstition. Nietzsche, in contrast, argues that the so-called knowledge of the essence of things is a creation of the mind, which can neither be justified by nor rely upon rationality alone. Enlightenment must turn to myth in order to fulfill science's ultimate goal, the explanation and justification of all phenomena. However, Nietzsche contends with irony that the mystagogue of science, Socrates, might have saved the world from the consequences of a gruesome practical pessimism: "For if we imagine that the whole incalculable sum of energy used up for the world tendency had been used *not* in the service of knowledge but for the practical, i.e., egoistic aims of individuals and people, then we realize that in that case universal wars of annihilation and continual migration of peoples" would have weakened the will to live and led to mass suicide and "genocide motivated by pity."[102] While Socrates accelerated the decline of culture, he also paradoxically saved civilization from physical self-destruction.

In his chapter on Socrates in *Twilight of the Idols*, Nietzsche returns to the motif of Socrates as the supposed rescuer of and cure for Greek culture, a cure, however, that does not halt the progress of the disease. Nietzsche criticizes Socrates and the Socratic school of thought as pseudo-Greek representatives of decline, symptoms of decay, and agents of dissolution.[103] Reinforcing his earlier argument, Nietzsche no longer blames Socrates for the death of tragedy, because Socrates had no choice: either he had to become absurdly rational or he would have to perish. A decadent due to excessive rationality, Socrates is a part of the decaying Greek culture, but his making "a tyrant of reason" became a matter of life and death, since rationality was meant to be a saviour and the last effort for self-preservation. This is why Socrates was compelled to construct that bizarrest of equations: reason equals virtue which equals happiness.[104] Socrates, the philosopher of the rabble, made dialectics, which is one of the most effective tools to set in motion the dynamics of *ressentiment*, into the dominant mode of thought. Dialectics, by Nietzsche's account, is a "pitiless instrument" with which "one can play tyrant; one compromises by conquering. The dialectician leaves it to his opponent to demonstrate he is not an idiot: he enrages, he at the same time makes helpless. The dialectician *devitalizes* his opponent's intellect."[105] Expressing the philosophy of the mob, dialectical thought serves to act out the *ressenti-*

ment of the masses and represents the performance of domination. Nietzsche detects a certain fanaticism in the deployment of rationality by Socrates and the Socratic school, and contends that this indicates the pathological rigor of a decadent morality. The formula that equates reason, morality, and happiness supports the dependency upon reason and the necessity of repressing the instincts. Although Socrates employed rationality to combat suffering and to stem the decline of Greek culture, Nietzsche argues that Socrates ultimately only increased suffering and hastened this decline. Socrates exercised fascination, because he seemed to be a physician who offered a cure. However, his cure of rationality is poison and exemplifies a self-destructive form of life. Like Christian morality, his cure attempts to eradicate the symptoms of human suffering without ever being able to even ascertain its cause. The cure of rationality just redistributes the symptoms of decay and ultimately destroys its own viability in the process.

In the aphorism entitled "Criticism of Modernity," Nietzsche defines decadence as the instinctive preference for "that which leads to dissolution, that which hastens the end,"[106] and identifies decadence as a process reaching from Socrates to the establishment of the modern state. As the first decadent, Socrates cannot step outside of decadence but can only alter its expression; he represents merely another symptom of the same disease.[107]

> Socrates was a misunderstanding: *the entire morality of improvement, the Christian included, has been a misunderstanding.* . . . The harshest daylight, rationality at all cost, life bright, cold, circumspect, conscious, without instinct, in opposition to the instincts, has itself been no more than a form of sickness, another form of sickness— and by no means a way back to "virtue," to "health," to happiness. . . . To *have* to combat one's instincts—that is the formula for *décadence.*[108]

Socrates' proclamation of rationality as the highest and most privileged faculty of recognition and reflection opposes art and life. Socrates not only furthers the internalization and repression of the instincts, but is also instrumental in the destruction of Greek tragedy. Aesthetic Socratism—that is, Socratism spilling over into the realm of the aesthetic—destroys the expression of genuine art by insisting upon the rationalization of art. Introducing the will to truth and the drive for theoretical knowledge to tragedy, it becomes naturalistic, inartistic, and sober artistry.[109] Paralleling Socrates' dictum "knowledge is virtue," aesthetic Socratism promotes this law: "To be beautiful everything must be intelligible."[110] Thus, even in art, knowledge becomes an absolute virtue, bringing about the degeneration of tragedy through reasonableness and rationalistic method. Euripides, the embodiment of aesthetic Socratism, ruined tragedy by turning it into a dramatized epos.

Directly opposed to the Dionysian, the Socratic is the death warrant of tragedy. Restraining the vibrant, unmediated life force of the Dionysian reinforces the internalization, rationalization, and repression of nature and the instincts, and turns tragedy into drama and a further symptom of decadence. In his "Excursus" to the *Dialectic*, Adorno explicates in a Nietzschean manner this internalization and rationalization that lead the individual into a cycle of self-destruction. In order to avert physical annihilation by the forces of nature or the will of the gods, Odysseus must repress his instincts and engages in similar tyrannical excesses as the Socratic, theoretical type. Nietzsche draws a line from Socrates to Richard Wagner, the decadent artist *par excellence*, whose connection to decadence and to Socrates shall be explored in chapter four.

Nietzsche's criticism of Socrates as the embodiment of enlightenment, logocentrism, and theoretical culture is unrelenting. Through their search for legitimation and their claims to truth, Socrates and enlightenment become involved in the fabrication of myths and fictions about life, because they do not recognize and accept the limits of rationality. Unlike Nietzsche, who admits that he might be only replacing one error with another, enlightenment thought insists upon replacing *wrong* judgments with *right* ones. The figure of Socrates exemplifies the self-righteousness of enlightenment as much as it does its limits; his thought is testimony to the dialectic of the enlightenment, the point at which enlightenment reverts to myth. However, Nietzsche holds out the hope for the overcoming of the tyranny of reason and metaphysics, for a *New Enlightenment* and a *Socrates who practices music*. Nietzsche's own philosophizing with the hammer and unswerving urge to expose erroneous claims attest to his interest in the ideals of enlightenment, one ideal of which, as Adorno prefers to think of it, being the movement of the sovereign mind. While Nietzsche provides a positive vision of the *New Enlightenment* and the music-practicing Socrates, the authors of the *Dialectic* offer, as David Couzens Hoy points out, only the "vague assertion that the only antidote to Enlightenment is more enlightenment," thus admitting "the parasitism of the critical activity on the traditional conception of theory."[111] In other words, the authors were aware that they cannot step outside of enlightenment but must remain enclosed within it.

2

Writing History:
Nietzsche, Foucault, and Genealogy

More than twenty years after writing the *Dialectic*, Adorno and Horkheimer restated their support for their earlier ideas and expressed their hope that the *Dialectic*, as a critique of philosophy, offers more than the documentation of a historically outdated perception of enlightenment. Although admitting that they "would not now maintain without qualification every statement in the book," they nevertheless feel that their assessment of the transition to the world of the administered life was not too simplistic.[1] Although they accept that some formulations are no longer appropriate to contemporary experience, they claim that the "sinister trend" drawn out by the *Dialectic* continues. Bringing the book up to date would require nothing less than a new book, for Adorno and Horkheimer understand truth as bound to contingencies of time and place. There can be no universal and stable truth, because "the core of truth is historical."[2] With these criteria and qualifications in mind, an exploration of the writing of history has to consider the methodological implications of the *Dialectic*'s radical critique of enlightenment. Because of his reception and continuation of Nietzsche's genealogical project, the work of Michel Foucault invites a closer examination of the advantages and disadvantages of genealogy for the writing of history. Foucault's reflections on history and genealogy can serve as a productive medium for the attempt to uncover the moments of resistance and protest in Nietzsche's and Adorno's counternarratives to traditional history and philosophy.

A critique of enlightenment that merely analyzes the content of enlightenment thought alone is insufficient, because enlightenment ideology not only functions through argumentation, but also bears on the methodology and the manner of representation. In order to lay bare enlightenment's ideological presuppositions, it is necessary to find a method that resists the formal constraints imposed by enlightenment rationality, such as logic, identity thinking, and thinking in terms of progressions, first principles, telos, and cause. Nietzsche's genealogical model offers an alternative to the *Bildungsroman* of reason and enlightenment by narrating and interpreting the course of history and the historical transformation of phenomena from a different perspective. Genealogy attempts—not without creating its own pitfalls—to overcome the limitations and trappings of rationality and to recognize the failure of universal history to account for the dialectic of enlightenment and for the regressive dimensions of so-called progress. As Habermas and others have pointed out, there are many similarities between the interpretations of phenomena in the *Dialectic* and in Nietzsche's *On the Genealogy of Morals*. These works, however, contain not only similar lines of argumentation, but also similar ways of arguing. Beyond their common goal of exposing ideological presuppositions and errors of judgment, they engage in similar methodological and self-reflective enterprises, adding a performative aspect to their work. Accompanied by its aphoristic style of writing, which sets the antitotalitarian, antisystematic, and antimetaphysical tone in resistance to traditional philosophical discourse, the genealogical method, in its formulation of an alternative history of civilization, proposes alternative forms of writing history.

Inseparably bound to its radicalized critique of ideology and rationality, the *Dialectic*'s and the *Genealogy*'s strategic re-presentation of history reconstructs historical narration in order to expose the erroneous claims of enlightenment. By making visible the *Dialectic*'s strategic maneuvers, the concept of genealogy provides a useful analytical tool for a deeper understanding of Adorno and Horkheimer's philosophical project. More importantly, in conjunction with the Nietzschean drive towards the reevaluation of all values, it shall be argued here that genealogy rescues the *Dialectic* from merely reenacting enlightenment's reversion to myth. Interpreting the *Dialectic* in terms of genealogy not only rescues it from falling victim to its own claims of enlightenment's collapse into myth, but also provides the critical impetus for Adorno and Horkheimer's resolve to enlighten enlightenment. As a radical counternarrative, the *Dialectic* presents a genealogy of enlightenment that attempts to deliver itself from metaphysics, to investigate the ideological moments of rationality, and to challenge the notion that rational forces propel history toward enlightenment. To argue that the genealogical impetus and the Nietzschean drive "rescue" the *Dialectic* is to oppose Habermas's strong and consistent critique of the concept of genealogy. Instead of denouncing Nietzsche's influence and the radicalized critique of enlightenment and ideology, these factors are understood here as a productive and consistent resistance to enlightenment's inflated estimation of history and rationality.

In *The Gay Science*, Nietzsche maps out a genealogical program for the industrious or, as he calls them in the *Genealogy*, the honeygatherers of the spirit—*Honigsammler des Geistes*—who want to study matters of morality.[3] Genealogies, Nietzsche contends, are painstaking studies carried out in a meticulous fashion. Every phenomenon has to be considered in detail and must be thought of as a singular event in a particular time and at a particular place. The studious must collect evidence in order to determine the active and reactive forces in the struggle for dominance and to recognize those mechanisms designed to acquire and maintain power. Genealogists bring to light that which has been hidden, repressed, or forgotten by conventional history. To examine phenomena as expressions and matters of morality is to open up an immense field of work: "All kinds of individual passions have to be thought through and pursued though different ages, peoples, and great and small individuals; all their reason and all their evaluations and perspectives on things have to be brought into the light."[4] Striving toward distinctions in terms of time, manner, and place, Nietzsche emphasizes the need for an examination, within specific geographic and historical contexts, of individual passions and particular phenomena usually deemed insignificant by traditional history. The emphasis upon individual passions of great and small individuals forecloses the idea of a monumental history focusing exclusively upon the heroes and major events as perceived by traditional history. Nietzsche encourages the industrious to pursue subjects previously ignored by historians: "So far, all that has given color to existence still lacks a history: where is a history of love, of avarice, of envy, of conscience, of pious respect for tradition, or of cruelty? Even a comparative history of law or at least of punishment is so far lacking completely."[5] Nietzsche further suggests studies on such topics as the divisions of the day, the consequences of a regular schedule of work and of life in monasteries, and the moral effects of different foods. The genealogist, according to his view, ought to study the basic drives, needs, and motivations underlying human existence, including the reason, passion, and superstition involved in the formation of a view of the world. Yet another stage of research would be to ascertain the errors behind conventional reasons, moral judgments, and the social order.

Eric Blondel asserts that Nietzsche takes as models the so-called moralists of the eighteenth century, such as La Rochefoucauld, Montaigne, and Pascal, and in a fashion similar to theirs generalizes in his observations of *the* woman, *the* Christians, *the* priests, and *the* Jews. His general approach "means to show the unity and secret motives of their ways, thoughts, and impulses, describing and evaluating them according to the disparity between their facade and their deeper psychology."[6] As in the moralist tradition, Nietzsche is fond of employing the spirited style of maxims and aphorisms sprinkled with psychological and valuative generalizations. Genealogy, as Blondel points out, combines a number of approaches toward its subjects. As a psychological genealogy it reveals, uncovers, and unmasks the psychological origins of cultural ideals. As an investigation into the physiological origins of ideals, genealogy follows the transformations of ideals; as a philological study, it attempts a reading, decoding, and interpretation of hidden meanings.

While searching for the value of values, genealogies also evaluate, refute, and judge. Genealogies examine values, concepts, and words not in terms of their claim to truth, but rather in relation to their value for life. Genealogy shifts the emphasis from the accurate representation of historical events to an exploration of the functions of traditional values, judgments, and conventions. With its critical negativity toward existing value judgments and its aim to formulate a life-affirming counterhistory, the concept of genealogy continues the project of critical historiography outlined in "On the Advantage and Disadvantage of History for Life."[7] Here Nietzsche insists that history must not be reduced to an intellectual phenomenon representing and conserving the events of the past, but should be pursued for the sake of life. As a science, history constitutes a "final closing" and does not serve the future as a "powerful new life-giving influence."[8] Life, however, requires the service of history, just as it requires the act of forgetting. Both the awareness and forgetting of history are necessary in order to overcome inertia and to allow for human action. Excessive historical awareness suffocates life and is detrimental to those who must act in the present: "For with a certain excess of history life crumbles and degenerates, and finally, because of this degeneration, history itself degenerates as well."[9] As is the case with Socrates and the decadents, excess and overabundance lead to decay and self-destruction. History must serve life and must therefore be selective in its awareness of the past and its uses. Nietzsche distinguishes between three kinds of history: the monumental, the antiquarian, and the critical. The monumental view of the past possesses the advantage of espousing the knowledge that it was once possible for the great to exist, and that such greatness may well be possible again. Complete truthfulness is to monumental history's disadvantage, since its primary concern is to monumentalize great events and to stylize its actors into grand heroes of history. Monumentalization sacrifices truthfulness at the expense of the historical reality to be retold: "it will always approximate, generalize and finally equate differences; it will always weaken the disparity of motives and occasions in order, at the expense of the *cause*, to present the *effect* monumentally, that is, as exemplary and worthy of imitation."[10] For this reason monumental history disregards as much as possible causes, differences, and nuances and focuses instead upon those events' effects that can serve as great models for the present and the future. The disadvantages of monumental history are its deceptions through analogies and tempting similarities and its encouragement of fanaticism.

Antiquarian history is the history of the preserving, reverent, and loyal soul who loves to look back to origins. Nietzsche describes the antiquarian as a kind of *Biedermeier* personality, who cherishes ancestral furniture and bestows dignity upon the small, limited, and obsolete. Antiquarian history is content with tradition and firmly against the restless cosmopolitan selection of and search for novelty. Since it knows merely how to preserve the past, it undervalues change and the processes of becoming. Due to its conventionality, antiquarian history stands in the way to new life, new art, and new standards by affirming identity and continuity in history. The reverence of antiquarian history toward its object clearly demonstrates the need for the third kind of history, critical history, which is required from time to time "to shatter and dissolve something."[11] The critical historian serves life by shattering old values and views, facilitating the renewal of life. This is achieved by dragging his subject "to the bar of judgment, interrogating it meticulously and finally condemning it."[12] Nietzsche sees every past as worthy of condemnation. Occasionally, it is necessary to become aware of the injustice of the existence of some phenomenon, privilege, caste, or dynasty and to decide to which extent a thing deserves destruction:

> Then its past is considered critically, then one puts the knife to its roots, then one cruelly treads all pieties underfoot. It is always a dangerous process, namely dangerous for life itself: and men or ages which serve life in this manner of judging and annihilating a past are always dangerous and endangered men and ages. For since we happen to be the results of earlier generations we are also the results of their aberrations, passions and errors, even crimes; it is not possible quite to free oneself from this chain. If we condemn those aberrations and think ourselves quite exempt from them, the fact that we are descended from them is not eliminated. At best we may bring about a conflict between our inherited, innate nature and our knowledge.[13]

Thus critical history is propelled by the negativity, the radical criticism, and the drive for destruction necessary to allow the rise of the new. Just as Adorno and Horkheimer acknowledge that they are part of the process of enlightenment they criticize, Nietzsche also notes that the critical historian never stands entirely apart from and outside of the criticized object of study. Despite one's condemnations, one always remains a part, an inheritor, and a result of the condemned. However, the conflict initiated by the critical historians implants, under the best of circumstances, new habits and instincts. Here and there a victory is achieved over convention, but the critical historian may console him or herself with the realization that these new instincts and habits will one day be displaced by others. Critical historians know that what is believed to be the "first nature" was, at some time or another a "second nature."[14] Nietzsche suggests here that there is no absolute "first nature" and no absolute distinction between so-called first and second natures.

History itself has no inherent meaning, Nietzsche argues, but only has meanings ascribed to it, which in turn are transformed in a continuous process of interpretation and reinterpretation. The need for critical history arises from an awareness that one is "oppressed by some present misery and wants to throw off the burden at all cost."[15] This oppression by some present misery describes not only the condition for the production of critical history, but also by extension the historical conditions under which both the Nietzschean concept of genealogy was developed and the *Dialectic* was written. Nietzsche's call for a critical history, which destroys and deconstructs contentional values and values systems previously perceived as natural and universal, anticipates his later conception of genealogy. Critical history arises from human suffering, and as Nietzsche claims in the *Genealogy*, morality also results from an interpretation, or rather a misinterpretation, of suffering. Human beings invented the ascetic ideal as a moral value in order to give a meaning and purpose to their suffering: "The meaninglessness of suffering, *not* suffering itself, was the curse that lay over mankind so far."[16] In its construction of a master narrative, history also functions as an interpretation of human suffering that gives meaning to the hardships of human existence. However, the interpretation of suffering cannot eliminate it. In the same way that Socrates' rationality ultimately hastened the decay of Greek culture and merely exchanged one expression of decadence for another, the moral interpretation of suffering in terms of the ascetic ideal brought only "deeper, more inward, more poisonous, more life-destructive" forms of suffering, namely suffering under the perception of guilt.[17] There is, however, a distinction between the "present misery," *gegenwärtige Noth*, which motivates critical history and the suffering, *das Leiden*, leading to the invention of morality. While both generate reactions to the travails of life, critical history represents, in the service of life, a productively destructive and creative approach toward the interpretation of human suffering, while morality, reverting to a defensive, life-negating reaction, turns suffering into a redemptive virtue. Critical history and genealogy engender action, creation, and protest against oppression, while morality conforms to and justifies oppression. In claiming that what is believed to be static and universal are historical phenomena interpreted and reinterpreted over time, Nietzsche continues his attack upon metaphysical foundations and the inherent meaning ascribed to the past. In his later work, Nietzsche identifies the dynamic displacing interpretation as the will to power, which underlies human actions and reactions. The genealogical studies assume that there exists a basic link between power and meaning, and they investigate the relationship between language, forms of discourse, and the structures of power maintaining the fictions about reality. As symptomatologies, genealogies reject the idea of a rational foundation for values and phenomena. Genealogies forego positivist research and examine their subject, in Nietzsche's case morality, as a symptom of and a sign for a larger complex. Questioning the value of the values themselves, genealogy investigates values in terms of "the conditions and circumstances in which they grew, under which they evolved and changed (morality as consequence, as symptom, as mask, as tartufferie, as illness, as misunderstanding; but also morality as cause, as remedy, as stimulant, as restraint, as poison)."[18] In this quotation, "morality" can be replaced by an infinite number of subjects: in Foucault's case with punishment, madness, pleasure, or institutional discourse, and in the *Dialectic*'s case with enlightenment, myth, fascism, capitalism, and the culture industry. In *Twilight of the Idols*, Nietzsche pronounces "symptomatology" as the appropriate method for the philosophers who place themselves beyond good and evil. Nietzsche affirms *"there are no moral facts whatever"* and that "morality is only an interpretation of certain phenomena, more precisely a *mis*interpretation."[19] Both religious judgment and moral judgment belong to a single level of ignorance, at which the distinction between the real and the imaginary is lacking. Moral judgments can never be taken literally, because they in themselves contain nothing but nonsense. However, as semiotics they are of incalculable value: "Morality is merely sign-language, merely symptomatology."[20] Similarity, Foucault and Adorno and Horkheimer treat the subjects of their investigations as symptoms not of a single cause, but as complex signs within a multifarious network of interactions.

Nietzsche asks for the origins and values of values, for *Herkunft, Ursprung,* and *Werth* of morality. His search for origins opposes, as Foucault shows, the postulation of universal historical meaning and undermines metaphysical foundations. As a language of signs, moral values are bound to an economy of signs and are constantly undermined and displaced by new meanings. Nietzsche insists that genealogy must account for these transformations and displacements of language, discourse, and meaning in terms of a struggle for power. Although the origin and the use of a phenomenon might appear inseparably bound to each other, genealogy must differentiate between origin and utility, because the origin of moral values has no direct and logical connection to its past and present application and usefulness:

> the cause of the origin of a thing and its eventual utility, its actual employment and place in a system of purpose, lie worlds apart; whatever exists, having somehow come into being, is again and again reinterpreted to new ends, taken over, transformed, and redirected by some power superior to it; all events in the organic world are a subduing, a *becoming master*, and all subduing and becoming master involves a fresh interpretation, an adaptation through which any previous "meaning" and "purpose" are necessarily obscured or even obliterated.[21]

The history of a phenomenon must separate origin and utility and must be interpreted as a flexible chain of events governed by the various processes of domination and overcoming. Nietzsche affirms that the manner in which institutions, social or political customs, art, or religion make use of values and practices reveals nothing about their origins. By renouncing the belief that an understanding of the origin can be deduced from the demonstrable purpose of a thing, form, or institution, genealogy calls into question conventional meanings and reads the history of a phenomenon as a "continuous chain of signs of ever new interpretations and adaptations."[22] Just as there is no connection between origin and utility, the causes for the emergence of a phenomenon are not necessarily even related to one another, and may, "on the contrary, in some cases succeed and alternate with one another in a purely chance fashion."[23] The processes of transformation which a phenomenon undergoes are by no means "its *progressus* toward a goal, even less a logical *progressus* by the shortest route and with the smallest expenditure of force," they are rather "independent processes of subduing, plus the resistances they encounter" for the purpose of defense.[24] Undermining the fiction of historical progress, Nietzsche describes history as a process of transformation involving active and reactive forms of subjugation, deviance, and opposition. The forms of these processes of becoming are as fluid as the meaning ascribed to them.

Employing the example of punishment to demonstrate his point, Nietzsche implicitly calls into question the notion of *praxis* whose ideological moments were such a widely debated topic within the Frankfurt School. He discerns two elements in his discussion of the practice of punishment: one is the relatively stable characteristic, namely the action, the custom, or habit of doing; the other element is the fluid one. It concerns the meaning, utility, and expectation attached to the action. In accordance with the postulated difference between origin and utility, Nietzsche critiques a notion of praxis that centered upon the implementation of principles and the direct translation of theory into practice. Since origin and utility are two separate aspects of a practice, there are multiple reasons not only for its coming into existence but also for its perpetuation. Nietzsche contends that punishment was—contrary to the assumptions of naive genealogists of law and morals—not invented to punish. However, because of the various displacements of meanings attached to punishment, it is impossible to disentangle the history of punishment and render it definable. Punishment has no meaning in and by itself; the meaning of the act of punishment is flexible and substituted by appropriate and useful meanings in a certain instance and at a certain time. Nietzsche provides some examples of the multiple meanings attached to the practice of punishment in the following passage:

> Punishment as a means of rendering harmless, of preventing further harm. Punishment as recompense to the injured party. . . . Punishment as the isolation of a disturbance of equilibrium, so as to guard against any further spread of the disturbance. Punishment as a means of inspiring fear of those who determine and execute punishment. Punishment as a kind of repayment for the advantages the criminal has enjoyed. . . . Punishment as the expulsion of a degenerate element. . . . Punishment as a festival. . . . Punishment as the making of a memory. . . . Punishment as payment of a fee. . . . Punishment as a compromise with revenge. . . . Punishment as a declaration of war.[25]

Like other institutionalized values and practices, punishment is not reducible to one coherent concept. The genealogist has the task of examining the various functions and contexts, mapping out the displacements of application, and finally shedding light onto the experiences, discursive practices, and bodies of knowledge connected to a phenomenon. There lies no monocausality behind a certain praxis, nor is there a single function that a certain practice fulfills nor a unique goal toward which it is directed.

As he does with his genealogy of words and moral concepts such as good, noble, bad, and evil, Nietzsche unveils the plurality of meaning behind seemingly singular terms. Language, the multifaceted, falsified, and falsifying system of signs, distorts reality; words and concepts have no meaning in themselves, but meaning is appropriated in a struggle of self-assertion. Subject to change in the course of history, good and bad, like other concepts, are designations leading back to conceptual transformations: "'good' derives from 'noble' in the sense of 'aristocratic' and 'privileged' and 'bad' is a transformation of 'low', 'common', 'plebeian'."[26] This heritage of good and bad undermines the assumption that good and bad are universal moral values, and exposes the complicity between language, the appropriation of values, and power. Those in power claim the "good" for themselves and allocate the "bad" to the others, either to those who do not hold power or, as a *ressentiment* phenomenon, to those in power. Entirely dependent upon the individual's and society's point of view, concepts denoting superiority in terms of political and financial influence are transformed into concepts denoting the superiority of moral postures and attitudes.

Genealogy is both an exegetical and interpretative strategy. Nietzsche makes it clear that interpretation is a human activity and a part of life, because life continuously engages us in giving form and assigning meaning. Itself an "open and mobile strategy of interpretation,"[27] the genealogical method traces the forces of these interpretive processes and undermines currently "binding" interpretations: "It is a method designed to initiate a critical and constructive stance to the original question itself, deepening the question and leading to a violence towards other interpretations and a radicality towards definitions of reality."[28] Thus, genealogy does not attempt to identify falsehoods and errors in order to replace them with truth, but offers instead alternative interpretations that will eventually be replaced by other interpretations. Rejecting the claim to truth raises the question of legitimation and validity. On some level, it puts into question the purpose of the whole genealogical and critical enterprise, since the replacement of one error with another does not appear to be a very promising and productive mode of criticism and, on the contrary, seems to compromise criticism by rendering it—if judged by the standard of a resultant truth—an exercise of futility. However, Nietzsche did not advocate a complete relativism in regard to the merit of different interpretative possibilities. Although he avoids making claims to truth and undermines judgments of good and evil, he does accept the possibility of a multiplicity of truths and is deeply committed to truthfulness. Rather than denoting a concept of authenticity—which for many reasons is problematic in the context of Nietzsche's love of irony, the mask, and the surface—Nietzsche's call for truthfulness might be more appropriately described in terms of Adorno's notion of integrity of thought. Nietzsche's call for amorality, which Adorno dismissed as a historically outmoded reaction

against the tyranny of bourgeois and Christian values, stands in ironic opposition to his demand for truthfulness and integrity.

Nietzsche's perceptive critique of the linguistic process of naming and his
demand for the reevaluation of all values reveal his radically subversive aim. His
critique calls into question the exchange of the valuative standards of morality,
such as "good" and "evil," for such physiological standards as "healthy," "sick,"
"strong," and "weak." The question is whether the shift of emphasis from moral
values to designations of the body improves upon the systems of traditional normativity and is as revolutionary as Nietzsche himself seems to think, or whether
it merely substitutes designations without substantially changing the structures of
thought supporting such oppositional constructs and judgments. For Nietzsche
there are, of course, no value-free designations or concepts, because judging and
assigning value, one of the fundamental human activities, is inseparable from
life. In Nietzsche's work "life" functions as a generalized concept for all forms
of existence on earth, and he rarely distinguishes between public and private
spheres. On the one hand, resisting categorizations of the life world makes visible Nietzsche's protest against the codification of modern spheres of values and
influences. On the other hand, insisting on the inseparable nature of existence
makes Nietzsche's call for the affirmation of life problematic, because this affirmation of an undifferentiated life world stands in contrast to the critical enterprise of deconstructing conventions, institutions, and traditions. However, the
focus upon the legitimation of reinterpretations and reevaluations poses, in the
Nietzschean sense, the wrong questions. If one accepts that only objectively
valid interpretations can make a claim to a final truth—and that no such interpretation exists or ever can exist—interpretations of relative validity will have to
do. Similar to the *Dialectic*, genealogy recognizes that it is parasitic on the interpretations it challenges, and what Daniel W. Conway asserts concerning Nietzsche's genealogy also holds true for the *Dialectic*: "genealogical interpretations
are logically dependent upon the authoritative interpretations they seek to sup-
plant."[29] Nietzsche's strategy, through which he constructs his genealogies in
relation to the authoritative rival interpretations, suggests that genealogies must
be viewed in the context of a relative validity and that their merit must be
assessed in terms of their success in displacing other interpretations. In Conway's
view, genealogy is successful if it "effectively supplants or discredits the dominant interpretation of the historical phenomenon in question"; its achievements
cannot be measured in relation to its approximation of objective validity, but
depends upon "calling into question the authoritative interpretation it challenges."[30]

Foucault is one of those honeygatherers of the spirit committed to the task
of researching the processes by which values become established, conserved, and
subverted. Expounding on the critical potential of genealogy, his outline of the
workings of genealogy presents a productive interpretation of Nietzsche that also
has implications for the *Dialectic*'s genealogy of enlightenment. However, as

many critics have noted, Foucault's project represents a limited, partial, and specific appropriation of Nietzsche's concept of genealogy. Gary Shapiro remarks that Foucault's reading of the *Genealogy* overlooks the plurality of voices in Nietzsche's text and fails to question the identity and voice of the genealogist. Rather than presenting a univocal point of view, the voice of the genealogist alternates with a series of historical and fictional voices, such as the Oedipal scientist, the tragic dramatist, the buffoon of world history, and the real and imaginary witness summoned to testify to the manufacture of ideals.[31] Benjamin Sax maintains that for Foucault genealogy became a generic term for the study of activities on the level of discourse and practice relating to the institutional deployment and articulation of the human sciences, whereby in Nietzsche no such unity of methods exists.[32] Foucault investigates the interaction of discourse and practice, that is how practice modifies, distorts, or creates discourse and how discourse in turn directs, undermines, or masks practice.[33] Although genealogy, according to Sax, marks a refinement of Foucault's thought and historical research, his concept of genealogy tends to limit the diversity of meaning that Nietzsche accorded to phenomena. Therefore, Sax concludes that the emphasis on the similarities between Foucault's and Nietzsche's use of the genealogical method, even when suggested by Foucault himself, "is misinformed and misguided, proving a false means of evaluation."[34] Against those who lament the gap between Foucault and Nietzsche, it could be argued that Foucault has, admittedly and fortunately, not attempted to imitate Nietzsche and has developed from the notion of genealogy his own methodological conceptions and style of investigation. His work presents the single most productive attempt to think and rethink the implications of genealogy for contemporary criticism. Thus, Foucault's work will be treated here as a possible interpretation of Nietzsche, which provides a better understanding of Nietzsche's texts, and as an advancement of ideas that take their points of departure from Nietzsche's work and that explore its possible potentials and implications.

In *Discipline and Punish*, Foucault takes on the Nietzschean challenge for a study of punishment. As seen in his histories of madness and sexuality, the study of punishment analyzes its subject in Nietzschean terms; it explores subjects excluded from historical accounts and the conditions of their existence in light of criteria that have been ignored by traditional historical research. For Nietzsche, these criteria include such diverse psychological, physiological, and ideological fields of influence as passion, fear, superstition, climate, nutrition, self-preservation, and the will to power. For Foucault they include the desire to control that which lies outside the norms of civilized society, to avert chance occurrences, and to limit the power of opposition. The archeological digging for hidden, forgotten, and repressed information poses the challenge of researching marginalized subjects, and it includes the search for the various layers and levels of representation, interpretation, and subversion accumulated over time. Foucault's later works are marked by an increasing emphasis on genealogy rather than archeology, and they might be called "translations of the *Genealogy* into the worlds of the prison and surveillance, psychiatry and biopower."[35] Shapiro maintains that Foucault's distinctive contribution to contemporary thought might be described as the extension of the genealogical approach to the human sciences and their associated disciplines and practices. By tracing the "capillary" forms of power in these fields, Foucault exhibits the taste for the documentary, which Nietzsche describes in the preface to the *Genealogy*, and engages in "the laborious side of the outrageous attempt to raise the question of the value of morality."[36]

Foucault describes *Discipline and Punish* as an attempt to present the displacements of application, function, and effects in connection with the practice of power. This project is "intended as a correlative history of the modern soul and of a new power to judge; a genealogy of the present scientifico-legal complex from which the power to punish derives its bases, justifications and rules, from which it extends its effects and by which it masks its exorbitant singularity."[37] Foucault thus takes up the challenge to write a history of morality that goes beyond investigating a rationally directed history. In the tradition of Nietzsche, Foucault wants to unveil the "singularity of events outside of any monotonous finality," and thus expose the irrationality behind the teleological narratives of history.[38] The task is not to dissolve an event in the construction of an ideal continuity, but to assert "events in terms of their most unique characteristics, their most acute manifestations."[39] An event of history should not be seen as the result of the rational decisions of individuals, "but a reversal of a relationship of forces, the usurpation of power."[40] In order to accomplish this task, the genealogist cannot rely upon speculation, but must rather engage in a fastidious type of research, which Foucault defines in the following Nietzschean terms: "Genealogy is gray, meticulous, and patiently documentary. It operates on a field of entangled and confused parchments, on documents that have been scratched over and recopied many times."[41] Genealogies require patience, attention to detail, and relentless erudition. Genealogists neither seek an ultimate truth, nor do they see things in terms of opposition, in black and white. They probe the spaces and nuances of gray that Nietzsche outlined in the *Genealogy*: "For it must be obvious which color is a hundred times more vital for the genealogist of morals than blue: namely *gray*, that is, what is documented, what can actually be confirmed and has actually existed, in short the entire long hieroglyphic record, so hard to decipher, of the moral past of mankind."[42] Foucault maintains that in contrast to Paul Ree and the English moralists, who described the history of morality as a linear development and assumed that words retain their meanings, desires their direction, and ideas their logic, Nietzschean genealogy acknowledges that "the world of speech and desires has known invasions, struggles, plundering, disguises, and ploys."[43]

In contrast to Habermas, who interprets Nietzsche's genealogy as a nostalgic search for origins, Foucault's reading of Nietzsche opposes such a grounding and rejects both a search for origins and the postulation of a telos. Through his analysis of Nietzsche's use of the words *Ursprung* and *Herkunft*, Foucault affirms that Nietzsche undermines historically and metaphysically grounded claims to truth. Nietzsche refuses the ontological and teleological grounding of his thought, and "rejects the metahistorical deployment of ideal significations and indefinite teleologies."[44] Nietzsche challenges the pursuit of the origin, *Ursprung*, because he did not search for the essence of things, which would presume the existence of a priori, immobile forms resistant to historical determination and transformation:

> if the genealogist refuses to extend his faith in metaphysics, if he listens to history, he finds that there is "something altogether different" behind things: not a timeless and essential secret, but the secret that they have no essence or that their essence was fabricated in a piecemeal fashion from alien forms. Examining the history of reason, he learns that it was born in an altogether "reasonable" fashion—from chance.[45]

Furthermore, genealogical analysis shows that the concept of liberty is, as Nietzsche claims in *Human, All Too Human*, an invention of the ruling classes and not fundamental to human nature. What is found at the historical beginning is not an identity of origin, but disparity and the dissension of things.

Nietzsche's request for genealogical investigations further expresses the need for a history that disrupts presumptions of continuity. The forces of history are not controlled by destiny or reason; they respond to "haphazard conflicts."[46] Historical moments are not the result of rational developments, but rather of chance, discontinuity, and rupture. Neither reason nor the rational individual rules history. Nietzsche and Foucault converge in their assertion that history is interpretation and in their identification of claims to truth as claims to power. Freed from the claim to absolutes, genealogies evade metaphysics and adapt a sense of history with "the acuity of a glance that distinguishes, separates, and disperses, that is capable of liberating divergence and marginal elements—the kind of dissociating view that is capable of decomposing itself."[47] This "historical sense" of self-decomposition gives rise to three distinct modalities of history: Genealogy is parodic, directed against reality, in that it opposes the theme of history as reminiscence or recognition; genealogy is dissociative, directed against identity, in that it opposes history as continuity or representative of a tradition; and finally, genealogy is sacrificial, directed against truth, because it opposes history as knowledge.[48]

In Foucault, as in Nietzsche, the link between power and language presents the defining moment of genealogy. Power encompasses all practices, actions, and institutions; it is complex and exists only through its functions. In *Beyond Good and Evil*, Nietzsche contends that the will to power is a hypothetical proposition demanded by "the conscience of *method*."[49] Ultimately, the will to power is nothing more or less than an expression of passions and drives, an expression, however, which defines and determines thought: "Suppose nothing else were 'given' as real except our world of desires and passions, and we could not get down, or up, to any other 'reality' besides the reality of our drives—for thinking is merely a relation of these drives to each other."[50] Nietzsche proposes to undertake the experiment of making do with only one form of causality: the will to power, "a moral of method which one may not shirk today."[51] Genealogical studies represent such an experiment of "positing the causality of the will hypothetically as the only one";[52] they are interpretations for which the will to power provides a guiding principle. However, Nietzsche concedes that the will to power is itself an interpretation, a hypothetical construct, and an operational procedure whose existence cannot be proven, but whose use is required by the genealogical method. The will to power can therefore be described, as Sax does, as a genealogical unity and not as a metaphysical or ontological one. Foucault expands Nietzsche's construct of the will to power and analyzes the complex relationship between power and knowledge as it manifests itself in institutional discourses and practices. In the analysis of discourses, genealogy studies the discontinuous processes of discourse formation in relation to power. Foucault operates on the assumption that in every society "the production of discourse is at once controlled, selected, organized and redistributed according to a certain number of procedures, whose role is to avert its powers and its dangers, to cope with chance events, to evade its ponderous, awesome materiality."[53] The genealogical method exposes the procedures controlling discourse formation, which are modes of control and suppression designed to avert the constitution and proliferation of those discourses detrimental to the exercise of established power.

Although the critical potential of Foucault's project of genealogy oppose traditional notions of identity, continuity, progress, and truth owes a great deal to Nietzsche, there are obvious differences between his and Nietzsche's approaches to their subject. While Foucault emphasizes Nietzsche's parodic, dissociative, and sacrificial uses of genealogy, Nietzsche's work itself evades any proposed structural procedure; Nietzsche's genealogies are aphoristic, open-ended, and highly speculative in their claims, while Foucault presents clearly outlined research projects with detailed, analytic descriptions. Foucault follows Nietzsche's call for a meticulous documentary, a call Nietzsche himself ignores. In his work, Foucault establishes clearly definable historical periods, while Nietzsche perceives "overlappings, strange continuities, and terminological confusions both within an age and between them."[54] Sax notes apparently marked differences between Nietzsche's and Foucault's interpretation of texts. Where Nietzsche discovers "rich and competing readings of texts and institutional practices, Foucault provides single . . . and rather flat renderings of them."[55] A second contrast becomes apparent, according to Sax, when the question of language and discourse is connected to that of power. The genealogical coupling of discourse and power in Foucault "is not as simple as it is in Nietzsche; for it involves the linkage of rational, reflective discourses with non-discursive, institutional practices."[56] Although the play of domination in Nietzsche is not as simple and reductive as Sax argues, Foucault's analysis of power indisputably supercedes Nietzsche's in complexity and specificity. In Nietzsche, the multiplicity of meanings on the semantic level cannot be reduced, as Sax claims, to a single force or cause, such as the ascetic priest. The dynamics of domination, the formation of discourses, and the creation of values are motivated by a number of overlapping reasons. Although the cause is "hypothetically" and ultimately reduced to the will to power, such intertwined factors include the struggle for power, the will to self-preservation and domination, the fear of nothingness, or the attempt to alleviate suffering.

Since neither Foucault nor Nietzsche takes for granted the identity of phenomena, they search instead for the non-identical. Genealogical study explores dissensions, disparities, and differences and avoids participating in a rational enlightenment narrative. Nor does such a method center on the rational individual's realizing his or her freedom and liberty in a progressive enlightenment fashion. Genealogies displace the universalized accounts of history and create counternarratives that reject and subvert the ideological presuppositions of enlightenment. Foucault's laborious projects reflect not only his interest shared with Nietzsche and Adorno in the displacement of enlightenment ideals, but also his concern with finding an appropriate method of research and mode of thought for his enterprise. Foucault orients himself in Nietzsche's theoretical reasoning on the concept of genealogy, which he interprets and turns into a productive approach for his own work. Provoking criticism from Habermas, who asserts that Foucault repeats Nietzsche's fateful mistake of confusing claims of truth with claims to power, Foucault's continuation of the Nietzschean project owes its critiques of positivism, science, and history and his entire concept of an "erudite-positivistic historiography in the appearance of an antiscience to his reception of Nietzsche."[57] Habermas's biographical explanation for Foucault's "misguided" reliance upon Nietzsche strikingly resembles his account of the origins of Adorno and Horkheimer's Nietzscheanism. Habermas maintains that Foucault's theory of power and domination are the result of a combination of historical and biographical circumstances. While Adorno and Horkheimer were led astray by their experience of fascism, which prompted them to give up faith in the emancipatory potential of enlightenment, Foucault's supposedly erroneous judgments are connected to his sudden disappointment with political action in the wake of the 1968 student revolt, which, according to Habermas, "makes the concept of a historiography of the human sciences as a critique of reason biographically intelligible."[58]

Habermas views Foucault's Nietzschean critique of scientific and historical thought as bearing the traces of postmodernism. Habermas's claim of Foucault's postmodernism must, however, undergo some qualification, since as late as 1983 Foucault himself did not seem to understand the German controversy surrounding modernism and postmodernism. In an interview with Gérard Raulet, Foucault indicates that he has neither a clear grasp of the supposed collapse of reason, nor does he fully understand the postulated opposition between post-modernist and modernist positions. Contrary to what Habermas identifies as the postmodern position in the *Philosophical Discourse of Modernity*, Foucault asserts that there is no radical announcement of an end of reason in his work: "there is no sense at all to the proposition that reason is a long narrative which is now finished."[59] Foucault labels the traditional opposition of rationality and irrationality "blackmail," because it renders impossible a rational critique of rationality, and he commends the Frankfurt School for having resisted such blackmail.[60] The traditional conception of rationality is only one possible interpretation of rationality; for Foucault, reason is self-created, "which means that humans develop forms or conceptions of rationality as part of their larger project of evolving an understanding of themselves given specific historical conditions."[61] Foucault does not want to destroy reason, but rather wishes to demonstrate reason's role as a historical construct in the formation of discourses and practices. Genealogies show, as Foucault maintains in the interview with Raulet, "how that-which-is has not always been," and "why and how that-which-is might no longer be that-which-is."[62] For Habermas, however, the genealogical project represents a radical critique of reason that lapses into irrationality. Subsequently he equates the radicalized critique of rationality with irrationality, just as he equates a radicalized critique of science with an antiscientific attitude and postmodernism with antimodernism.

Habermas's main contention against genealogy is its linkage of power to truth: "the entire weight of the problematic rests on the basic concept of power that lends both the archeological prospecting and the genealogical disclosures their dimension of being a critique of modernity. Nietzsche's undeserved authority lies in his "utterly unsociological concept of power," which Foucault and other postmodern thinkers borrowed.[63] Foucault, Habermas maintains, relinquishes the philosophy of the subject through a theory that explains the emergence of knowledge from practices of power. A method of this kind thus surrenders the idea of autonomous spheres of values and autonomous forms of discourses:

> Genealogical historiography clears away the autonomy of self-regulating discourses as well as the epochal and linear succession of global forms of knowledge. The danger of anthropocentrism is banished only when, under the incorruptible gaze of genealogy, discourses emerge and pop like glittering bubbles from a swamp of anonymous processes of subjugation.[64]

Habermas portrays genealogy and its hypothetical grounding in the will to power as an ahistorical mode of perception, typical of aesthetic modernity, which falls back to myth. While foregoing a recognition of the particularity of an epoch, Nietzsche constructs a "heroic affinity of the present with the most remote and the most primitive."[65] In contrast to Foucault, who makes great efforts to disassociate Nietzsche from a search for origins, Habermas interprets Nietzsche's genealogy as a nostalgic return to an archaic origin, and postulates that Nietzsche favors the ancient and the archaic. Nietzsche supposedly falls into this trap, because he rejects all rational criteria for assessing claims of validity:

> The more *primordial* is considered the more worthy of honor, the preferable, the more unspoiled, the purer: It is deemed better. *Derivation* and *descent* serve as criteria of rank, in both the social and the logical senses. In this manner, Nietzsche bases his critique of morality on *genealogy*. He traces the moral appraisal of value, which assigns a person or a mode of action a place within a rank ordering based on criteria of validity, back to the descent and hence to the social rank of the one making the moral judgment.[66]

In asserting that Nietzsche's genealogy assigns value to phenomena according to their closeness to the origins, Habermas profoundly misreads Nietzsche. Nietzsche's work neither displays a nostalgic longing for nor a glorification of the archaic. Nietzsche insists that no fundamental line can be drawn between a first and second nature, between origin and derivation. The *Genealogy of Morals* insists that no single origin can be found, but that the so-called original moment of the appearance of a phenomenon is the result of a play of heterogeneous forces: "There are, always already, at least two languages of morality."[67] While Habermas supposes that the rejection of a progressive and teleological history entails a nostalgic valorization of the archaic, Foucault's genealogical project is vigorously committed to avoiding the temptations of both nostalgia and progress: "Genealogy is the articulation of differences, of affiliations that never reduce to a system or totality and of the transformations of power/knowledge in their unplanned and unpredictable concatenations."[68] Clearly, Habermas's opposition to the genealogical study is connected to his rejection of Nietzsche and postmodern thought. For Habermas, genealogies embody the renunciation of enlightenment ideals, because they enact an unacceptable radicalized critique of modernity.

GENEALOGICAL COUNTERNARRATIVES TO ENLIGHTENMENT

Alongside this genealogical framework comes the recognition that historical narratives are artificial constructs unable to represent the past as it was; they allow for only a limited number of possibilities of looking at the reality behind history. With this turn from archeology to genealogy, Foucault acknowledges the fictional character of his historical writings and recognizes the myth-making function of historical and genealogical narratives. As the work of Hayden White so cogently outlines, historical writing shares the use of narrative techniques with other forms of narration, including fictional accounts of events, and since events cannot be portrayed and represented in the way they actually happened, the past can only be reconstructed according to the intellectual and narrative means available in the present. Historical events are subject to interpretation within a certain historical and cultural framework that must rely upon narrative and mythological structures in order to define itself. In his later writings, Foucault comes to acknowledge the inevitability of producing myth in historiographic writing, and he accepts "Nietzsche's notion of history as something that propagates, or at any rate ought to propagate, myth that will be useful in the present."[69] Myths are useful for Foucault, if they disturb the traditional, metaphysical, and so-called rational order of things. Foucault justifies the production of philosophical-historical narrative by articulating a notion of historiography which does not search for foundations: "on the contrary, it disturbs what was previously considered immobile; it fragments what was thought unified; it shows the heterogeneity of what was imagined consistent with itself."[70] Narratives that fulfill these functions are useful and need not deny their relationship to fiction by hiding behind pseudoscientific pretensions. In an interview given in 1977, Foucault remarks that the problem of fiction is of importance to his work:

> I am well aware that I have never written anything but fictions. I do not mean to go so far as to say that fictions are beyond truth. It seems to me that it is possible to make fiction work inside truth, to induce truthful effects with a fictional discourse, and to operate in such a manner that the discourse of truth gives rise, "manufactures," something that does not yet exist, that is, "fictions" it.[71]

Foucault acknowledges that narratives, including genealogical narratives, are inseparable from fiction and cannot operate independently from their mythmaking function; however, in his view, this does not affect the truthfulness of the narrative, for fictional discourses can reveal, manufacture, and "fiction" truth into being. With his statement, Foucault blurs the boundaries between "truth" and "fiction" in terms of their production through both writing and interpretation. Since every interpretation can only make a limited claim to truth, new interpretations replace, in Nietzsche's words, "the improbable with the more probable, possibly one error with another."[72] According to Foucault's standards, the myths created by Nietzsche in his genealogical explorations are to be considered useful, firstly because they acknowledge the creation of myth and do not pretend to produce historical truth, and secondly because they disturb and subvert the so-called rational order of things and conventional ways of thinking.

NIETZSCHE AND THE *DIALECTIC OF ENLIGHTENMENT*

The *Dialectic* uniquely illustrates the impossibility of completely separating truth from fiction and history from myth. Here Adorno and Horkheimer go beyond admitting that their writings consist of fictions by demonstrating the entwinement of myth and enlightenment not only by way of rational argumentation but also through their method and style of presentation. In the interpretation of myth, enlightenment constitutes itself as both a moment of emancipation and regression. The liberating element of enlightenment demythologizes the world and frees the individual from superstition and the belief in magic. This is the element of enlightenment represented by the epic style of narration, found both in the grand metanarratives of Homer and Adorno and Horkheimer. However, following the degeneration of reason to instrumental rationality, the emancipatory element follows the epic narrative in its reversion to myth. The increasing alienation of the self-sacrificing individual and the domination of nature act out the regressive tendencies of enlightenment. Myth and enlightenment are entangled and cannot be perceived as progressive opposites in terms of a Hegelian dialectic. Thesis and antithesis cancel each other out, and the dialectic of myth and enlightenment becomes negative. When enlightenment reaches its limits, it returns to myth, since myth has always contained elements of bourgeois enlightenment. The *Dialectic* not only presents its central thesis of the entwinement of myth and reason in the form of an argument, but also enacts it through the representational entwinement of mythical and enlightenment narratives. By using mythical and epic narratives, such as Homer's *Odyssey*, to reconstruct the history of Western civilization, Adorno and Horkheimer perform their thesis. Seen in the context of critical theory, the *Dialectic* attempts to construct a genealogical counternarrative that is to replace the authoritative *Bildungsroman* of the Enlightenment, while the aphoristic style sets the antitotalitarian, antisystematic, and antimetaphysical tone in resistance to traditional philosophical, scientific, and historical discourses. In addition to an alternative history of civilization, the *Dialectic* offers alternative forms of discourses about history. A critique of enlightenment that produces a thematic analysis of content is insufficient, since the ideology of enlightenment also pervades the formal, stylistic, and methodological aspects of historical representation.

The *Dialectic* shares a dominant characteristic of myths in that it presents its interpretation of the world in narrative form; Adorno and Horkheimer create an interpretive narrative about the stories called history. In Adorno's first excursus, Odysseus's adventures become metaphors for the historical processes of civilization. The interpretation of Homer's epic is meant to yield genuine insights into the historical developments and transformations leading to the present condition of society. In his contribution to a collection of essays discussing the *Dialectic*'s contemporary relevance, Herbert Schnädelbach defines the *Dialectic* as a social myth in the tradition of Hegel's narrative of the cunning intrigues of the world spirit, Marx's march of the historical modes of production, Wagner's *Ring*, Nietzsche's *Genealogy*, and Freud's *Totem and Tabu*. In contrast to the myths of nature (*Naturmythen*), these social myths (*Sozialmythen*) presume the demythification and disenchantment of nature, and their narrative interpretations and explanations of human existence no longer count on the active and intentional intervention of nature, but rather understand natural occurrences as the conditional framework of human action.[73] At the same time, social myths stand in contrast to theoretical explications of phenomena. Concerned with individual and collective actions and reactions, social myths render events in narrative forms and posit themselves between history, fiction, and theory. They attempt to find what is behind the stories about history. Modern social myths, by Schnädelbach's account, operate on the hermeneutic premise that becoming and understanding are interconnected processes and that we can only understand something if we know how it became what it is. In the manner of the hermeneutic circle, *Verstehen* participates in *Werden*, and *Werden* anticipates *Verstehen*.

As Schnädelbach points out, social myths produce grand metanarratives about *the* Enlightenment, *the* rational, and *the* modern and thus tend to mystify modernity. In its narrative passages and interpretation of Homer's *Odyssey*, the *Dialectic* can be said to present such a social myth of disenchanted nature that wants to provide insights into historical processes and human behavior. However, the *Dialectic*'s contribution toward enlightening enlightenment consists not so much in its construction of a grand metanarrative as in its genealogical investigation, which exposes the ideologies of enlightenment and additionally undermines stylistically and methodologically the grand enlightenment narrative. As a counternarrative to enlightenment, it explicates the connections between events and their preconditions as a continuous process of formation and transformation. The narrative style resists the expectations of theoretical rationalizations and scientific positivism by incorporating the process of interpretation into the narrative itself. Insights come not by presenting a definitive theory or a final interpretation, but by interpretative efforts that enlighten about enlightenment, by offering not only alternative points of view but also alternative ways of thinking. The inherent rationality of myths and the myths of rationality serve as integral and necessary aspects of the antitotalitarian critique of enlightenment.

Nietzsche provides the *Dialectic*'s main frame of reference and is the most frequently cited thinker. Its explications of the correlation between the exchange principle and sacrifice, moral judgments and identity thinking, the constitution of subjectivity and the history of rationality, debt and guilt, revenge and justice, take up the themes and arguments of the *Genealogy* and furnish yet another reply to Nietzsche's demand for historical studies of morality. Similar to Nietzsche, the *Dialectic* searches for undatable historical beginnings while rejecting ontological grounding, and for both the *Genealogy* and the *Dialectic* "the origin lies at a place of inevitable loss."[74] While deconstructing traditional concepts of history, including the notions of origin, telos, and progress, both genealogies reconstruct history as a process propelled by the drive for self-preservation and claims to power and legitimation. They question the value of existing values and attempt to shed light upon the conditions and circumstances under which values are created and displaced. The notion of the origin as a place of inevitable loss attests to the regressive tendency of value displacements. Nietzsche poses the following question: "What if a symptom of regression were inherent in the 'good,' likewise a danger, a seduction, a poison, a narcotic, through which the present was possibly living *at the expense of the future?*"[75] Adorno and Horkheimer inquire into enlightenment's symptoms of regression, and Nietzsche's advocation of a symptomatology of morality resonates throughout the *Dialectic*. If we replace "morality" with "enlightenment," Nietzsche's description of the genealogical project may also apply to the *Dialectic*: *enlightenment* "as consequence, as symptom, as mask, as tartufferie, as illness, as misunderstanding"; but also *enlightenment* "as cause, as remedy, as stimulant, as restraint, as poison."[76] The subjects under examination in the *Dialectic*, such as subjectivity, rationality, science, myth, and metaphysics, are not investigated as immutable and universal phenomena, but rather as flexible metaphors reverberating throughout history. Through its postulation of reason's entwinement with myth and liberation's reversion to repression, the *Dialectic* confirms Nietzsche's contention that phenomena neither develop nor logically progress toward a goal by the shortest, most efficient route, but rather move in a succession of more or less profound, more or less mutual processes of subjugation, resistance, and defensive transformations. The meaning of these processes is even more fluid than the form they take.

Although Adorno and Horkheimer affirm in the introduction to the new edition of the *Dialectic* their intellectual affinity and the intensity of their cooperation, the *Dialectic* contains different, if not conflicting, Nietzsche interpretations. "No outsider will find it easy to discern how far we are both responsible for every sentence. We jointly dictated lengthy sections; and the vital principle of the *Dialectic* is the tension between the two intellectual temperaments conjoined in it."[77] However, despite their protestation of mutual cooperation, nowhere is the tension and disparity between the two intellectuals more obvious than in the Nietzsche interpretations of "Excursus I" and "Excursus II," both of which explore from very different perspectives Nietzsche's thought as the completion of the enlightenment. "Excursus II," written mainly by Horkheimer, presents a rather cynical view of Nietzsche's completion of enlightenment. Nietzsche and Marquis de Sade are portrayed as having taken the Enlightenment to its absurd consequences, and thereby, it could be inferred, belong to its self-destructive movement. Horkheimer's "Excursus" draws connections between de Sade's and Nietzsche's crusade against Christianity and morality, including their rejection of the notion of compassion. Unlike Adorno, who is always quick to point out fascist misinterpretations of Nietzsche, Horkheimer connects Nietzsche to the fascist movement by identifying him as the intellectual predecessor of its ideas on violence and domination. Nietzsche "maliciously celebrates the powerful and their cruelty" and holds the weak to be most responsible for the spread of life-negating Christianity and for circumventing natural law by means of cunning.[78] By elevating the cult of strength to a world-historical doctrine, German fascism took it to an absurd extreme, and the realization of Nietzsche's assertions of the morality of the masters and the slaves "both refutes them and at the same time reveals their truth, which—despite all his affirmation of life—was inimical to the spirit of reality."[79]

In contrast, Adorno's critique of enlightenment is informed by a positive Nietzschean perspective. His excursus draws upon Nietzsche's critique of enlightenment and rationality and the genealogy of morals in order to outline the self-destructive constitution of modern subjectivity. Unlike Horkheimer, Adorno decisively separates Nietzsche from the anti-enlightenment and anti-intellectual attitudes associated with fascism. While Nietzsche's relationship to the Enlightenment and to Homer, the latter whose epic combines elements of the bourgeois enlightenment with mythology, remained ambiguous, that of the prefascists did not. Nietzsche perceived enlightenment as the universal movement of the sovereign mind as well as a live-negating, nihilistic force, and Adorno contends that in prefascist thought only the second element survived and became subsequently perverted into a nihilistic ideology.

For Adorno, Homer's work represents the entwinement of myth and reason and emphasizes their common ground of domination and exploitation. Homer's narrative, especially of the adventures, shows a close relation to myth: "the Homeric spirit takes over and 'organizes' the myths, but contradicts them in the process."[80] The epic rationalizes myth, translating it into a novel of the bourgeois enlightenment. The hero of the epic reveals himself to be a prototype of the cunning bourgeois individual. As the "basic text of European civilization" showing the mutual implication of enlightenment and myth, Homer's epic demonstrates myth's "aspects of deception which triumphs in the fraudulence of Fascism."[81] In Homer, epic and myth and form and content expound and elucidate one another, and this "aesthetic dualism" attests to a historical-philosophical tendency, which Adorno describes by referring to *The Birth of Tragedy*: "The Apollonian Homer merely continues that general human artistic process to which we owe individuation."[82] In a process analogous to Nietzsche's, Adorno's "Excursus I" expands the concept of enlightenment by defining it as a process whose beginning cannot be located at any particular point in time. There is no origin and no definite beginning, for one can only ascertain that "the lines from reason, liberalism, and the bourgeois spirit go incomparably farther back than historians who date the notion of the burgher only from the end of medieval feudalism would allow."[83] The history of enlightenment is a history of the subject attempting to free itself from the bondage of mythological superstition. Caught between the will to liberation and the need for self-preservation, the subject enlists rational thought to gain control over nature and the self. However, domination over nature and the self and the denial of nature in the self are only attained at a price: the sacrifice of the self: "Man's domination over himself, which grounds his selfhood, is almost always the destruction of the subject in whose service it is undertaken; for the substance which is dominated, suppressed, and dissolved by virtue of self-preservation" is the one meant to be preserved.[84]

As with Nietzsche's *Genealogy*, Adorno's "Excursus" interprets the history of civilization as a history of the internalization of the instincts and the introversion of the principle of sacrifice. He also interprets sacrifice and renunciation in relation to claims to power. The sacrifice is both external and internal; sacrifices appeasing the gods and mythical creatures are made in the name of physical self-preservation, but each external sacrifice brings with it an internal sacrifice, that of the renunciation of nature in the self and its needs and desires. Sacrifices cheat the god to whom they are offered, and their rational irrationality constitutes the deception in sacrifice whose prototype is Odyssean cunning. The substantiality of sacrifice is semblance and illusion, and its trickery elevates the frail individual to the status of a vehicle of a divine substance. Sacrificial practices subject the god to the primacy of human ends, dissolve his power, and find yet another expression in the sacrifices practiced "by the disbelieving priests on the believers."[85] Without direct reference to Nietzsche, Adorno maintains that Odysseus functions simultaneously as a sacrifice and a priest. As a symbolic communication with the deity, the sacrifice has a representational function, and, as Adorno speculates in the manner of the *Genealogy*, represents not a primal component of the individual but a practice whose origin can be found in the history of domination. Sacrificial violence turns against nature and the self, while the subjected internalize violence and "repeat upon themselves the injustice that was done them, enacting it again in order to endure it."[86] By calculating his own sacrifice, Odysseus, the priest, negates the power to whom the sacrifice is made. In his way he redeems the life he forfeited, and as Nietzsche's ascetic priest, turns sacrifice and self-renunciation, *Entsagung*, into his most potent instrument and supreme licence for power.[87] Odysseus is a priest in the Nietzschean sense because he uses restraint, cunning, and deceit to achieve his goals while at the same time transforming himself into the object of sacrifice by renouncing his self in order to persevere and dominate. As power-hungry hermits and innovators of ideas, the ascetic priests exercise cruelty toward themselves, and are possessed with their ideal not only in faith, but also in their will, power, and interest: "His *right* to exist stands or falls with that ideal."[88] The ascetic priest finds a perverted kind of pleasure and feeling of triumph in his self-renunciation, and in his ability to renounce his own ego. Such renunciation represents "a violation and cruelty against *reason*—a voluptuous pleasure that reaches its height when the ascetic self-contempt and self-mockery of reason declares: '*there is* a realm of truth and being, but reason is *excluded* from it!'"[89] According to Nietzsche, the ascetic priest's negation of life is a life-preserving defensive device that affirms the will to power:

> *the ascetic ideal springs from the protective instinct of a degenerating life* which tries by all means to sustain itself and to fight for its existence; it indicates a partial physiological obstruction and exhaustion against which the deepest instincts of life, which have remained intact, continually struggle with new expedients and devices. The ascetic ideal is such an expedient . . . life wrestles in it and through it with death and *against* death; the ascetic ideal is an artifice for the *preservation* of life.[90]

The life-negating ascetic ideal and the preservation of life are not opposed, but are rather entwined. The exercise of power affirms life; the priest, a master of negation and seemingly an enemy of life, invents new ideas and transforms values. In his struggle for self-preservation and claims to power, the priest must fight against his opposition. He will not be spared from a fight with the beasts of prey, but it will be a violent war of cunning and of the minds rather than a war of physical violence.[91] In his adventures, Odysseus also oscillates between self-preservation and self-negation, and "artifice is the means by which the adventuring self loses itself in order to preserve itself."[92] He has to deny his inner nature in order to gain control over the outer nature and other human beings, and he sacrifices present gratification in the hope for a future reward. Physically weaker than the forces opposing him, Odysseus takes on the role of Nietzsche's ascetic priest and fights a war of mental cunning, while the physical challenges he faces are mere athletic exercises. Self-preservation and physical strength are dissociated, and Odysseus' athletic achievements are those of "the gentleman who, free from practical cares, can as a self-possessed master devote himself to training."[93] Odysseus can never engage in direct conflict with the mythic forces and must instead rely upon rationality to affirm his superiority. Avoiding physical struggle, Odysseus divorces his body from the conflict and restrains it with the force of his rationality. As a knowing survivor, Odysseus takes great risks, and in the manner of Nietzsche's "What doesn't kill me makes me stronger,"[94] he becomes stronger, more cunning, and more unyielding as his life continues.

Odysseus's gifts and sacrifices are part of his cunning and his often deceitful plans are deeply rooted in the principle of exchange. The gift resembles a sacrifice in its purpose of paying for forfeited blood or of sealing a covenant of peace. They are commodities exchanged for some equivalent. Barter, in Adorno's view, secularizes sacrifice. The magic schemata of sacrificial rituals bear already the marks of rational exchange; sacrifices are a performance that aim at controlling and manipulating the gods, who are, ironically, dethroned by the rituals in their honor.[95] In the history of civilization, sacrifice is thus not merely an irrational religious ritual, but a form of self-serving rationality and exchange. Sacrifice is never a selfless act of giving, for the sacrifice is made with the expectation of a return of the investment, either in form of goods or favors such as, for instance, the protection from destructive forces. In this way, sacrifice prefigures the capitalist principle of exchange and, like bourgeois enlightenment, requires sobriety and common sense, "a proficient estimate of the ratio of forces."[96] However, all power in class society is tied to a nagging consciousness of its own impotence against physical nature and its many social descendants, and "only consciously contrived adaptation to nature brings nature under the control of the physically weaker. The *ratio* which supplants mimesis is not simply its counterpart. It is itself mimesis: mimesis unto death."[97] The pattern of Odysseus's cunning represents the mastery of nature through adaptation, and in this way, imitation enters into the service of domination. As a principle of bourgeois disillusionment, renunciation represents the internalization of the sacrifice already present in the "estimation of the ratio of forces which anticipates survival as so to speak dependent on the concession of one's own defeat, and—virtually—on death. The nimble-witted survives only at the price of his own dream, which he wins only by demystifying himself as well as the powers without."[98]

Adorno examines Odysseus's self-preserving sacrifices, gifts, and contracts as exchanges that lead to the emergence of the internalized mechanisms of self-denial and self-restraint representing the subject's involvement in an exchange with himself. Although the forms, expressions, and rationale of the sacrifice change over time, the transitory, irrational practice continues to exist because of its elements of rationality: "the practice of sacrifice lasted longer than its specific rational necessity—itself already untrue. It is this gap between rationality and irrationality that needs cunning to cover it over. All demythologization is colored by the inevitable experience of the uselessness and superfluousness of sacrifices."[99] Like Nietzsche, Adorno affirms the fluidity and multiplicity of utility and the already inauthentic origin of a practice. The mythological idea of identity—the exchange of goods or favor of equal value—rationally constructs the principle of exchange, which simultaneously implies deceit and the desire for unfair advantage and revenge. If truly identical things were exchanged, the practice of exchange could not continue to exist: "Zarathustra postulates that human beings will be delivered from revenge. Revenge is the mythological model of exchange; as long as exchange is a medium of domination, myth will dominate."[100] The sacrifice functions as a demythologized form of revenge, and the continuation of the mythological theme of revenge in the exchange principle negates the bourgeois belief in progress. Based upon thinking in equivalences, the exchange of goods or favors and the infliction of damages or punishments are carried out under the assumption that one adequately compensates for the other: "everything has its price; *all* things can be paid for."[101] Unequal and non-identical objects and phenomena are turned into commodities by creating equivalents and forcing identities.

Nietzsche's examination of the relationship of debt and guilt interprets materialistically the emergence and continued transformation and transvaluation of phenomena that later operate in Adorno's genealogy of exchange and sacrifice. The morality of guilt and bad conscience, Nietzsche claims, is based upon materialistic principles of exchange. The concept of guilt (*Schuld*) arises from debts (*Schulden*) that must be repaid. As the internalization of guilt, the internal control mechanism of bad conscience ensures the payment of debt. Physical coercion is thus no longer necessary, nor is it exercised directly by those in power, because the coercion is imposed by the indebted subject on itself. Bad conscience acts as the cultural and moral memory of society, and the continued emphasis on self-sacrifice, renunciation, and alienation draws attention to the debt that must be paid. A sense of guilt and personal obligation is basic to all forms of civilization, having "its origin, as we saw in the oldest and most primitive personal relationship, that between a buyer and seller, creditor and debtor: it is here that one person first encountered another person, that one person first *measured himself* against another."[102] Buying and selling is part of the oldest human experience, out of which a kind of astuteness developed, as well as human pride and the feeling of superiority in relation to other animals. "Setting prices, determining values, contriving equivalences, exchanging—these preoccupied the earliest thinking of man to so great an extent that in a certain sense they constitute thinking *as such.*"[103] The practice of exchanges and contracts brought about the emergence of moral values and concepts such as guilt, justice, liability, duty, and compensation, "together with the custom of comparing, measuring, and calculating power against power."[104] The idea that everything can be bought and sold became the defining moment of human interaction. The individual's feelings of self-worth represent the "oldest and naivest moral canon of *justice*, the beginning of all 'good-naturedness,' all 'fairness,' all 'good will,' all 'objectivity' on earth."[105] Justice does not therefore manifest itself as a universal ideal of rational human beings who wish to be just, but rather as a materialistically motivated contractual concept of morality that permits "parties of approximately equal power to come to terms with one another" and to reach a settlement that compels "parties of lesser power to reach a settlement among themselves."[106]

For Adorno, cunning rationalizations, contracts, and exchanges are fundamental to the history of civilization. That these series of exchanges in the service of self-preservation alienate the self and destroy subjectivity becomes apparent in his interpretation of the siren episode in the first excursus. In order to avoid falling prey to the seductive power of the sirens' song, Odysseus has himself bound to the mast of the ship. He has wax put in the ears of his rowing companions so that they can neither hear nor be tempted to react to the sirens' song or to Odysseus's screams begging to be released. Odysseus accepts the superior strength of the sirens' song and resorts to having his technically enlightened self restrained. Unlike the rowers, he can listen to the sirens, but has carefully prepared himself not to fall under their spell.[107] Odysseus finds a loophole in the ancient contract, which does not specify whether one passes by the sirens chained or unchained, and he cunningly defies the sirens, well aware that he is helpless against their mythical power. He fights a defiant battle with rational means: "Defiance and infatuation are one and the same thing, and whoever defies them is thereby lost to the myth against which he sets himself. Cunning, however, is defiance having turned rational."[108] Odysseus's cunning is based upon the recognition and acceptance of his own weakness; his use of rational thought and his ability to calculate compensates for the disadvantage of being human. Odysseus does not try to sail a different route to avoid the sirens, nor does he not presume the superiority of his knowledge and listen freely to the song. Chained to the mast, Odysseus is the prototype of the bourgeois individual whose survival depends upon the conformity to the structures of power, and although his cunning enables him to persevere, he must restrain himself. Odysseus knows the limitations of his ability to reason and the unpredictability of his desires, and thus restricts his own movements. His intelligence is a mere means of survival and does not represent an emancipatory step toward the liberation from the power of myth; it is the result of the repression of his inner nature, instincts, and drives. Through his instrumentalization of reason, Odysseus allows himself to partake in the experience of art, the song, but nonetheless restrains himself from responding to it or coming under its influence. Unlike his oarsmen, he does not put wax in his ears. The song of the sirens, though heard, is rendered powerless and "becomes a mere object of contemplation—becomes art."[109] Separated from nature and divorced from its magic power, the sirens' song turns into art suffering from its depreciation. Odysseus longs for the mythical powers from which he wishes to free himself, and his rationality operates at the expense of art: "Since Odysseus' successful-unsuccessful encounter with the Sirens all songs have been affected, and Western music as a whole suffers from the contradiction of song in civilization—song which nevertheless proclaims the emotional power of all art music."[110] Odysseus's men, who cannot listen and know only of the song's danger but nothing of its beauty, are condemned to the physical labor of rowing, while Odysseus, the master, is a prisoner presented with a concert: "Thus the enjoyment of art and manual labor break apart as the world of prehistory is left behind. The epic already contains the appropriate theory. The cultural material is in exact correlation to work done according to command; and both are grounded in the inescapable compulsion to social domination of nature."[111] Odysseus and the oarsmen represent different social classes connected only through their will to survive and to dominate nature: "Just as he cannot yield to the temptations to self-abandonment, so as proprietor, he finally renounces even participation in labor, and ultimately even its management" while his men remain enslaved and unable to enjoy their labor because it is performed under pressure, in desperation, and under the deprivation of the senses.[112] The restriction and impoverishment of sensual experience prefigures the regression of the masses and "their inability to hear the unheard-of with their own ears, to touch the unapprehended with their own hands," a form of deprivation that leads to a new form of delusion, bourgeois delusion, which deposes the conquered mythic form.[113] The replacement of one delusion by another enforces the belief in conformity and adherence to the status quo.

According to Homer, the sirens' song promises knowledge about everything that had ever happened on earth. Those who hear the song will be wiser and happier, will know the mystery of the world, and finally be freed of the anxiety connected to uncertainties. But in Nietzsche's view it is not the all-embracing knowledge of mythic totality alone that makes the sirens' song so irresistible; connected to the unifying knowledge of the world is the illusion that the one who has heard the song is a better and higher being. "You are more, you are higher, you are of different origin,"[114] such is the promise made in the sirens' song to those willing to surrender and devote themselves to the sirens. As in aesthetic

Socratism, the privileging of knowledge over the aesthetic experience brings art under the sway of morality, for knowledge is equated with virtue. In his description of the virtues of the free spirits and the "new philosophers" in *Beyond Good and Evil*, Nietzsche cites the promise of becoming a higher being to illustrate the irony of enlightenment thought. If the rational processes of demystification are based on simultaneous self-preservation and self-negation, self-glorification and the loss of the self are also part of the same mechanism. A truly free spirit must overcome Odysseus's desire to listen to the sirens' song and the desire to know everything; his ears have to be sealed. The free spirit liberates himself from two illusions: that it is possible to know everything and that knowledge equals virtue whose acquisition makes one a higher, better being. For Nietzsche, the sirens' song is a metaphysical trap, and in contrast to those caught in this trap, the free spirits possess the will and the strength to recognize and accept two opposing tendencies: one embracing the heterogenous nature of phenomena and the other striving toward simplicity and ignorance: "it is the will from multiplicity to simplicity"; "an apparently opposite drive serves this same will: a sudden erupting decision in favor of ignorance"; "also the occasional will of the spirit to let itself be deceived"; and finally, "that by no means unproblematic readiness of the spirit to deceive other spirits and to dissimulate in front of them, that continual urge and surge of a creative, form-giving, changeable force: in this the spirit enjoys the multiplicity and craftiness of its masks."[115] This will to appearance and simplification is countered by the sublime inclination toward profundity, multiplicity, and thoroughness, "with a *will* which is a kind of cruelty of the intellectual conscience and taste."[116] Meanwhile, there still remains plenty of garish intellectual finery and cheerful luxury:

> These are beautiful, glittering, jingling, festive words: honesty, love of truth, love of wisdom, sacrifice for knowledge, heroism of the truthful—they have something that swells one's pride. But we hermits and marmots have long persuaded ourselves in the full secrecy of a hermit's conscience that this worthy verbal pomp, too, belongs to the old mendacious pomp, junk, and gold dust of unconscious human vanity, and that under such flattering colors and make-up as well, the basic test of *homo natura* must again be recognized.[117]

The free spirit, because it must renounce the vanities of traditional philosophy and its decorative jargon, has the difficult duty of liberating himself from the self-deception buried under layers of misconception and of becoming "master over the many vain and overly enthusiastic interpretations and connotations that have so far been scrawled and painted over the eternal basic text" of human nature.[118] Hardened in the discipline of science, man must stand "before the *rest* of nature, with intrepid Oedipus eyes and sealed Odysseus ears, deaf to the siren songs of the old metaphysical bird catcher" promising superiority over nature and other men.[119] Nietzsche's ironic inversion of the two mythical motifs, the seeing Oedipus and the deaf Odysseus, maps out a path of resistance against metaphysics and enlightenment ideology. Odysseus's cunning rationality is dependent upon myth and the structures of metaphysics, for he still wants to hear the sirens' song and longs for the universal knowledge and self-enhancement it promises. Odysseus remains a victim of enlightenment ideology. The new philosopher, and presumably the *New Enlightenment*, go beyond these confines that still impede Odysseus. Although Odysseus, following his calculating sense for self-preservation, finds a way to withstand the seduction of the sirens, he has not freed himself from believing in their mythical promise. Vainly, Odysseus still clings to the illusion of universal knowledge and believes in the disclosure of mythical secrets. However, the new philosopher, the free spirit, and truly enlightened human being are not seduced by the gold dust of human vanity, close their ears to the enticing call, and become deaf to the siren song of metaphysics. Nietzsche's hope for free spirits and a *New Enlightenment* presents a vision of enlightenment liberated from the seductive power of myth and rationality underlining the Adornoan negative utopia of an enlightenment freed from domination. If Nietzsche, as Adorno claims, shares the *Dialectic*'s recognition of the element of bourgeois enlightenment in Homer,[120] he can also be said to oppose, resist, and subvert it.

Nietzsche's and Adorno's genealogies present a critical historiography of enlightenment that escapes traditional philosophy, history, and theory. They point out the displacements of mythical thought into modern rationality. Rather than a continuous progression toward a telos, history is described by the genealogies as a process of overcoming, subduing, and cunning, whose instrument is rationality. Like Nietzsche, Adorno emphasizes the "discontinuous, chaotically splintered moments and phases of history,"[121] and shows how the perception of historical necessity was developed into a means for justifying the status quo and for enforcing conformity. Both Nietzsche and Adorno share a materialistic view, tracing moral values and phenomena back to their undatable origin in the rational principle of exchange that had always already been the result of displacements and transformation. Adorno's and Nietzsche's counternarratives of enlightenment want to evade the enticing charm of metaphysics and defy the limits of rational thought by demonstrating the entwinement of myth and reason and by employing an open and mobile strategy of interpretation that does not derive its legitimacy from a claim to power and truth. This strategy legitimizes itself by challenging established authoritative interpretations and by offering new ways of thinking about the evolution of human civilization. Neither the *Dialectic* nor the *Genealogy*, however, completely divorce themselves from the history of civilization they are describing and the dominant ideologies they attempt to displace. They do not step outside of enlightenment or the Western tradition of thought, for they are "parasitic" and cannot exist independently. Since Nietzsche and Adorno maintain that values are the result of interpretations and misinterpretations, they can only propose alternative interpretations and displacements and must thematize the interpretive process in order to make visible their own fallibility. The displacements of interpretation are achieved by rational argumentation as well as through form, method, and style. For Nietzsche and Adorno, a critique of rationality and ideology not only signifies an argumentative attack on the subject, but also includes an attack on the formal and stylistic expressions of enlightenment ideology. Although there are obvious differences between Foucault's laborious projects and the speculative interpretations of Nietzsche and Adorno, his conception of genealogical studies outlines the critical potential of Nietzsche's and Adorno's examination of the acute manifestations of phenomena, examinations that lay bare the rationalizations of history and enlightenment's inherent ideological presuppositions toward history, such as progress, origin, telos, continuity, and necessity. The *Dialectic* subverts monumental and antiquarian forms of writing history and seeks to avert its shortcomings, which are the effacement of differences in the monumental model and the devaluation of change and the process of becoming in the antiquarian model. In line with Nietzsche, Adorno and Horkheimer construct a critical history, one which avoids its dangers, namely, the tendency to negate through simple opposition existing interpretations and phenomena to such a degree that it fails to recognize that it is part of the very tradition it is criticizing. In Foucault's terms, the genealogy of the *Dialectic* is parodic, dissociative, and sacrificial: its narrative asserts itself against the drive toward reminiscence, the illusionist creation of identity and continuity, and is willing to sacrifice claims to truth. The *Dialectic* affirms and performs the entwinement of myth and enlightenment. Myth is utilized for enlightening enlightenment, proving the thesis that myth always contained elements of enlightenment; enlightenment's entanglement with myth is brought to light by exposing enlightenment's ideology, which always contained mythical elements and which must, in order to justify itself, always revert to myth. By enacting enlightenment's, and even the enlightenment of the enlightenment's, complicity with myth, the *Dialectic* constructs a critical history that acknowledges its own entanglement in both myth and enlightenment. The critical and genealogical impetus of the *Dialectic* avoids both its reversion to the grand narratives of history and its relapse into myth.

3

The Critique of Metaphysics and the
Ideological Moments of Rationality

In Adorno's writings, Nietzsche acts primarily as a critic of ideology, and his frequent references to him attest to Nietzsche's impact on Adorno's critique of the ideological moments of rationality and metaphysics. Adorno cites Nietzsche in various contexts as a critic of systematic philosophy and of rational and metaphysical concepts such as truth, logic, identity, continuity, substance, and appearance. Like Nietzsche, Adorno questions what he names the *Metaphysik des Bleibenden*, the belief in and privileging of that which is thought to be permanent. In Nietzsche Adorno saw a thinker who resisted the traps of identity thinking, a concern central to *Negative Dialectics*. Furthermore, Nietzsche's critique of concepts (*Begriffe*), that is the subsumption of the non-identical in language, is integral to Adorno's critique of metaphysics and his antitotalitarian notion of a constellation. The following chapter will discuss the major thematic underpinnings of Adorno's references to Nietzsche; the citations stem from various contexts within Adorno's work and confirm their shared interest in a radical critique of—and resistance to—the ideologies of metaphysics and enlightenment. However, the present discussion also takes into account Adorno's critique of Nietzsche and his repeated comments that Nietzsche did not quite manage to escape the pitfalls of metaphysics and ideology.

METAPHYSIK DES BLEIBENDEN

According to Adorno, Nietzsche's work exposes the ideology of universality and permanence, *die Metaphysik des Bleibenden*: "Nietzsche's work is brimful of anti-metaphysical invective."[1] With Nietzsche, Adorno argues against the ideological allocation of truth to substance and illusion to appearance, a move that divorces truth from the processes of becoming; when the permanent is posited as the true, the beginning of truth becomes the beginning of deceit.[2] The metaphysical grounding upon first principles and the insistence upon and privileging of permanence are constituents of its ideology. In *Stichworte*, Adorno views in Nietzsche a witness to the metaphysical prejudice of Western civilization, which asserts that only first principles can lay claim to truth, thus devaluing that which has evolved and matured in the course of history.[3] In *Aesthetic Theory*, Adorno contends that the traditional equation of truth and being, which Nietzsche demolished, should be turned on its head: "Truth exists exclusively as that which has become."[4] By equating the permanent with the true, the onset of truth is always also the onset of deception.[5] The privileging of permanence and the accompanying mistrust and devaluation of the transitory are, according to Adorno, part of the desire for eternal life. "Lust—which wants eternity, according to a luminous word of Nietzsche's—is not the only one to balk at passing."[6] It is not only the human, all-too-human desire for stability and drive for legitimation and normativity motivating such prejudices, it is also the result of the *Verblendungszusammenhang*, the total context of delusion, instituted by the metaphysical and religious traditions, especially the mystical tradition, all of which promise the immediate experience of the eternal. While Adorno repeatedly affirms on the one hand the historical constructedness and transitory nature of truth, he argues on the other that a certain stability is by necessity one aspect of truth, "for it is a feature of truth that it will last, along with its temporal core. Without any duration at all there would be no truth, and the last trace of it would be engulfed in death, the absolute."[7]

The same holds true for the work of art. Although it does not contain an eternal truth, its truth content is, despite its temporal core, also not entirely perishable, for the assertion of truth's complete instability and demise would be falling back onto another absolute; but truth can exist only if freed from absolutes and metaphysical prejudice. Clearly, Adorno's critical emphasis upon the assumption against becoming is prevalent, because it is likewise a prevalent prejudice of traditional philosophy and religion. However, in mentioning the stable aspect of truth, he forestalls the conclusion that he is operating with simple reversals.

Adorno cites Nietzsche's aphorism *"What is perfect is supposed not to have become"* from *Human, All Too Human*,[8] in which Nietzsche charges that we are unaccustomed to asking how great art came into existence, but are trained to "rejoice in the present fact as though it came out of the ground by magic."[9] The artist, in Nietzsche's view, knows that the work only achieves its full effect when it arouses the spectator's belief in improvisation and the miraculous suddenness of coming into being. Great artists accordingly promote this illusion by introducing elements of "rapturous restlessness, of blindly groping disorder" as a means of deceiving the spectator.[10] Adorno sees an irreconcilable contradiction in what Kant called art's purposefulness without purpose, but the contradiction between its being—what is—and becoming—what is made—is a vital element of art, one that circumscribes its law of development. However, the process of becoming represents also art's "shame": by following the patterns of material production, art cannot evade the question "for what" it is made.[11] Art's apotheosis of making rests in its entanglement with production and rational purposefulness on the one hand and its negation of all purpose and its claim to a existence in and for itself on the other hand. Works of art try to silence the question of their motivation and their modes of creation, yet the more they distance themselves from the process of becoming and their material production, the more fragile they become: "the endless pains to eradicate the traces of making, injure works of art and condemn them to be fragmentary."[12] Following the decay of magic, art employs technique to produce illusion and to reproduce the magic of being and perfection. Adorno's critique of Wagner's works reiterates this point through his insistence that the attempts to erase the traces of production mark the descent of art into commercialism. Similarly, Nietzsche criticizes Wagner for denying to the listener the experience of his music as a process of becoming. Both Nietzsche and Adorno maintain that experiencing art as a process of becoming is vital to the aesthetic experience; its erasure indicates the degeneration of art into kitsch and simultaneously testifies to the reproduction of the metaphysical bias against *Werden.*

With regard to their rejection of such a prejudice, Nietzsche and Adorno bear a common respect for Heraclitus, the philosopher who does not view substance and transitoriness as antagonistic concepts. With recourse to Heraclitus, Adorno and Nietzsche argue against Plato for whom the transitoriness of appearances belongs to the domain of illusion.[13] The metaphysical tradition after Heraclitus disconnects substance from the transitory and equates it with the eternal, and "only Nietzsche protested."[14] Adorno quotes extensively from the first five aphorisms in the chapter "Reason in Philosophy" from *Twilight of the Idols*, in which Nietzsche attacks the narratives of unity, substance, and permanence. These aphorisms not only contain Nietzsche's most trenchant critique of metaphysics, but are also cited by Adorno almost in their entirety. That these are the longest direct quotations of Nietzsche found in Adorno's works points toward their centrality for Adorno's undertaking. In order to examine Adorno's use of Nietzsche's antimetaphysical arguments, it is therefore necessary to refer extensively to Nietzsche's text.

According to Nietzsche, one of the idiosyncrasies of philosophers is their lack of a historical sense. They operate with "conceptual mummies," because they are desperate to delineate a difference between the real world and the world of appearances,[15] and think that they honor phenomena by dehistoricizing them: "They kill, they stuff, when they worship, these conceptual idolaters—they become a mortal danger to everything when they worship. Death, change, age, as well as procreation and growth, are for them objections—refutations even. What is, does not *become*; what becomes, *is not*."[16] Philosophers believe in that which *is* to the point of despair, but since they cannot ascertain it, they claim that their senses deceive them and prevent them from recognizing what really is. The presumed immorality of the senses is countered by the "escape from sense-deception, from becoming, from history, from falsehood."[17] Heraclitus stands apart from the rest of the philosophers, who reject "the evidence of the senses because these showed plurality and change."[18] He valued sense perceptions, although he falsely claimed that the senses lie. Our senses do not lie, Nietzsche contends, for "it is what we make of their evidence that first introduces a lie into it, for example the lie of unity, the lie of materiality, of substance, of duration."[19] According to Nietzsche, the interference of reason is the true cause for the falsification of sense perceptions, because "in so far as the senses show becoming, passing away, change, they do not lie."[20] However, Heraclitus will always be right in his claim that being is an empty fiction: "The 'apparent' world is the only one: the 'real' world is only *lyingly added*."[21]

Nietzsche then castigates the philosophers for an additional idiosyncrasy: that of mistaking the last for the first. He suggests that they unfortunately place the highest concepts, "that is to say the most general, the emptiest concepts, the last fumes of evaporating reality, at the beginning *as* the beginning."[22] This behavior indicates once again the philosopher's glorification of being; the higher cannot be allowed to grow out of the lower, and in fact should not be permitted to have grown at all. Everything of the first rank must therefore be presumed to be *causa sui*, the cause of itself. Higher concepts are not permitted to locate their origins in something else, because such a principle of origin would count, in the eyes of the philosophers, as "an objection, as casting a doubt on value."[23] The postulation of the "stupendous concept 'God'" is required in order to assure that these supreme concepts presumed to have not become and to be *causa sui*, such as the unconditioned, the good, the true, the perfect, are not incommensurate with one another. The last, thinnest, emptiest is placed as the first, as cause in itself, as the most real being. Nietzsche wonders how "mankind should have taken seriously the brain-sick fancies of morbid cobweb-spinners!"[24] Here Adorno interrupts briefly his citation of Nietzsche and comments that what Nietzsche labelled "fancies" is in reality the result of the untamed nature of life. The misery brought about by metaphysics is the result of domination and does not, as Nietzsche claims, originate in the spirit alone. The victory of the higher, continues Adorno in his Nietzschean argumentation, is codified by the victorious with the claim that the higher is the better and that the better must triumph. Those who are subjugated are supposed to believe that whatever survives is of higher rank than that which is defeated.

In the fifth aphorism, Nietzsche asserts that *we* new philosophers, "I say 'we' out of politeness," view the problem of error and appearance differently:

> Change, mutation, becoming in general were formerly taken as proof of appearance, as a sign of the presence of something which led us astray. Today, on the contrary, we see ourselves as it were entangled in error, *necessitated* to error, to precisely the extent that our prejudice in favour of reason compels us to posit unity, identity, duration, substance, cause, materiality, being; however sure we may be, on the basis of a strict reckoning, *that* error is to be found here.[25]

Although Adorno confirms Nietzsche's view, he nonetheless contends that Nietzsche underestimated what he had recognized and therefore remained caught in a contradiction that could have been resolved by a self-reflection of thought. Adorno portrays Nietzsche as underestimating the opposition of the stable and the chaotic, of appearance and substance, of being and becoming. Nietzsche failed to recognize that these oppositions are themselves proclaimed by metaphysics, and to continue operating in these oppositional terms means to retain metaphysical structures of thought. By positing chaos in opposition to stability, Nietzsche's critique fails to reflect upon the metaphysical grounding of such an opposition. By Adorno's account, nature itself—and here his argument parallels the one about truth—has moments of identity, substance, and permanence, for without these moments the domination of nature would not be possible:

> Opposing the solid to the chaotic and mastering nature would never succeed without a moment of solidity in the subjugated. Or else it would constantly expose the subject as a lie. Just skeptically disputing that moment as a whole and localizing it in the subject, is no less subjective hubris than the absolutization of the schemata of conceptual order.[26]

In Adorno's view, the projection of sheer chaos is just as much a product of the imagination as its reverse, the projection of order. Adorno thus resists the Nietzschean tendency to declare all reality chaos, and opposes the claim from "On Truth and Lie in an Extra-Moral Sense" that nature knows no forms or concepts.[27] The proclamation of chaos perpetuates rather than undermines the structures of identity thinking, because identity thinking tends to privilege universal categories, such as the concept of nature as chaos and civilization as order. In the context of Adorno's perception of particularity and universality, Peter Dews points out that in contrast to Nietzsche, "Adorno's philosophical effort is directed towards moving beyond the split between bare facticity and conceptual determination, through an experience of the contradiction which that split itself implies."[28] Adorno, it should be noted, does not accuse Nietzsche of perpetuating metaphysical prejudices, but rather of underestimating the power and presence of metaphysical structures in very particular instances. In Nietzsche's work Adorno recognizes a very potent protest against metaphysics, and he pays tribute to

Nietzsche, who mocks the differentiation between appearance and substance, as the unreconciled opponent of the theological inheritance of metaphysics.[29] Adorno's remarks about the metaphysical residues in Nietzsche's thought imply that Nietzsche is no *Überwinder*—a thinker who overcomes—of enlightenment and metaphysics in the sense of finality and completion, but rather that overcoming enlightenment and metaphysics is a continuous process of critical labor, for, as Nietzsche himself points out repeatedly, the shadow of God lurks everywhere. Adorno's Nietzsche reception also foreshadows the assertions of many postmodern thinkers that the escape from metaphysics and compulsive identity thinking is a slow procedure and not a sudden occurrence. The Heideggerian twisting-out of metaphysics is a fitting metaphor for this gradual process; after all, the metaphysical tradition and its manifestations in language and thought patterns remain the frames of reference through which thought is expressed.

CONCEPTS AND IDENTITY THINKING

Nietzsche's essay "On Truth and Lie in an Extramoral Sense," addresses the relationship between language and truth and describes the process by which language and concepts are formed. According to this essay, these come into being through a kind of consensus theory of truth, and Nietzsche concludes that convention determines the use of words and concepts. As a creative activity, linguistic representation also establishes relations and cannot claim to truly represent or express the thing-in-itself: "The 'thing in itself' (for that is what pure truth, without consequences, would be) is quite incomprehensible to the creators of language and not at all worth aiming for. One designates only the relations of things to man, and to express them one calls on the boldest metaphors."[30] Nietzsche determines truth as a relational phenomenon and argues that human expression knows nothing of the thing itself, but knows only metaphors and concepts with which it circumscribes the object. Concepts formed by language inadequately express reality and know nothing of the origin and substance of a phenomenon. Words and concepts are the result of the drive to form metaphors and are merely empty shells sustained by convention and forgetfulness. Through the conventional usage of language, human beings form a consensus concerning what is considered true, but in forgetting that their truth is based only upon this conceptual agreement, they also forget that it is only an illusion. Affirmations perceived to represent objective statements, such as 'the stone is hard', are merely the result of subjective nerve stimuli, while the categorization of things by gender provides yet another example of the arbitrary nature of concept formation.

Nietzsche's explication of the concept formation process renders a precise and distinct description of what Adorno identified as identity thinking:

> Every word immediately becomes a concept, inasmuch as it is not intended to serve as a reminder of the unique and wholly individualized original experience to which it

owes its birth, but must at the same time fit innumerable, more or less similar cases—which means, strictly speaking, never equal—in other words, a lot of unequal cases.[31]

Every concept is formed by a reductive process that excludes the individual and particular and favors larger categories. Universalizing and generalizing phenomena, the individual object or experience is reduced to a concept applicable to many other objects or experiences. Expressions through language equate the merely similar:

> Every concept originates through our equating what is unequal. No leaf ever wholly equals another, and the concept 'leaf' is formed through an arbitrary abstraction from these individual differences, through forgetting the distinctions; and now it gives rise to the idea that in nature there might be something besides the leaves which would be 'leaf'—some kind of original form after which all leaves have been woven.[32]

No leaf, however, turns out to be a correct and reliable copy of the original form. Why, Nietzsche asks, do we speak of honesty under these circumstances when we know nothing of an "essence-like quality named 'honesty,' we know only of numerous individualized, and thus unequal actions which we equate by omitting the unequal."[33] Thus the creation of words and concepts subsume unequal phenomena under a forced unity, making the non-identical commensurable.

For Adorno, identity thinking is also inherent to conceptualization, a process constituted by subsumption and abstraction. Related to conceptualization in its concealment of mechanisms of domination, the metaphysics of numbers is an integral part of identity thinking and a major component in the establishment of a hybrid order: "Concepts themselves involve subsumption and thus contain numerical ration. Numbers are an arrangement for making the non-identical, dubbed 'the Many' commensurable with the subject, the model of unity. They bring the manifold of experience to its abstraction."[34] Identity thinking excludes the different, foreign, diverse, and heterogeneous, while non-identity thinking, for which Adorno uses the model of constellations, gives expression to the conceptless (*das Begriffslose*), and to what is repressed, reduced, forgotten, and eliminated by the abstract nature of concepts and categories. Art, and especially music, are renderings of the non-identical that escape language and concepts. In contrast to conceptual identity, aesthetic identity stands by and supports the non-identical repressed in everyday life.

In the realm of philosophy, Adorno envisions constellations of thoughts as an alternative to the hierarchical order of philosophical and metaphysical systems. Like the constellation of the stars, a constellation of thought and phenomena constitutes a mobile relation between things unfixed by hierarchies and categories. However, the manifestation of identity is an integral part of thought itself, and thus thought can never stand completely outside the processes of conceptualization and abstraction. It must therefore continually resist identity thinking through self-reflection and contradiction.

To think is to identify. Conceptual order is content to screen what thinking seeks to comprehend. . . . Aware that the conceptual totality is mere appearance, I have no way but to break immanently, in its own measure, through the appearance of total identity. Since that totality is structured to accord with logic, however, whose core is the principle of the excluded middle, whatever will not fit this principle, whatever differs in quality, comes to be designated as a contradiction. Contradiction is non-identity under the aspect of identity.[35]

Although excluded by conceptual totality, the non-identical becomes visible through the awareness of the illusory nature of totality and identity and the recognition that envisioning non-identity and divergence is only possible with a referent, namely identity and unity: "What we differentiate will appear divergent, dissonant, negative for just as long as the structure of our consciousness obliges it to strive for unity."[36] Hoping to rescue the divergent and dissonant—the non-identical—Adorno opposes Hegel's absolute idealism and posits contradiction as an indication for the untruth of identity, and "the fact that the concept does not exhaust the thing conceived."[37] Like logic, identity thinking is an instrument of domination that subsumes phenomena under concepts, and thereby robs the non-identical of the possibility of expression. In philosophical thought, identity thinking, "the passion for equating the non-synonymous" serves to establish hierarchies that exclude opposition; in social reality, it serves to enforce conformity. Adorno is aware that "no theory today escapes the marketplace" and suspects that the aspiration of his own theory to do just that would deteriorate into self-righteous "self-advertising."[38] Just as there is no escape from the traps of metaphysics and identity thinking, there is no escaping capitalist reality. However, there are, according to Adorno, ways to resist conceptualizations that eradicate the remainder. Salvaging thought from conformity to social, economic, metaphysical, and scholastic pressures, Adorno revitalizes Benjamin's conceptualization of the relationship of ideas to phenomena, which he compared to the relationship of constellations to the individual stars.[39] As Buck-Morss points out, Adorno—with the aid of Marxism—reworked Benjamin's concept of constellation by translating Benjamin's mystic-influenced theory into a dialectic and materialist one.[40] Without positing a metaphysical realm beyond history and above human existence, the concept of a thought constellation allowed Adorno— in the tradition of Benjamin—to confront the question of the possibility for truth.[41] Giving consideration to the multitude of transitory and particular phenomena, constellations resist systems and the Platonic and Hegelian devaluation of the empirical realm in favor of viewing truth as nonempirical absolutes.[42] In his "A Portrait of Walter Benjamin," Adorno even refers to Nietzsche as a precursor to the notion of a constellation:

The later Nietzsche's critical insight that truth is not identical with a timeless *univer-sal*, but rather that it is solely the historical which yields the figure of the absolute, became, perhaps without his knowing it, the canon of his practice. The programme is formulated in a note to his fragmentary main work, that "in any case the eternal is more like lace trimmings on a dress than like an idea." By this he in no way intended the innocuous illustration of concepts through colourful historical objects. . . . Rather, his desperate striving to break out of the prison of cultural conformism was directed at constellations of historical entities which do not remain simply interchangeable examples for ideas but which in their uniqueness constitute the ideas themselves as historical.[43]

Nietzsche's and Adorno's critique of identity thinking thus reflects not only their radical skepticism toward rationality, philosophy, and systems but is also intimately connected to their view of truth as a historically contingent phenomena. As Anke Thysen phrases it, it attests to their shared recognition of the forms of domination mediated by the concept of identity.[44] However, their suspicions toward identity thinking and systematic rationality are accompanied by their affirmation that thought can never be fully controlled and subsumed by them. Adorno cites Nietzsche to demonstrate that language and thought also contain a playful element that resists positivist claims to factuality and truth. Nietzsche affirms perception and expression as a creative activity and aesthetic behavior, and in his essay on truth and lie, Nietzsche argues that there is no causality or correctness of perception between the subject and the object, but rather an aesthetic operation, which transfers and translates perception into expression. While concepts are the burial sites of perception, the drive to form metaphors pushes human beings beyond the bondage of conceptual thought. Involved in a continuous process of transference, human beings confuse categories and mix up concepts, and thereby create new metaphors and metonyms. Through this confusion of words and categories, the unsubsumable and disorderly remainder come into play, providing the free-spirited intellect with the opportunity to mock and destroy the old boundaries of language and concepts:

> that enormous framework and hoarding of concepts, by clinging to which the needy man saves himself throughout life, is to the freed intellect only a scaffolding and a toy for his most daring feats; and when he smashes it to pieces, throws it into confusion, and then puts it together again ironically, pairing the most alien, separating the closest items, then he reveals that . . . he is no longer led by concepts but by intuitions.[45]

Similarly, Adorno argues that thought does retain the trace of the different and non-identical that can be rescued through art and, in the realm of thought, through the aesthetic/philosophical constellation. There always exists a beyond and above that which is expressed; thought aims beyond its target because it never quite reaches it. A transcending thought takes into account its own inadequacy and knowingly extrapolates order by overextending itself.

> While thought relates to facts and moves by criticizing them, its movement depends no less on the maintenance of distance. It expresses exactly what is, precisely

because what is is never quite as thought expresses it. Essential to it is an element of exaggeration, of overshooting the object, of self-detachment from the weight of the factual, so that instead of merely reproducing being it can, at once rigorous and free, determine it. Thus every thought resembles play, with which Hegel no less than Nietzsche compared the work of the mind.[46]

This element of play—the awareness of the potential for disorder and irresponsibility and the pleasure derived from the volatility and fleetingness of thought—represents the nonbarbaric side of philosophy, the side that exhibits a disinterest in domination and subsumption, acknowledges its distance to reality, and values the moments of non-identity. If thought tries to conceal this distance from reality and assumes the guise of factual representation rather than interpretation, it denies thinking as such and becomes ideology.

LOGIC AND SYSTEMS

Nietzsche's and Adorno's critique of identity thinking is closely linked to their critique of logic and philosophical systems. Logical thought is yet another fiction of rationality that confines reason to instrumental functions and reduces thought to positivist operations. Both Nietzsche and Adorno argue that oppositions, such as the logical and illogical, are metaphysical structures of thought that inhibit the enlightenment of the enlightenment. As the opposition between rationality and irrationality—which Foucault attacks as blackmail—it constitutes the ideological moments of rationality which must, in the interest of self-preservation and self-legitimation, seek recourse in myth. Like Adorno, Nietzsche recognizes that concepts such as order, unity, and logic have no existence by and in themselves but always need as a point of reference a notion of disorder, disintegration, and the illogic that allows for a determination by comparison. Nietzsche asserts the entwinement of the logical and the illogical and argues that logic comes into existence out of illogic. Those who resisted operations of logic, the tendency to equate, and "subsumed things too slowly" had a lesser probability of survival.[47] "The dominant tendency, however, to treat as equal what is merely similar—an illogical tendency, for nothing is really equal—is what first created any basis for logic."[48] Likewise, it was necessary to develop the concept of substance, "which is indispensable for logic although in the strictest sense nothing real corresponds to it."[49] Thus, the fiction of logic is built upon a number of other fictions, and although Nietzsche attempts to undermine thinking in oppositions, he nevertheless sees that judgments are made possible only by giving consideration to opposing values. He asks:

[H]ow can something originate in its opposite, for example rationality in irrationality, the sentient in the dead, logic in unlogic, disinterested contemplation in covetous desire, living for others in egoism, truth in error? Metaphysical philosophy has hitherto surmounted this difficulty by denying that the one originates in the other and assuming for the more highly valued thing a miraculous source in the very kernel and being of the "thing in itself."[50]

Instead of postulating absolutes and substances as the origin of values and phenomena, Nietzsche puts forward the relational and transformational aspect of their development. Oppositions are nothing more than customary exaggerations of popular or metaphysical interpretations, and Nietzsche recommends that one should unlearn the habit of thinking in oppositions. As a first step, this would entail acknowledging that good and evil, true and false, reason and unreason, logic and illogic develop in a dynamic relationship with each other: knowledge originates from error, logic from illogic, and reason from irrationality. As a mechanism of survival, logic is connected to identity thinking, and Nietzsche views them both as forms of subjugation arising from the will to survival, the will to power, and a need for order and normativity. Rooted in instinct and desire, the illogical drive to logical thought and identity thinking instrumentalizes rationality in the service of self-preservation. According to Adorno, logic and its manifestation in science and positivism reduce thought to a technical process of utility, while at the same time refusing to accept the diversity of phenomena and the multiplicity of meaning.

> The exclusiveness of logical laws originates in this unique functional significance, and ultimately in the compulsive nature of self-preservation. And self-preservation repeatedly culminates in the choice between survival and destruction, apparent again in the principle that of two contradictory propositions only one can be true and only one false.[51]

Adorno stresses with Nietzsche the reductive nature of logical thought that becomes a means of survival, and he too criticizes logic as oppositional either-or thinking devised to maintain hierarchical orders. In *Hegel: Three Studies*, Adorno agrees with Nietzsche's assessment that nothing exists in reality that corresponds to logic.[52] Logic, Nietzsche contends, depends on presuppositions that not only find no reflection in the real world but also suppress a sense of history and change: "for example on the presupposition that there are identical things, that the same thing is identical at different points of time."[53]

Systems of thought, be they philosophical, political, metaphysical, scientific, or religious, give voice to the rage against the non-identical. By setting their own rules of inclusion, systems, like logic, protect themselves against the incommensurable. Adorno sums up his critique of the system most pointedly in his inversion of Hegel's affirmation of totality; in opposition to Hegel, Adorno writes that "The whole is the false,"[54] a motto that could sum up Nietzsche's entire project. Belonging to the realm of administration, systems are ordering schemata that have various compensatory functions: "According to Nietzsche's critique, systems no longer documented anything but the finickiness of scholars compensating themselves for political impotence by conceptually construing their, so to speak, administrative authority over things in being."[55]

Philosophical systems compensate for a lack of power and control, and as part of the administered world, they create the illusion of order, logic, and reason and thus participate in the context of delusion. Systems interpret and portray the world as a rationally ordered and controllable phenomenon and situate themselves within the prevailing structures of power. They are constructed in order to conquer the fear of chaos and the unknown, and to exclude, as Foucault has shown in his analyses of institutions and discourses, the non-identical as the Other. Similar to institutionalized discourses, systematic philosophy produces in its narratives an order and a logic lacking in reality. Systems and logic become strategic devices for the creation of a fictitious order that can only be a narrative and not a substantial order. Systems become ideological not because they invariably contain falsehoods, breaks, inconsistencies and contradictions, but because their attempt to hide them and erase their traces which only causes them to become more entangled in ideology.

> Whenever something that is to be conceived flees from identity with the concept, the concept will be forced to take exaggerated steps to prevent any doubts of the unassailable validity, solidity, and acribia of the thought product from stirring. Great philosophy was accompanied by a paranoid zeal to tolerate nothing else, and to pursue everything else with all cunning of reason.[56]

As in the case of logic, the drive to systematization originates in prehistory, in the life-preserving rationale of animals. Human beings devise systems and hierarchical orders to justify their attacks upon others, upon those who stand outside of a particular order or system. Systems also legitimize the desire to attack the Other by declaring it evil and worthy of destruction. Although the will to power and self-preservation manifest themselves through systems and hierarchies, only part of the desire to destroy the Other is motivated by the need for physical survival. To risk attacking an opponent requires additional impulses; Adorno maintains that these additional impulses come from the rage against the victim—the different that can neither be absorbed nor subsumed. In order to justify and sustain the rage, the victim has to be classified as the evil Other. This not only justifies the attack, but also conceals the animalistic drive and ideological zeal behind the crusades for morality and justice. Furthermore, these strategies of vilifying the Other cover up, as Adorno has pointed out with regard to the dynamics of anti-Semitism, the dynamic of self-hatred leading to the hatred of others, to a transference of hatred from that which one hates in the self to its false projection onto the Other.[57] Philosophical systems represent the intellectual rather than the physical rage against the victim, and when they incorporate morality into systems, they express their contempt for humanity. Systems, including moral laws, operate on the basis of rationalizations. On the one hand, such rationalizations idealize totality and total inclusion, while on the other they marginalize the non-identical as potential threats to the coherence of the whole.

The august inexorability of the moral law was this kind of rationalized rage at non-identity; nor did the liberalistic Hegel do better with the superiority of his bad conscience, dressing down those who refused homage to the speculative concept, the hypostasis of the mind. Nietzsche's liberating act, a true turning point of Western thought and merely usurped by others later, was to put such mysteries into words. A mind that discards rationalization—its own spell—ceases by its self-reflection to be the radical evil that irks it in another.[58]

The pressure exerted by the philosophical system is paralleled by the demands of social institutions and moral laws, and, according to Adorno's Nietzschean genealogy, these forms of pressure originate not in human reason, as traditional philosophy claims, but in the human desire for survival. In his critique of the jargon of authenticity, Adorno makes use of Nietzsche to testify to the dishonesty of systems, and reproaches philosophical systems for the jargon they employ. The language of systems is indifferent toward the individuality of the subject and fulfills a predetermined function: to create a totality and to justify the existence of the system itself. The language of systems becomes metaphysics, because language is not generated according to the needs of the individual elements but according to preestablished hierarchical ordering principles.[59] The creation of exclusionary systems, such as jargon, logic, identity thinking, and the privileging of substance and permanence are powerful tools that simultaneously construct and obscure ideology.

The structure of immanence as absolutely self-contained and all-inclusive is necessarily always already system, irrespective of whether it has been expressly deduced from the unity of consciousness or not. Nietzsche's mistrust of *prima philosophia* was thus also essentially directed against system builders. "I mistrust all systematizers and I avoid them. The will to a system is a lack of integrity."[60]

Nietzsche's, Adorno's—and Foucault's—radicalized critiques of ideology examine systems' mechanisms of exclusion in a variety of contexts and explicate the repressive nature of systems not only in the realm of philosophy but also within sociopolitical reality. In their attempt to leave nothing out, systems come to resemble the demagogue, whose irrational authority is mediated by rationality and whose claim to power is advanced by argumentative logic and coercion.[61] Systems, as part of every aspect of life, enforce conformity and act as unifying, totalitarian forces in metaphysics and philosophy as well as in the realm of administration and material production. The complicity of systems with metaphysics and instrumental rationality indicates how it is impossible for systems to ground and justify themselves without resorting in the end to myth and ideology. Both Nietzsche and Adorno expose how metaphysical presuppositions, identity thinking, and instrumentalized reason can neither legitimize thought nor ground claims to power, because these presuppositions obscure truth rather than express it.

TRUTH AND LEGITIMATION

The following does not propose to investigate whether or not Adorno, as some critics claim,[62] ultimately rejected Nietzsche's notion of truth. Such an undertaking would presuppose a unequivocal concept of truth in Nietzsche's work and a more or less unequivocal acceptance or rejection by Adorno. Since neither possibility is the case, a comparison of the two positions toward truth can be credible only if it recognizes that the search for truth in Nietzsche and Adorno, as an experiment and adventure, finally eludes exact definition and determination by necessity. However, one can safely claim—at the risk of sounding trite— that Nietzsche's radical skepticism toward all claims to truth has a profound impact upon Adorno's work. With regard to absolute claims to truth, this skepticism includes the critique of identity thinking, instrumental rationality, logic, systems, the postulation of metaphysical principles, and of the traditional correspondence theory of truth. Both thinkers undermine the correspondence theory with their assertion that the representation of phenomena through language and concepts does not correspond to reality. Inherent in their contention of the semiological impossibility of truth are the critiques of the *Metaphysik des Bleibenden*, concepts, language, logic, and systems as well as a rejection of any and all metaphysical and ontological theories of truth. "What, then, is truth?" Nietzsche asks, and then answers:

> A mobile army of metaphors, metonyms, and anthropomorphisms—in short, a sum of human relations, which have been enhanced, transposed, and embellished poetically and rhetorically, and which after long use seem firm, canonical, and obligatory to people: truths are illusions about which one has forgotten that this is what they are; metaphors which are worn out and without sensuous power; coins which have lost their pictures and now matter only as metal, no longer as coins.[63]

Truth is not a static expression of the things-in-themselves, but rather a mobile and dynamic strategy of establishing relations. Truth is deception whose illusionary character has been forgotten, or, in Adorno's terms, truth is ideology because the non-identical and the element of untruth are repressed and hidden. However, both thinkers affirm the possibility of truths. They agree that truth is historically contingent and a matter of perspective and interpretation. Truth is not a static, universal, or metaphysical entity, and there is, of course, always the possibility of error; in fact, truth is based upon error. Nietzsche points out that we are "entangled in error, *necessitated* to error,"[64] while Adorno argues that without the risk and the present possibility of error, truth is objectively not possible. Stupidity of thought arises when the courage inherent in the process of thinking is repressed; this stupidity is, however, not a private affair but rather testimony to the scars of social mutilation.[65] Nietzsche's pathos knew this, Adorno maintains, and his adventurous and imperialistic credo of living dangerously meant to promote thinking dangerously.[66]

The risky undertaking of searching for truths gives rise to both truths and errors, which are inseparable from the historical moment in which they arise. Since history is not a self-correcting development toward emancipation but a dynamic process of continuous transformation, truths must undergo transformations as well and are neither final nor subject to evaluation in terms of final goals or ultimate standpoints. Philosophy's tendency toward systematization and the postulation of abstract and supposedly permanent and stable concepts hinders the extraction of its truth content. Hegel, and after him only Nietzsche, recognized the historicity of truth and dismissed the identification of philosophical content and abstraction with eternal truth, thus liberating truth from traditional metaphysical appropriations.[67] In rejecting the static view of truth proclaimed by the *Metaphysik des Bleibenden*, which conflicts with a dynamic view of history, Nietzsche uses the plural "truths" rather than the singular "truth" to indicate the heterogeneity and multiplicity of his understanding of truth. Nietzsche draws a distinction between the absolute, ultimate truth proclaimed by metaphysics and *truths*, which are produced by the dynamic interaction between thought and reality; "everything has become: there are *no eternal facts*, just as there are no absolute truths. Consequently what is needed from now on is *historical philosophizing*, and with it the virtue of modesty."[68] Instead of dispensing with the concept of truth, Nietzsche revises it by emphasizing—despite his warnings against the disadvantages of an excessive accumulation of historical knowledge—the need for a historical perspective. Truths are possible only as moments of truth in history, and a modest philosopher would admit to this.

Adorno perceives Nietzsche as a critic of metaphysical, scientific, and positivistic notions of truth and attributes to him, against the allegation of relativism and the everything-goes mentality, a critical notion of truth. Adorno identifies certain criteria that make it possible to distinguish between ideology and truth:

> Essence is what must be covered up, according to the mischief-making law of unessentiality; to deny that there is an essence means to side with appearance, with the total ideology which existence has since become. If a man rates all phenomena alike because he knows of no essence that would allow him to discriminate, he will in a fanaticized love of truth make common cause with untruth. He will join hands with Nietzsche's despised scientific stupor that will not bother with the dignity of objects to be dealt with.[69]

The failure to accept any differentiation between opinions, ideological suppositions, and truths serves only to support positivist fallacies and to insult critical judgment. To dismiss all truths as mere opinions is to deny qualities and differences, and brings truths under the constraints of plausibility and common sense. The claim that all truths are merely opinions confirms the mythical superstition that reality is a chaos of arbitrary ideas and forces that blindly drive society toward destruction. Adorno sees this claim as testifying to Nietzsche's grandiose anticipation of the self-destruction of truth by an unreflected process of enlightenment.[70] Identifying truth with the formation of a popular consensus is just as false as denying the existence of truth outright: both views relegate truth to opinion. To substitute the notion of a normative truth, however problematic it may be, with the more comfortable truth of a consensus and an average represents yet another version of the self-destruction of truth. The slogan, "'Thirteen million Americans can't be wrong',"[71] stylizes truth into a fetish of the average, champions the idea of truth as a middle ground, and claims truth as a right of the majority. It exiles truth to the realm of quantity and numbers, a move that ultimately leads to the commodification of the so-called truth through the ideology of the culture industry. It is the task of philosophy, Adorno insists, to enunciate the distinction between truths and opinions, at a time when society no longer does so. Philosophy is the place for the reflection and self-reflection of truth, and it must resist truth's reification and the tendency to place it abstractly against mere subjectivity. The reified consciousness of society, however, is losing its ability to critically unfold truths through a reciprocal mediation between subject and object.[72]

Adorno blames traditional metaphysics and positivism for the destruction of this critical notion of truth. He criticizes metaphysics' attempt to hold on to the notion of absolute truth and positivism's capitulation to facts, figures, and the status quo. The two forms of consciousness, the latter bowing before factuality and the former deceiving itself by seeing itself as the sovereign of facts, represent the torn halves of truth that, however, do not add up to truth.[73] Nietzsche narrates the history of truth as a history of errors: over an immense period of time the intellect produced nothing but errors. A few of these errors proved to be useful and were subsequently passed down from one generation to the next until they became the basic endowment of the species. These errors include the following: "that there are enduring things; that there are equal things; that there are things, substances, bodies; that a thing is what it appears to be; that our will is free; that what is good for me is also good in itself."[74] The errors facilitating survival provided stability and order, and skepticism toward these errors posing as truth—the "weakest form of knowledge"—came into existence relatively late in the history of civilization,[75] and only after it became apparent that the debasement of these errors called truth also contained the possibility of their utility. Intellectual curiosity, the pleasure of intellectual play, skepticism, and doubt found their place as a useful need among others. Thus the desire for intellectual struggle assisted in legitimizing the desire for truth:

> A thinker is now that being in whom the impulse for truth and those life-preserving errors clash for their first fight, after the impulse for truth has proved to be also a life-preserving power. Compared to the significance of this fight, everything else is a matter of indifference: the ultimate question about the conditions of life has been posed here, and we confront the first attempt to answer this question by experiment. To what extent can truth endure incorporation? This is the question; that is the experiment.[76]

Now that truth can be thought, the real question is the extent to which truth itself can survive its assimilation into life. The difficulty implied by living with truth is that neither truth nor life might survive the experiment. The significant struggle between truth and life-affirming errors leads to the central problem of Nietzsche's genealogy of truth: "the problem of the value of truth."[77]

Since truth originates from error and the will to truth from the will to deception, the metaphysical prejudice against appearance and illusion is a temporary value judgment in need of reevaluation. It is possible "that a higher and more fundamental value for life might have to be ascribed to deception, selfishness, and lust."[78] Thus an error and the falseness of a judgement are not necessarily objections to such errors and judgments; at issue is their life-affirming status. We are fundamentally inclined to regard the false metaphysical judgments as the most indispensable for us, since "without accepting the fictions of logic, without measuring reality against the purely invented world of the unconditional and self-identical, without a constant falsification of the world by means of numbers, man could not live."[79] To renounce these false judgments is to renounce and to deny life: "to recognize untruth as a condition of life—that certainly means resisting accustomed value feelings in a dangerous way; and a philosophy that risks this would by that token alone place itself beyond good and evil."[80] The value and outcome of the risky experiment of living with truth is still undecided. However, the philosopher's will to truth is of value only to himself. Philosophy represents the philosophers' tyrannical drive to power; philosophers are spokesmen for their prejudices, which they baptize "truth," and they are very far from exhibiting the good taste and courage of conscience to admit this. The will to truth at any price, the will to unveil, uncover, and bring to light whatever is kept concealed for good reason is a repulsive pleasure that does not necessarily lead to the discovery of truth: "We no longer believe that truth remains truth when the veils are withdrawn."[81] The Greeks rejected this indecency because they knew how to live: "What is required for that is to stop courageously at the surface, the fold, the skin, to adore appearance, to believe in forms, tones, words, in the whole Olympus of appearances. Those Greeks were superficial—out of profundity."[82] The provocation and irony behind Nietzsche's adoration of surface and appearance points toward the more bitter irony of truth itself. On the semantic level, it is impossible to formulate truth because linguistic representation demands abstraction and conceptualization. However, Nietzsche does not deny the possibility of truth: errors and false judgments can be corrected. It does remain uncertain whether or not this correction is in the best interests of life, and whether truth can even survive or is still truth once it becomes uncovered.[83] By questioning the possibility of the apprehension of truth, Nietzsche projects the discovery of truth as a process of infinite deferral. If truth is no longer truth once it is uncovered, the search for truth never reaches its final goal, for the apprehension of truth is sabotaged by the dissimulation, or, to put it in Derridian terms: "Truth, unveiling, illumination are no longer decided in the appropriation of the truth of being, but are cast into its bottomless abyss as non-truth, veiling, and dissimulation."[84]

Both Nietzsche and Adorno are in agreement when they argue that wishful thinking and the will to self-preservation frequently serve as foundations for the so-called truth. In their critiques of philosophical systems, they assert that systematic thought is unfit to discover truth, since self-interests and the desire for self-preservation interfere with critical self-reflection. Like the conclusions and results of systematic thought, the wish to affirm a phenomenon often motivates the need for justification, and identity thinking and logic often act as strategies of legitimation. The will to and longing for truth, already under suspicion because it implies the desire for order, stability, universality, and control, guarantees neither objectivity nor truth. According to Adorno, Nietzsche's insight is still valid today: that the justification of a contention that arises from the desire to prove its legitimacy is an argument against the contention rather than for it.[85] Although philosophers often sacrifice truth for wishful thinking, Nietzsche hopes they are truthful and proud investigators of the soul, who "have trained themselves to sacrifice all desirability to truth, *every* truth, even plain, harsh, ugly, repellent, unchristian, immoral truth."[86] Both Nietzsche and Adorno highly value intellectual honesty, truthfulness, integrity, and modesty. Like Nietzsche, who is modest enough to admit to the possibility of error in his own thought, Adorno holds that every truth has the possibility of error inscribed on it. According to Adorno, no productive thought can ever be proven and no truth can ever be completely legitimized. "Every thought which is not idle, however, bears branded on it the impossibility of its full legitimation."[87] Adorno agrees with Nietzsche that metaphysical thought is especially prone to mistake wishful thinking for truth. In the *Antichrist*, Nietzsche voiced the strongest argument against theology and metaphysics: "that hope is mistaken for truth; that the impossibility of living happily, or even living at all, without the thought of an absolute, does not vouch for the legitimacy of that thought."[88] Feelings of happiness and pleasure thus present one of the strongest grounds for suspicion towards claims to truth. Adorno carries his suspicion against pleasure and enjoyment so far as to assert that they can turn an objectively existing phenomenon into a lie. The fifth aphorism of *Minima Moralia* expresses *in nuce* the complex relationship of truth, lie, and reality in connection with a call to distrust all forms of pleasure, spontaneity, impetuosity, all loss of self-control, because such a surrender implies pliancy toward and complicity with existing conditions:

> Even a blossoming tree lies in the moment its bloom is seen without the shadow of terror; even the innocent "How lovely!" becomes an excuse for an existence outrageously unlovely, and there is no longer beauty or consolation except in the gaze falling on horror, withstanding it, and in unalleviated consciousness of negativity holding fast to the possibility of what is better.[89]

The possibility of truth arises from negativity and not from affirmation. Even the beauty of nature is a lie if it is not perceived as a negative contrast to the ugliness of social reality. For Adorno, pleasure represents an affirmation of life, and he argues that under the present conditions joy can exist only in complicity with ideology. Understandable within Adorno's project of negativity, this equation of pleasure and consumerism, joy and ideology seems as reductive as his equation of an uncomplicated style of writing and ease of communication on the one hand and the loss of intellectual vigor on the other; similarly reductive appear the association of the products of the culture industry with the total loss of subjectivity and a totalized context of delusion. Although pleasure and wishful thinking must arouse suspicion of claims to truth, Adorno nevertheless concludes, that the idea of truth cannot exist without hope: "In the end hope, wrested from reality by negating it, is the only form in which truth appears. Without hope, the idea of truth would be scarcely even thinkable, and it is the cardinal untruth, having recognized existence to be bad, to present it as truth simply because it has been recognized."[90] The idea of truth is always connected to the hope for a better reality; truth must negate the false conditions of existence and reject the mere recognition of reality as representing the truth. Hope, for Adorno, is thus not a joyful anticipation of a better future, but rather the somber glance of negativity upon the present. Hope and the vision of a better reality are extracted *ex negativo* from the recognition of a reality separated from truth.

Nietzsche claims that the hope for health and the intoxication of convalescence after a long period of exhaustion and suffering motivated him to write *The Gay Science*, in which he labels philosophy a physiological misunderstanding that reveals more about the philosopher's life, body, and state of health than about truth and reality. Nietzsche recommends that philosophers laugh at themselves, "as one would have to laugh in order to laugh *out the whole truth*"; however, to do so "even the best so far lacked sufficient sense for the truth, and the most gifted had too little genius for that."[91] But laughter may yet have a future, Nietzsche contends, since it may yet form an alliance with wisdom. For Adorno, the alliance of laughter and philosophy is both absurd and impossible. Although he argues that the tasks of philosophy must be redefined, this redefinition excludes "joyful wisdom," which is in his view a contradiction in terms. Before lapsing into intellectual neglect through its transformation into a discipline of method and abstraction, "the teaching of the good life" had been regarded as the task of philosophy.[92] But "life" has become a private sphere of consumption and a mere appendage of the process of material production, and whoever "wished to know the truth about life in its immediacy must scrutinize its estranged form, the objective powers that determine individual existence even in its most hidden recesses."[93] Nietzsche's laughter and Adorno's sobriety in the search for truth constitute the significant difference in mood and attitude between the former's gay science and joyful hope for convalescence and the latter's "melancholy science"[94] at the abyss of twentieth-century thought.

ADORNO'S CRITIQUE OF NIETZSCHE

Adorno's critical reading of Nietzsche's thought is most apparent and concentrated in his *Minima Moralia*. Maurer remarks that although Nietzsche is omnipresent in Adorno's work, he appears only occasionally openly and by name. The case of Karl Marx represents another suppression of reference, who is never even mentioned in the *Dialectic* despite his enormous influence upon Adorno's work. As one critic remarked, the name Marx comes up in the *Dialectic* only in connection to the films of the Marx brothers. In most of his works, Adorno filters his own thoughts through Nietzsche and cites him to reinforce his arguments. Because Nietzsche is seldom invoked at an argument's beginning but is usually brought into play at the end of a thought process, Peter Pütz argues that Adorno identifies in Nietzsche a philosopher of the end, and perhaps of a new beginning.[95] Adorno also frequently remarks on the misinterpretation and misappropriation of Nietzsche by other thinkers or political factions, and he chooses to detail his own disagreements with Nietzsche primarily in *Minima Moralia*.

Adorno takes Nietzsche to task for his misogynist attitude and writings on women, and further contends that the historical circumstances have changed significantly enough to warrant a reversal and reevaluation of the ascetic ideal and the value of amoralism. Another area of disagreement concerns Nietzsche's assessment of decadence, which shall be discussed in the context of Adorno's and Nietzsche's critique of Wagner in the following chapter. However, Adorno's most pronounced critique of Nietzsche is seen in his objections against *amor fati* and Nietzsche's call for the affirmation of life. Here the gap widens between the gay science of laughter and affirmation and the melancholy science of negativity. For Adorno, the affirmation of life is synonymous with the affirmation of the degrading conditions of human existence and the false reality created under capitalism, and by extension fascism. Synonymous with conformity, the affirmation of life is under the present circumstances no longer possible. However, since truths and realities are subject to historical processes, negativity can only appropriately express nonconformity at a particular moment in history. Adorno appreciates Nietzsche's radical negativity with regard to metaphysics and enlightenment, but argues adamantly against any demand for affirmation and any positive utopian vision.

AMORALITY AND THE ASCETIC IDEAL

Although Adorno accepts that there are no universal and absolute laws of morality, he nevertheless retains the notion of moral action. Morality is not grounded in rationality, but rather in the dictates of human decency. Adorno and Horkheimer dispute in the *Dialectic* the possibility of arguing rationally against so-called immoral acts, and cite "the impossibility of deriving from reason any fundamental argument against murder."[96] In his examination of Hegel's notion of morality, Adorno agrees with Hegel's rejection of a pure moral consciousness. Hegel knew that the individual is on the one hand a socially functioning being whose actions are determined by his work within particular socioeconomic contexts, while on the other he is a being with individual tastes, tendencies, and predispositions. The interests of these two sides do not necessarily concur, and therefore pure moral actions, of which the individual believes him- or herself to be the only judge and master, are suspect, ambiguous, and self-deceptive.[97] Adorno sees Hegel's notion of morality as a prelude to Nietzsche's, and contends that modern analytic philosophy has brought home an aspect of Hegel's speculations in that it recognizes that the individual's self-perception is based on rationalization and deception:

> Hegel derived the transition from pure moral self-consciousness to hypocrisy— which then became the focus of Nietzsche's critical attack on philosophy—from its moment of objective untruth. Historically, of course, formulations like the one in the *Phenomenology* about the "hard heart" . . . represent a prelude to Nietzsche's notion of *ressentiment*, of morality as "revenge."[98]

In his aphorism "A word for morality," Adorno suggests that Nietzsche advocates a form of amorality that is at present historically outdated: "Amoralism, with which Nietzsche chastised the old untruth, is itself now subject to the verdict of history."[99] In Adorno's view, the restrictive prohibitions of religion and morality have lost their inherent authority. He understands Nietzsche's plea for amorality, the rejection of Christian morality, and the assertion of strength and abundance, as signs of nonconformity at a time when the decay of religion and metaphysics was less pronounced and material production was still underdeveloped. In a highly developed capitalist economy, however, due to a change in objective preconditions, such drives for abundance, strength, and the will to enrich oneself are now conformist attitudes. In the face of consumer society's plenitude, in which all restrictions appear superfluous, the ascetic ideal becomes once again a viable alternative to the gluttonous opulence of the consumer age. The wilful gesture of seizing opportunities and taking what one wants, exemplified by the ruthless drive of Nietzsche's blond beast, no longer enunciates the aristocratic will to self-determination, but rather articulates bourgeois complacency:

> The implied meaning of the master-morality, that he who wants to live must fend for himself has in the meantime become a still more miserable lie than it was when a nineteenth-century piece of pulpit-wisdom. If in Germany the common citizen has proved himself a blond beast, this has nothing to do with national peculiarities, but with the fact that blond bestiality itself, social rapine, has become in face of manifest abundance the attitude of the backwoodsman, the deluded philistine, that same "hard-done-by" mentality which the master-morality was invented to combat.[100]

The excesses of strength and force of the master-morality are part of fascist and capitalist ideology, an ideology that pervades all classes of society, including the targets of master-morality, the disadvantaged. The morality of the slaves has absorbed the morality of the masters, and the virtue of refined and noble manners (*die Tugend der Vornehmheit*), has been detached from the morality of the masters. Under present conditions,

> true distinction has long ceased to consist in taking the best for oneself, and has become instead a satiety with taking, that practices in reality the virtue of giving, which in Nietzsche occurs only in the mind. Ascetic ideals constitute today a more solid bulwark against the madness of the profit-economy than did the hedonistic life sixty years ago against liberal repression.[101]

Adorno understands Nietzsche's advocacy of amorality and his proclamation of the virtues of nobility, coupled with his opposition to the ascetic ideal, as useful forms of protest against the norms of nineteenth-century society. However, resisting a profit-oriented society and the domination of the exchange principle requires opposition to excess. Such forms of opposition include the practice of giving rather than taking, and abstinence rather than indulgence. Today, the amoralist may at last permit himself "to be as kind, gentle, unegoistic and open-hearted as Nietzsche was already back then."[102] Although Nietzsche's call for amorality was an effective strategy deployed against prevailing values, it was nevertheless a mask that does not reflect Nietzsche's personality: "As a guarantee of his undiminished resistance, he is still as alone in this as in the days when he turned the mask of evil upon the normal world, to teach the norm to fear its own perversity."[103] Adorno suggests that Nietzsche did not practice the amorality that he preached, and that he played the devil's advocate in order to further enlighten about enlightenment. His appeal to amorality was designed to expose and undermine the absurd hypocrisy of moral laws. However, in order to continue the path of nonconformity in late capitalist society, the strategy must change in the face of new circumstances warranting a reversal of Nietzsche's mask of amorality.

AMOR FATI

Adorno's critique of *amor fati* contains his most strongly worded disagreement with Nietzsche. Considering the centrality of negativity to Adorno's thought, it is not surprising that the affirmation of life and the injunction to love one's fate encounter Adorno's resistance. It is indeed Nietzsche's most serious transgression, for which Adorno can find neither excuses nor explanations. Neither a consideration of changing historical circumstances nor a recognition of his mask can rescue Nietzsche's *amor fati*. The concept of *amor fati*, argues Adorno, is incoherent and conflicts with Nietzsche's critical analysis of theological and metaphysical prejudices. On the one hand, Nietzsche refutes the Christian proof by efficacy, that faith is true because it brings pleasure, while on the other he advocates the acceptance and love of fate. The proof of pleasure, by Nietzsche's account, is proof of pleasure and nothing more; there is no reason why true judgments should produce more enjoyment than wrong ones. Despite this insight into the dubious nature of deriving grounds of legitimation from pleasure and enjoyment, Nietzsche taught *amor fati*, a myth that "debars Nietzsche's critique of myth from truth."[104] In the *Antichrist*, Nietzsche makes his strongest argument against the metaphysical and theological concept of truth, and further insists that wishful thinking is often confused with truth and used to legitimize it. Since Nietzsche recognized no basis for the assumption that right judgments are more desirable than wrong ones, there is, according to Adorno, no reason to love life: "We might well ask whether we have more reason to love what happens to us, to affirm what is because it is, than to believe true what we hope."[105] The notion of *amor fati* escapes the critical rigor that Nietzsche employed against concepts of truth and the mechanisms of legitimation. Adorno asks if it is "not the same false inference that leads from the existence of stubborn facts to their erection as the highest value, as he criticizes in the leap from hope to truth?"[106]

Nietzsche's argument that wishful thinking does not legitimize truth must be applied to *amor fati*: to love something does not justify its existence. While Nietzsche relegates the origins of blissfulness and happiness to the lunatic asylum, Adorno argues that the idea of *amor fati* should be conceived as originating in prison. "The love of stone walls and barred windows is the last resort of someone who sees and has nothing else to love. Both are cases of the same ignominious adaptation which, in order to endure the world's horror, attributes reality to wishes and meaning to senseless compulsion."[107] *Amor fati* indicates resignation, renunciation, conformity, the grotesque glorification of absurdities before the powers that be and a concession to the status quo. To affirm existing conditions as fate depicts them as immutable forces, and to love this so-called fate would mean loving the existing conditions just because they exist. Conversely, the recognition of existence as "bad" or "false" does not legitimize its presentation as truth. *Amor fati*, however, reproduces this "crime of theology that Nietzsche arraigned without ever reaching the final court."[108] Adorno finds the lineage of *amor fati* in the Christian values of sacrifice and self-sacrifice, already severely criticized by Nietzsche himself. The church has preached the acceptance of one's fate for centuries; it renders the individual powerless and promotes the subjugation of will to the postulated higher powers. Instead of resisting the will to domination and manipulation by the priests, *amor fati* sanctions them. Nietzsche maintains that the sacrifice of the innocent for the sins of the guilty is among the most repulsive and barbaric sacrificial acts. Adorno, turning Nietzsche against Nietzsche, remarks: "Nothing other, however, is love of fate, the absolute sanctioning of an infinity of such sacrifice."[109] *Amor fati* perpetuates theological myths and is, in Adorno's view, incompatible with the rest of Nietzsche's phi-

losophy and his rigorous criticism of Christianity and metaphysics. His advocacy
of *amor fati* causes Nietzsche, whom Adorno otherwise admires for his dissociation from "complicity with the world,"[110] to revert to myth, because he fails to
take the final step toward the total rejection of the prevailing power systems. For
Adorno, hope and truth do not reside in the acceptance and love of fate, but are
actively and perpetually "wrested from reality by negating it."[111] Through *amor
fati*, Nietzsche renounces negativity and refuses to take the last step toward an
unmitigated negation of reality. Nietzsche's refusal thus provokes Adorno's most
substantial disagreement with him.

WOMEN AND GENDER

Most of Nietzsche's remarks on women reflect the prevailing views of his
time. Adorno's critique of Nietzsche's view of women concentrates on Nietzsche's essentialist notion of femininity, and argues that the so-called feminine
nature is, in fact, not natural but rather the product of male violence. Adorno criticizes Nietzsche for accepting an unverified image of the feminine and for ultimately allowing his thought to fall under the sway of bourgeois society.
Nietzsche's mistake, in Adorno's opinion, was to say "the feminine" when speaking of women. However, although Adorno criticizes Nietzsche's notion of femininity, he himself tends to reproduce some aspects of bourgeois ideology: he
replaces the essentialist view with a totalized notion of a socially constructed
femininity. Adorno's failure to question some of his own stereotypical assumptions about women renders virtually irrelevant the nature versus nurture argument, because the end result of the social-constructivist argument (i.e., the
negative view of women as seductresses and gullible manipulators) does not significantly differ from the essentialist standpoint. Firstly, Adorno seems inclined
to overlook the differences between male-constructed images of femininity and
real women; secondly, he seems unaware of the fact that his own observations
represent male constructs. His analysis of women focuses on behavior patterns
that have more in common with stereotypical, male perceptions than with social
reality. Adorno analyzes the deployment of so-called feminine behavior, such as
flashing eyes and impulsiveness, as if these actions exemplified the typical and
representative behavior of real women. Instead of questioning these stereotypical male perceptions, Adorno reinforces and reproduces them and thus undermines—despite his forceful arguments against Nietzsche—the credibility of his
critique. Adorno's characterization of women as seductresses, accomplices, and
victims does not significantly diverge from the conventional, essentialist notions.
The question therefore arises as to the viability of refuting the supposed "naturalness" of feminine traits by relegating the very same or similar traits to the
realm of social construction, without taking into account the ideological gesture
underlying any postulation of femininity, be it essentialist or socially con-

structed. To confront Adorno with his own arguments with regard to *amor fati* and the legitimation of fate as truth: one could say that recognizing the social constructedness of femininity, deeply ingrained in the societal context of delusion, does not provide the legitimation "to present it as truth simply because it has been recognized."[112] Given Adorno's limited engagement with issues of gender, it is somewhat surprising that Nietzsche's view of women provoked Adorno to add to his critique of Nietzsche's concept of *amor fati* and the claim to amorality a third critical aphorism on women. Adorno treats issues of gender mostly as asides or to illustrate and enhance his critique of enlightenment, rationality, the sacrifice, or bourgeois delusion. Furthermore, women are entirely absent from his canon of modernity; he neither grants recognition to women's accomplishments in philosophy, literature, politics, or art, nor does he discuss or criticize the works of contemporary female artists and writers. Especially conspicuous is the absence of women in his *Notes to Literature*, in which women find no mention next to Samuel Beckett, Franz Kafka, Heinrich Heine, Walter Benjamin, Thomas Mann, and other great thinkers and writers of modernity.[113] Although a number of women were affiliated with the Frankfurt School, they held positions behind the scenes and none of them attained a position of prominence. On the whole, the Frankfurt School was a men's club, where the wives supported their husbands while serving as secretaries and editors.[114]

Nietzsche's derogatory comments on women have been widely publicized, cited and discussed. Occasionally they occur as passing asides, while on other occasions they are expansive diatribes that link the emancipation of women to the general decay of European culture. Nietzsche invokes women for contrast, and almost always compares them unfavorably to men: "In revenge and in love, woman is more barbarous than man"[115] and "indescribably more evil than man."[116] Nietzsche likens women to cows, cats, hyenas, and other animals,[117] and he ascribes to them a large number of undesirable traits, among them "much pedantry, superficiality, schoolmarmishness, petty presumption."[118] However, women supposedly love Nietzsche, except, for course, for emancipated women, those "*abortive* females . . . who lack the stuff for children."[119] A woman with scholarly inclinations is probably sterile or has "usually something wrong with her sexually."[120] Nietzsche reduced women's role in society to the reproductive realm: Motherhood is not only woman's primary function, but also the solution to her problems and the problems caused by her. Nietzsche contends that "everything about woman has one solution: that is pregnancy."[121] Nietzsche's most famous (or notorious) statement about women is the old women's advice to Zarathustra, which recommends the domination of women by physical violence: "You are going to women? Do not forget the whip!"[122]

Beyond Good and Evil contains two seemingly contradictory—and by now also famous—associations between women and truth. The first remark begins the preface: "Supposing truth is a woman—what then?"[123] Comparing the dogmatic philosopher's search for truth with the male pursuit of women, Nietzsche notes that dogmatists are as inexpert about women as they are about truth. As is the case with truth, the obscure and elusive phenomenon of woman escapes definition if one tries to win her over with improper methods. Truth as woman thus stands in opposition to the dogmatic truth of philosophy. This woman-as-truth metaphor can be said to represent a figure of resistance to metaphysical and rational absolutism and to oppose a fixed model of identity. A second aphorism maintains that nothing is "more alien, repugnant, and hostile to women than truth—her great art is the lie, her highest concern is mere appearance and beauty."[124] Given Nietzsche's dislike of dogmatic truth, his admiration for Greek superficiality, and his arguments against the devaluation of appearance in favor of substance, it could be and has been argued—as it is possible with many of his contradictory statements on women—that Nietzsche's remarks are not as misogynist as they might initially appear. For example, critics have argued that the old woman's advice about the whip is not straightforwardly misogynist, because it is uttered by a fictional character within the framework of a fictionalized philosophy, a philosophy that may contain "at least potentially a mark of irony."[125]

On the basis of these numerous contradictions and ambiguities which characterize the possibly ironic remark about the whip and his ambiguous position toward truth in relation to women, many critics have reevaluated Nietzsche's view of women. In the wake of Derrida's *Spurs*, they have attempted to contextualize, recontextualize, and contrast Nietzsche's derogatory remarks within Nietzsche's thought. Many others follow Derrida's footsteps in their inscription of woman as a figure of displacement and undecidability; in *Spurs*, Derrida draws a connection between the essentialist notion of woman and the dogmatic understanding of truth: "woman is but one name for that untruth of truth."[126] Derrida relegates Nietzsche's remarks about women to the realm of style and thereby avoids ascribing to Nietzsche's texts an essentialist, fixed notion of womanhood: "Still, one might wonder whether that [the link between women and style] doesn't really amount to the same thing—or is it to the other."[127] Nietzsche's thought utilizes a plurality of styles, according to Derrida's argument, and this heterogeneity of expression evades all attempts to posit fixed identities and a stable truth. Derrida emphasizes the volatility rather than the continuity of Nietzsche's remarks on women, and thus rationalizes their misogynist implications.

The publication of *Spurs* in 1978 marks Nietzsche's entry into the discourse of gender and feminism. In recent years, the literature on Nietzsche and women has exploded, and Derrida's figure of undecidability has led many to conclude that there is an "irreducible ambivalence in Nietzsche's attitude toward the feminine."[128] Undecidability, heterogeneity, plurality, and irreducible ambivalence are, however, dissatisfying responses to the majority of Nietzsche's statements testifying to an unambiguous, one-sided, and unmediated degradation of women. To focus on truth, style, and metaphor and to glorify women as figures of undecidability suspends issues of gender in the realm of contingency, strips Nietzsche's writings of their cultural context, diminishes the actual struggle of actual women against male domination, and, last but not least, turns patriarchy into a palatable enterprise.[129] Turning the social and political issues pertaining to woman into a question of style and claiming, as Derrida does, that Nietzsche's style of writing is feminine, prompted Rosi Braidotti to pose the following question: "Isn't it strange that it is precisely at the time in history when women have made their voices heard socially, politically, and theoretically that philosophical discourse—a male domain *par excellence*—takes over 'the feminine' itself?"[130] Another critic, Keith Ansell-Pearson further asks whether it is "not Derrida who castrates woman by turning the issue of woman's emancipation from a question of politics (of power) into one of style."[131] Not once, this critique continues, does Derrida engage in a discussion of the historical, theoretical, or practical struggles of feminism, and he "simply refuses to take seriously the fact that Nietzsche meant what he said and that he believed that women should have neither political power nor social influence."[132]

Much of the recent work on Nietzsche and women mirrors the problems inherent in Derrida's *Spurs*. Indeed, *Spurs* and Luce Irigaray's *Marine Lover of Friedrich Nietzsche*, which is influenced by Derrida, have become the foundational texts of the debate. Robert C. Holub pointed out that one of the strategies of most current essays on Nietzsche and women is to repeat various misogynist statements from Nietzsche, claim that they are inexcusable, and then proceed to demonstrate that "Nietzsche's philosophical position is more beneficial to feminism than his derogatory comments are deleterious."[133] Several participants in this discussion point out that usually derogatory terms, such as falsehood, lie, and deception, are not necessarily negative terms in Nietzsche's thought. It therefore follows that his insulting descriptions of women might not be so misogynist after all, but may be "expressing profound truths about woman as 'the other'."[134] Not without justification, Holub criticizes these moves as "excessive rhetorical gymnastics."[135]

By and large, the writings on Nietzsche and women far surpass Adorno's critique in their complexity and their attention to detail. Although it remains open to debate whether or not Adorno avoids other traps or offers a viable alternative, he does unequivocally condemn Nietzsche's views, while most contemporary writings on the subject are far less judgmental and attempt to rescue Nietzsche from a position where Nietzsche is, in Adorno's opinion, beyond rescue. Adorno devoted only one aphorism in *Minima Moralia* to this critique of Nietzsche's view of women, and his other sparse comments on women dispersed throughout *Minima Moralia* and the *Dialectic* allow for the conclusion that despite his critique of Nietzsche, Adorno himself does not operate with a functioning concept of gender. The same might be said of critical theory as a whole.

A few feminist critics, for the most part in Germany, have in recent years turned to the task of examining the question of gender in relation to the *Dialectic*. The conclusions vary somewhat, but most critics find that despite the *Dialectic*'s sharp critique of enlightenment, instrumental rationality, and the

domination of the male logos, it ultimately reverts to the male myth of andro-
centric philosophy. Christine Kulke argues that the *Dialectic* allocates to the feminine the role of the self-sacrificing victim. In her view, Horkheimer and Adorno
do not extend the dialectic of victim and perpetrator, which characterizes their
analysis of National Socialism, to gender relations.[136] Similarly, Helga Geyer-
Ryan and Helmut Lethen maintain that although Adorno and Horkheimer
demonstrated how the domination of instrumental rationality and the subjugation
of women are complicitous, they reduce women to victims of and collaborators
with oppression within the dialectic of enlightenment.[137] These findings should,
however, not lead to the conclusion that the *Dialectic* is unproductive and
entirely without implications for feminism and feminist theory. Its unrelenting
criticism of enlightenment philosophy, its debunking of the myths of the logos,
instrumental rationality and the *Bildungsroman* of reason, and its unmasking of
metaphysics and moral prejudice are all, like Nietzsche's thought, fundamental
to any contemporary critique of ideology, and consequently also to the formulation of feminist theory. Because Adorno and Nietzsche make it possible to
explore the constitution of ideology and claims to power and legitimation, their
thought also offers a window of opportunity through which feminist claims to
power and legitimation can be examined. Just as Marx may provoke a rethinking
of the structures of economic and material domination and Freud the rethinking
of the role of sexuality in view of feminist theory and practice, Nietzsche and
Adorno may offer productive ways to question the myth of enlightenment and
the functions of morality and ideology.

However, in light of Nietzsche's nauseating misogynist attitudes and the
Dialectic's inscription of women as victims and accomplices, deriving a pro- or
protofeminist perspective would indeed require both thinkers to be rewritten.
Although the reinterpretation and rewriting of texts is a truly Nietzschean project
for the free spirits, it does demand that the interpreter leave behind the letter of
the text. This necessity to go beyond the text illustrates the peculiar state of the
current debates. Participants in the ongoing Nietzsche debate want to overcome
the attitude of many Nietzsche scholars, including Walter Kaufmann's, that
Nietzsche's view of women is philosophically irrelevant. However, to go beyond
Kaufmann has in some cases also led to a space beyond Nietzsche and to certain
stylistic and argumentative excesses, some of which render incomprehensible the
critical discourse on Nietzsche for the readers trained in the analytic tradition of
interpretation.

Burgard's introduction to the volume *Nietzsche and the Feminine* clearly
reflects the problematic nature of this discourse. Burgard comments that many of
the essays in the volume resist introduction and outline. It is almost impossible
for the editor to summarize adequately the content of some essays and to render
cogently their arguments. Burgard only resists the texts' resistance to commentary "for the reader's convenience."[138] In the case of two essays, Burgard's struggle against the texts' resistance to introduction and outline gives way to "brief

and uncharacteristically general summary," and he relinquishes further ground in his battle by resorting to a summary that "succumbs to direct quotation."[139] Confronted with Irigaray's text, Burgard finally resigns from his role as commentator to "commentary's beyond": "In Irigaray's case—the case of a text that goes to commentary's beyond—I give . . . up."[140] In his short self-analysis, Burgard comes to the conclusion that perhaps the most likely reason for giving up is that Irigaray's text "must speak for itself."[141] Burgard's progressive resignation is symptomatic of the current state of scholarship concerning Nietzsche and women, for it is part of a debate that challenges traditional notions of interpretation and criticism and those discourses grounded in logic and rationality.

That the text, entitled "Ecce Mulier? Fragments"[142] must, in Burgard's estimation, speak for itself without commentary and introduction is a result not only of its unique style, metaphorical affluence, and lyrical quality, but also of its resistance to being understood in rational-analytical terms. Irigaray's major work on Nietzsche, *Marine Lover of Friedrich Nietzsche*, is widely discussed among feminist theorists today, and many critics have taken up the challenge of commenting on commentaries beyond. Kelly Oliver delivers a reading of Irigaray's response to Nietzsche and Derrida's *Spurs* that centers on the problems of the feminine as a figure of undecidability and ambiguity, the logic of castration, the reappropriation of the functions of the maternal, and the economy of giving and the necessary forgetting of the maternal giving of life, the last of which is termed by Julia Kristeva the abjection of the mother.[143] Oliver suggests that "the maternal body and its relation to the fetus and placenta can provide a model for an intersubjective theory of subjectivity as a process of exchanges."[144] In order to arrive at her "intersubjective model of subjectivity" after departing from Nietzsche, Oliver travels a path of so many detours, including Hegel, Freud, Lacan, Irigaray, Kristeva, Derrida, Cixous, and the important figures of North American Nietzsche scholarship, that Nietzsche himself becomes another detour, immeasurably removed from his own text.

In her recent work *To Nietzsche: Dionysus, I love you! Ariadne*, Claudia Crawford engages in a dialogue with Nietzsche and Irigaray by emulating the latter's style and weaving together multiple voices, some of which are identifiable as belonging to Nietzsche, Irigaray, Ariadne, Dionysus, Baudrillard, Deleuze, and Derrida.[145] The intermingling of dialogues distances Nietzsche even further from his own texts, and despite the fascination such discourses on Nietzsche arouse in terms of their novelty of style, their mental acrobatics of argumentation, and attention to detail, they may also represent a source of confusion for the reader, and not just for those unfortunate readers who have to comment on them. Thus, Burgard's "I give . . . up" becomes the peculiar opening statement for a discussion that should not, as Burgard himself suggests, end with "calling a misogynist a misogynist and leaving it at that."[146] The distance from Nietzsche's texts, the tendency toward incomprehensibility, and the reproduction of figures of undecidability inherent in many of the newer readings on Nietzsche and women testify to the difficulty of defining Nietzsche's relationship to the feminine. There remains the further difficulty of those critics who attempt to make Nietzsche's writings fruitful for feminist theory.

Reading texts against the grain and against the author's intentions can be productive enterprises. Every text can be said to contain the negation of its own claims, a negation that can be activated through critical activity in a way that undermines and subverts a text's own presuppositions. However, at some point such interpretations gain a degree of independence from the text, and it becomes necessary to reflect upon the difference between interpretation and revision, although there is, of course, no clear dividing line between the two, and every interpretation always already transgresses that boundary. In his review of Burgard's volume, Holub responds polemically to the discrepancy between Nietzsche's direct insults of women and the clever twists of some of his critics: "If Nietzsche can be recruited for women, then why not Schopenhauer, or Otto Weininger? If textual politics is the result of the most clever tricks we can play with an author's text, then there is no limit—but also no impact—of 'the political'."[147] Nietzsche has always received attention from very diverse factions of thinkers and activists, including anarchists and feminists such as Erich Mühsam, Max Stirner, and Emma Goldman. Despite his numerous diatribes against socialism, anarchism, women's emancipation, and democratization, Nietzsche's radical critique of metaphysics, morality, and religion and his proclamation of liberated individualism were of great interest to early feminists activists like Goldman and Helene Stöcker.[148] Like Adorno, Stöcker found Nietzsche's radical critique of ideology and morality fruitful, thus indicating a path of reception less traveled by current scholarship on Nietzsche and women, but one that may ultimately prove to be more productive.

Adorno's critique of enlightenment is one of the most radical indictments of patriarchal structures. The *Dialectic* sees the relationship between rationality and the nature of things as patriarchal; in other words, rationality serves the domination and subjugation of nature because it knows no limits to the domination of creatures and nature. Although Adorno and Nietzsche both affirm that the male world projects its own image of femininity and seeks to dominate women, in both cases this insight seems to have ultimately lessened their respect for women. Against the youth who claims in the *Gay Science* that women corrupt men, the sage smiles and states that men corrupt women and that all the failings of women should be atoned by and improved in men: "For it is man who creates for himself the image of woman, and woman forms herself according to this image."[149] Women, the crowd suggests, need to be educated better, to which the sage replies "men need to be educated better," and beckons the youth to follow him.[150] The youth, however, does not. Similarly, Adorno writes, "the feminine character, and the ideal of femininity on which it is modelled, are products of masculine society,"[151] and agrees with Nietzsche that woman forms herself according the male image. Male-dominated society entirely forms and sustains the ideals of womanhood and "breed[s] in woman its own corrective. The feminine character is a negative imprint of domination. But therefore equally bad. Whatever is in the context of bourgeois delusion called nature, is merely the scar of social mutilation."[152] As scars of social mutilation, women exhibit feminine traits attributed to nature that are actually the result of the degenerative processes of male-dominated society. What passes for nature in civilization, Adorno argues, is by its substance furthest from nature, and so-called instinctual feminine behavior is forced upon women by male violence. Even if women play the roles accorded to them by man, they are more or less willing collaborators who make use of the seductive powers accorded to them:

> One need only have perceived, as a jealous male, how such feminine women have their femininity at their finger-tips—deploying it just where needed, flashing their eyes, using their impulsiveness—to know how things stand with the sheltered unconscious, unmarred by intellect. Just this unscathed purity is the product of the ego, of censorship, of intellect, which is why it submits so unresistingly to the reality principle of the rational order. Without a single exception feminine natures are conformist.[153]

Femininity and so-called feminine behavior do not originate in a natural inclination, but rather constitute a strategy of a will to power, or on a more basic level, a survival strategy in male society. This strategy postulated by Adorno parallels the one of "the weak" asserting themselves against "the strong" that Nietzsche outlined in the *Genealogy*, and it parallels—albeit under the guise of social criticism—Nietzsche's numerous derogatory remarks about women. Adorno's women fit the mold: they are cunning, yet ignorant seductresses and their behavior and identity is determined and confined by the conditions created by masculine society. Feminine behavior is not the unconscious, irrational, and innocent expression of an essential female nature, but rather a product of the ego and a rational means to an end. Since femininity is an exclusively male construct, Adorno sees its deployment by women as conformist without exception and does not allow for its subversive potential. In his view, the behavioral patterns conform to male norms and submit themselves easily to the male postulation of reality and rational order.

Adorno criticizes Nietzsche for failing to unmask the ideology of so-called feminine nature. While Nietzsche exposes the claims to naturalness concerning morality and metaphysics, he overlooks the ideological foundation of the so-called feminine nature: "The fact that Nietzsche's scrutiny stopped short of them, that he took over a second-hand and unverified image of feminine nature from the Christian civilization that he otherwise so thoroughly mistrusted, finally brought his thought under the sway, after all, of bourgeois society."[154] Nietzsche betrayed his own insights and fell into the error of saying the feminine (*das Weib*), when speaking of woman. "Hence the perfidious advice not to forget the whip: femininity itself is already the effect of the whip."[155] In criticizing Nietzsche for attributing an essential nature to *das Weib*, Adorno points out that both condescension toward and veneration of femininity function in the same insulting way, because "the glorification of the feminine character implies the humiliation of all who bear it."[156]

As products of male domination and as effects of the whip, women bear the scars of civilization constituted through the doubled deformation of the already damaged subject. Within the dialectic of enlightenment women are entangled, more deeply than men, in the societal context of delusion. Women appear more susceptible to the culture industry's manipulations and have utterly internalized both the norms of society and the illusory standards and precepts portrayed by the culture industry. The emancipation of women, Adorno argues, has been distorted by masculine society and the continued existence of traditional social structures. The participation of women in salaried employment and in every conceivable supervised activity only "conceals continuing dehumanization" and the fact that working women have "as much or as little independence as men."[157] In business and in the family, women retain their status as objects. Women do not protest these conditions and "willingly, without any countervailing impulse, . . . reflect and identify themselves with domination."[158] Women neither question nor recognize their entrapment within the structures of power; not only do they willingly take part their own domination, but also seem to happily participate in their oppression, as long as they are pacified by consumer products.

> Instead of solving the question of women's oppression, male society has so extended its own principle that the victims are no longer able even to pose the question. Provided only a certain abundance of commodities are granted them, they enthusiastically assent to their fate, leave thinking to the men, defame all reflection as an offence against the feminine ideal propagated by the culture industry, and are altogether at their ease in the unfreedom they take as the fulfillment of their sex. The defects with which they pay for it, neurotic stupidity heading the list, help to perpetuate this state of affairs.[159]

Women, it appears, are subjected not only to the general bourgeois context of delusion, but also to a specific male-created context of delusion that functions within and in cooperation with the larger context. By not endowing women with an essential nature and natural defects, as Nietzsche does, Adorno differentiates between sex and gender; however, in avoiding biological arguments, he does not escape creating another essentialism. Femininity and the defects of women are the symptoms of the degenerative processes of civilization and male domination over nature, and woman becomes the sign, the trace, and the scar of a bad existence. At bottom, Adorno, like Nietzsche, does not differentiate between male perceptions of femininity and real women. Women, in Adorno's perception, are the embodiment of the male images of femininity. With this postulated absorption of women by the images of femininity created by masculine society and the culture industry, he duplicates Nietzsche's relegation of the feminine to the realm of appearance. The problematic aspect of Adorno's argument is that superficiality, dissimulation, the art of calculated manipulation, and stupidity remain female traits, albeit not natural ones. Adorno cites these traits as if they were representative of the behavior of all women, and he does not counterbalance his generalizations with more positive images. A more constructive aspect of Adorno's critique would be to bring his argument to the conclusion that femininity, disassociated with nature, is a performance. However, Adorno's insistence that this performance, the setting in scene of the male image, is conformist without exception blocks this path toward thinking productively about gender performance or seeing it as a potentially subversive act.[160] Since women supposedly identify completely with their oppressors and are inextricably entangled in the totalized context of delusion, their recognition or questioning of their own predicament is precluded; there remains only the hope of the hopeless, the hope wrested from negation, which would allow for women to improve their lot within the present structures of society. However, under these circumstances, attempting to correct the defects of civilization seems as futile as attempting to correct nature.

In their "neurotic stupidity," women become totalized objects, victims, and products of male domination and commodity fetishism, whose progress toward emancipation has not only been hindered by masculine society but also been negated by women themselves. The emancipation of women has been subsumed and absorbed by and integrated into the present social and political structures. For Adorno, as for Nietzsche, women have no solidarity among themselves. Bourgeois women turn against their "hysteric sisters who undertook, in their stead, the hopeless attempt to break out of the social prison which so emphatically turned its four walls to them."[161] Within the current state of affairs, their granddaughters would "smile indulgently over these hysterics, without even feeling implicated, and hand them over to the benevolent treatment of social welfare. The hysteric who wanted the miraculous has thus given way to the furiously efficient imbecile who cannot wait for the triumph of doom."[162] Hysteria, the female protest against bourgeois society, has given way to heartless institutionalization and the reliance upon the state to care for those who can no longer cope. Through its interpretation of hysteria as social protest and his contrasting it to the supposed complacency of the "furiously efficient imbecile," Adorno's imagery of social and moral deterioration furnishes hysteria with an aura of nobility that has more to do with the male idealization of this self-destructive illness than with the real experiences of stricken women. Because of its apparent negativity and resistance to social pressures, Adorno falls into the trap of valuing women's self-destructive and self-sacrificing behavior as morally superior.

The institution of marriage, in theory "one of the last possibilities of forming human cells within universal inhumanity,"[163] is subjugated to the alienated orders of rights and properties. The failure of a marriage exposes this somber base of rights and properties, "the husband's barbarous power over the property and work of his wife, the no less barbarous sexual oppression that can compel a man to take life-long responsibility for a woman with whom it once gave him pleasure to sleep."[164] The husband, who must take responsibility for a woman because he once enjoyed sexual relations with her, seems no less oppressed by his own barbarous power than the woman, for he no longer experiences sexual pleasure with his wife but must, nevertheless, take lifelong responsibility for her. Interesting is, firstly, Adorno's choice to postulate a connection between the breakup of a marriage and the presumed fact that the man no longer feels pleasure when sleeping with his wife and, secondly, his implicit bemoaning of the— seemingly unjust—lifelong responsibility a man must take for his wife.

Falling back into a biologistic argument, Adorno ascribes to women "an archaic frigidity" that is based upon the apparently natural "female animal's fear of copulation."[165] According to Adorno, women "undergo" love in unfreedom, "as objects of violence."[166] Particularly among the petty bourgeoisie, women have retained a memory of the physical pain of sexual intercourse, although civilization has removed immediate fear and physical pain. Society, however, "constantly casts woman's self-abandon back into the sacrificial situation from which it freed her."[167] Through sexuality, women sacrifices herself and is sacrificed and becomes the *Opfer* in the double sense of the word: as the sacrifice and the victim. A woman is right to use a man's advances, for once persuaded she pays the price after a "brief triumph of refusal."[168] As with his understanding of hysterics' self-destructive behavior, Adorno idealizes a gesture of denial and self-denial as morally superior. He gives no consideration to the possibility that the refusal of sexual relations might also suggest the self-sacrifice, repression, and denial of female sexuality. Thus, Adorno casts women as passive and asexual beings incapable of experiencing pleasure. Women are right to reject men's sexual advances, because it is "the only prerogative left by patriarchal society to women."[169] Once again taken in by the idea of negation and refusal, Adorno ignores here the fact that as a sign of bourgeois propriety this refusal is already culturally encoded, and, like hysteria, constitutes a form of denial that perpetuates rather than escapes the norms of bourgeois society.

While men might attain satisfaction, true pleasure is today beyond the reach of both men and women. The experience of pleasure presupposes the "limitless readiness to throw oneself away," and neither women with their fear nor men with their arrogance are capable of doing so.[170] Since neither men nor women are willing and able to throw themselves away, to perform the ultimate self-sacrifice, they are denied happiness. The subjective capacity as well as the objective possibility for happiness do not exist, since they "can only be achieved in freedom,"[171] that is not under the present conditions of unfreedom. This view of women as victims of male dominance on the one hand and collaborators with male violence on the other is paralleled in the *Dialectic*. In his travels, Odysseus is torn between spirit and nature, rationality and sensuality, pleasure and duty, hedonism and abstinence, and self-denial and self-preservation. The bourgeois subject constitutes itself through rationality's capacity to repress the instincts and sacrifice pleasure and sensuality. As the prototype of the bourgeois male, the hero Odysseus must resist the seduction by the female forces who promise him sensual pleasures and gratification. The contradictions and entanglements of the patriarchal-bourgeois relation between the sexes are exemplified by Odysseus's encounter with Circe, the courtesan-enchantress who seduces men by tricking them into believing in the pleasure she promises, while ultimately giving herself only to the one who resists her. Circe tempts Odysseus's men, promises pleasure and "destroys the autonomy of the one she makes happy."[172] By surrendering to her, the enchanted men liberate their repressed nature and behave like wild animals. However, since they have already undergone the process of individuation by way of repressing their instincts, their liberation from repression constitutes a reversion to myth, which the civilized epic cannot represent as anything other than the unseemly degradation of men. In the course of the ritual to which Circe subjects men, she recalls that ritual to which patriarchal society repeatedly subjects her: "Like her, women under the pressure of civilization are above all inclined to adopt the civilized judgment on women and to defame the sex. In the confrontation of enlightenment and myth, the traces of which are preserved in the epic, the powerful temptress is already weak, obsolete and defenseless."[173] As powerful temptresses, women represent a danger to men, whose capitulation to women's powers must cost them their selfhood. Once their repressed nature is unleashed by the enigmatic, powerful figure of irresistibility, who is simultaneously powerless and weak, men lose their identity, or, in Freudian terms, must fear castration by the *femme fatale*. The alleged danger that women pose to male identity represents the true myth, a myth that has survived long into the twentieth century. The studies of Klaus Theweleit, Jacques Le Rider, and Bernd Widdig, for example, all investigate the crisis of male identity and the fear of a feminization of culture at the beginning of our century.[174]

The cunning and rational Odysseus recognizes the danger and resists Circe's magic. In turn, he is rewarded with the pleasures that are only deceptively promised to the men who do not resist her. Odysseus's renunciation of nature is thus not only the foundation for preserving his autonomy and subjectivity, but is also the basis for possessing and dominating Circe, for Circe subjects herself to the will of the man who resists her: "on the pleasure that she ensures, she sets a price: that pleasure has been disdained. The last of the courtesans shows herself to be the first female character. In the transition from saga to story, she makes a decisive contribution to bourgeois frigidity."[175] The deformation of femininity in bourgeois society manifests itself in coldness and submission, thus integrating itself into patriarchal rationality. Circe's power of prophecy about the dangers to be encountered by Odysseus is put into the service of patriarchy and is "ultimately of advantage only to male survival."[176]

The ambiguity of women's role as partisan of male survival on the one hand and seductress on the other is inscribed in the categorization of women as wives and prostitutes: "Prostitute and wife are compliments of female self-alienation in the patriarchal world: the wife denotes pleasure in the fixed order of life and property, whereas the prostitute takes what the wife's right of possession leaves free, and—as the wife's secret collaborator—subjects it again to the order of possession: she sells pleasure."[177] The wife and the prostitute are not necessarily two separate roles, but are rather present in the ambiguous behavior of every woman: Circe, the seductress, eventually acts like a bourgeois housewife, while Penelope, Odysseus's wife, acts like a courtesan when she suspiciously sizes up the returning Odysseus, estimating the chances that he might really be an old beggar or a god trying to deceive her.

The defects of civilization (such as neurotic stupidity, consumerism, frigidity, cold-heartedness, and the assignment of women to the role of victim and collaborator, wife and prostitute) subjugate gender relations to the principle of exchange. The "furiously efficient imbeciles" are engrossed by consumer society, and the absence of women from the canon of modernity indicates women's positioning in the mass culture of modernity. As Adorno sees it, women are the "superior" consumers, easily distracted from and pacified by consumer products. Excluded from the realm of high culture as artists and writers, women in the nineteenth and early twentieth century were judged both inferior readers or second-rate writers, while the decorative arts and crafts and acting were perceived to be suitable female activities. Actresses did not produce, but continued to play the role accorded to them by society: to imitate, reproduce, and submit themselves to the will of the male director. The theater, Nietzsche claims, is the art form of the masses *par excellence*,[178] and is as such already excluded from high culture. In turn, the masses were gendered and represented as a regressive, feminine phenomenon—a threat to high culture, male identity, and political authority. The works of Hans Blüher, Gustave Le Bon, Sigmund Freud, Elias Cannetti, and Thomas Mann testify to this view as well as that of Otto Weininger, who along with Nietzsche saw in the feminization of culture the cause of the general decay of Western civilization. Andreas Huyssen relates aesthetic modernity's fear of being "devoured by mass culture through co-option, commodification, and the 'wrong' kind of success" to the male fear of an engulfing femininity projected onto the masses.[179] Nietzsche's work, especially his polemic against Wagner, abounds with ascriptions of feminine characteristics to the masses and strongly decries the modern tendency toward commodification and feminization: "Wagner, the theater, the mass, women—all become a web of signification outside of, and in opposition to, true art."[180]

Wagner himself, Nietzsche claims, is an actor, a man of the theater. This postulation feminizes Wagner, the man and artist, and underlines Nietzsche's argument that decadent art represents the feminization of modern culture. The theater is no place for a true artist, but rather a place for the herd crying out for democracy, socialism, and emancipation, a place for women, youth, and the masses. Acting might be an appropriate and somewhat acceptable creative outlet for women, but the artist working for the theater loses his artistic sensibility, because he no longer works in solitude and without witnesses. The same holds true for the audience, which is no longer constituted by a number of individuals contemplating a work in solitude. A member of a theater audience becomes a neighbor and a member of the voting public. Although women and youth are Wagner's greatest admirers, his art corrupts the youth and is calamitous for women.[181] They are seduced by Wagner's music, "music as Circe," and taken in by the theatricality of his music dramas. However, the theater is "always only *beneath* art, always only something secondary, something made cruder, something twisted tendentiously, mendaciously, for the sake of the masses . . . the theater is a revolt of the masses."[182] Nietzsche links women and adolescent boys, who in their adoration of Wagner are willing to be seduced by and submit to his music, to the crowd with corrupted tastes for whom the theater stages a revolt. Wagner is an expert in "all the feminisms from the *idioticon* of happiness" and offers the "forgetting of your manhood under a rosebush."[183] Wagner enacts the decay of the artist and the decay of art. The musician-turned-actor developed the female talent for lying, and his music expresses the decline of male potency and the—feminine—hysteria caused by a weakening of the instincts.

When the Frankfurt School and other theorists of modern culture undertook the terminological shift away from the term "mass culture," they abandoned the explicit gendering of mass culture as feminine. Adorno and Horkheimer's rejection of this term and its replacement by the term "culture industry" forestalls the mistaken impression that mass culture is a culture by the masses, rather than a culture produced for the masses as consumers.[184] However, despite this shift in emphasis and the abandonment of the explicit gendering of popular culture, Adorno still ascribes to women the role of consuming, imitating, and reproducing in her self-presentation, an image prescribed by images of male culture and the culture industry. Women as artists and audience are absent in Adorno's discussions of high culture, but are present as both actresses and gullible television viewers in his discussions of Hollywood. In his approach of gender and his attitude toward women, Adorno thus perpetuates rather than undermines Nietzsche's and modernity's positioning of women and the "persistent gendering as feminine of that which is devalued."[185]

The frustrated attempts at women's emancipation are of course in line with the *Dialectic*'s argument on the regressive and self-destructive process of enlightenment. Although Adorno puts forth the notion of progress in high art, he continuously negates it in the social realm. Confronted with fascism, Stalinism, and the excesses of late capitalism, Adorno seems to deliberately blind himself against some of the potential sources of resistance against the destructive process of civilization. Although Adorno resists ascribing to women an essential nature, his portrayal of female character fixes femininity no less than arguments for women's essential female nature. As the scars of societal deformation, women are the images and mirrors of male domination and are subject to double jeopardy: as victims of male domination within the dialectic of enlightenment, they buy into the myth of male power, support patriarchy, and self-destructively defame their own sex. In the end, Adorno's reproach of Nietzsche for taking over a secondhand and unverified image of femininity does not lead to the formulation of a constructive alternative point of view, and it could be argued that Nietzsche's view of women as mean-spirited saboteurs of male culture accords more power and possibilities of subversion to women than Adorno's perception of women as victims of and collaborators with the male-dominated degenerative process of enlightenment. However, Adorno provides insights into mechanisms of male domination within the dialectic of enlightenment, mechanisms toward which Nietzsche was—by and large—either gender biased or gender blind.

4

Wagner's Aesthetics as the Origin of Totalitarianism or the Advantages and Disadvantages of Decadence for Wagner

———

Biologically, modern man represents a *contradiction of values*; he sits between two chairs, he says Yes and No in the same breath.
                    —Nietzsche in *The Case of Wagner*

Both [art and the products of the culture industry] are torn halves of an integral freedom, to which however they do not add up.
                    —Adorno to Walter Benjamin

While in exile in London and New York between 1937 and 1938, Theodor Adorno wrote his book of essays *In Search of Wagner*, whose subject he described as "the classic of the Third Reich."[1] In the announcement to this volume, Adorno explains that this work is part of the interdisciplinary effort of the Institute of Social Research to resist National Socialism, by converting indignation and shock toward the rise of Nazism into an understanding of its origins. Considering the magnitude of the collective repression of the past, Adorno finds that this task had not lost its urgency by the time the Wagner book was published in its present form in 1952.

> The aim was to shake off the notion of a mere historical accident and to uncover the origin of fascist totalitarianism within the social processes that supported it. The

117

source of Hitler's ideology was to be researched without regard for its relation with appropriated cultural values. The work of Richard Wagner forced itself to the forefront of this task.[2]

Adorno conceives Wagner's aesthetics as rooted in the original landscape of fascism, and the concept of the *Gesamtkunstwerk* as a foreshadowing of Hitler's authoritarian organization of the state. Wagner's operas are calculated works of art primarily concerned with the production of effects. The music is subordinated to the technical requirements of the stage production and serves only to dramatize bombastic gestures. On a political level, this subordination and utilization of these artistic elements points toward the aestheticization of politics and the instrumentalization of art as propaganda; on a cultural level it anticipates the commodification of art and the reification of music.

Although writing from different historical, social, and political perspectives, Adorno's and Nietzsche's interpretations of Wagner share a profound critique of modernity and modern art. Adorno shares Nietzsche's view that Wagner's work represents the ambiguity of the modern condition, and their critiques exhibit a measure of supplementarity. Both are using Wagner as a foil to come to terms with their own tendencies and positions: in acknowledging his own tendency toward decadence, Nietzsche defines himself in opposition to the decadence he sees in Wagner, while the musician Adorno, aside from exploring the origins of fascist ideology, appears to wrestle with the composer Wagner in order to develop and later revise his understanding of modern music. In some ways, their writings on Wagner act as diagnostic surrogates for a critique of modernity. More specifically in Adorno's case, this critical engagement concerns itself with the postulated separation of culture into autonomous art and the culture industry, the connection between aesthetic modernism and the commodification of art, and opens up questions about the interdependent emergence and genealogy of both high art and the culture industry. Both Nietzsche and Adorno approach Wagner as representative of modern artistic developments and as a phenomenon that needs to be analyzed and exposed, because by laying bare the ideological foundations of Wagner's music dramas they hope to gain insights into the defining moments of modernity. While Adorno wants to investigate the "social-anthropological type" embodied in Wagner's work,[3] Nietzsche's first methodological move is to deprive Wagner of his individuality, to turn him into a representative and paradigmatic character, to transform him into *The Case of Wagner*, on which he conducts a case study illustrating the pathology of modern decadence.[4] Nietzsche and Adorno undertake a two-pronged attack by focusing simultaneously on art and ideology and by establishing an inseparable link between the two. Through their critiques they demonstrate not only the entwinement of art and ideology in Wagner, but also the necessity for forms of criticism that recognize the aestheticization of ideology and the ideology of the aesthetic. Nietzsche criticizes in Wagner the European-decadent artist on the one hand, and the *reichs-*

deutsche anti-Semite, who bowed before the Christian cross, on the other. Similarly, Adorno's project attempts to shed light upon the original landscape of fascism by delivering a detailed analysis of Wagner's music.

Nietzsche's critique of Wagner, whom it virulently attacks in its attempt to come to terms with decadence, also functions as a critique of modernity. This double aspect also applies—with qualifications—to Adorno, whose critique of Wagner is inextricably bound to his critique of modernity, but for whom the concept of decadence presents no critical category through which Wagner could be criticized. In fact, Adorno's and Nietzsche's critiques differ significantly from each other on this question of decadence. In evaluating the repressive moments of Wagner's work, Adorno positions Wagner not in the context of decadence, but rather in the context of his distinction between autonomous art and the culture industry. It will be argued here that Adorno's differentiation of these two spheres of artistic production is not as rigid as it might seem in parts of his *oeuvre*, and that his analysis of Wagner is the site at which this opposition actually becomes untenable.

Before moving on to Wagner, it is necessary to outline briefly the following two frameworks: Nietzsche's approach to decadence and Adorno's division between modern, "high" art, and the culture industry. In this reading, Adorno's encounter with Nietzsche bridges the gap between nineteenth- and twentieth-century thought, and not only adds new dimensions to the critique of Wagner, but also prefigures a formulation of critical theory. However, this reading neither suggests that Adorno provides the answers to the impasses in Nietzsche's thought, nor defends or condemns Adorno for his apparently dogmatic judgments. Andreas Huyssen, who also asserts that Adorno undermines his own scheme of separating culture into two spheres, sees Adorno's theoretical limitations caused by historical as well as theoretical blindnesses, which were shaped not only by the experience of fascism, exile, and Hollywood, "but also quite significantly by cultural phenomena of the late nineteenth century, phenomena in which modernism and culture industry seem to converge in curious ways rather than being diametrically opposed to each other."[5] By reversing Adorno's strategy of identifying elements of the culture industry in l'art pour l'art, Jugendstil, and Wagner, Huyssen sees a way to explore "how modernism itself appropriates and transforms elements of popular culture."[6] The following traces Nietzsche's and Adorno's important confrontations with Wagner, including the changes in their reception of Wagner, in order to reflect upon the possibilities their arguments hold for a critique of contemporary culture that subscribes neither to rigid antimodern or anti-postmodern positions nor to wholesale condemnations of contemporary—that is, commodified—culture.

NIETZSCHE'S CRITIQUE OF MODERNITY
AND WAGNERIAN DECADENCE

Nietzsche's break with Wagner has received much critical attention and represents an interesting chapter in the history of ideas. Numerous attempts have been made to interpret Nietzsche's complex and changing relationship to Wagner, including many that examine the relationship in light of the biographical material, such as Nietzsche's and Wagner's correspondence and Cosima Wagner's diaries. In opposition to some biographers of Nietzsche and Wagner, Mazzino Montinari insists upon the philosophical basis of the conflict between Nietzsche and Wagner and takes issue with the biographical interpretations of the "deadly insult" that Wagner, according to Nietzsche's letter to Franz Overbeck, had inflicted upon him.[7] In a letter to Malwida von Meysenbug, written one week after Wagner's death in February 1883, Nietzsche describes his ambiguous reaction to Wagner's death and elaborates on the nature of the "deadly insult":

> Wagner's death has upset me terribly. . . . It was hard to have to be someone's enemy for six years, someone whom one has admired and loved as deeply as I have loved Wagner. . . . Wagner has insulted me in a deadly manner—I want to tell you this—I have perceived his return, his crawling back slowly to Christianity and to the church as a personal affront to me: my whole youth and its direction appeared stained, in as far as I had honored an intellect capable of such a step. . . . What could have happened between us, had he lived longer! I have horrible arrows on my bow, and Wagner was one of those types who could be killed with words.[8]

According to Montinari, this letter proves that the "deadly insult" has nothing to do with Wagner's speculations about Nietzsche's supposedly abnormal sexual behavior, as Martin Gregor-Dellin and Curt Paul Janz claim in their respective biographies of Wagner and Nietzsche.[9] In 1877, Wagner had written to Otto Eiser, one of Nietzsche's physicians, expressing the suspicion that Nietzsche's shortsightedness and headaches were caused by excessive masturbation. Trying to convince the friendly physician Eiser of his diagnosis, Wagner calls himself a "physicianly friend" and advises Eiser to speak to Nietzsche "in all seriousness, without concealing from him the primary cause of his illness."[10] Disregarding all rules of professional discretion, Eiser explained in his answer that Nietzsche was infected with the virus causing gonorrhea and had been advised to practice coitus for therapeutic reasons. Nietzsche heard about Wagner's speculations and Eiser's indiscretion and remarks in a letter to Peter Gast that Wagner is full of wicked ideas in claiming that the changes in Nietzsche's philosophy were caused by unnatural excesses and homoerotic pedophilia.[11] Dismissing this letter, Montinari insists that critics should lay to rest the rumors that the personal rift between Wagner and Nietzsche was caused by anything but their philosophical and intellectual differences, and he pleads with researchers to accept the fact that Nietzsche's break from Wagner was a logical consequence of these differences. Peter Wapnewski takes up Montinari's claim that Nietzsche had to break with Wagner in order to reclaim and develop his own ideas and argues that in order to liberate himself, Nietzsche had to sacrifice Wagner, and with Wagner, a substantial part of himself.[12] In the words of these critics—Walter Kaufmann takes a similar point of view—Nietzsche's break with Wagner resembles an episode of a *Bildungsro-*

man in which the hero must leave behind the comforts of familiarity and authority in order to fulfill a higher calling. Common to these critics is, along with the claim that there is no substantial break or change, the emphasis upon the continuities in Nietzsche's work.

In his examination of the stages of Nietzsche's Wagner reception, Thomas Baumeister maintains that there is a continuity in Nietzsche's critique of Wagner.[13] He argues that *The Birth of Tragedy*, despite its enthusiasm for Wagner, outlines already the direction taken by Nietzsche's later criticism. By interpreting tragedy as an expression of a pessimism of strength originating from an overabundance of life forces, Nietzsche delineates the motifs that dominate his later works, including his critiques of decadence and Wagner. Nietzsche judges attitudes toward morality, life, and views of the world according to his own valuative standard, which asks whether they, in his estimation, affirm life or negate it and can stand firm against life's absurdities. He distinguishes between those values and attitudes capable of turning suffering into a stimulant for a richer and more powerful life and those that cannot.

Nietzsche himself reflected upon the continuity of his views on art, and by extension on Wagner, in his "Attempt of Self-Criticism" of 1886, in which he distances himself from some aspects of *The Birth of Tragedy* and reiterates others. While admitting to what he calls the "storm and stress" failings of his youthful enthusiasm, he claims that *The Birth of Tragedy* contains the seeds that bear fruit in his later works. Emphasizing the importance of his discovery of the Dionysian force in art, Nietzsche restates his admiration for Greek culture and its life-affirming pessimism that does not signal degeneration, decay, and a weakening of the instincts, but rather a pessimism coming from strength. More importantly, Nietzsche reconceptualizes the Dionysian by freeing it from its metaphysical implications. He retracts his early proclamation of a metaphysics of art, a so-called *Artistenmetaphysik*, which he now sees as the naive expression of his youthful temper. Written as if it were a dialogue with Richard Wagner, Nietzsche now finds *The Birth of Tragedy* an impossible book and considers offensive his claim that the world is justifiable only as an aesthetic phenomenon. However, his errors reveal already a spirit that will one day fight at any risk against all interpretations assigning a moral ground and moral significance to existence.[14] Despite its metaphysical afflictions, one discovers that in *The Birth of Tragedy*

> perhaps for the first time, a pessimism "beyond good and evil" is suggested . . . a philosophy that dares to move, to demote morality into the realm of appearance—and not merely among "appearances" or phenomena (in the sense assigned to these words by Idealistic philosophers), but among "deceptions," as semblance, delusion, error, interpretation, contrivance, art.[15]

In hindsight, Nietzsche perceives his idea of a purely aesthetic interpretation and justification of the world as an opposition to Christian morality, which negates, judges, and damns art by relegating it to the realm of lies. Behind Christian modes of thought lurks a hostility towards life itself, and instead of falling into the traps of Christianity by offering "metaphysical solace" through art and ascribing to it functions, such as protection, healing, and redemption, the anti-Wagnerian Nietzsche now wants to teach laughter and the art of worldly consolation.

> It was against morality that my instinct turned with this questionable book, long ago; it was an instinct that aligned itself with life and that discovered for itself a fundamentally opposite doctrine and valuation of life—purely artistic and *anti-Christian*. . . . As a philologist and man of words I baptized it, not without taking some liberty . . . I called it Dionysian."[16]

The Birth of Tragedy's project of affirming life through art is thus tied to the project of exposing morality and moral judgments as interpretations based upon fiction, deception, and error. As is the case with art, morality is an illusional construct; however, while art is a life-affirming construct, morality is a construct hostile to life. Although he collapses the distinction between appearance and substance by postulating that moral values are nothing more than imposed interpretations and the inevitable creation of illusion, dissimulation, and falsification, Nietzsche nevertheless insists on readily facing and enduring life's harsh realities rather than fleeing from them, a retreat justified by declaring appearances illusory and therefore unworthy of reflection.

It could be argued that *The Birth of Tragedy* itself undermines its own metaphysical presuppositions, and by extension the positive functions ascribed to Wagner's art. In the last few sections, Nietzsche emphasizes the aspects of play, affirmation, and the "playful construction and destruction" that come from the discharge of original passion.[17] Here the world of appearances is no longer understood as a medium through which redemption is possible, but rather as the manifestation of a vitality that simultaneously creates and destroys. In combination with the symbol of the music-practicing Socrates, which shall be discussed later, these contentions clearly foreshadow Nietzsche's later positions on Wagner and decadent art, which he then sees as nihilistic expressions of the modern spirit that neither withstand nor enhance life, but generate the need for redemption.

Following Montinari, Baumeister points out some of the difficulties with Nietzsche's work in praise of Wagner, *Richard Wagner in Bayreuth*, and maintains that it contains *in nuce* Nietzsche's later critique of Wagner. In this work, Nietzsche begins to develop his aesthetic and ethical reservations toward various Wagnerian faults, among them egocentrism, extravagance, excessive sensuality, the will to power, acting and dilettantism. However, in *Richard Wagner in Bayreuth*, Nietzsche claims that Wagner was either in the process of sublimating or overcoming these problematic tendencies. The publication of the posthumous fragments from the year 1874 by Colli and Montinari, which contain the notes and reflections to *Richard Wagner in Bayreuth*, further indicates Nietzsche's difficulty with writing an uncritical tribute to Wagner and show Nietzsche's distance from Wagner by making visible the suppressed subtext of the laudation. He speaks of Wagner's anti-Semitism and tyrannical mentality: striving for legitimacy, Wagner's tyrannical attitudes are based on the feeling of "false omnipotence,"[18] while "the danger for Wagner is great, if he does not accept . . . the Jews."[19] Other themes of his later critiques that are strongly indicated in the notes, but suppressed or excused in the laudation, include the excessive search for effects, and the tendency to flee from the world and to negate life. As the artistic expression of Schopenhauer's philosophy, Wagner's music exhibits the dull drifting without purpose, the ecstacy, the despair, the sound of suffering and desire, but "seldom a cheerful ray of sunshine."[20] Nietzsche already characterizes Wagner as an actor and a rhetorician without the power of conviction. Convinced of it in his later years, Nietzsche wonders about Wagner's dilettantism and questions his musical abilities: "Absurdly, I have often doubted if Wagner has any musical talent at all."[21] Thus, beneath the admiring surface of *Richard Wagner in Bayreuth* hide his reservations, reservations that will eventually shatter Nietzsche's confidence in Wagner and lead to one of the most interesting intellectual duels of modernity.

According to Montinari, Nietzsche is incapable of fulfilling his own premise of an unqualified veneration and borrows heavily from Wagner's own writings; he characterizes Wagner through Wagner, thereby producing a collage composed of citations from Wagner's works: "Wagner is being portrayed and explained by Wagner."[22] Driven by the will to a renewal of art and culture, *Richard Wagner in Bayreuth* casts an idealized and utopian picture of Wagner and his potential future. In him Nietzsche sees the possibility for the renewal of art and music, which in turn could effect the renewal of culture and civilization as such. The direction Nietzsche charts is a challenge to Wagner, a challenge that he cannot meet. Nietzsche implicitly sets himself up for his later disappointment, which translates not only into a sharp and relentless criticism of Wagner, but also into a reevaluation of the function of art. Nietzsche leaves behind the metaphysics of art found in *The Birth of Tragedy* and enters, with *Human, All Too Human*, which was written in the first period of disenchantment with Wagner, into a phase of deep skepticism toward art and the artist. This break with Wagner parallels the beginning of this period of distrust toward art and the privileging of science. *Human, All Too Human* must be read, to a certain extent, as a reaction to Wagner and as a compensatory backlash against his earlier admiration for him. Due to his developing skepticism toward art, Nietzsche confronts his overestimation of the potential for cultural renewal through Wagner's music; this change becomes especially evident in a *Nachlass* fragment from 1878:

> I wish that fair-minded people will consider this book as a kind of atonement for the
> dangerous aesthetics which I have supported earlier and whose aim was to turn all

aesthetical phenomena into "miracles"—I have done damage to Wagner's fans and perhaps to Wagner himself, who tolerates everything, however unfounded it may be, which promotes his art.[23]

Disavowing all metaphysical grounding, Nietzsche returns to a positive evaluation of art in his later years. However, art, the aesthetic view of the world, and the artistic perception of life appear in the later works as essentially promising possibilities, which can make existence more bearable, but, as with all other attempts at interpretation, cannot by itself explain, justify, or legitimize existence. In a posthumous fragment from 1886, written ten years after *Richard Wagner in Bayreuth* and in the same year—and in a similar tone and with similar expressions—as his self-critique of *The Birth of Tragedy*, Nietzsche characterizes the aesthetic view of the world as a antimetaphysical, but also an artistic, pessimist-buddhist, skeptical, scientific, and yet not positivistic one.[24] The artistic view of the world, he maintains, is as flawed and incomplete as all competing scientific, religious, and morally interpretive approaches that sublimate different instincts and drives to domination. By his account, the artistic view of the world must seek insights into the psychology of the artist and into the nature of his sublimation; it must include a critique of the artistic drive to play, the desire for change, and the absolute egocentrism of the artist.[25] Again, Nietzsche's words seem to be coined by his disappointment with Wagner, for now he insists on investigating the link between the work of art and its producer. By discussing the shortcomings of the artistic view of life in relation to the flaws of the scientific, religious, and moral views, Nietzsche makes it clear that his hope for renewal no longer rests on the realm of the aesthetic alone. His disappointment with Wagner, or rather, the rapid deterioration of his idealized and utopian vision of him, provoked a swift reinterpretation of the function of art. In departing from Wagner and metaphysics, Nietzsche explored the critical potential of his own work by taking issue against himself.[26]

> As I proceeded alone I trembled; not long after, I was sick, more than sick, namely, *weary*—weary from the inevitable disappointment about everything that is left for us modern men for enthusiasm, about the universally *wasted* energy, work, hope, youth, love—weary from nausea at the whole idealistic lie.[27]

However great his disappointment and loss of enthusiasm, the break with Wagner in 1878 was never complete, just as there was no complete change of in Nietzsche's thought. Nietzsche's analysis of Wagner, Dieter Borchmeyer points out, remains unsurpassed and presents an enduring challenge.[28] In *Ecce Homo*, Nietzsche describes the time of the break-up as a time of crisis, for which *Human, All Too Human* is his monument. Wagner was no longer Wagner, but had turned into a Wagnerian himself: "The Wagnerian had become master over Wagner."[29] As one of Nietzsche's "particular blunders," Wagner was only a sign for a larger confusion of his instincts, and in the process of rethinking his philosophical positions, it was time "to recall and reflect on myself."[30] Nietzsche repeatedly claimed that no one was as closely related to him as Wagner. In a letter to Overbeck in 1886, Nietzsche reiterates that Wagner might have understood him better than anybody else, and that Wagner was the only one so far, or at least the first one, who had a feeling for what Nietzsche is all about.[31]

Nietzsche had always admitted to his ambivalent love-hate relationship with Wagner and his music, and despite his condemnations, he confessed to his affinity not only to Wagner, but also to decadence: "Well then! I am, no less than Wagner, a child of this time; that is, a decadent: but I comprehended this, I resisted it. The philosopher in me resisted it."[32] Nietzsche's attempts to come to terms with decadence and the so-called modern illnesses, nihilism and pessimism, have indeed left a decisive mark in his later work, and his attacks on Christianity, metaphysics, and rationality are all inextricably bound to his critique of decadence. Aside from his emphasis on a healthy lifestyle, Nietzsche's ruminations on climatic and bodily influences upon the quality of intellectual activities—such as the air one breathes and the role of digestion—represent one aspect of his attempt to overcome these modern illnesses. His struggle with Wagner represents another. However, the two are, of course, interconnected, for being modern and decadent is an expression of a physiological contradiction,[33] and Nietzsche promises to write a chapter "Toward a Physiology of Art" in which he would explore the decay of art and the artist in terms of physiological degeneration. Wagner's music, Nietzsche claims, has negative physical effects on the listener: it inhibits circulation, obstructs the stomach with phlegm, and overexcites the nerves.[34] The spirit of decadence, which Nietzsche cites as the prevalent mark of modernity, is a sign of physical as well as spiritual degeneration. Rooted in the devaluation of the body, the instincts, and the rationalization of everyday life, the spirit of decadence has brought about the modern disenchantment with life and a renewed need for art. After abandoning the *Artistenmetaphysik* of *The Birth of Tragedy* and the more scientifically oriented phase, during which he was suspicious and distrustful of art, the later Nietzsche reemphasizes the notion that art should be a life-affirming force and a stimulant that must resist decadent tendencies and protest the ideologies of the status quo.

Nietzsche's critique of Wagner represents at the same time one of the most powerful critiques of modernity. Wagner personifies for Nietzsche the modern artist *par excellence*, the Cagliostro of modernity, and the decadent hysteric who like no other exemplifies the *Zeitgeist*.

> Through Wagner modernity speaks most intimately, concealing neither its good nor its evil—having forgotten all sense of shame. And conversely: one has almost completed an account of the value of what is modern once one has gained clarity about what is good and evil in Wagner. . . . Wagner sums up modernity.[35]

Wagner's work contains the major forces of modernity, namely the process of increasing rationalization, which becomes visible in his compositions and stage productions, and the tendency toward decadence. Nietzsche saw modernity as the result of a continuous process that had begun with the decline of Greek culture, and his notion of modern decadence reaches from the theoretician and dialectician Socrates to the musician-actor Wagner. Socrates and Wagner are part of the same phenomenon, that of descending life, and their contributions to Western civilizations were timely expressions of decaying cultures. Socrates embodies the myths of scientific rationality based upon notions of enlightenment, such as progress and the *promesse de bonheur* of a rational society, while Wagner incarnates the nihilistic view of a world that can only hope for redemption. Similar to Adorno, who interprets Odysseus's adventures as the exploits of a rationality that exemplifies modernity's progress in terms of a dialectic of enlightenment, Nietzsche does not view modernity as a consistent entity with a definite beginning and end; Socratism, understood here as representing the emphasis upon rationality and its zeal to correct being, is a process of world-historical dimensions extending beyond the constraints of a historical epoch. "Boring" Plato, who combined all forms of style in his dialogues with his "frightfully self-satisfied" and "childish kind of dialectics," was the first decadent of style,[36] yet the beginnings of decadence lie in the Socratic cult of rationality. For Nietzsche, as Ernst Behler points out, Socrates and Socratism were fundamental phenomena of human life and historical development: "It was the conviction that the realm of ideas could reach into the deepest abyss of being and that it could not only explain being, but also correct it. With this Nietzsche describes the most significant characteristics of modernity."[37]

As already discussed in the previous chapters, Nietzsche viewed Socrates' belief in the explicability of nature, the universal healing power of knowledge, and his theoretical view of the world as bringing about the demise of tragedy and the tragic view of ancient Greek culture. However, as we have seen in his critique of Wagner, his critique of the decadent Socrates is not an unequivocal condemnation. Walter Kaufmann, for example, argues that Nietzsche admired him and felt genuine kinship.[38] Nietzsche's appraisal of Socrates, according to Kaufmann, is not as harsh and negative as some critics have claimed: "As a dialectical thinker, Nietzsche affirms as necessary and admires even what must be overcome. His admiration does not arrest his thinking, and his critique does not detract from his admiration."[39] As with the Wagner of *Richard Wagner in Bayreuth*, Nietzsche admires what must be overcome, whether his critique of Wagner detracts from his admiration and whether it did, at times, arrest his thinking is open to debate. Citing Nietzsche's critique of Socrates as proof, Kaufmann argues for a continuity in Nietzsche's thought in general and opposes the division of Nietzsche's work into three different phases, of which the second one, with its privileging of science and enlightenment, is said to represent a temporary departure from true Nietzscheanism. Kaufmann contends that Nietzsche's repudiation of nationalism and racism and his appreciation of the Enlightenment and Socrates are persistent features of his thought, and categorizing Nietzsche's work by periods is a simple and expedient way for scholars "to explain away" Nietzsche's break with Wagner.[40]

In line with Kaufmann's argument for a continuity in Nietzsche's work is the relative continuity of his critique of Wagner, as discussed in connection with the themes and motifs of *The Birth of Tragedy* and the posthumous fragments, including the notes to *Richard Wagner in Bayreuth*. However, Kaufmann's claim to continuity must not deter scholars from recognizing the differences in emphasis and argumentation in the course of Nietzsche's work. His criticism of Socrates is continuous and certainly more prevalent and apparent than the remarks which seem to rehabilitate him. In *Twilight of the Idols* Socrates appears as an ugly foreigner, a would-be criminal, and a symptom of decay; responsible for Greek culture's decline in *The Birth of Tragedy*, Socrates becomes, however, also a figure of hope: the Socrates who practices music, *der musiktreibende Socrates*, ideally combines theoretical thought and art, and thus symbolizes not only the death of tragedy, but also the possibility of its rebirth. The harmonious coexistence between science and art, however, can only come about after science and theoretical explications have reached their limits and "the claim to universal validity [is] destroyed by the evidence of these limits."[41] Having reached its limits, scientific thought reverts to myth, because by itself it can neither justify its existence nor prove its conclusions. This is also the point at which rationality, thrown back upon itself, is in danger of becoming decadent.

Socrates, like other decadents, devalues the instincts by advocating reason at all costs, thus offering a cure that only accelerates the decline of civilization. Because of his weakened instincts, it is impossible for him to halt this decline and overcome decadence.

> It is self-deception on the part of philosophers and moralists to imagine that by making war on *décadence* that they therewith elude *décadence* themselves. This is beyond their powers: what they select as an expedient, as a deliverance, is itself only another expression of *décadence*—they *alter* its expression, they do not abolish the thing itself.[42]

In a similar fashion, Wagner offers a cure that also only hastens the decline. More than any other artist, Wagner can exploit the need for a "cure" for art while spreading the modern diseases, and he is unique in his ability to alter and to play with the expressions of decadence. In order to resist decadence, Nietzsche had to resist the modern "cures" that only worsen the sickness by fighting off self-destructive, modern ideas: "For such a task I required a special self-discipline: to take sides against everything sick in me, including Wagner, including Schopenhauer, including all of modern 'humaneness'."[43] However, Wagner and his decadent afflictions are indispensable for the philosopher, for where else, Nietzsche asks, could one find such an eloquent guide to the modern soul?

The ambiguity of Nietzsche's evaluation of decadence is partly mirrored by the ambiguity of the concept itself. Nietzsche never used it as a completely

derogatory and negative term, and the indecisiveness delineates not only Nietzsche's multiperspectivism, but is "significant in its very necessity."[44] Decadence,
a *metahistorical*, rather than an ahistorical term, transgresses the boundaries of
historical periodizations and is tied to the history of Western civilization. As a
paradigm for Nietzsche's critique of Wagner, it profoundly affects his thought by
shedding new light upon the ideological functions of art and the role and function of the artist as a bearer of ideology. Decadence in Nietzsche cannot be understood as a purely aesthetic category, but must be viewed in the context of his
heterogenous critiques of all aspects of life, including his critiques of rationality,
morality, metaphysics, philosophy, Christianity, and history.

In his critique of art, Nietzsche always treats the ideological implications of
decadence as a view of life for which artistic expressions are merely a symptom.
Through his association of modernity and decadence, Nietzsche is in accordance
with the leading theorists of decadence, who used the term for attacking or
defending either classical or modern aesthetics. However, when it describes an
ideological phenomenon tied to the genealogy of morality and Christianity, span-
ning such diverse figures as Socrates and Richard Wagner, decadence takes on
dimensions pointing not only beyond the aesthetic parameters set by literary theorists, but also toward Nietzsche's idiosyncratic utilization of the term. To take
Nietzsche's position fully into consideration within the discussion of European
decadence and to ascertain the influence of theories of decadence upon Nietzsche
is, therefore, an insufficient means of grasping the significance, complexity, and
depth it acquires in Nietzsche's work.

However, the frequent and heterogeneous employment of the term "decadence" suggests that it was indeed Nietzsche's good fortune when he discovered
Paul Bourget's "Théorie de la décadence" in the *Essais de psychologie contemporaine*, which he read in the winter of 1883/84. The similarities between Bourget's text and *The Case of Wagner* have been noted by several scholars, and
some, unwilling to call such congruencies "borrowing" as Kaufmann does, have
accused Nietzsche of plagiarism.[45] Be it as it may, it can be argued that Nietzsche's discovery of Bourget, who, despite his conservatism was an admirer of
decadent art, expedited the reconceptualization of art toward Nietzsche's later
antimetaphysical physiology of art.

Dieter Borchmeyer claims that the specificity of Nietzsche's stance on decadence lies firstly in his combination of its modern and positive evaluation on the
one hand with the traditional, negative evaluation of decadence on the other, and
secondly in the replacement of the Apollinian-Dionysian polarity with the
Dionysian-decadent.[46] Although Borchmeyer underscores the ambiguity and
idiosyncratic use of the concept of decadence, his contention that Nietzsche
replaced the Apollinian-Dionysian dichotomy with the Dionysian-decadent
should not remain unquestioned. The nature of the relationship between the
Apollinian and the Dionysian is incompatible with that of the Dionysian and the
decadent and the latter can, therefore, not function as a replacement for the for-

mer. In a constant struggle with each other, the Apollinian and the Dionysian are nevertheless harmonizing drives functioning interdependently within the metaphysics of art. The relationship between the Dionysian and decadent is not a dynamic interchange striving for reconciliation, for decadence is an affliction, a symptom of a larger illness rather than one part of a reconcilable duality. The antagonism between the Apollinian and the Dionysian is not destructive, since "these two tendencies run parallel to each other . . . and they continually incite each other to new and more powerful births."[47] The real opposing force of the Dionysian is, as Nietzsche postulates toward the end of *The Birth of Tragedy*, "the murderous principle" of "aesthetic Socratism" whose supreme law is summed up in the following dictum: "To be beautiful everything must be intelligible."[48] Aesthetic Socratism, however, lies outside the sphere of the "two art-impulses," the Apollinian-Dionysian, and destroys the effect of both.[49] Instead of the Apollinian art of contemplation, aesthetic Socratism produces "cool, paradoxical thoughts," and instead of Dionysian ecstasies, it arouses "fiery affects."[50] Since Socrates' cult of rationality denotes, as we have seen, the beginning of decadence, the relationship of the Dionysian and the decadent bears obvious similarities to that of the Dionysian and aesthetic Socratism. Instead of a replacement of the Apollinian-Dionysian view of art with the Dionysian-decadent, there seems to be a shift in the conceptualization and description of the antagonistic forces from Socratism to the more encompassing term decadence. Socratism becomes subsumed under the heteronomous concept of decadence, of which it denotes merely a possible tendency.

Both aesthetic Socratism and decadence function as polarizing terms. In addition to his knowledge of Bourget, Nietzsche began using the term *decadence* after becoming familiar with the theories expounded by other writers such as Charles Baudelaire and Théophile Gautier. In the polemic introduction to his Edgar Allen Poe translation, Baudelaire redefines decadence by transforming the derogatory term used against modern art by conservative defenders of classical aesthetics into a designation for the modern condition in general and the modern condition of art in particular. In traditional usage, decadence has as its paradigm the decline of Roman civilization and generally denotes the decay of culture. In Baudelaire's usage it refers to a variety of themes and motifs. Baudelaire praises the exuberance and the colorful play of decadent art and reevaluates the motifs of decline and decay, exemplified and metaphorized by a setting sun. As signs of a descending culture, these images are valued as highly as the classical motifs.[51] The aesthetization of decay and horror and the creation of an artificial paradise lead Baudelaire to praise Poe as a modern, antimimetic writer and to recognize Wagner as a fellow decadent, the most sincere representative of the modern disposition.[52] Baudelaire applauds the orgiastic portrayal of myth in *Tannhäuser*, calling it a titanic flight with a nervous intensity, the intensity of passion and willpower.[53]

Nietzsche also saw Wagner in the context of European and especially French *décadence*. He had already established a connection between Baudelaire and

Wagner even before he discovered Baudelaire's essay on Wagner's *Tannhäuser* and became aware of the fact that Wagner and Baudelaire had corresponded. In a posthumous fragment of 1885, he named Baudelaire a sort of Richard Wagner without music.[54] While noting the difference between French and German decadence, Nietzsche sees similarities in the "development of the European soul" and in Baudelaire's poetry and Wagner's music: to both expression is paramount, and in the name of expression both sacrifice everything else; both dependent on literature; and both are highly educated human beings who are nervous, diseased, and tormented.[55] Nietzsche names Baudelaire a "typical decadent," and the first "intelligent" supporter of Wagner.[56] He speaks of France as the center of artistic innovation: "As an *artist* one has no home in Europe, except Paris: the *délicatesse* in all five artistic senses that is presupposed by Wagner's art, the fingers for *nuances*, the psychological morbidity are found only in Paris."[57] Nietzsche appreciates the "French" Wagner and despises the German one; "what did I never forgive Wagner?" Nietzsche asks, "that he condescended to the Germans—that he become *reichsdeutsch*."[58] The Germans, according to Nietzsche, have no sense for nuances and style and lack an understanding of the enormous ambition of the French artists.

In line with Bourget, Nietzsche uses organic functions as models to remark metaphorically upon the disorder and lack of coherence and unity in decadent works of art, which produced the shortcomings of the artistic style of decadence. The part is no longer subordinated to the whole, and as a result the now independent cell no longer subordinates its energy in order to ensure the functioning of a whole organism. Bourget views the emancipation of the individual elements as a process of disintegration and decay. During the different stages of decomposition from a unity to ever-smaller parts, individual elements gain their independence at the expense of a dissolution of context. The emancipation of the individual element results in the disintegration of the whole, and the newly established anarchy constitutes the decadence of the ensemble.

> A decadent style is a style where the unity of the book decomposes in order to give way to the independence of the page, where the page decomposes to give way to the independence of the phrase, and the phrase to give way to the independence of the word.[59]

In a strikingly similar manner, which has provoked the plagiarism charges, Nietzsche describes how such a lack of coherence and the emancipation of the individual elements come about at the expense of the whole. Due to his association of aesthetic with political and moral values, he adds a decidedly political component to this model by drawing parallels between the literary style of decadence and the notion of equality. Democratization and the enlightenment ideal of equality thus become yet another aspect of decadence. The anarchy of atoms is the result of a disintegration of the will; however, unlike Bourget, Nietzsche speaks in terms of an expansion of the individual elements rather than a decomposition of the whole. In Bourget, the page becomes independent because of the disintegration of the whole; in Nietzsche, the independence of the page causes the disintegration of the whole, so that

> life no longer dwells in the whole. The word becomes sovereign and leaps out of the sentence, the sentence reaches out and obscures the meaning of the page, the page gains life at the expense of the whole—the whole is no longer a whole . . . the anarchy of atoms, disintegration of the will, "freedom for the individual," to use moral terms—expanded into a political theory, "*equal* rights for all." Life, *equal* vitality, the vibration and exuberance of life pushed back into the smallest forms; the rest, *poor* in life.[60]

The individual element leaps out and gains life while obscuring the meaning of the whole. Pushing the exuberance and overabundance of life into the ever-smaller elements, the whole is drained of its energy. It is therefore the expansion of the individual element and the inability of the whole to contain these elements that lead to the decomposition of the whole. Kaufmann claims that his reading of Bourget did not add a new aspect to Nietzsche's work. In a footnote Kaufmann mentions that Nietzsche had used the term decadence in connection with Cervantes' *Don Quixote* years before reading Bourget, whose theory of decadence merely strengthens a previously present motif. Referring to the similarities to Bourget, Kaufmann comments: "The generalization seems justified that Nietzsche's 'borrowing' is usually of this nature."[61] Instead of defending Nietzsche's "borrowing" practices in regard to Bourget, a close reading of the above two passages can sufficiently ascertain the similarities and the differences between the two interpretations of decadence and its disintegrative forces. Along with Bourget, Nietzsche affirms that the individual gains life at the expense of the whole; however, for Nietzsche, the "paralysis, arduousness, torpidity *or* hostility and chaos" caused by the destruction of the whole, which becomes a lifeless "composite, calculated, artificial, and artifact," results from the expansive dimensions of the part rather than the decaying features of the whole.[62] Nietzsche did not plagiarize or borrow from Bourget, but rather appropriated and reinterpreted Bourget's theory of decadence to serve his own purposes.

Borchmeyer argues that both Baudelaire's and Nietzsche's employment of the term *decadence* represents a continuation of the "Querelle des Anciens et des Modernes." However, while Baudelaire comes out on the side of the moderns, Nietzsche combines the traditional negative position on decadence with a positive reevaluation: "Since his [Nietzsche's] notion of the classical excludes the traditional academic domestication by including the Dionysian elements, he judges the phenomena of decadence fairly critically without falling behind the aesthetic positions which had been reached since Baudelaire."[63] Although Nietzsche virulently attacks decadence and the life-negating forces of modernity, his admiration for these fanatics of expression, who radicalized and idealized the realm of the aesthetic, is equally strong. Mingling and mixing the arts, they are great inventors who redefined the role and function of the artist; they seduce and entice, display the sublime and the gruesome and are the great discoverers of effects, displays, and decorations. These "last great seekers" belong, like Wagner, to the tradition of late French romanticism:

> Literature dominated all of them up to their eyes and ears—they were the first artists steeped in world literature—most of them were themselves writers, poets, mediators and mixers of the arts and senses (as a musician, Wagner belongs among painters; as a poet, among musicians; as an artist in general, among actors); all of them were fanatics of expression "at any price" . . . all of them great discoverers in the realm of the sublime, also of the ugly and gruesome, and still greater discoverers concerning effects, display, and the art of display windows—all of them talents far beyond their genius—virtuosos through and through, with uncanny access to everything that seduces, allures, compels, overthrows; born enemies of logic and straight lines, lusting after the foreign, the exotic, the tremendous, the crooked, the self-contradictory . . . on the whole, an audaciously daring, magnificently violent type of higher human beings who soared, and tore others along, to the heights—it fell to them to first teach their century—and it is the century of the *crowd!*—the concept of "higher man."[64]

Nietzsche's colorful and forceful characterization of decadence returns almost word for word in *Nietzsche contra Wagner*, where, however, the artist no longer teaches the masses the concept of "higher man," but the concept of the "artist."[65] In this work an additional qualification underscores the ambiguity of his praise of the geniuses by appending the words: "But sick . . .";[66] the ellipsis at the end further underlines the ambiguous quality of the decadent art and indicates that sickness is the prevalent feature of decadence and the decadent artist.

Decadence, then, is a term that places everything it signifies in the obscure twilight of undecidability. Decadent art is courageous, sublime, and glorious, yet it is sick. Decadent artists are likewise sublime and seductive geniuses, yet they too are sick. Similar to Nietzsche's philosophy, decadent art speaks against the ideals of progress, logic, and rationality, yet decadence goes too far; its excesses lead to nihilistic and pessimistic views and sensibilities, which are embodied in statements such as Cosima Wagner's: "I long for ruin and decline."[67] As Weineck has pointed out, by using the word meaning "apart from" (*abgerechnet*) in his self-description, Nietzsche implies that decadence is a surplus rather than a deficiency: "Apart from the fact that I am a decadent, I am also the opposite."[68] Decadence is not a lack, a too-little, but rather an excess, a too-much;[69] it is, as the comparison with Bourget indicates, the expansion and the excesses of the individual elements that yield a destructive power over the whole. As a symptom of dissolution and decay, decadence is a sickness caused by the overabundance of energy in the sovereign parts. Nietzsche promises to show in a chapter of his projected main work "On the Physiology of Art," which was never written or published in this form, that the deterioration, including the deterioration of the artist's character, has physiological causes and represents a form of hysteria.[70]

Despite identifying it with an effort to fight the moralizing tendency of art and the subordination of art to morality, Nietzsche is opposed to the concept of *l'art pour l'art*. In its eccentric revolt against prevailing moral standards, *l'art pour l'art* liberates art from any purpose, including the mission of the moral betterment of mankind; *"l'art pour l'art* means: 'the devil take morality'."[71] Although he agrees with the project of freeing art from morality, Nietzsche objects to the claim that art has no purpose. "Art is the great stimulus to life: how could it be thought purposeless, aimless, *l'art pour l'art?*"[72] Declarations of art's purposelessness rest upon preconceptions and misunderstandings of the nature of art. Through this notion of *art for art's sake*, the hostility toward morality falls victim to prejudice, since "rather no purpose at all than a moral purpose" is its slogan.[73] Nietzsche makes a similar claim in *The Birth of Tragedy*, the *Genealogy of Morals*, and elsewhere when he contends that the will always needs a goal, and rather than willing nothing, it wills nothingness.[74] Art inevitably praises, glorifies, selects, and privileges and thus points toward the desirability of life. For Nietzsche, art affirms life, and the convergence of *l'art pour l'art* and decadence can be found in their failure to affirm life, *l'art pour l'art* because it renounces all purpose, and decadence because its pessimism, arising from a position of weakness, negates life. Similar to the works of *l'art pour l'art*, Wagner's music dramas likewise fail to affirm life and thus testify to the morbid and nihilistic qualities of modern life.

> Wagner's art is sick. The problems he presents on the stage—all of them problems of hysterics—the convulsive nature of his affects, his overexcited sensibility, his taste that required even stronger spices, his instability which he dressed up as principles . . . all of this taken together represents a profile of sickness that permits no further doubt. *Wagner est une névrose.*[75]

Nietzsche's strategy of pathologizing and subsequently disqualifying certain works of art stands in a long line of denunciations that include Goethe's remark regarding the sickness of the Romantics, Georg Lukács's attack on the art of the turn of the century, Expressionism, and Kafka, and finally Jürgen Habermas's exclusionary crusade against postmodernism. According to Nietzsche, Wagner puts into music his neurosis, which contains the three stimulants of modern exhaustion: the "brutal," the "artificial," and the "innocent (idiotic)."[76] Music is no longer an expression of the free and independent spirit but of the talent for lying; subordinated to action, it becomes the slave of ruthless actions and insincere attitudes. Wagner's music is the opposite of what Nietzsche described as "great style," the height of artistic development that comes about through the victory of the beautiful over the monstrous.[77] The art of "great style" rejects admiration and forgets to be convincing; it wants to master its chaos and force it to become form. Its ambition is to become law.[78] However, Nietzsche indicates that the opposition of "great style" and Wagner might only be a reflection of the opposition to "great style" inherent in all modern music. Nietzsche poses the

question: Is modern music, "a sister of the baroque style," not already decadence?[79] Modern music is the counter-Renaissance of art, and decadence is its
social expression.[80]

Because there is much that is valuable, new, and admirable in decadent art,
Nietzsche speaks of decadence as "a word, that, as we understand it intuitively
amongst ourselves, is not meant to condemn, but merely to name."[81] However,
despite this assertion that he was naming rather than judging, Nietzsche did use
the term *decadence* as a standard of criticism, and a stringent one at that. By
maintaining a link between morality and aesthetics, decadence is an artistic quality, a characteristic of the artist, and an expression of philosophical and moral
positions and attitudes. No matter how innovative and valuable decadent art may
be, its aesthetic qualities remain rooted in Christian morality, nihilism, and pessimism. However, since decadent art gives rise to the new, it is but one way to
induce change. As a regressive moment, decadence is not pointless. In *The
Genealogy of Morals*, Nietzsche argues that the confrontation between the
decaying aristocratic morality of the masters and the expanding Christian morality of the slave brings about shifts in power relations and a renewal of culture. In
an aphorism from *Human, All Too Human*, Nietzsche asserts the importance of
the weak, deformed, and sick elements for the advancement of society. Being
more perceptive, sensitive, and wise, they guarantee the intellectual growth of
the community. By not conforming to the norm, they represent the wounds and
scars that "inoculate" the entire social organism with the new. Progress depends
upon a disturbance of unity and the injuries inflicted by the weak, but also upon
the strength of the whole to absorb the injuries without destroying itself.[82]
Whether modern society is able to absorb the shocks of decadence is open to
debate. Nietzsche's insistence on the affirmation of life seems to indicate that, in
his estimation, the potential for survival exists.

Nietzsche claims that he was able to withstand the attack and overcome
decadence, because he was strong enough to absorb the injuries inflicted upon
him while taking advantage of decadent delights and Wagner's music. He argues
that "The world is poor for anyone who has never been sick enough for this
'voluptuousness of hell'."[83]

> I think I know better than anyone else of what tremendous things Wagner is capa-
> ble—the fifty worlds of alien ecstasies for which no one besides him had wings; and
> given the way I am, strong enough to turn even what is most questionable and dan-
> gerous to my advantage and thus to become stronger, I call Wagner the great bene-
> factor of my life.[84]

On the one hand, life is impoverished for those who were never able to experience the rapture of the aesthetic experience; however, those who long for it
excessively are entwined in a process of self-destruction. The "voluptuousness of
hell" and the pleasurable ecstasy of modern art can be beneficially enjoyed by
those who are strong and healthy and for whom weakness and sickness are only

temporary states of mind. Once again, the motto is: "What does not kill me makes me stronger."[85] The sickness and weakness of the will inherent in modern art is not a regrettable, dispensable, or correctable characteristic of modernity, but rather its defining moment.

QUESTIONS OF CULTURE

Unlike Nietzsche, Adorno did not use the term *decadence* as a framework for a critique of Wagner. The morbid and nihilistic quality of decadent art constitutes, on Adorno's account, a resistance to the requirements of the healthy and strong. Decadence defies the image of the all-powerful blond beast, and thus creates a space for criticism by mocking the disparity between reality and its idealized representations. Adorno appreciates decadence for some of the same reasons that Nietzsche despises it. Nietzsche's praise of the creative energy of decadence ends with the regretful phrase "but sick . . . ," because decadence fails to affirm life. As discussed earlier, nowhere is the gap between Nietzsche's and Adorno's thought more apparent than in the former's call for the affirmation of life and the acceptance of *amor fati*. To accept one's fate, which is determined by the rules of an unjust society, and to affirm life under the present historical and social conditions is synonymous with succumbing to the forces of domination. In Adorno's critique of Wagner, it will become apparent that Wagner's decadence saves and redeems him from complete subsumption under political and aesthetic ideologies.

Fascist ideology and the opposition between autonomous art and the products of the culture industry, rather than decadence, come into play in Adorno's critique. However, his attempt to analyze the origins of totalitarianism through the medium of Wagner is a problematic enterprise, for it can neither explore completely the roots of fascism nor appreciate fully the complexity of Wagner's work. Written in exile under the immediate threat and experience of fascism and in recognition of the futile hopes for a successful opposition, *In Search of Wagner* is colored by the events then taking place in Nazi Germany and stands at the beginning of a lifelong preoccupation with analyzing and resisting totalitarianism in every possible respect. Beyond the political ideologies of anti-Semitism and National Socialism, Adorno engaged in the struggle against totality and totalitarianism in his entire *oeuvre*, which includes not only *Negative Dialectics* and the critiques of metaphysics and philosophy, such as the critiques of identity thinking, epistemology, and positivism, but also such diverse subjects as culture, art, the culture industry, literature, music, writing and style, superstition and astrology, and the study of the authoritarian personality.

Terry Eagleton argues that the horror of the experience of fascism lingers in Adorno's work "as a distorting as well as illuminating perspective."[86] As a victim of anti-Semitism, Adorno is afflicted by a survivor's "paralysing historical guilt" that gives rise to "tiresome bouts of *haut bourgeois* anti-technological nostalgia" and the projection of "trivializing" correspondences between the age of technology and fascist maltreatment.[87] An "overreaction to fascism" is the rather infelicitous phrase with which Eagleton characterizes Adorno's work.[88] Describing *Minima Moralia* as a "bizarre blend of probing insight and patrician grousing" and pointing toward the inverse proportion of "the breathtaking subtlety of Adorno's disquisitions on art" to "the two-dimensional crudity of some of his political perceptions," Eagleton posits two different Adornos, one "somewhat more defeatist than the other."[89] One Adorno retreats from the nightmare of history into the aesthetic and asks for a subsistence in the "near-intolerable strain of an absurdist, self-imploding thought," and the other is the theorist who hopes for a realm beyond the aesthetic and for whom "the aesthetic offers a paradigm, rather than a displacement of emancipatory political thought."[90] Of course, there are not two Adornos, but only one whose work may be interpreted to exhibit both of these tendencies. Adorno's paradoxical, deliberately contradictory thought moves at times along the borders of the intolerable, yet there seems to be no other place for a type of thinking that must refuse to be subsumed, totalized, and instrumentalized. That Adorno's thought was profoundly shaped by fascism, and that he goes through great pains in his attempts to resist all totalizing tendencies is without question; however, the postulation of an "overreaction to fascism"—a term in all probability unfathomable for Adorno and, as a matter of fact, to the author of this study—could be considered a new strain of "near-intolerable," absurdist thought.

In Adorno's *In Search of Wagner*, Wagner becomes not just the site of a confrontation between art and fascist ideology but also between the avant-gardist, high art of modernity and the products of the culture industry of late capitalism. *In Search of Wagner* implicitly undermines the belief in an absolute, irreconcilable opposition between high and low culture, and shows their common origin. Belonging to both the realms of high and low culture, Wagner's music dramas demonstrate the entwinement of the two and attest to the paradoxical nature of modern culture. As Huyssen points out, Adorno's 1938 Wagner essay can not only be read "as an account of the birth of fascism out of the spirit of the *Gesamtkunstwerk*, but also as an account of the birth of the culture industry in the most ambitious high art of the nineteenth century."[91] By surrendering the autonomy of art and the artist to ideological and economic forces, Wagner enters the cultural commodity market. Driven by economic interests, the false totality created by his *Gesamtkunstwerk* and the phantasmagorical mythology of his stage productions mark the beginnings of the culture industry and, despite the fact that in the end they refuse, as Adorno argues, an unqualified affirmation of reality, exemplify the notion of culture as ideology. Culture consoles, appeases, and lies about the harsh realities of life and the social conditions under which it is produced.

> Among the motifs of cultural criticism one of the most long-established and central is that of the lie: that culture creates the illusion of a society worthy of man which

does not exist; that it conceals the material conditions upon which all human works rise, and that, comforting and lulling, it serves to keep alive the bad economic determination of existence. This is the notion of culture as ideology, which appears at first sight common to both the bourgeois doctrine of violence and its adversary, both to Nietzsche and to Marx.[92]

Aiding in the preservation of the status quo, modern culture produces legitimizing narratives propelled by ideological and material forces alike. However, to subscribe to the view that culture is entirely determined by ideological and economic interests would be like throwing out the "baby with the bathwater," as the title of the aphorism cited above indicates. It is important to recall the paradoxical involvements of culture in order to keep in perspective Adorno's Wagner critique and his association of Wagner with the culture of totalitarianism and late capitalism. Culture appeases and lies, but is also bears thought that opposes and resists the ideology it perpetuates. This argument runs counter to the impression of a sharp division of culture into high art and mass culture propagated by the essay on the culture industry, whose grim diagnosis seems to espouse the view of totalized domination and manipulation. Huyssen notes that the concept of the culture industry and his insistence on a fundamental separation between the products of the culture industry and modernist art are based on theoretical assumptions and historical experiences that are open to debate. Politically, Huyssen argues, adherence to the classical culture industry thesis can only lead to "resignation or moralizing about universal manipulation and domination," while "theoretically, adherence to Adorno's aesthetics may blind us to the ways in which modern art, since the demise of classical modernism and the historical avant-garde, represents a new conjuncture that can no longer be grasped in Adornoan or other modernist categories."[93] This debate surrounding the relationship between autonomous art and the culture industry continues to haunt contemporary criticism. Led by Benjamin and Adorno in the thirties, the positions were, in summary, between interpreting technology and the "mechanical reproduction" of art as progressive developments and as potential agents of emancipation and the view that the new cultural technologies, such as film, radio, and the recording industry, are part of a repressive system of manipulation guided by economic and ideological motives. While Benjamin emphasizes the potential power of art, and especially film, to mobilize the masses,[94] Adorno categorically states that movies and radio need no longer pretend to be art: "The truth that they are just business is made into an ideology in order to justify the rubbish they deliberately produce."[95] Adorno discounts the argument that technological advances further the cause of emancipation and claims that this view not only overlooks the question of ownership, but also underestimates the relation of material possession and ideological interests: "Interested parties explain the culture industry in technological terms. . . . No mention is made of the fact that the basis on which technology acquires power over society is the power of those whose economic hold over society is greatest. A technological rationale is the rationale of domination itself."[96] Adorno wants to expose both the progressive and the regressive aspects of art and the products of the culture industry: "Both bear the stigmata of capitalism, both contain elements of change. . . . Both are torn halves of an integral freedom, to which however they do not add up."[97] While Adorno criticizes Benjamin for underestimating the regressive moments of the culture industry on the one hand and the progressive moments of autonomous art on the other, one might claim that the reverse is true for Adorno. The essays on the culture industry, including the above-cited skepticism concerning the combination of art with technology and the writings on aesthetic theory, attest to the fact that art and the products of the culture industry are never treated in the value-neutral fashion suggested by the phrase "torn halves." Adorno's charge against Benjamin in reverse portrays Adorno's position much more accurately: Adorno underestimated the progressive moments of the products of the culture industry while simultaneously overestimating the progressive moments of autonomous art.

However, it seems that no one undermines the insistence upon the fundamental difference between the products of the culture industry and autonomous art more consistently and effectively than Adorno himself. He did so in his essay on Wagner, and throughout his *oeuvre*. One part of the term "culture industry" is, after all, the word "culture." As much as Adorno dislikes it, the culture industry is not only part of the economic apparatus but also part of culture. In *Minima Moralia*, for example, Adorno argues that cultural criticism cannot reduce culture to economic and ideological forces, because in doing so cultural criticism runs the risk of turning into ideology itself. A dogmatic critique of the culture industry in terms of its utter determination by these forces would therefore only revert to ideology: "To identify culture solely with lies is more fateful than ever, now that the former is really becoming totally absorbed by the latter, and eagerly invites such identification in order to compromise every opposing thought."[98] A similarly paradoxical challenge to the non-identification of culture with its potentially existing ideology returns later in *Negative Dialectics*, in which Adorno contends that all art after Auschwitz is garbage, because it has become the ideology that it potentially always had been by restoring itself after what had occurred in its realm: "Whoever pleads for the preservation of the radically culpable and shabby culture becomes its accomplice, while the man who says no to culture is directly furthering the barbarism which our culture showed itself to be."[99] Since within the culture of modernity no form of artistic production can be separated from its function as a commodity and a carrier of ideology, the distinction between autonomous, "high" art and the products of the culture industry becomes blurred.

While showing the traces of commodity fetishism, autonomous art negates reality and protests against ideology; freed from religious, political, and other functions, art is an autonomous sphere of value. However, since society itself is unfree, the "freedom" of autonomous art is contradictory. Because of its pacifying and affirmative quality, art must resist its own principles in order to avoid affirming existing conditions. No art, Adorno argues, will be conceivable without the moment of anti-art. Ironically, the existence of an autonomous sphere of art rests upon the increasing commodification and reification of art, processes that become possible only in a market economy: "The emergence of 'genuine' modernism," Huyssen points out, "is seen as resulting from a deterioration within forms of high art, a deterioration which bears witness to the increasing commodification of art."[100] In capitalist society, autonomous art is thus "always already permeated by the textures of that mass culture from which it seeks autonomy";[101] Wagner is the strong case in point. Peter Osborne, who reads, and some might say misreads, *Aesthetic Theory* as a "materialist metaphysics of modernism," contends that Adorno's diagnosis of modernism's crisis perceives the threat of the "tendential elimination of the autonomy" and the "inherently degenerative character" of high art generated by this threat to its autonomy.[102] Since for Adorno the autonomy of art is a precondition for the possibility of an authentic aesthetic experience, which holds the "promise of the idea of truth and a prefigurative anticipation of a state of reconciliation and a transformed subjectivity," and since this autonomy cannot exist, Osborne argues that the crisis of modernity "produces the necessity for, but denies the actual possibility of, a postmodern art."[103]

Autonomous art resists society's obsession with the principle of exchange and carries with it the refusal to be consumed. It offers the possibility of knowledge, experience, and modes of understanding which defy integration into a concrete political and social reality; Adorno speaks of the cognitive character of art, the *Erkenntnischarakter der Kunst*.[104] Art, and especially music, give expression to the unsayable, to that which cannot be formulated by discursive language. The aesthetic experience provides a unique form of recognition and understanding, a nonconceptual understanding that stands in contrast to the conceptual operations of instrumental rationality. However, the nondiscursive aesthetic experience does not signify the recognition of the "truth" content of art, and would be rendered impotent unless interpretive rationality, that is, philosophical criticism, uncovers that which points beyond the fleeting moment of the aesthetic experience.[105]

The need of artworks for interpretation in the construction of their enigmatic truth content indicates "their failure with regard to their own element of rationality."[106] Paradoxically, art positions itself to articulate the unsayable lying beyond the borders of discursive rationality, but in order to recover the unsayable, art needs to enlist rational thought and language, that is, criticism and philosophy. However, art will always elude final interpretations and conceptual determinations. Despite its dependence, art constitutes the space for the "escape" from the domination in an administered world of commodities. As the systems of manipulation and domination increase in sophistication, art is the last frontier for salvaging, as Andrew Bowie puts it, "at least some aspects of subjectivity in a world increasingly dominated by mechanisms which threaten to abolish it."[107]

Rüdiger Bubner contends that Adorno's concept of the aesthetic experience remains mysterious, because Adorno evades the question of how art achieves its effects. He criticizes Adorno for his predetermination of the aesthetic experience as a moment of criticism and negativity.[108] If authentic art is seen exclusively as negating reality, then the aesthetic experience, which opens up consciousness to new, previously unperceived possibilities and accentuates new modes of perception, is reduced to the function of criticism, and the alternative modes of understanding suffer from the restriction upon the "free play of reflection."[109] Similarly, Hans Robert Jauß argues that Adorno shortchanges the aesthetic experience by dictating not only the categories of negation and affirmation, but also the appropriate modes of the reception of art.[110]

In *Aesthetic Theory*, Adorno is rather suspicious of the pleasure connected with the aesthetic experience and the reception of art, because pleasure is and has been traditionally associated with identification and catharsis as well as the mindless reception of the products of the culture industry: those who fetishize the enjoyment of art are philistines,[111] and their "relation to artworks is ruled by whether and to what degree they can, for example, put themselves in the place of the actors as they come forth; this is what all parts of the culture industry are based on and they foster it insistently in their customers."[112] In his rejection of aesthetic hedonism, he goes so far as to suggest the abolition of the concept of aesthetic enjoyment as constitutive to the reception of genuine art.[113] Through its negativity, art evokes a better praxis and alternatives to the existing conditions. However, since this possibility for a better praxis reflects back onto the present conditions, it is, in Adorno's view, inappropriate to derive pleasure from art. The moment of pleasure in art should rest in its protest against "the universally mediated commodity character."[114] Art's *promesse du bonheur* does not lie in the pleasure it provides to those admiring it, but rather in the recognition of the possibility for alternatives to domination. Therefore, the aesthetic experience is only autonomous if it rejects all inclinations for enjoyment and gratification. However, should the last trace of pleasure be erased, then answering the question of why art exists would pose a dilemma.[115] The concept of pleasure is a deficient compromise between the social function of art and its antithetical position to society,[116] and it attributes to art a form of use value that imitates sensual desires. Although he cannot entirely separate the aesthetic experience from gratification and pleasure, Adorno nevertheless claims that those who understand art indulge less in its pleasures: "Actually, the more they [artworks] are understood, the less they are enjoyed."[117] Seeking a supplement to the sensual pleasures withheld from him by social reality, the average bourgeois, with his objectified and reified consciousness that contrasts to that of the expert, wishes his art to be lush and gratifying. Art is thus no longer an object of contemplation and reflection, but a commodity:

> While the artwork's sensual appeal seemingly brings it close to the consumer, it is alienated from him by being a commodity that he possesses and the loss of which he must constantly fear. The false relation to art is akin to anxiety over possession. The fetishistic idea of the artwork is as property that can be possessed and destroyed by reflection has its exact correlative in the idea of the exploitable within the psychological economy of the self.[118]

Unlike a commodity, authentic art cannot be assessed on the basis of its material, psychological, or pleasure value, nor can it be perceived as devoid of any connection to reality. Art's double nature, as belonging to an autonomous realm and existing as *fait social*, allows it to be an element of resistance and negativity. Art is the social antithesis of society and cannot be deduced directly from it. Art is neither an immediate reflection of society, nor its direct negation or absolute other. Although it will always contain the traces of these conditions, a work of art cannot be reduced to the social conditions under which it was produced. It criticizes social reality not through discursive argumentation or analysis or by a social engagement, as proposed by advocates of *littérature engagé*, but merely through its existence. In "Commitment," an essay published in *Notes to Literature*, Adorno states that art does not necessarily point out alternatives, but through nothing else but its form can it go against the course of the world, "which continues to hold a pistol to the heads of human beings."[119] The *Erkenntnischarakter* of art, its ability to foster understanding, lies in these unresolved contradictions, and only critical reflection upon a work of art can bring to light the traces of the different and the new. Art critiques reality not because it reflects it, but because it distances itself from it. It gives expression to the other, the heterogenous, the non-identical and the unresolvable remainder that resist subsumption and domination. Great works of art, because they enunciate what ideology hides, tendentiously reconcile the contradictions of reality without claiming an illusionary dissolution. Neither the concept of *littérature engagé*, which Adorno criticized in response to Sartre and Brecht, nor that of *l'art pour l'art* does justice to this interdependence of art and reality; both fall back into ideology. The former displays the barbarism of art assigned an ultimate and concrete purpose: art as didactic tool or propaganda. The latter is guilty of the barbarism originating from the craving for pleasure. In his view, each of these alternatives negates itself or each other in their relationship to social reality: tendentious art, which as art is necessarily held separate from reality, abolishes this difference, while art for art's sake, through its absolute aesthetic, denies that indelible connection to reality.[120]

As opposed to the products of the culture industry, authentic works of art make no attempt to eradicate their differences from reality; they insist upon and make visible their illusory quality. The antagonisms and contradictions of social reality find their reflections in form, material, and technique. Unresolved social antagonisms return as immanent problems of form, and together with the advancement of the artistic material and technique, they constitute the social-historical basis for a work of art. Works of art are "windowless monads" that are not necessarily conscious of society, but nevertheless stand in an interdependent relationship with it: "the works of art, and notably music, which is far removed from concepts, represent society. Music, one might think, does this the more deeply the less it blinks in the direction of society."[121] The nonconceptual and nondiscursive character of music make society's imprint upon it much more complex and subtle. Music exemplifies the paradoxes of modern art, and like other forms of art, music depends upon the development of the material.

In his *Philosophy of Modern Music*, Adorno insists upon the entwinement of form and content in music. Every musical form is a sediment of content that bears witness to false reality and to the repression of and in history: "In them there survives what is otherwise forgotten and is no longer capable of speaking directly. What once sought refuge in form now exists without definition in the constancy of form. The forms of art reflect the history of man more truthfully than do documents themselves."[122] Bound to the historical context and its historical tendency, both the aging and the advancement of musical material show the traces of social-historical processes. Consequently, the composer's struggle with the material becomes his dialogue with society. While some modes of musical expression age, and thus become regressive, others advance and widen the horizon with new techniques. In the face of the new possibilities of expression, traditional techniques, such as tonality, sound like impotent clichés. However, they are not only old-fashioned and untimely, but also false because they no longer fulfill their function of resisting and negating reality. The state of technique represents itself in every beat, and the composer is a mere agent who gives voice to suffering and negative experiences by following the self-propelled dynamic of the material. In order to master this task, the composer must do what the music demands of him: "But such obedience demands of the composer all possible disobedience, independence, and spontaneity. This is the dialectical nature revealed in the unfolding of the musical material."[123]

Dissonance is modernity's most prevalent expression of the disparity between existing conditions and the possibility of a better reality. A signum and invariant of modernity, dissonance is the original aesthetic phenomenon signifying ambivalence and an immanent play of forces. Within the work of art, such an interplay of oppositions parallels reality's play of power over the subject: "Dissonance elicits from within the work that which vulgar sociology calls its social alienation."[124] By signalling the emancipation from the classical ideal of harmony, dissonance expresses modern alienation and reification and allows works of art to unfold their truth content. Dissonance is the inherent tendency and desire of all art and has only been repressed by society's pressure for affirmation.[125] By opening up a space for the non-identical and contradictory, dissonance rebels against seamless illusion and reveals the truth about harmony and the harmonizing forces.

For modern art, dissonance is the most appropriate mode of expressing polarities and various levels of alienation, which manifest themselves in several ways: between society and art, between autonomy and commodification, between the artist and the audience, between the artist and the material, and finally, while important in the context of Adorno's understanding of the artwork as a product of social labor, between the forces and relations of production. Since in Adorno's view artworks arise from society through a dialectic of subject and object, he faces, as Lambert Zuidervaart points out, the constant challenge "to show how three dialectical levels interrelate: a dialectic in society between forces and relations of production, a dialectic within artistic production between artists and materials, and a dialectic within artworks between their content and form."[126]

Adorno's selective canon of modern art, which includes only a fairly limited number of artists of the avant-garde, results directly from his estimation of how well these artists reflect upon these dialectical relationships. In contrast to the products of the culture industry and to some modern art, genuine and autonomous art makes visible the breaks and gaps on every level. Adorno's harsh judgments have been criticized as elitist and arbitrary, and it is indeed difficult at times to shake off the feeling that Adorno merely seeks to legitimize his own literary and musical tastes. However, most of his preferences and rejections result from thorough philosophical reflection, and the reasoning behind these evaluations becomes intelligible within the context of Adorno's philosophical agenda. While Beckett and Kafka stand of course at the top of his modern literary canon, surrealism, dadaism, *l'art pour l'art*, and *littérature engagé* are disqualified from the modern artistic canon.[127] Although Adorno argues against both *l'art pour l'art* and *littérature engagé*, as seen in his sharp critique of Sartre and Brecht, it becomes clear where his preference lies. Brecht's art transmits ideological messages, and by forcing reality upon art, he makes real conflicts appear inoffensive. As a carrier of ideology, *littérature engagé* has lost any claim to autonomy. The works standing under the banner of *l'art pour l'art* are not necessarily inherently ideological, but ideology can utilize their denial of negativity, as in the case of advertising and propaganda. Adorno's musical canon is as discriminating and distinct as his literary canon. Especially noteworthy is his exclusion of the works of Stravinsky and, of course, every form of so-called popular music, including jazz. Instead, the Vienna School of Arnold Schönberg provides the framework for all of Adorno's writings on music. Schönberg's music is the incarnation of modern, autonomous art and gives expression to the ambiguity of the modern condition by overcoming traditional limits and advancing new techniques, such as atonality, the twelve-tone row, and dissonance. As a model of the modern artist, Schönberg's "composition emerged out of an unresolved contradiction between the subjective freedom of the composer and the objective demands of the material."[128]

As Martin Jay points out, Adorno's dialectic of enlightenment began in musical terms with the work of Bach, whose work stands at the beginning of the secularization process. Not surprisingly, Beethoven, whose work is often linked with high bourgeois culture and German Idealism, represents the height of "bourgeois humanism, the clearest embodiment of practical reason in sensuous terms, the greatest realization of active subjectivity in objective musical material."[129] Beethoven's return to the religious mass indicates the failure of bourgeois enlightenment, his use of contrapunctual forms questioned genuine autonomy, and by finally disappointing the audience's expectations, "he registered the growing alienation of the artist from the public."[130] In contrast to Beethoven, Wagner regresses into myth and the acceptance of fate, his gestures are static and atemporal, and his work eventually broke down into a commodity, thus displaying the decay of musical forms and the loss of the possibility of genuine autonomy after Beethoven.

Beethoven's work bears the mark of modernity, and stands at the beginning of genuine, autonomous modern art. Similar to Baudelaire's poetry, it registers alienation, instead of attempting a false reconciliation. Both Beethoven and Baudelaire reject the affirmative and free themselves from the slavish restraints imposed by tradition. This loss of tradition relates to an objective condition of modernity, because it demands the authority of the new. The abstraction of modern art mirrors the abstract relations of society; modernity does not merely negate outdated forms and styles, but negates traditions as such. However, in its constant search for the new, art demonstrates parallels to the mechanism of the commodity market. The modern obsession with the new relates to the demands of the marketplace, but the new soon loses its novel status when it falls victim to circulation and reproduction. Baudelaire's work is the first to codify the only possibility for autonomous art to respond:

> in the midst of the fully developed commodity society, art can ignore this tendency only at the price of its won powerlessness. Only by immersing its autonomy in society's *imagerie* can art surmount the heteronomous market. Art is modern art through mimesis of the hardened and alienated; . . . Baudelaire neither railed against nor portrayed reification; he protested against it in the experience of its archetypes. . . . The power of his work is that he syncopates the overwhelming objectivity of the commodity character—which wipes out any human trace—with the objectivity of the work in itself, anterior to the living subject: The absolute artwork converges with the absolute commodity.[131]

Therein lie the paradoxes faced by modern art: to negate without explicit, discursive criticism, to show the traces of reification without reproducing it, and to recognize commodification by ignoring it. Modern art must affirm its autonomy, even if genuine autonomy is an illusion of bourgeois ideology. However, this illusion is constitutive to the self-consciousness of modern art, whose freedom is the cunning of its reason.[132]

THE CULTURE INDUSTRY

The culture industry produces works neither from the masses nor by the masses, but rather *for* the masses. By invoking the concept of the culture industry, Adorno and Horkheimer want to avoid the ambiguity of such terms as low art, mass culture, and popular art, which imply the participation of the masses or a grounding in traditional folk art. The essays on the culture industry in the *Dialectic of Enlightenment* intend to "demonstrate the regression of enlightenment to ideology"[133] and the reduction of enlightenment and rationality to the calculation of effects and the techniques of production and distribution. The ideology of the culture industry idolizes the status quo and the power mechanisms that facilitate domination through technology. The culture industry's own admission of its commercial nature and presentation of a qualified truth function as a convenient excuse to avoid responsibility for its lies. Adorno and Horkheimer's analysis aims to expose the products' inherent claim to be aesthetic embodiments of truth in order to illustrate the inanity of these truth-claims.

In contrast to autonomous art, the products of the culture industry deny alienation by blurring the differences between reality and illusion. They hide their illusory character by erasing the traces of production, the traces of becoming, of being made. The business of the culture industry is to produce illusions and to sell them as realities; taking on the characteristics of advertising, culture eliminates its difference to practical life and completely erases the possibility of an autonomous, aesthetic reality. Products of the culture industry are made to function as substitutes for reality and assume a "parasitic character"[134] in their liquidation of all opposition to empirical reality. The culture industry creates standardized products that supposedly reflect the needs and desires of the consumer. However, these apparent needs and desires are already the result of the manipulation by the industry, whose use of technology enables it to plan and organize the responses of the audience. In its glorification of the use and advancement of technology, the culture industry is silent about "the fact that the basis on which technology acquires power over society is the power of those whose economic hold over society is greatest. A technological rationale is the rationale of domination itself. It is the coercive nature of society alienated from itself."[135] In other words, the industry conceals the fact that it reproduces the power mechanisms of capitalist society, not only hiding its deployment of technology as a means of production and distribution by those who own or control it, but also concealing its use as a tool for manipulation and the expansion of influence. The culture industry is consumed by the exchange principle, turning culture into a totalized commodity: "Culture is a paradoxical commodity. So completely is it subject to the law of exchange that it is no longer exchanged; it is so blindly consumed in use that it can no longer be used."[136]

Commercial culture completes the subsumption of culture under the sphere of administration, and mockingly satisfies the call for a unified culture. Devoid of any critical potential, the products of the culture industry posit imitation of and obedience to the social hierarchy as an absolute. The products of the culture industry are part of the administered world and of the *Verblendungszusammenhang*, which genuine art opposes. Giving testimony to the regressive elements of enlightenment, the culture industry's products embody the myths of modern society, such as progress, freedom, and individuality. The subtitle of the essay on the culture industry, "Enlightenment as Mass Deception," leaves no doubt as to Adorno's assessment of its subject:

> Today aesthetic barbarism completes what has threatened the creations of the spirit since they were gathered together as culture and neutralized. To speak of culture was always contrary to culture. Culture as a common denominator already contains in embryo that schematization and process of cataloging and classification which bring culture within the sphere of administration.[137]

Administered culture uses intellectual and artistic creations to occupy the senses of the workers from the time they leave the factory to the time they punch the clock in the morning. Culture becomes entertainment; amusement becomes an ideal in itself and a substitute for subjective interiority. The affinity between business and amusement becomes apparent in the latter's specific role to defend society: "To be pleased means to say Yes."[138] Amusement recreates a false sense of happiness, suppresses reflection, and hides the position of powerlessness. It promises liberation from one's troubles, without, however, providing liberation from reality, but rather from thought and negation: "Pleasure always means not to think about anything, to forget suffering even where it is shown. Basically it is helplessness. It is flight; not, as is asserted, flight from a wretched reality, but from the last remaining thought of resistance."[139] Ironically, consumers invariably insist upon the very ideology that enslaves them, and their "misplaced love" for the wrongs under which they suffer is "a greater force than the cunning of the authorities."[140]

In its fusion of culture and entertainment, the culture industry relies upon schemata and stereotypes. Its products are the recurrence of the same, and the differences are the illusionary differences of essentially similar and sometimes identical consumer products. Everything becomes standardized to accommodate easy consumption. Sameness also rules the relationship to the new; the new is dismissed as an untried risk, while talk of novelty and surprise is endless. The tempo and dynamics of the industry and its incessant movement only mask the eternal return of the same. New is only that "the irreconcilable elements of culture, art and distraction, are subordinated to one end and subsumed under one false formula: the totality of the culture industry. It consists of repetition."[141] The innovations of the culture industry are nothing more than improvements in technique and the modes of mass reproduction, while the rationality of power hides behind the veil of bourgeois quaintness, *die heile Welt*. The consumer is made to believe that he has a choice, and that he has control over his choices: "All are free to dance and enjoy themselves, just as they have been free, since the historical neutralization of religion, to join any of the innumerable sects. But freedom to choose an ideology—since ideology always reflects economic coercion—everywhere proves to be freedom to choose what is always the same."[142]

The culture industry conceives of the consumer not as an individual with individual needs and tastes, but as one of the masses, a member of a species, who signifies only those attributes by which he can be replaced by somebody else: he becomes a substitute and a copy.[143] Its products aim at the momentary and illusory satisfaction of needs, and their effectiveness relies upon the promise of gratification. Gratification is endlessly promised, but infinitely deferred: "The culture industry perpetually cheats its consumers of what it perpetually promises."[144] The individual and individuality are illusory constructs of the culture industry and are only tolerated so long as the "complete identification with the generality is unquestioned."[145] The products of the culture industry are not concerned with individual elements and their interaction but with producing effects. Technological advances are used to establish a false identity between the universal and the particular. The individual elements can no longer liberate themselves from the whole as part of an emancipatory process, as is possible in autonomous art, in which the emancipation of the individual signifies a protest against subsumption and a critique of the status of the whole. The individual elements within these culture industry products are absorbed into a false totality, and style, which in the culture is a negation of style as such, is thereby eliminated. These products are not struggling for the reconciliation between the universal and the particular or the rules of form and the specific demands of specific materials, through which style emerges in genuine art. Due to a tension between the part and the whole, the subject matter and the material, and representation and society, the culture industry offers false reconciliation through its products. When these discordant elements become identical, the universal substitutes for the particular.

> The development of the culture industry has led to the predominance of the effect, the obvious touch, and the technical detail over the work itself—which once expressed an idea, but was liquidated together with the idea. When the detail won its freedom, it became rebellious and, in the period from Romanticism to Expressionism, asserted itself as free expression, as a vehicle of protest against the organization. . . . The totality of the culture industry has put an end to this.[146]

Adorno's critique of the culture industry mirrors Nietzsche's complaint concerning the predominance of effect in Wagner's works. In contrast to Nietzsche and Bourget, however, who decried the emancipation of the individual elements because it leads to the dissolution of the whole, Adorno does not affirm a process of decay and disintegration, but perceives the emancipation of the individual element as a truly emancipatory process resisting subsumption under the authority of the whole. In Bourget's perception, the disintegration of the whole made possible the emancipation of the individual elements; by Nietzsche's account, the expansion of the individual element leads to the breakdown of the whole. For Adorno, the emancipation of the individual element signifies negativity and the resistance against repression and subordination. However, in his view, the culture industry has eliminated the possibility of escaping integration:

Though concerned exclusively with effects, it crushes their insubordination and makes them subserve the formula, which replaces the work. The same fate is inflicted on whole and parts alike. The whole inevitably bears no relation to the details. . . . The so-called dominant idea is like a file which ensures order but not coherence. The whole and the parts are alike; there is no antithesis and no connection. Their prearranged harmony is a mockery of what had to be striven after in the great bourgeois works of art.[147]

Like Wagner's music dramas, the totality of the culture industry's products is constructed by way of formulas and a predetermined idea of harmony, which specifically prevents an integral connection between individual elements, because it imposes an artificial order rather than a constellation of individual elements. The whole and the parts do not stand in a dialectic relationship to each other. In modern music, Adorno complains, the single harmonic effect has "obliterated the awareness of form as a whole."[148] This imposed harmony stands in contrast to Beethoven, whose works achieve a nontotalitarian wholeness. In his *Introduction to the Sociology of Music*, Adorno describes Beethoven's music as a "dynamically unfolding totality."[149] As Martin Jay points out, it seems surprising that Adorno, who is hostile to any affirmation of totality, unequivocally favors it with regard to music.[150] Jay explains that Adorno saw a sharp distinction between totality in theoretical terms and totality in musical terms: "Whereas the former is essentially conceptual and thus threatens to dominate the non-identical and heterogeneous particulars subsumed under it, the latter is non-conceptional and thus less inclined to eliminate otherness."[151] Another way of explaining Adorno's preference for musical totality is to postulate that Beethoven's work embodies a vision of reconciliation, harmony, and unity established through a nonrepressive and nonsubsumptive relationship between the whole and the parts. Unlike the preestablished, standardized, and static harmony of the products of the culture industry, the totality in Beethoven's works is dynamically achieved by an unforced reconciliation.

Despite the fact that Beethoven proved himself to be a rather shrewd businessman, his works stand in absolute opposition to commodification and constitute a most extreme renunciation of the market.[152] Beethoven did not cover up the opposition between autonomy and commodification, but integrated it into his work. To cover up the opposition is to succumb to ideology. The principles of Beethoven's aesthetics, and that of idealist aesthetics, which asserts purposefulness without purpose, reverses the demands of the marketplace and insists on a purposelessness for a purpose.[153]

The essays on the culture industry in the *Dialectic* reiterate substantial components of Adorno's critique in "On the Fetish Character in Music and the Regression of Listening" written in 1938. Rather than focusing on the visual products of the culture industry, this essay explores the commodification of music. It laments the decay of musical forms, the emphasis on melody and repetition, the loss of aesthetic totality, and the preoccupation with effects. This critique further includes an attack on the standardized productions and reproductions of music on the one hand and the infantile regression of listening on the other. Finding its precursor in Wagner, modern music relies upon climaxes and repetitions to make itself memorable, and the performances of classical music are reduced to vulgarized presentations.[154] Within the culture industry, music mainly functions within advertising. It is used to advertise products, including those products that the consumer needs in order to listen to the reified music. Music has become the fetish of late capitalism. The fetish character of the commodity is, according to Marx, the result of the alienation of the producer from the product. Products are not produced for personal use, but rather for the exchange with other products. Capitalist production is geared toward the production of goods that are to be exchanged; labor is a commodity, and the principles of exchange dominate not only the relation to the commodity, but also the relationships between human beings. The fetishization of the commodity is thus the veneration of a reified product, whose use value is displaced by its exchange value. Adorno claims that despite its seemingly immediate relationship to the goods, the realm of culture is completely dominated by the exchange value, because the use value of the product is nothing more than an illusion perpetuated in order to increase consumption. The change in the function of music reflects the reified relation between art and society, in which the exchange value disguises itself as the object of enjoyment. In the world of commodity fetishism, enjoyment that does not have its basis in exchange mechanisms takes on subversive features.

The regression of listening is evident in the conformist behavior of the consumer. According to Adorno, it would be impossible to verify the fetishization of music through surveys, because the ability to listen to music has regressed to a point at which the listeners are completely unaware of the depth of their regression and the manipulation of their listening habits by the culture industry:

> In music as elsewhere, the discrepancy between essence and appearance has grown to a point where no appearance is any longer valid, without mediation, as verification of the essence. The unconscious reactions of the listeners are so heavily veiled and their conscious assessment is so exclusively oriented to the dominant fetish categories that every answer one receives conforms in advance to the surface of that music business which is attacked by the theory being "verified."[155]

The fetishism of music finds its counterpart in the regression of listening. Contemporary listening is arrested in an infantile stage: by being denied the freedom of choice and the burden of responsibility, the listening subject is incapable of a conscious perception of music. In fact, modern music negates even the possibility for a conscious perception.[156] The simultaneous loss of the *Erkenntnischarakter* of music and the regression of listening denies the listener the possibility for a genuine aesthetic experience. The audience listens "atomistically and dissociate what they hear, but precisely in this dissociation they develop certain capacities which accord less with the concepts of traditional aesthetics than with those of football and motoring."[157] The regression is a withdrawal from the possibility of a different and oppositional music. The culture industry does not merely turn away listeners from more important music, but confirms them "in their neurotic stupidity."[158] The popularity of "light" music and the regression of listening cuts across class lines; in America, according to Adorno, one finds even so-called liberals and progressives among the advocates of "light" popular music. Because of the popularity and the broad spectrum of its effects, most of them defend popular music as "democratic";[159] however, this "masochism" of listening is nothing more than a pseudo-pleasure and an identification with power.[160] The conformism of the listener finds a parallel in the absolute authority of the conductor, whose rule reminds of that "of the totalitarian *Führer*."[161] The conductor reduces the musical parts to a common denominator: "At one stroke he provides norm and individualization: the norm is identified with his person, and the individual tricks which he perpetrates furnish the general rule. The fetish character of the conductor is the most obvious and the most hidden."[162] This theme of the composer-conductor is an integral part of the critique of Wagner, in which Adorno further explores his identification of Wagner's role as conductor with the behavior of a tyrant.

Adorno's portrayal of the culture industry and its products contrasts sharply with his delineations of the role of high art in society. The products of the culture industry deny the possibilities promised by autonomous art: they affirm rather than negate society and forfeit the hope for criticism and a genuine aesthetic experience. The immediacy of the moment of the aesthetic experience and the critical reflection upon the work of art are, however, preconditions for the unveiling of a work's truth content. Theoretically, it is futile to argue that the products of the culture industry retain some semblance of truth, since this truth would remain unrecoverable. The commodified standardization, which is achieved by utilizing technology, effects, and formulas, eradicates art's potential to gain knowledge and understanding, namely, its *Erkenntnischarakter*. Simultaneously, the infantile regression in viewing and listening habits eliminates the ability to reflect critically. One could argue that Adorno reproduces the culture industry's view of the audience as substitutes, copies, and members of a species rather than a group of individuals. Manipulated and dominated by the culture industry, the audience has regressed to a stage of infantility, and now the culture industry only confirms their "neurotic stupidity"[163] as evidenced by their willingness to be subservient, to conform, to consume, and to accept the status quo. The regressed listener shares these characteristics with women, whom Adorno describes in *Minima Moralia*—as discussed in chapter 3—in very similar terms. This points to a rather unfortunate affinity between Nietzsche and Adorno: through his description of the regressed listener, Adorno implicitly draws a connection to what could be called the "regressed women," and Nietzsche finds women listeners—in this instance female Wagnerians—to embody the regressed listener depicted by Adorno in such derogatory terms.

As Huyssen points out, Adorno's analysis of increasing commodification is persuasive when it describes its effects in all cultural products; however, it becomes reductive when it denudes the products of their specificity and imagines the consumer in a state of passive regression.[164] Huyssen argues that cultural products cannot be totalized commodities without use value which only retain an exchange value, because in this case it would be impossible for them to "fulfill their function in the processes of ideological reproduction."[165] Cultural products do preserve their use value for capital, and therefore "also provide a locus for struggle and subversion. Culture industry, after all, does fulfill public functions; it satisfies and legitimizes cultural needs which are not all *per se* false or only retroactive; it articulates social conditions in order to homogenize them. Precisely this process of articulation can become the field of contest and struggle."[166] This process of articulation would need to restore critical negativity and the possibility for experience and reflection, for to deny this possibility in the age of a consumer culture would deny the potential of art to be more than entertainment. It seems today that the invasion of the sphere of autonomous art by the culture industry, to whose beginning Wagner's works testify, has become an indisputable fact. However, to claim that this invasion is now complete, to postulate a total collapse of the two realms into one, or to deny all differences between autonomous art and commercial art is both shortsighted and reductive. Adorno's analysis of Wagner confirms these differences and reaffirms the possibility for the existence of art in a commodified culture.

Wagner's music dramas enact the entwinement of the regressive and progressive aspects of modernity and also demonstrate that one cannot be had without the other. In their return to archaic forms and ideas, they exemplify the regressive nature of commingling myth and reason, while simultaneously advancing the progressive and the regressive developments in music. Wagner's rationally organized music dramas make use of the newest technological inventions; structurally and musically they reinforce the tyranny of instrumental rationality. In the reproduction of mythological images, they fall back into myth and bear witness to the myth of enlightenment. Wagner's works mark the ambiguity of the modern condition and establish an inseparable link between its regressive and progressive aspects, between myth and modernity. In his greatest moments, Wagner draws his force from the irreducible contradiction between regressive gestures and progressive constructions. This makes clear "that progress and reaction in Wagner's music cannot be separated out like sheep and goats. The two are indissolubly intertwined."[167]

THE SEARCH FOR WAGNER'S CASE

Despite claims to the contrary, Adorno's critique of Wagner is, to say the least, ambiguous and not entirely consistent. The 1933 essay "Notiz über Wag-

ner" ("Note on Wagner"), *In Search of Wagner* (1938), and three essays written
in 1964 and 1966 explore similar themes and issues, and while they may not contradict each other, they nonetheless exhibit remarkable shifts in emphasis. While
In Search of Wagner focuses to a great extent on the regressive elements in Wagner's work, the later essays emphasize almost exclusively his progressive side
and his contributions to the advancement of music. The earlier work analyzes
Wagner as a social character and draws parallels between his persona as an artist,
the expression of the social character in the music, and the rise of commodity
culture and fascism. These aspects of Adorno's critique of Wagner, which are of
primary interest for this study, are barely acknowledged in the later essays. The
difference between the various writings can certainly be explained by the changing historical circumstances, a factor that Adorno does acknowledge. The 1933
"Notiz über Wagner" praises Wagner's musical accomplishments and damns the
Wagnerkult,[168] *In Search of Wagner* reflects his attempts to explore the roots of
fascism and the frustrations of exile, and the essays published in the sixties are
written to honor Wagner's work: "Wagners Aktualität"[169] ("Wagner's Timeli-
ness") was a lecture delivered at the Berlin Wagner festival in 1964 and later
printed in the program of the Bayreuth festival, and "Wagner und Bayreuth," a
speech from 1966 dedicated to the memory of Wagner, endorses Bayreuth as a
forum for the actualization of the truth content in Wagner's work.[170] As this short
account demonstrates, the motivation for writing these essays on Wagner as
well as the audience addressed varied over time. Adorno's "Wagners Aktualität"
provoked a lively Wagner discussion in *Die Zeit*, a then and now prominent liberal weekly, to which Adorno reacted with a postscript to the discussion, entitled "Nachschrift zu einer Wagner-Diskussion" ("Postscript to a Discussion on
Wagner").[171] In this piece Adorno insists that his position on Wagner has not
changed and pledges his continued belief in the ideas expressed in *In Search of
Wagner*; however, he also defends his right to reclaim his thoughts of the thirties
and to resume a dialectical critique. Such a critique attempts to decipher Wagner's music within its social context by taking into account historical changes,
which he sees reflected as objective changes in Wagner's work itself. Adorno
reaffirms the status of *In Search of Wagner* as a rescue effort and an attempt to
extract from the obscurity of the subject that which is true. He claims firstly that
aesthetic form and social untruth are inseparably bound to each other in Wagner's
work and that secondly the political and the aesthetic moments of his work cannot be separated. However, these aspects cannot be equated: the aesthetic
moments have to be separated from the political to the extent that the work of
art belongs to the realm of illusion and semblance and is not to be identified
with reality. Wagner's work combines a politics of catastrophe with disinterested
pleasure, but his nationalism now should no longer be seen as an immediate
threat.[172] As proof of his allegiance to his older work, Adorno cites how he
allowed the chapter on instrumentation from *In Search of Wagner* to be reprinted
unchanged in the 1964 Bayreuth program brochure. However, because this chap-

ter contains by far the most positive and laudatory comments on Wagner's work, Adorno's argument is not entirely convincing, nor does it irrefutably counter his critics' assertion that Adorno's perception of Wagner has in fact substantially changed.

In "Wagners Aktualität," which provoked the discussion and led to Adorno's response in the postscript, he appears to be rather defensive about his early work on Wagner. He speaks of the changes in historical circumstances and of a changed attitude toward Wagner's works as a whole. There is an involuntary, ironic reversal to Nietzsche in Adorno's explanation for these changes in attitude toward Wagner. While Nietzsche admits to his "youthful error" in his admiration for Wagner, Adorno sees his—although he does not refer to it explicitly as an error—in his harsh judgment of him. As the Wagner of the sixties no longer represents the generation of parents, but rather of the grandparents, there no longer exists, according to Adorno, the need to reject Wagner as a sign of revolt in the conflict between the generations. The historical distance has also brought about an affective distance to Wagner's work, and although his works still possess potentially nationalistic elements, this potential in Wagner's art begins to recede because the immediate political threat of nationalism has abated.[173] Most striking, however, is Adorno's claim that not only the historical circumstances and the reception of Wagner have changed, but also the work itself. Adorno justifies this claim for an *objective* change in Wagner's work by reminding the reader that works of art are not static entities, but are in a state of constant transformation. They form a field of tension for all possible forces and intentions, in which *objectively* old layers fall off, new ones emerge, and others become obsolete and become extinct.[174] Whether these are indeed *objective* changes within the works themselves or matters of changes in perception and reception remains open to discussion. In any case, Adorno contends that Wagner's work is not limited to its political content, which indeed remains unsalvageable. By exposing the politics of Wagner's work, Adorno's critique claims to have eroded one layer, from under which another came to the surface.[175]

It is worth mentioning that Adorno's brief essay, "Notiz über Wagner," written five years before *In Search of Wagner*, precedes his later writings in its focus upon Wagner's musical accomplishments and the "revolutionary" quality of his works. Adorno argues that the best way to honor Wagner is by performing him in a meaningful way, that is by disregarding the Wagner cult and by emphasizing the progressive elements of his music. According to Adorno, these progressive elements include his use of dissonance and counterpoint, the polyphony of his melodies, the nuances of sound and color, his rigorous use of form, and the enigmatic connection of the old and the new. Although Wagner's music reflects the structures of the society in which and for which it was written, its dynamic points simultaneously beyond contemporary reality to a possible future. Wagner is, as Nietzsche had claimed as well, a magician, and his treasures will be discovered by those who can read his secret writing and understand the "stenography of runic inscription," the leitmotif.[176] Although his view of the world rests upon the antithesis of guilt and redemption, Wagner's demystification of the power of myth should receive its proper emphasis.

Adorno's review of Ernest Newman's biography of Richard Wagner entitled "Wagner, Nietzsche, and Hitler," published in *The Kenyon Review* in 1947, provides rare insights into his estimation of Wagner, Nietzsche, his perception of the relationship between Nietzsche and Wagner, and their final break with one another in 1876. Adorno's remarks shall be cited in detail here, because they illustrate in a remarkably lucid manner those aspects of Nietzsche's thought most significant to Adorno. Although Adorno feels that Newman himself might dispute this, his biography of Wagner gathers "tremendous evidence for the thesis which might be epitomized by saying that Wagner, as a human being, crystallized to an amazing extent the Fascist character long before Fascism was ever dreamed of."[177] Despite the biographer's apologetic attitude toward Wagner's work and writings, products which even Newman compares to Hitlerism at times, the portrayal of Wagner's personality reveals that in his private life the artist resembled a fascist agitator. Wagner displays the "same mixture of the ideology of 'faith' and the readiness to betray his closest friends so significant for the sociology of the Fascist racket."[178] Adorno interprets Wagner's choice of Bayreuth as the home of the Wagner festivals as a confirmation of the "politico-fascist motive" in the desire for the "monopolization of public opinion."[179] While plotting continuously, Wagner senses "in the authentic Fascist way conspiracies everywhere."[180] Anticipating the patterns of anti-Semitism, Wagner brings forth the argument that Jews provoke anti-Semitic reactions against them due to their feelings of inferiority and oversensitivity.[181] According to Adorno, these patterns reveal their full meaning only fifty years after Wagner's death with Hitler's rationalization of his persecution of the Jews as defensive actions. Wagner shows one of the most sinister features of the fascist character, "the paranoid tendency of projecting upon others one's own violent aggressiveness."[182]

Adorno retells Newman's account of Nietzsche's flight from Bayreuth in 1876. Newman claims that Nietzsche left for health reasons and not for reasons of philosophical and artistic disillusionment; Newman perceives the latter explanation as one of Elisabeth Foerster-Nietzsche's many attempts to rewrite and manipulate history. Adorno's comments on these speculations anticipate Montinari's plea to biographers to accept the philosophical basis of Nietzsche's break with Wagner:

> There might still be some quibbling about precise dates but there can be no doubt that Nietzsche's alienation from Wagner goes back far behind the first Bayreuth festival, that it was caused by Nietzsche's own philosophical development rather than by his headache or his narcissistic disappointment in Bayreuth, and that the features he incriminated in Wagner, though "private" ones, are deeply related to the basic issue, Nietzsche's growing insight into the ideological character of Wagner's work, his conformism to middle class society.[183]

Interestingly enough, Adorno identifies Nietzsche's charges against Wagner as "private" ones, but continues to argue that the break is related to Nietzsche's growing insight into the ideological character of Wagner's work and not into the ideological character of Wagner the man. Adorno defends Nietzsche against some of Newman's unchallenged claims that Nietzsche made a negligible contribution to philosophy and that he was intellectually lazy. It is Adorno's contention that the traditional division of labor between the historian of the mind and the philosopher leads Newman to accept the criteria of official philosophy, which are

> precisely those which were subject, by Nietzsche, to the most penetrating critical analysis, that the latter's failure to comply with the rules of the game of academic thinking is not due to a lack of strength and self-discipline but rather to a lack of naivety and conformism. Nietzsche, one of the most advanced enlighteners of all, sensed in the "system" and what it entailed the same apologetic desire he sensed in the religion of redemption, or, for that matter, in the truly systematic totality of the Wagnerian music drama.[184]

Adorno aligns himself with the "most advanced enlighteners of all," who likewise disregard the strict borders of academic disciplines, resist systematization, and condemn systematic totality. Nietzsche turned against the accepted values of society, such as Christian love and pity, which Wagner ultimately reaffirmed, because he recognized the "barbarian momentum inherent in official cultural values," and not because of a "complicity with a dawning relapse into barbarism."[185] Like Wagner's work, Nietzsche's positive doctrines, such as the "spiteful" cult of power, the contempt of the masses, and the concept of the *Übermensch* fell prey to fascist ideology: "But his negativism, with regard to the logico-systematic tradition of philosophy, to traditional morality and to affirmative art, nevertheless also expressed the humane in a world in which humanity had become a sham."[186] To be sure, Adorno resists judging works on the basis of their manipulative acceptance by fascism and insists on the relevance of a work's objective implications. For him there is no doubt that Wagner's work "down to the most intimate details of musical technique, lends itself eagerly to Nazi falsification," while

> conversely, Nietzsche was not only overtly opposed to the Nazi in Wagner and everywhere, but his incessant attack on rationalizations and lies, his unique demonstration of the repressive character of occidental culture, comes closer to ultimate reconciliation than the vernacular of those who praise reconciliation in order to perpetuate injustice.[187]

While Nietzsche's work also lends itself to National Socialist manipulation, its objective import is, in contrast to Wagner's, implicitly and explicitly antifascist. Adorno's regard for Nietzsche is based on the latter's skepticism, radical critiques, and negations of traditional values rather than on the "doctrines" of the will to power, *amor fati*, the affirmation of life, and the concept of the *Übermensch* at the center of the fascist reception of Nietzsche. Unlike Nietzsche, Wagner encouraged Nazi falsification through his propagandist gestures. As the ideologist of the ascetic ideal, for whom redemption is tantamount to annihilation, he was much more obsessed by power than the philosopher who exposed the will to power. However, Adorno does agree with Newman's assessment of Nietzsche's "musical backwardness and dilettantism," since Nietzsche failed to recognize those elements which transcend, against Wagner's conscious will, his bombastic Germanic *Weltanschauung*.

Adorno's comments on Newman's biography outline the strategy of *In Search of Wagner*, which moves freely among ideological, social, and aesthetic considerations. This rescue effort certainly is, as Adorno claims, an attempt to make visible those aspects of Wagner's work that have either escaped ideology or can, against Wagner's own intentions, be turned against its ideological underpinnings. Unlike the later essays, which are concerned with recovering Wagner's progressiveness in musical technique, *In Search of Wagner* primarily explores the relationship between fascism and details of musical technique. As do all his writings on music, *In Search of Wagner* transcends traditional categories of musical criticism. Adorno's analyses of music consistently relate music back to society by drawing parallels between the development of music and social processes. Adorno's writings are preoccupied with music, and it could be argued that in many of his writings, especially the *Aesthetic Theory*, art becomes synonymous with music. Several music critics have pointed out the shortcomings of Adorno's Wagner critique in terms of musical theory. His criticism of music, and cultural phenomena in general, is at once immanent and transcendental, a philosophically eclectic approach that, as Martin Jay points out, makes his writings on music difficult to classify. As musical theorists, Carl Dahlhaus and Rainer Cadenbach point out that this eclectic strategy leads Adorno to formulate inaccuracies, misjudgments, and misinterpretations of musical phenomena.[188] While Adorno can be considered a sociologist of music, he transcends sociology because of his indebtedness to the philosophy of negative dialectics and to the introduction of psychological categories.[189] Jay proposes that one could speak of a musical philosophy, with the necessary caveat that it not be confused with the tradition of philosophical aesthetics. The major premises underlying Adorno's musical criticism are the direct consequence of his understanding of the relationship between music, and, by extension, art and society. His writings must also be understood in the context of the Marxist concepts of base and superstructure; criticism must move from the individual work to the larger social-economic context, from intrinsic to extrinsic analysis. Fredric Jameson describes this approach in the following way: "Such thinking thus recognizes an obligation to transcend the limits of specialized analysis at the same time that it respects the object's integrity as an independent entity."[190]

As Jay sees it, Adorno operates under the premises that music is a historical phenomenon that reflects, but does not *mirror*, society as a whole and that the aesthetic merit and social content of music are inseparable.

The dialectic of art and society effectively undermines the claim of art's autonomy. As a negation of society, high art reflects the social processes through their very negation. Neither the products of the culture industry nor high art exist independently of society; both reflect, one affirmatively and the other negatively, the same base structure and social processes which gave rise to their existence. Adorno's analysis of Wagner illustrates the inseparability of the aesthetic and the social on the one hand and the entwinement of art and the culture industry on the other. Although Nietzsche is not, as Huyssen claims, entirely oblivious to the commodification of culture, his critique of Wagner is more concerned with Wagner's conformity with the tastes and desires of his contemporaries than with the implications of commodification. Despite their differences, Nietzsche's and Adorno's critiques nevertheless focus on many similar issues and complement each other in these key respects.

Both Nietzsche and Adorno focus their attention on the totalitarian moments of Wagner's works, mainly because they criticize Wagner the artist as well as those aspects of this work that implicitly express his complicity with traditional values and political ideologies. Adorno devotes a chapter to Wagner as social character, and despite his claim that Nietzsche's incrimination of Wagner were "private" ones, his own charges against Wagner appear somewhat much more "private" than Nietzsche's, since Adorno presents more personal details about Wagner's private life than Nietzsche. However, in their discussions of Wagner both Nietzsche and Adorno tend to attach great significance to Wagner's personality as revealed through his work, but both refrain from indulging in overtly personal recriminations regarding his character. The chapter on Wagner's social character is essentially an expanded version of the points cited above in connection with Newman's biography. Of course, Wagner the man cannot be separated from Wagner the artist, just as the artist cannot be considered separately from his work: Wagner's tyrannical mentality finds reflection in the *Gesamtkunstwerk*, the leitmotif, and the preoccupation with effects in the musical compositions as well as in the stage productions, all of which can be seen as totalitarian aspects of his work.

In the epilogue to the Wagner discussion, Adorno defends his interest in Wagner as a social character by maintaining the distinction between forms of biographical inquisitiveness which invade the private sphere unnecessarily and a legitimate interest in the social character of the artist. *In Search of Wagner* explores, according to Adorno, the relationship between the person and the work down to the smallest detail of musical gesture, while refraining from cheap gossip.[191] An investigation into social character brings to light the issues through which the private person can be identified as an exponent and site of social tendencies. Adorno describes Wagner's social character as that of a hypocritical beggar. Wagner, who came from the "Bohemian milieu of dilettantish artists,"[192] begs for sympathy and for money. He developed a virtuosity that enabled him "to achieve bourgeois goals at the cost of his bourgeois integrity."[193] Wagner was deceptive and lacked character, two weaknesses that lead deeply into his work. His lack of restraint in begging, which suggests his identification with the those in power and his dependence upon bourgeois norms, finds expression in the absence of tension in his musical harmonies:

> The power of the existing order over the protester is so great that he is no longer capable of separating himself from it or even of putting up any genuine resistance: and in the same way there is an absence of tension in Wagner's harmony as it descends from the leading note and sinks from the dominant into the tonic. It is the fawning stance of the mother's boy who talks himself and others into believing that his kind parents can deny him nothing, for the very purpose of making sure that they don't.[194]

Full of self-praise and pomp, features that Wagner's productions share with the fascist mass spectacle, Wagner denounces the victims in private and in his work. Wagner has the sadistic desire to humiliate through his cruel sense of humor. Adorno cites numerous characters from Wagner's music dramas that are insulted and ridiculed, including Mime and Alberich of the *Ring*. The object of Wagner's insults is not simply ridicule: "in the excitement caused by the laughter at his expense the memory of the injustice that he has suffered is obliterated. The use of laughter to suspend justice is debased into a charter for injustice."[195] Wagner's anti-Semitism constitutes itself from this contradiction between mockery of the victim and self-denigration. His seemingly idiosyncratic hatred of Jews is of the type that Walter Benjamin had in mind when he defined "disgust as the fear of being thought to be the same as that which is found disgusting."[196] Investigating the rumors of Wagner's Jewish ancestry, which circulated in Germany during Wagner's lifetime, Newman found that they all lead back to Nietzsche. Adorno contends that the rumors can be explained with Nietzsche's recognition of what Benjamin later defined as fear and disgust. Nietzsche, who despised Wagner's anti-Semitism, had seen through the idiosyncracies of Wagner's hatred, he "knew the secret," and he finally broke the spell by naming it.[197]

Although Adorno denies this later in the "Nachschrift" of 1964, he does appear to agree with Nietzsche that Wagner is a multifaceted dilettante. Adorno cites Thomas Mann's "The Sorrows and Grandeur of Richard Wagner," which takes up Nietzsche's charge of Wagner's dilettantism, and he contends that the indignant reaction to Mann's mention of the word *dilettante* in connection with Wagner proves that it touches a raw nerve. Mann writes:

> Observing him with passion and admiration one might say, at the risk of being misunderstood, that Wagner's art is a case of dilettantism that has been monumentalized by the supreme effort of the will and intelligence—a dilettantism raised to the level of genius.[198]

In the "Nachschrift" Adorno claims that his critics have not read his text carefully enough and that his argument was that Wagner touched the sphere of dilettantism, but grew out of it and eventually escaped it. The ambiguity of the parts from *In Search of Wagner* which surround the Mann citation and to which Adorno refers in his self-citation of the "Nachschrift" allows indeed for the interpretation that Wagner escaped dilettantism. However, since Adorno speaks in fact just two pages later of the "dilettantish features of Wagner's character" and of Wagner's inability to overcome the "fundamental stance of the amateur";[199] those critics suggesting Adorno's agreement with the charge of dilettantism in the *Die Zeit*'s Wagner discussions have done so with some textual evidence.

Adorno certainly agrees with Mann's and Nietzsche's assessment of the essentially amusical nature of Wagner's relationship to music. Adorno maintains that the early Wagner made "clumsy errors in part writing and in linking chords" and diagnoses "slips in modulation" and "harmonic balance" in his later work.[200] Wagner takes up attitudes, and the music becomes subordinated to rhetoric, "parasitical upon language," while it "slavishly follows the curve of the linguistic flow."[201] In Wagner, music degenerates to a commentary to the stage action and thus takes on a similarly illustrative role as music in films. By reducing it to an interpretive function, music is drained of "all the energies that make it a language remote from meaning, pure sound," and thus loses its integrity.[202] Wagner's music mirrors the relationship of writing to the word, in that its expression does not present itself, but is itself the object of presentation.[203] Nietzsche contends that Wagner abandoned all style in music by instrumentalizing it as theatrical rhetoric, a mere expressive medium that underscores gestures and the picturesque. Wagner, Nietzsche notes with irony, is the Victor Hugo of music as language; music becomes language, instrument, and *ancilla dramaturgica*.[204] Wagner abandons style by regressing to the elementary: "what he wants is effect, nothing but effect."[205] Adorno criticizes these dramatic gestures in a similar fashion, because they cannot be developed but only repeated and reinforced. The element of gesture articulates reified, alienated reality that is drawn into the artistic effect and into the relationship with the public.[206] Nietzsche asks if Wagner could be seen as a musician at all; Wagner, a genius of the theater and a scenic artist *par excellence*, does not belong to the history of music:

> Wagner was *not* a musician by instinct. He showed this by abandoning all lawfulness and, more precisely, all style in music in order to turn it into what he required, theatrical rhetoric, a means of expression, of underscoring gestures, of suggestion, of the psychologically picturesque. . . . Wagner's music . . . is simply bad music, perhaps the worst ever made.[207]

Nietzsche saw in Wagner an actor who became a musician in order to act out his tyrannical mentality, while Adorno sees Wagner's musical gestures as manifestations of the "unlimited symbolic power" Wagner held over the masses. Wagner was also the first composer to write in the grand style music for the bourgeois profession of the conductor.[208] The fundamental gesture of Wagner's music is beating and striking blows, and "through such a system of gestures Wagner's social impulses are translated into technique."[209] Nietzsche and Adorno are both in agreement regarding their understanding of the beat of Wagner's music: it exemplifies his regression to the elementary and the barbaric. Wagner's music has the tendency to disguise the estrangement between the composer and the listener by incorporating the listeners into his work as an element of "effect": "As an advocate of effect, the conductor is the advocate of the public in the work. As the striker of blows, however, the composer-conductor gives the claims of the public a terroristic emphasis."[210] However, the Wagnerian gestures are mere translations onto the stage of the imagined reactions of the audience, such as murmuring, applause, the triumph of self-confirmation and the waves of enthusiasm. Thus the archaic muteness of the gestures is a "highly contemporary instrument of domination."[211] In this way the composer-conductor both represents and suppresses the bourgeois individual's demand to be heard.

Both Nietzsche and Adorno question Wagner's integrity; Wagner sold himself out by appealing to the taste of the masses and by taking a self-satisfied and complacent attitude toward authority.

> The dilettantish features in Wagner's character are inseparable from those of his conformism, of his resolute collusion with the public. Enthroned as conductor, he is able to enforce this collusion whilst maintaining the appearance of strongly individual opposition, and to establish the power of impotence in the realm of aesthetics.[212]

Behind Wagner's aesthetization of powerlessness, Adorno suspects economic self-interest. His eagerness to please his audience and his sponsor plays a role in Wagner's rather cynical self-denunciation that provoked Nietzsche's break with him, which occurred, in Nietzsche's words, when "Richard Wagner . . . suddenly sank down, helpless and broken, before the Christian cross."[213] Adorno describes this capitulation in the following way:

> As important as the question of whether there really was a connection between the production of *Parsifal* and the economic interest of the founder of Bayreuth, is his gesture of self-immolation: not only does he beg shamelessly; he is also prepared to accuse himself of fraud and so plays almost wilfully into Nietzsche's hands.[214]

Since Wagner caters to the values of bourgeois society and Christian and political institutions, his artistic productions are predetermined by the prospect of success. Like the consumers of the products of the culture industry, Wagner's audience is the object of calculation: "democratic considerateness towards the listener is transformed into connivance with the powers of discipline: in the name of the listener, anyone whose feelings accord with any yardstick other than the beat of the music is silenced."[215] The audience's estrangement from the composer-conductor is inseparable from the calculation of the effect on this audience, and like the consumers of the culture industry's products, the audience itself becomes the "reified object of calculation by the artist."[216] Wagner overwhelms his audience, just as the individual characters in his works are overwhelmed by powerful forces. The pretentious quality of his work heightens the impression of futility and defeat and satisfies the needs for a bourgeois mythology. Ironically, the power of the bourgeoisie over Wagner is so complete that it is impossible for him to achieve the ideals of bourgeois propriety. Nietzsche calls Wagner "the most *impolite* genius in the world,"[217] and like Adorno, remarks upon the calculation of effects and the complicity of the masses with the forces manipulating them:

> We know the masses, we know the theater. The best among those who sit there— German youths, horned Siegfrieds, and other Wagnerians—require the sublime, the profound, the overwhelming. That much we are capable of. And the others who also sit there—the culture crétins, the petty snobs, the eternally feminine, those with a happy digestion, in sum, the *people*—also require the sublime, the profound, the overwhelming.[218]

Nietzsche disliked the theater, because it represents for him on the one hand a form of entertainment for the masses, yet satisfies on the other the tastes of those who think of themselves as educated, refined, and above the masses. Nietzsche's perception of the theater in many ways foreshadows Adorno's critique of the culture industry. In accordance with his critique of decadence, Nietzsche maintains that Wagner's music is a numbing intoxication that takes revenge on life. It is music for the sick who need a god and savior, and it provides idiots with the logic for a conceptual understanding of life.[219]

Both Adorno and Nietzsche criticize Wagner for advocating the ascetic ideal, which they see as part of his self-denunciation. For Nietzsche this asceticism found expression in Wagner's grovelling before the Christian cross, while for Adorno, Wagner's promotion of asceticism forms a mere pretense for the perpetuation of bourgeois morality. Adorno contends that Wagner's self-proclaimed attempt to find a balance between the "unrestrained sexuality" of his early work and the ideal of asceticism has nothing to do with a mature artistic development, because this balance is "achieved in the name of death."[220] Wagner equates pleasure and death, and thus a reconciliation between sexuality and asceticism is not possible in life, but only at the moment of death. Similarly, Nietzsche argues that Wagner's seductiveness lies in the reconciliation of beauty and disease and that the ascetic ideal invoked by Wagner's works expresses impoverishment and exhaustion. In the third essay of the *Genealogy*, Nietzsche asks for the meaning of the ascetic ideal for the artist. The answer: the ascetic ideal means either nothing or so much that the multiplicity of meaning reverts to meaninglessness. In the artist, the ascetic ideal does not deserve attention, because artists do not stand independently enough in and against the world for their values to be taken seriously: "They have at all times been valets of some morality, philosophy, or religion; quite apart from the fact that they have unfortunately often been all-too-pliable courtiers of their own followers and patrons, and cunning flatterers of ancient or newly arrived powers."[221] However, judging by Nietzsche's numerous remarks, Wagner's surrender to the ascetic ideal, which culminated in *Parsifal*, does seem to warrant some attention. In Wagner, Nietzsche takes it—to some extent—seriously, because it is dishonest, deceptive, and lacks genuineness. For Nietzsche, *Parsifal* is symptomatic for the hatred of knowledge and sensuality, and, as Sarah Kofman observes, "it marks neither the apotheosis of the artistic life nor the summit of art, but rather an artist's renunciation of himself and his ideals, which had until then linked together the spirituality and sensuality in his art and his life."[222] In fact, the ascetic ideal is opposed to art and is fundamentally anti-artistic. Art, as Nietzsche defines it in the *Twilight*, is the great stimulus to life, and the ascetic ideal, according to the *Genealogy*, is the will to nothingness. However, the human will, in Nietzsche's view, needs a goal and "it will rather will nothingness than not will" at all.[223] The ascetic ideal signifies the will to power through negation, self-cancellation, and a return to "morbid" Christian values.[224] By stylizing suffering into the highest value, asceticism combines, as in Wagner's works, pleasure with suffering. Poverty, humility, chastity are the slogans of the ascetic ideal, which seeks pleasure in decay, pain, voluntary deprivation, and self-sacrifice. As the highest affirmation of life, art opposes the ascetic ideal's "intellectual perversity,"[225] embodied by its hostility toward sensuality and its negation of life. Under the influence of Schopenhauer's nihilism and theory of the sovereignty of music, Wagner began to see himself as an ascetic priest, a mouthpiece for the things in themselves, "a telephone from the beyond" uttering metaphysics.[226] He subsequently underwent the "most distinctive corruption of an artist" by placing himself in the service of the ascetic ideal.[227]

For Adorno, Wagner's adherence to the ascetic ideal parallels his struggle with bourgeois morality, a collusion ultimately affirmed by his siding with those in power. By reproducing Schopenhauer's pessimism, Wagner dissents from the rebellion against the deleterious conditions of society. In Wagner, the will itself is not negated, but only

> the objectification of the Will in the Idea, in the phenomenal world. The Will itself, in other words the essence of the undirected social process, continues to be accepted in a spirit of compliant admiration. The individual then acquiesces without demur in his own annihilation, deeming it the work of that Will which has ceased to oppose itself to itself as Nature.[228]

Adorno sees a contradiction between Wagner and Schopenhauer. For Schopenhauer, the idea's renunciation of its own Will-to-Life comes from its recognition of injustice and therefore represents a break with the vicious circle of blind fate, while in Wagner the will turns into blind fate. For Wagner, pleasure assumes the features of death and destruction, and in return death, serving as an advertisement for itself, is celebrated as a "soaring joy" and the greatest good. In contrast, Adorno notes that "[i]n Schopenhauer, suffering appears as a 'mere phenomenon,' its very shabbiness and meanness make its seriousness evident. In Wagner it is trivialized by the accoutrements of grandeur."[229] According to Adorno, Wagner's role as an artist exemplifies the changing function of the individual under bourgeois ideology. The bourgeois individual seeks to escape destruction in the hopeless struggle with the authorities by siding with them. In this way, Wagner's own career parallels and reflects the decay of the bourgeoisie and the rise of fascism. The impotent petitioner becomes the tragic panegyrist: "For the focal points of decay in the bourgeois character, in terms of its own morality, are the prototypes of its subsequent transformation in the age of totalitarianism."[230] Nietzsche comments on Wagner's obedience training of the audience and shares Adorno's detestation of the authoritarian and anti-Semitic tendencies in Wagner's work: "since Wagner had moved to Germany, he had condescended step by step to everything I despise—even to anti-Semitism."[231] Like Adorno, Nietzsche does not hesitate to draw direct parallels between Wagner and the rise of totalitarian ideologies, nor does he shrink from relating Wagner's work to political and historical reality. He writes that the ideal of decadence requires virtue in the form of

> training, automatism, "self-denial." . . . It is full of profound significance that the arrival of Richard Wagner coincides in time with the arrival of the "*Reich*": both events prove the very same thing: obedience and long legs.—Never has obedience been better, never has commanding. . . . Wagner understood how to command.[232]

Wagner's concept of the *Gesamtkunstwerk* is simultaneously an expression and instrument of the power demanding obedience. Both Nietzsche and Adorno saw in this concept a rationally constructed attempt at artificial wholeness that in the end lacks free will. Wagner creates a false identity and disregards particularity and the interest of the individual. Without realizing that the social conditions necessary for the survival of unity are absent, Wagner wants to will an aesthetic unity into being. Wagnerian totality and the *Gesamtkunstwerk* are doomed to failure, because they subordinate the individual elements and subsume the non-identical. The stylistic failure of the music drama is the result of his arbitrary combination of different elements and genres, which disregards the individuality and the internal requirements of the artistic material and tries to hide them. Instead of creating style, Wagner strives for stylization: "The whole no longer achieves unity, because its expressive elements are made to harmonize with each other according to a pre-arranged design. . . . The formal premises of an internal logic are replaced by a seamless external principle in which disparate procedures are simply aggregated in such a way as to make them appear collectively binding."[233] Adorno contends that Wagner's seemingly unified totality, which turns out in the end to be a mere illusion, owes its existence to the extirpation of the individual. Wagner was the first to place the uneven development of the arts, and indeed irrationality itself, into a rationally constructed frame-work. Wagner's music dramas pave the way for the listener's adaptation to the order of bourgeois rationality, that is, the culture industry, which privileges sight over hearing. Hearing becomes a kind of "dozing" that is subject to "psycho-rational control."[234]

Wagner's unity represents for Nietzsche an artificial construct: "The whole no longer lives at all: it is composite, calculated, artificial, and artifact."[235] Wag-ner creates an impenetrable mixture of effects that forces the audience to surren-der. According to Nietzsche, the operas hypnotize the audience into resignation; "into mute, rigid, deaf resignation, self-forgetting, self-extinction."[236] For Adorno, the basic idea of the *Gesamtkunstwerk* is revealed in the mental flight, the abdication of everything unequivocal, and the negation of individuality. Adorno links the *Gesamtkunstwerk* directly to totalitarian ideology and the regression of listening. Evocative of the fascist dictum that subordinates the par-ticular to the so-called common good, the *Gesamtkunstwerk* forces a reconcilia-tion between its various artistic elements and its genre. Its eclectic combination of old and new elements offers constantly new stimuli that nevertheless never affront the "well-worn habits" of regressive listening.[237] Wagner's music dramas construct something resembling an epic totality and simulate the unity of the internal and external, the subject and the object "instead of giving shape to the rupture between them. In this way the process of composition becomes the agent of ideology."[238] As Adorno sees it, the principle of false identity forbids the con-struction of a unity from the contradictions of art forms alienated from each other. Furthermore, the *Gesamtkunstwerk* signifies the victory of technology and rationality over the aesthetic and foreshadows the technical productions of the culture industry. Wagner's call for a style of declamation is as symptomatic of his hostility to standard musical forms as of the need to synthesize the arts; "but as in the case of the leitmotif this too prepares the ground for the technical, rational work of art."[239] Similar to the products of the film industry, Wagner's elaborate and phantasmagoric stage productions aim toward a total illusion, and Adorno, using a Nietzschean turn of phrase, speaks of "the birth of film out of the spirit of music."[240]

The concept of the *Gesamtkunstwerk* is related to Wagner's interpretation of Hegel's philosophy. Nietzsche argues that Wagner understands the German taste for Hegel and puts it into his music, which in turn seductively proffers the Hegelian idea of the absolute. It is thus the predominance of the realm of the idea and ideals that brought about Wagner's popularity:

> It was not with his music that Wagner conquered them, it was with the "idea"—it is the enigmatic character of his art, its playing hide-and-seek behind a hundred sym-bols, its polychromy of the ideal that leads and lures these youths to Wagner; it is Wagner's genius for shaping clouds, his whirling, hurling, and twirling through the air, his everywhere and nowhere—the very same means by which Hegel formerly seduced and lured them![241]

For Adorno, Wagner is a Hegelian *Weltgeist-Regisseur*, for whom the individual is a mere puppet in the hands of the World-Spirit, who manipulates him or her by means of technological rationality.[242] Wagner's work is a metaphor for the totality of world history, but it fails to articulate dialectically the antagonism between the universal and the particular, just as it is devoid of any hope for an altered condition in which the recurrent antagonism might vanish.[243] Wagner's flight from the philosophy of history ends, beyond self-glorification and the legitimization of claims to power, at the identification of resistance with domination. Adorno's rejection of Wagner's *Gesamtkunstwerk* might well be seen as the most pointed instance of his famous critique of totality in *Minima Moralia*, in which he converts Hegel's dictum "The whole is the true" to "The whole is the untrue."[244] The *Gesamtkunstwerk* not only expresses metaphysics, but produces it, and can be seen as no longer in conformity with the Hegelian definition of art as the sensuous manifestation of the idea. Instead, the sensuous is arranged to appear to be in control of the idea. The technological intoxication is generated from the fear of sobriety and the need to feel in control.[245]

Wagner's totalitarian *Gesamtkunstwerk* erases the boundaries of genre not out of artistic necessity, but rather out of desire for effects. With Wagner's intentions in mind, Adorno thus differentiates Wagner's *Gesamtkunstwerk* from the attempts of the Romantics to overcome the boundaries between genres, periods, and disciplines. Nietzsche contends that the Romantic ideal of the *unendliche Melodie* (endless or infinite melody) has become in Wagner "infinity, but without melody,"[246] and compares *Parsifal* with the suffocating "rumination of moral and religious absurdities," a phrase employed by Goethe to describe the danger threatening all Romantics.[247] Adorno argues that the Romantic concept of synesthesia neither fuses elements by assimilation and subjugation nor attempts to erase the differences between the components of their artistic mixtures or between art and reality. The *Gesamtkunstwerk*, however, denies the particularity of its elements in favor of an illusory unity and hides this orchestrated and forced reconciliation, which has been imposed by the arbitrary will of the artist; in this way, the totalizing process of composition parallels the establishment of ideology. With their use of phantasmagoria, Wagner's *total works of art* are the early miracles of modern technology, which immortalize the moment in history between the death of Romanticism and the birth of realism. They anticipate the products of the culture industry, because the miracles and wonders of technology render the works as impenetrable as the daily reality of reified society. The works, through their magic, function like commodities that satisfy the needs of the culture market.[248] It is Adorno's view that there are only scenes in Wagner's work directly affected by the conditions of commodity production. However, the music in these scenes takes the greatest care to disguise its production in a passive, visionary presence. The phantasmagoria gives Wagner's work dreamlike features that pose as the deluded wish-fulfillment of potential buyers. However, phantasmagoria commodifies art not so much by producing illusions and promising the consumer gratification, but more by concealing the labor that has gone into making it. Thus, the use of phantasmagoria fetishizes the products of labor while rendering them no longer identifiable as such.[249] Wagner's technologically induced miracles are works of deception (*Blendwerk*), and by erasing the traces of production, aesthetic illusion takes on the character of the commodity. The quantification of industrial labor parallels the fragmentation into minute parts: "Broken down into the smallest units, the totality is supposed to become controllable, and it must submit to the will of the subject who has liberated himself from all existing forms."[250]

In addition to the technique of phantasmagoria, the leitmotif further enhances the commodification of his art. Wagner's compulsive and repetitive musical gestures, in Adorno's opinion, evade the necessity of creating musical time, thus violating musical characterization.[251] Nietzsche contends that Wagner was unable to create a totality, and was forced "to make patchwork, 'motifs,' gestures, formulas, doing things double and even hundredfold."[252] Adorno compares the leitmotif with an *idée fixe* that denies the possibility for change, since this particular musical gesture favors repetition over development. Wagner's repetition of musical motifs merely poses as development and raises the expectations of something new, which fails to materialize. According to Adorno, in this discovery lies the grain of truth in the otherwise unfounded charge of formlessness.[253] The formlessness is not, as Nietzsche claims, the product of chaos, but of a false identity. When identical materials appear and reappear as if they were something new, they negate the flow of time and "fail to do justice" to it.[254]

Wagner operates with musical formulas created for the stage,[255] which function like commercials: "anticipating the universal practice of mass culture later on, the music is designed to be remembered, it is intended for the forgetful."[256] In the leitmotif, genuinely constructed motifs are replaced by repetitious associations. Adorno contends that psychology later refers to this phenomenon as ego-weakness, a psychological state "on which Wagner's music is already predicated."[257]

By hiding the traces of production, the products present themselves as self-producing, and in the absence of any glimpse of the underlying forces or conditions of production, aesthetic illusion claims the status of being.[258] Hiding the processes of labor and production also implies concealing the intensified division of labor connected to the stage productions:

> The flawed nature of the whole conception of music drama is nowhere more evident than where it comes closest to its own foundations: in the concealment of the process of production, in Wagner's hostility towards the division of labour on which it is agreed that the culture industry is based. In theory and in the ideology of his works, he rejected the division of labour in terms that recall Nationalist Socialist phrases about the subordination of private interests to the public good.[259]

Adorno views works of art as consistently the result of the social division of intellectual and physical labor. The idea of sound from which the traces of production are removed leads more deeply into the commodity, and by exaggerating its claim to a "natural" character, Wagner's works actually become artificial. Wagner's *oeuvre* resembles the consumer goods of the nineteenth century, which attempted to conceal every sign of the labor gone into producing them, "perhaps because any such trace reminded people too vehemently of the appropriation of the labour of others, of an injustice that could still be felt."[260] The concealment of labor is the contradiction of all autonomous art, but in high capitalism, "with the complete hegemony of exchange-value and with the contradictions arising out of that hegemony, autonomous art becomes both problematic and programmatic at the same time."[261] Wagner does not have the good conscience to admit that his works are illusions, and thereby confirms what his ideology of artistic creation denies: "work is degrading."[262]

Nietzsche also criticizes Wagner's failure to admit to the constructedness of his operas and to offer his audience the possibility of experiencing the process of artistic creation. As a ironic gesture, he contrasts Wagner's to Bizet's music. Nietzsche tells Carl Fuchs in a letter that he is not serious about his estimation of Bizet, that he merely used him as an "ironic antithesis" to Wagner.[263] In *The Case of Wagner*, Nietzsche claims that, unlike Wagner, Bizet's music has a logic in its passion. In Bizet, the composition follows its own dynamic: "I actually bury my ears under this music to hear its causes. It seems to me I experience its genesis."[264] Bizet's music liberates the spirit and gives wings to thought; "it builds, organizes, finishes. . . . Without grimaces. Without counterfeit. Without the *lie* of the great style."[265] In contrast to Wagner, who repeats himself until one despairs, Bizet's music treats its listeners as intelligent human beings. Bizet's music is polite and subtle, while Wagner's tone is brutal and artificial. Wagner's music cannot be experienced as a process of becoming, but rather as a contrived entity:

> The danger reaches its climax when such music leans more and more heavily on a wholly naturalistic style of acting and gestures, which is no longer dominated by any law of plasticity, and wants *effect*, nothing more. *Espressivo* at any price, and music in the service, the slavery, of poses—*that is the end.*[266]

Wagner's role as an actor is a second reason for Nietzsche's repeated criticism. Nietzsche claims that Wagner's music dramas belong to the theater, which Nietzsche despised as mass entertainment, rather than to opera. Here he locates in Wagner the decay of art and the decay of the artist, which finds "expression in the formula: the musician now becomes an actor, his art develops more and more as a talent to *lie*."[267] In *Minima Moralia*, Adorno argues that Nietzsche should not have reproached Wagner for being an actor, because all art, including music, is related to drama and acting. What Nietzsche should have criticized is the "actor's denial of play-acting."[268] In Adorno's mind, Wagner cannot be reproached for acting, just as he cannot be reproached for creating illusions. The problem is therefore not the creation of illusions but the failure to admit to it. In the process by which the difference between illusion and reality is erased and the traces of production are concealed, the illusions become totalized.

The gestures, motifs, and the arrangements of musical time favor repetition over development, and these musical qualities are a reflection of Wagner's view of the world. The music dramas reproduce and reinforce his view of the futility of human action. Salvation is thus the only hope for change, and Nietzsche sees the need for redemption as the most honest expression of the decadent spirit in Wagner; it is the most convincing, "most painful affirmation of decadence in the form of sublime symbols and practices."[269] Redemption is the Christian's hope for deliverance from himself. Christianity itself cannot be refuted, in the same way that "one cannot refute a disease of the eye."[270] What should be discredited, however, is the falsehood with which Wagner seeks to cover up the contradiction between classical aesthetics and decadent art on the one hand and the morality of the masters and Christian morality on the other. Wagner's good conscience about the concealment of these opposites, his "lie" is, however, modern *par excellence*, in that "it almost defines modernity" and the ambiguity of the modern condition.[271] In light of the biologically divided state of modern man, it is not surprising that "in our times falsehood itself has become flesh and even genius."[272] Wagner's falsehood is his attempt to obscure the fact that he is a decadent. Decadence, however, is the only honest expression of Wagner, but Wagner refuses to face up to his decadent self and is therefore unable to overcome it.

Adorno remarks that Wagner's pessimism and the immutability of conditions portrayed in his works, which create the need for redemption, hypostasizes the metaphysical principle of meaninglessness into a meaning endowed upon a meaningless, empirical reality. Wagner's pessimism is the philosophy of the apostate rebel:

> What he retains from his rebellion is his insight into the evil nature of the world "as such," as an extrapolation from an evil present, as well as the further insight into the inexorable reproduction of that evil. He defects from rebellion simply by elevating this process to the status of an all-embracing metaphysical principle. As something immutable to all eternity, it derides all efforts to alter it and acquires the reflected glory of a dignity which it withholds from man.[273]

However, not all is lost for Wagner. What seemed somewhat unsalvageable in 1938, the time in which most of the chapters were written, was redeemed in Adorno's 1952 announcement for his complete essay collection *In Search of Wagner*. Although he had in the text of the book already defended Wagner against the voices criticizing his decadence, Adorno articulates in his short critical notice a way to rescue Wagner, by making the interesting move of reaffirming the critical potential of decadence. Adorno argues that the ambiguities and breaks of Wagner's work reflect the historical moment of their production. Where the breaks become visible, Wagner's works genuinely reflect the modern condition: "But the fault-line discernible in Wagner's work—his impotence in the face of the technical contradictions and the social conflicts underlying them, in short all the qualities that prompted his contemporaries to speak of 'decadence'—is also the path of artistic progress."[274] Adorno takes up once again the connection between decadence and artistic progress in the announcement, in which he argues that the morbid and nihilistic quality of decadent art constitutes a resistance to the requirements of the healthy, strong, and all-powerful blond beast. Here Adorno creates a space for criticism, a space where, against its own intentions, Wagner's work refuses to sanction the ideologies of power. In opposition to Nietzsche, Adorno does not condemn decadence as self-destructive, but instead maintains that it contains the seeds of the new and different. By affirming its critical potential, Adorno follows the tradition of Baudelaire and takes another step toward the positive reevaluation of decadence. Critics should be careful with their judgment of decadence with regard to Wagner, Adorno maintains, because

> whatever makes Wagner better than the social order (to whose dark powers he aligned himself) owes itself to decadence, to the damaged subject's incapability of playing sufficiently by the rules of the existing social order. In this way he fails to meet the expectations of health, cleverness, communication, and mutual understanding, and turns silently against the power in whose service his language stands. It is not the unshakably self-assertive form, but rather the decaying form that indicates the coming of the new.[275]

Adorno's argument echoes Nietzsche's view from the *Genealogy*, in which he argues that the "weak" slave morality will eventually reverse the relations of power, and of aphorism 224 in *Human, All Too Human*, which insists that the weak, deformed, and sick elements that defy integration and stand outside of the social consensus bring about change and give birth to the new. In *The Case of Wagner*, "the great corruption of music," Nietzsche denies the possibility for a positive reevaluation of sickness: "Sickness itself can be a stimulant to life: only one has to be healthy enough for this stimulant. Wagner increases exhaustion: that is why he attracts the weak and exhausted,"[276] and, one might add, the regressed listener. For Adorno, the refusal of the social requirement for health, efficiency, communication, and consent constitutes the critical moment of modern art. It is the decaying form and the injured subject that give expression to the non-identical and give rise to the new and the different by revealing "the trace of something better."[277] In contrast to Nietzsche, Adorno values the decadent negation of life, because for Adorno *life* constitutes itself in a concrete social-political context, from which it cannot be separated. To negate *life* is therefore also to negate the existing conditions and claims to power. It is this negativity that Adorno appreciates in art, including so-called decadent art, and, ironically, in Nietzsche's philosophy. While he strongly disagrees with Nietzsche's evaluation of decadence, he is most enthusiastic about Nietzsche's powers of negation. As one of the most advanced enlighteners of all, Nietzsche's thought is most potent in its radical negation of traditional values, his critique of totality and systems, and his refusal to comply with authority or conform to bourgeois ideology.

Through his critique of Wagner, Adorno shows the interconnection of the geneses of the culture industry and authentic, autonomous art on the one hand and the inseparable bond between the progressive and the regressive moments of art on the other. Adorno recognizes that the evolution of art, music, and "in particular the emergence of the autonomous sovereignty of the artist . . . is intertwined with the origins of the culture industry."[278] If one acknowledges the complicity of art with the culture industry, the celebration of the possibilities of autonomous art and the unrelenting critique of the culture industry point toward the impossibility of upholding a rigid separation. Since commodification invades autonomous art, it puts at risk art's negative and critical potential. Such an invasion simultaneously invites the question as to whether the products of the culture industry are not, in a dialectical fashion, invaded by the negativity of autonomous art. Seen within the dialectic of myth and enlightenment, autonomous art cannot be had without the culture industry. That Adorno wanted the one without the other, that he practically denied the products of the culture industry a critical potential, contradicts his own dialectic, but must, however, be seen in the context of his concerns for the dissolution of the subject. The old subject has dissolved "without yet giving rise to a new one"[279] and is neither resistant to manipulation and domination, and in Nietzsche's terms, nor healthy and strong enough to withstand the spread of the disease. Nietzsche's and Adorno's view of the audience as a gullible, manipulated object absorbed by a dialectic of regression does make it clear that their hopes for the possibility of change and the traces of the better do not rest with the masses.

According to the dialectic of myth and enlightenment, it is not improper to search for pockets of resistance within the culture industry or for points at which the culture industry, against its own intentions, turns against its own ideology. In the fast-paced climate of perpetual change, where something is "in" one minute and "out" the next, the commodification process makes it increasingly difficult to locate points of resistance before they turn into icons of conformity. Pessimism and the refusal to conform to artistic norms and standards have become marketable commodities in the film and music industry and the mass media. The nihilism expressed in the music, which rejects norms and standards, sells not only millions of albums, but also millions of gadgets and other paraphernalia. If decadence, as an *überhistorisches* phenomenon and as power of negation, is to be rescued from commercial and ideological subsumption, then it is imperative to formulate theories of culture that acknowledge the entwinement of the sphere of art and the culture industry without attempting to obliterate their differences. Adorno's Wagner critique suggests a mode of criticism that establishes a connection between art and the social-historical conditions under which it is produced, and it further suggests that criticism must undermine the traditional disciplinary boundaries between the arts, humanities, and the social sciences.

Nietzsche's critique of Wagner represents a productive basis for such an undertaking, since Nietzsche defied disciplinary boundaries as well. Nietzsche not only recognized the dialectic of enlightenment, but his astute critique of Wagner also locates in his work the dawn of modern art as well as the ideology of the culture industry. Nietzsche already perceives in Wagner what Adorno later criticizes in the culture industry, such as overwhelming and bombastic gestures, repetitions, the use of the leitmotif, and the attempt to cater to a mass audience. Nietzsche's diagnosis of modernity and the development of modern art has not been overtaken by history, although his evaluation of these phenomena may be seen as such. As Adorno shows, it is not the resistance against decadence but rather the resistance against the glorification of bourgeois values that protest against the norms of the administered world of capitalism. Philosophizing with the hammer, Nietzsche—who personally and professionally lived on the margins of society—offers the dynamite to blow apart bourgeois ideology. However, in the matter of decadence, he falls—to argue with Adorno—under the sway of the norms of the bourgeois society he despised.

EXCURSUS

The Critiques of *Bildung*

Nietzsche's and Adorno's respective critiques of *Bildung* constitute a significant aspect of their cultural criticism. Since education lays the foundations for consciousness, it is not only an integral part of culture and society but is also a formative element in social and political developments and the preservation of cultural memory. While passing pertinent knowledge and insights on to the next generation helps a society and culture survive, so too, as Nietzsche argues in the "Advantages and Disadvantages of History," does the repression of certain aspects of historical knowledge and consciousness. "Forgetting" some aspects of history and collective and individual experience is a prerequisite for political, social, and personal action. "Forgetting" becomes problematic, however, when selective memory becomes institutionalized repression. For Nietzsche, forgetting is, paradoxically, an active process of consciousness that is required to overcome the paralyzing influence of historical knowledge and to forestall the formation of bad conscience and self-castigation. Strictly speaking, it is of course impossible to turn forgetting into a conscious act, because if one forgets something, one forgets that one is forgetting. In criticizing the damaging surplus of historical knowledge passed on to the younger generation, Nietzsche argues—in opposition to both institutionalized excess and repression—for a critical view of history and a conscious choice of a culture to take control of its memory. Therefore, Nietzsche's emphasis upon forgetting should not be interpreted as a call for social amnesia, but rather as a pronounced opposition to the expansion of positivist rationality.

Although Nietzsche and Adorno favor the education of citizens, they critically view the institutionalization of education in light of a dialectic of enlightenment: education enlightens, but it also perpetuates bourgeois morality and the political status quo. Implicit in their critique of the educational system is their belief in a form of education marked by humanistic concerns for the emancipation of the individual. Their critiques of *Bildung* also make clear that neither Nietzsche nor Adorno abandons the idea of enlightenment. Furthermore, their engagement with this issue can also be read as a call for the emancipation of the educational systems from the political, social, and moral constraints imposed upon them by the state, society, and the church. However, both thinkers refuse to furnish advice regarding concrete reforms to the system. This refusal appears to be based upon the conviction that isolated reforms of the educational system alone would be ineffective, for in both thinkers the critique of *Bildung* is very much integrated into their critique of the modern condition.

The agendas of the state and the church determine the quality of education, and the quality of education in turn directly affects not only the political and social climate, but also the quality of cultural productions. The status of *Bildung* is therefore a measure of the future position and condition of culture. However, Nietzsche and Adorno clearly reject the exclusive relegation of *Bildung* to the realm of culture and morality, and clearly indicate its connection to economic developments. Both discuss the relationship between education, cultural conditioning, and economic status, and Nietzsche even shares Adorno's Marxist perspective on education when he speaks of a school system producing undereducated and more easily exploitable workers.

The word *Bildung* does not easily translate into the specific English term "education," for it includes, beyond the acquisition of knowledge, the development of the critical, moral, and creative faculties. *Bildung* aims not only at shaping and releasing the potential and talents of the individual, but also at molding character, behavior, and consciousness. It has a strong individualized component, and although *Bildung* propagates a shared body of knowledge, values, and judgments in its advancement of civilization and culture, its emphasis lies in the development of the individual's unique intellectual and creative capacities. In the realization of spiritual and moral nobility, the process of *Bildung* creates a human being in harmony with him- and herself and the world. The father of the German ideal of *Bildung*, Wilhelm von Humboldt, perceived it not so much as a goal to be achieved but as the purpose of human existence. His holistic concept emphasizes, in line with Kant, the duty of individuals to educate themselves to their true purpose, prescribed not by changing inclinations but by an eternal unchanging reason, which is the highest and most suitable formation of his powers to a whole.[1]

As a humanistic value, *Bildung* is associated with the project of enlightenment, classical and liberal arts education, and the rituals of high culture and the
bourgeoisie. While in the nineteenth century a knowledge of classical languages,
such as Latin and Greek, of science and mathematics, music, art, and literature
were essential components of a good education, today controversy arises over
which subjects should be included in the canon of learning. Today there is much
less agreement as to what and how subjects should be taught, which body of
knowledge should be shared, and with whom it should be shared. At its height in
the late eighties, recent discussions about the canon of knowledge still move
along ideological lines: while the so-called liberals, including feminists, Marxists, and multiculturalists, question the function of the canon as a ethnocentric,
sexist perpetuation of values, conservative cultural critics have advocated the
adherence to an—albeit expanded—cultural literacy project.[2] Confirming the
debate's continuation along outmoded party lines, is the recent remark by the editor of a major academic journal in the field of German studies: the editor portrays
cultural studies as inherently left-wing and the practice of close reading as inherently right-wing.[3]

The notion of *Bildung* includes the progressive as well as conservative
aspects of the educational process, for *Bildung* aims at nurturing the freedom of
the spirit on the one hand and the preservation of cultural values on the other.
While idealized notions of *Bildung* propagate it—not unlike genuine art—as a
value in itself and by itself, it contributes to social, political, and economic
progress. Nietzsche's and Adorno's questioning of notions of progress, enlightenment, and their deep distrust of rationality have put into question the project of
Bildung, provoking a reevaluation of its goals and purpose in modern society.
Although elitist and conservative on the one hand, Nietzsche's and Adorno's critiques of the educational institutions advocate a critical concept of *Bildung*, one
that fits neither the conservative nor the liberal mold and thus escapes one-sided
labelling.

Adorno's "Theory of Pseudo-Education" (*Theorie der Halbbildung*) is
closely connected to his critique of Enlightenment. In the *Dialectic*, Adorno and
Horkheimer use the example of Odysseus to illustrate how the emancipation of
the individual is inevitably bound to self-repression. The dialectical relationship
between liberation and subjugation render enlightenment and myth inseparable—enlightenment inevitably reverts to myth, and myth already contains within
it elements of enlightenment. In this way, "progress," in terms of the emancipation of the individual and the progressive development in history, is hindered by
regressive moves, among them the self-mutilation of the human spirit. Adorno
argues that *Halbbildung*, the contemporary replacement of *Bildung*, expresses
the individual's self-mutilation within modern culture. It is a level of *Bildung* that
further disenfranchises the disenfranchised, and at one point in the essay he
seems to privilege *Unbildung*, the state of being uneducated, over being partially
educated. He does bring forth a slightly more sophisticated variant of the ques-

tionable "ignorance is bliss" argument, which idealizes naïveté and intuitive knowledge in contrast to the corruption of the spirit. Adorno claims that the half-education dispensed to the masses by educational institutions hinders the emancipation of the individual while simultaneously severing ties to tradition. *Halbbildung* acts as an agent of conformity, and although it promises the expansion of the mind through education, it does not fulfill its promise, leaving the individual in a state of limbo between enlightenment and myth. It fails to effect true emancipation and destroys the intuitive understanding upon which unconscious and immediate action is based. Adorno's view of *Bildung*, or rather the institutions providing *Halbbildung*, parallels his view of the culture industry, which produces an almost inextricable web of ideological manipulations, fetishizes both myth and enlightenment, and thereby annihilates any emancipatory content. *Halbbildung* is bound to the principle of exchange and is an integral part of the web of bourgeois delusion: it is a state in which the spirit has been taken hostage by the fetish character of the commodity.[4] Indeed, *Bildung* itself becomes both a commodity and a financial investment into the financial future of the individual. With his critique of the commercialization of *Bildung*, Adorno foresaw one of the major trends of higher education today, namely that few today—at least in the North American context—can afford to spend tens of thousands of dollars on a liberal arts education with little hope of future financial reward. Certainly, Adorno could not have foreseen the extent to which institutions of higher learning have been forced in the last decades to bow to the pressures of the marketplace.

Since the question of *Bildung* is embedded in the social reality of the dominant exchange principle and the culture industry, Adorno is not overtly concerned with reforms of the educational system. To the disappointment of many of his students in the sixties, he refused to provide practical guidance for their struggle against the system and at times rejected their pleas for support. Many never forgave him for having students arrested during the sit-in at the Frankfurt Institute. Adorno's thoughts on education and pedagogy are entwined with his philosophical and political reflections, and he does not deliver recipes for the improvement of institutionalized education, but rather a profound indictment of modern civilization, of which the educational system is merely a symptom. Berndt Herrmann points out the difficulty of obtaining a coherent picture of Adorno's thoughts on education and maintains that Adorno's *Bildung* critique is a critique of the educational institution's microcosmic doubling of societal relations, which it does, however, not thematize. In Herrmann's view, Adorno aims at making visible the effects on the students of reality external to pedagogy, which are unreflectedly repeated by a pedagogy.[5]

More concretely, Adorno's critique of *Bildung* addresses the particularity of the German situation and the concerns regarding education after Auschwitz. Profoundly influenced by the recognition of humanism's failure to avert barbarism, Adorno begins his essay "Education after Auschwitz" by stating that the first and foremost goal of education is the demand that Auschwitz will never be repeated.[6] To achieve this requires the elimination of the political and social conditions fostering fascism and all forms of nationalism, racism, and anti-Semitism; as a further step it is necessary to gain an understanding of the individual and collective psyche that made fascism possible. In connection with his thoughts on education, Adorno refers repeatedly to Freud's theories of civilization, the psychology of the collective and the individual, early childhood development, and his own study of the authoritarian personality. Antifascist education, Adorno claims, must begin in early childhood. Education should not intend to mold a human being, for no human being has a right to mold another. It is also not the teaching of facts and figures, but *die Herstellung eines richtigen Bewußtseins*, the establishment of correct consciousness.[7]

Though less concerned with forming correct consciousness than Adorno's, Nietzsche's critique of *Bildung* nevertheless attacks the practices of institutionalized scholarship and testifies to his skepticism of the manifestations of cultural modernity, such as democratization and decadence. Like Adorno, Nietzsche affirms that real *Bildung* no longer exists:

> Our modern culture [moderne *Bildung*] is nothing living just because it cannot be understood at all without the opposition, that is: it is no real culture [gar keine wirkliche *Bildung*] at all, but only a kind of knowledge about culture [eine Art Wissen um *Bildung*], it stops at cultured thoughts [*Bildungs*-Gedanken] and cultured feelings [*Bildungs*-Gefühl] but leads to no cultured decisions.[8]

Nietzsche criticizes the impotence of academic institutions and the individual scholars and teachers alike. For Nietzsche, *Bildung* is an ideal related to the development of free spirits and to the education of the outstanding individual who carries the hope for the future. As Nietzsche has no concern for the woman of the future, it is the outstanding man who can become the model for the future—an individual of untimely ideas and actions, a being with transformational powers transcending contemporary constraints and the barbarism of modernity; a man who will contribute to the creation of a strong civilization.

Thoughts on the fate of *Bildung* and the state of education, including the institutions which administer it, can be found throughout Nietzsche's entire *oeuvre*; however, they are most pointed in the second and third of the *Unfashionable Observations*—"The Advantages and Disadvantages of History" and "Schopenhauer as Educator"—and in his public lecture series "On the Future of our Educational Institutions." As Timothy Murphy points out, all of Nietzsche's writings can be said to have a didactic purpose and aim, but in the above-named works Nietzsche criticizes *Bildung* in its institutional context by connecting it to the critique of modernity, ideology, culture, and the state:

> Nietzsche's entire corpus of works centers around, of course, the relationship between life and values. And in that respect his concerns would be those of a grand

teacher . . . who attempts through his criticism and example, to instruct humanity in a way to live. It would seem, moreover, that his very notion of philosophy cannot be understood but as being educative in nature. His specific aim is to alert humanity to and help humanity to avoid and overcome nihilism and decadence.[9]

It is important to note that the two untimely meditations most extensively critical of education and educational institutions were published between 1872 and 1874, during the years in which Nietzsche stood under the influence of Wagner, the subject of the fourth untimely meditation, and at the beginning of his already faltering academic career. Wagner's influence—and the idea of a culture's duty to foster first and foremost the unfolding of genius—and Nietzsche's own experience as teacher and scholar in institutions of higher learning are constitutive factors behind the *Observations* and the lectures. His ideal of *Bildung* also prefigures the later demand for free spirits and his hope for the *Übermensch.*

For both Adorno and Nietzsche, the ideal of *Bildung* was desirable as a never-ending process of learning, but whose potential had not only been unfulfilled but also distorted. In their critiques of culture and *Bildung* they sought to expose those concealed and unconscious mechanisms operating in the individual and in society which hinder the realization of *Bildung.* Both Adorno and Nietzsche see *Bildung*'s deterioration as symptomatic of society's deterioration as a whole and as the result of a deformation process rooted in the attempt of the political and economic powers to institutionalize their ideology. The application of the idea and ideal of *Bildung* toward political and materialistic goals initiated its downfall. Nietzsche contends that economic interests and the popular national-economic dogmas of contemporary society undermine the quality of *Bildung*, in that we have utility as the goal of education, which more precisely manifests itself in the form of the greatest possible production of profit,[10] while Adorno comments that the profit motive of *Bildung* has covered the entire culture like a mould.[11]

Blaming popularization for its degeneration, Nietzsche's and Adorno's concepts of *Bildung* are essentially elitist. Adorno, of course, defuses charges of implicit elitism by mentioning popularization's positive aspects, especially the fact that millions more people "fortunately" have access to education and, more concretely, to an education that enables them to follow Adorno's discussion of education.[12] While *Bildung* is a major factor in the preservation of bourgeois privileges, it is, paradoxically, designed to resist bourgeois elitism and the economic and ideological pressures on artistic, philosophical, and critical investigations. As Adorno points out, the bourgeois construct of *Bildung* proposes the idea of humanity without special status or extra advantages; once it becomes entangled in work deemed useful by society, *Bildung* violates itself.[13] Traditionally, *Bildung*—like art—was thought to be divorced from all utilitarian purposes. At the most, its goal could be to enable the individual to function as a free-thinking being. But according to Adorno, *Bildung* became simultaneously a sign of the emancipation of the bourgeoisie and a tool for the enforcement of social adaptation and political conformity. It allowed the exhibition of the relative power of the class that owned the means of production and sustained its privileges against the proletariat. *Bildung* has always been a status symbol; however, through its institutional integration and its ideological and economic utilization, the ideals of a humane society were lost. Once the idea of *Bildung* was popularized and institutionalized, it justified the prevailing conditions and became a state-administered instrument of power, thus furthering the dissipation of the visible borders between the classes. Adorno pronounces the end of the dream of *Bildung*, because of the lack of freedom from the dictates of means; *Bildung* became an apology for the world.[14] Traditionally a monopoly of the upper classes, *Bildung*'s transformation into so-called *Volksbildung* was to eliminate not only ignorance, but also political unpredictability. In this process of manipulation, the idea of *Bildung* did not simply disappear, but was turned into ideology: "the price for survival is practical involvement, the transformation of ideas into domination."[15]

No new concept of education was developed in order to fulfil the need and goal of educating the masses. *Bildung*, governed by market forces and the pressures of the culture industry, degenerated instead into *Halbbildung*. Since the broadening of *Bildung* trivialized and flattened the education process, mass-educated individuals lost part of their individuality, because true *Bildung* and the capacity for differentiation are equivalent.[16] The erasure of differences homogenized the masses without substantially changing society's power structures. As Adorno further argues, while there were no decisive changes with regard to the economic basis of relations determining the objective limits of *Bildung*, ideology transformed itself even more thoroughly. As part of the integration process, the masses are provided with the goods of education through countless channels, while the content of *Bildung* is adapted through market mechanisms to the consciousness of those who are denied access to the privilege of *Bildung*.[17]

Adorno's critique of the popularization of *Bildung* is based upon a critical and pessimistic assessment of the consciousness of the masses and the impact of a humanistic education. Public consciousness submits to the manipulations of a complex web of universal delusion, of which half-education has become a part. Intricately woven into the network of delusion and hidden behind complex mechanisms of domination, pseudo-education is not a medium for emancipation but an instrument of power. Half-education is the manipulative tool of both the culture industry and the educational system. However, it is not only the consciousness formed under the influence of the modern culture and *Bildung* industry, but also the privileged sensibility of high culture and humanistic education that failed to intervene and capitulated in the confrontation with inhumanity. Historical experience shows that a humanistic culture cannot prevent moral atrocities: "Auschwitz demonstrated irrefutably that culture has failed."[18] In a now-famous rhetorical gesture, Adorno declares contemporary culture to be ideological garbage that must be rescued:

All post-Auschwitz culture, including its urgent critique, is garbage. In restoring itself after the things that happened without resistance in its own countryside, culture has turned entirely into the ideology it had always been potentially.[19]

Auschwitz disqualifies culture from sustaining the illusion that humanism sustains a humane society; it also testifies to the ideological deformation of the ideals of culture, *Bildung*, and enlightenment. Auschwitz declares the bankruptcy of the project of modernity, for the progressive march of enlightenment through history has proven itself to be a descent into barbarism. As Jay points out: "the Holocaust has finally and irrevocably exposed the lie that supporters of culture and the humanities have promulgated for centuries in order to justify their existence: the claim that the pursuit of what we usually call 'high culture' is somehow a humanizing endeavor."[20] However, Adorno's devaluation of the impact of culture does not mean that the ideals of culture, and *Bildung*, are to be discarded. In a typical move, Adorno presents the predicament of culture, and by extension of *Bildung,* as an irreconcilable contradiction:

Whoever pleads for the maintenance of this radically culpable and shabby culture becomes its accomplice, while the man who says no to culture is directly furthering the barbarism which our culture showed itself to be.[21]

On the one hand, culture after Auschwitz is an ideological construct destined to be rubbish, while on the other, it is rubbish of which society cannot dispose without falling back into barbarism. Paradoxically, the ideological garbage called culture can neither be abandoned nor affirmed.

Bildung functions in a way similar to other myths of superiority. The illusion of *Bildung*, of being well-educated, satisfies the individual, collective, and narcissistic need of the *Bildungsbürger* to compensate for their lack of social control and their fear of the unknown. However, the unassimilated knowledge of half-education produces stereotypes instead of insights, and the half-knowledge acquired and used for economic ends underwrites the repression of opposition and critique. *Bildung*, which in the eighteenth century was a potential threat to the established order, was defused. Adorno argues that *Halbbildung* destroys unmediated subject-object relations, religious beliefs, and mythological imagery and provides instead cheap substitutes springing from a conglomerate of ideological notions.[22] In contrast to *Halbbildung*, *Unbildung* has a critical potential because imagination, naïveté, spontaneity, humor, and irony are qualities springing from that which has not been completely domesticated. Half-education, in its imposition of demystification and loss of imagery and tradition, testifies to the omnipresence of alienated consciousness, which leads to mental and spiritual desolation.

The conditions of material and cultural production in a capitalist society have abolished the dream of the autonomous subject, the subject of *Bildung*. The increasing imbalance of power removes the objective preconditions for autonomy.[23] As the autonomy of the individual ceases to exist, the autonomy of the realm of art and *Bildung* are lost to the culture industry: "Art's purposelessness consists in its having escaped the constraints of self-preservation. It embodies something like freedom in the midst of unfreedom."[24] The ideal form of *Bildung* escapes the confines of self-preservation as well, and represents a moment of freedom similar to that of art. However, like art, *Bildung* is now absorbed by a culture driven by the principle of exchange and commodification, and by subordinating themselves to economic interests, both the aesthetic and educational realms have lost the ability to resist or to stand in creative opposition to reality. Today's culture industry markets consumer products that legitimize themselves only through their profitability, while contemporary education seeks legitimacy by satisfying the demands of the job market. Like the pretentious pseudo-claims of *Halbbildung*, the products of the culture industry are only stereotyped translations and reproductions of art or *Bildung*, which further the impoverishment of the imagination, spontaneity, and critical thinking. The moralizing attitude of mass-produced kitsch extinguishes the last thought of resistance.

Nietzsche also sees the degeneration of *Bildung* in connection with the decline of contemporary culture. For him, as for Adorno, the invasion of economic and ideological motivations has decomposed the concept. Nietzsche asserts that in his time there exists a "misemployed and appropriated culture" and names four reasons for the failure of culture and *Bildung* to reach their goal, namely the "production of the genius": "the greed of the money-makers," "the greed of the state," "the greed of all those who have reason to disguise themselves behind form," and "the greed of the sciences," and "the men of learning."[25] Self-serving economic and political interests transform *Bildung* into ideology, which inhibits the independent, creative, and action-oriented type of thinking that could overcome metaphysics and reevaluate all values. Similar to Adorno's view, Nietzsche's concept of *Bildung* turns against the homogenizing tendencies of modern society. Gerhard Schmidt points out that the goal of Nietzsche's *Bildung* concept is not the attainment of the individual's majority as expressed by Enlightenment thought, but the differentiation among human beings; Nietzsche's idea is to make people unequal.[26] Fostering non-identity represents the critical framework for Nietzsche's antidemocratic stance and a way to resist the political and commercial pursuit of self-interest, which denies differentiation and individuality. The contemporary educational goal is the production of workers rather than thinking individuals. It is not the "age of finished, ripe and harmonious personalities but of common, maximally useful labour" in which

> men are to be trained for the purposes of the age to lend a hand as soon as possible: they are to labour in the factory of common utility before they are ripe, or rather to prevent their ever becoming ripe—because that would be a luxury which would withdraw a lot of strength from "the labour market."[27]

Rather cynically, Nietzsche pronounces the inhumane death of *Bildung* inflicted by crude, market-driven utilitarianism. In contrast to modern professional training, *Bildung* sets goals beyond the economic principles of acquisition and exchange, and is therefore diametrically opposed to the interests of society that seek to provide "a speedy education so that one may quickly become a money-earning being."[28]

Popularization and generalization ("*Ausbreitung und Verallgemeinerung*") of culture and *Bildung* serve the interests of the state, which seeks to release just enough of a generation's intellectual potential to make it useful servants of existing institutions. However, by leveling *Bildung* to *Allgemeinbildung*, the state proves its short-sightedness, since the creation and survival of a culture deserving of its name depends upon the great individual. The masses, according to Nietzsche, can never produce a great culture. While the majority of students can be satisfactorily served by the educational institutions' teaching skills that prepare their mastery over their own impoverishment, the truly outstanding individual has no chance to receive the kind of guardianship and attention needed for his advancement: one trend demands the greatest possible expansion of *Bildung*, while the other expects *Bildung* to relinquish its highest and most noble claims and enter the service of the state, with the result that utility becomes the goal and purpose of education.[29]

In order to counter the degenerative and destructive trends of *Bildung*—the broadening (*Erweiterung*) and dissemination (*Verbreitung*) that leads to its reduction (*Verminderung*) and weakening (*Abschwächung*)—the educational efforts of the future have to focus on narrowing and concentration of *Bildung* (*Verengung und Koncentration*).[30] *Bildung* has to become a concentrated effort taken up by the few individuals who are able to venture beyond the comprehension of knowledge and are willing to divorce their investigations from self-gratification or purpose-oriented thought: the eventual triumph of the desire to concentrate and consolidate *Bildung* originates in the fact that the forces of expansion and dilution run against the laws of nature, while education for the few is in harmony with them; the success of the latter impulses would serve as a foundation for a false and fabricated culture.[31] While the broadening and the dissemination of *Bildung* are mainly connected to Nietzsche's critique of the institutions, the reduction and the weakening of *Bildung* are evidence for the inadequacy of teachers and scholarship. In contrast to Adorno, who (albeit reluctantly) finds that "fortunately" a broad spectrum of the population now has access to education, Nietzsche rationalizes the exclusion of the masses from *Bildung* by establishing a hierarchy of the intellect. Most scholars and teachers have a false understanding of the common good and thus do not perform the role of a true educator. In fact, Nietzsche asserts that most advocates of *Bildung*, "*die Gebildeten*," are, in fact, its enemy: these opponents of true culture have as their goal the emancipation of the masses from the dominance of the few, but ultimately they are attempting to topple the holiest hierarchy in the intellectual realm: the servitude, obedience, and instinctual loyalty of the masses under the scepter of genius.[32]

Nietzsche pays special attention to the servants of the state and the church who do not provide *Bildung*, but rather a knowledge of *Bildung*. He is not only a sharp critic of academic institutions, but also of the practices of scholarship, and he questions the methods and motives of scholars and teachers. The scholarship within the individual disciplines has become specialized to the extent that it hinders the attainment and expansion of knowledge beyond small areas of research. A specialist within an academic field is comparable to a factory worker who works only with a limited number of tools, machines, and materials. The specialists have become so limited in their knowledge that they are no more than semi-thinkers, *Halbdenker*.[33]

Nietzsche takes the philosopher Schopenhauer as the example of the ideal teacher, because one can learn from him how to educate against the prevailing tendencies of modernity. Although Nietzsche praises Schopenhauer as a philosopher who was independent of the state, society, and public opinion, this praise has to be viewed with reservations. As part of the *Untimely Meditations*, the essay on Schopenhauer was undoubtedly inspired by Wagner's admiration for him. Martin Vogel claims that Nietzsche was not sufficiently familiar with Schopenhauer's philosophy either to praise or to criticize it and that Nietzsche's later disenchantment with Schopenhauer occurred when Nietzsche recognized the untenability of his illusions about him.[34] Nietzsche himself writes in *Ecce Homo* that the subject of the Third Essay is not "Schopenhauer as Educator," but rather "Nietzsche as Educator."[35] If one is to accept Nietzsche's claim, then Schopenhauer functions merely as a foil, or as Nietzsche maintains, as a famous, yet undiagnosed type that is useful in illustrating his points. As Plato did with Socrates, "one catches hold of an opportunity, in order to say something, in order to have at hand a few more formulas, signs, means of language."[36] However, even if the praises Nietzsche sings for Schopenhauer are not to be taken seriously and if one can, as Nietzsche suggests, substitute the name Schopenhauer with Nietzsche, the ideas of *Bildung* and the notion of the educator certainly must be given serious consideration.

Schopenhauer, Nietzsche claims, represented what every true philosopher with integrity should be, a total solitary: "Where there have been powerful societies, governments, religions, public opinions, in short wherever there has been tyranny, there the solitary philosopher has been hated; for philosophy offers an asylum to a man into which no tyranny can force its way, an inward cave, the labyrinth of the heart: and that annoys the tyrants."[37] Within Nietzsche's rather broad definition of tyranny, the philosopher is a towering figure of freedom who refuses, as Adorno formulated it in regard to the philosopher Nietzsche, to give his consent to the world. Despite his sharp criticism of philosophy and its practice within academia, Nietzsche retains a notion of philosophy as an sovereign space of reflection. The autonomy of thought is, however, compromised whenever a philosopher is dependent upon an institution for his livelihood. Schopen-

hauer functions, once again, as a positive example, because although Schopenhauer taught at the university, he was not financially dependent upon this institution. Nietzsche argues that Hegel's and Kant's philosophy suffered from their
employment in the academic system: "Kant was, as we scholars are accustomed
to be, cautious, subservient and, in his attitude towards the state, without greatness: so that, if university philosophy should ever be called to account, he at any
rate could not justify it."[38] The state bestows upon philosophers an office, rather
than freedom of inquiry. Philosophers who hold their positions because of
money, prestige, boredom, or loyalty to authority, disqualify themselves from
philosophy. Their ulterior motives make them slaves to material and ideological
thinking, and therefore steer them away from the truthful search for knowledge
and understanding. Philosophers of the university are seduced by the rewards
they receive. Furthermore, the state selects its "philosophical servants"[39] according to its own self-interest, and this self-interest does not necessarily include
freedom of thought, although it includes, for the most part, the appearance of
intellectual freedom. Instead of accepting their duty as teachers and developing
first-rate minds in their students, the second- and third-rate academic servants
divert, out of vanity and other self-seeking impulses, these young talents from
their talents. The *Zeitgeist* is such that university philosophers want to turn the
rare talents into servants, assistants, and instruments like themselves rather than
assist in the development of their higher natures. This *Zeitgeist* seduces its
thinkers and builds up a certain pseudo-solidarity among them:

> he [the philosophical servant] will be welcome to his own age, it will not fail to offer
> him laurels and rewards, powerful parties will bear him along, behind him there will
> be as many like-minded men as there will be before him, and when the man in the
> front line gives the word of command it will re-echo through all the ranks. Here the
> first duty is "to fight in rank and file," the second to treat as enemies all who refuse
> to fall in.[40]

Submissive scholars can not produce anything but useful knowledge, half-truths,
and errors, and the search for truth becomes a mere pretext for the kind of desire
and joy a hunter feels in tracking, encircling, and killing. Scholars, Nietzsche
suggests, follow the "sly fox's path in the realm of thought."[41] The search for
truth thus becomes a pleasure and the finding of the so-called truth a personal
victory: "Then, the man of learning is to a great extent also motivated to the discovery of *certain* 'truth,' motivated that is by his subjection to certain ruling per-
sons, castes, opinions, churches, governments: he feels it to his advantage to
bring 'truth' over to their side."[42] Since scholars and philosophers inside the acad-
emy disqualify themselves from fostering *Bildung*, Nietzsche sees the separation
of philosophy and the university as the first step to restore, firstly, *Bildung* and,
secondly, philosophy's authority and credibility. Nietzsche suggests the creation
of a higher tribunal outside the university, whose function would be to monitor
the educational process:

and as soon as philosophy departs from the universities, and therewith purifies itself of all unworthy considerations and prejudices, it must constitute precisely such a tribunal: devoid of official authority, without salaries or honours, it will know how to perform its duty free of the *Zeitgeist* and free from fear of it.[43]

Thus, Nietzsche perceives philosophy not only as the space for freedom of thought and freedom from any institutional form of tyranny, but also as a higher authority promoting and judging education. These tribunals of education would be staffed, of course, by independent scholars, who do not rely on the institution or the state for income and fame, and whose judgments are uninhibited by both economic and ideological pressures.

Considering the freedom from financial, institutional, and intellectual constraints and the outstanding mental capacity—which, in Nietzsche's opinion, most scholars do not have—the ideal independent philosopher and teacher would need to provide the basis for individualized *Bildung*. This concept of *Bildung*, with all its prerequisites, seems not only unrealistic, but also doomed to failure. What institutionalized education can provide is thus not *Bildung* but the absorption of massive amounts of facts and figures, while the overemphasis on historical knowledge amounts to little more than an exercise in memorization. The students are asked to comprehend in a few lessons what has taken centuries to evolve. Young people become lost in the concepts and terms that they are unable to understand and begin to feel disgust for their subjects. An excessive knowledge of history impairs students' development and renders them incapable of independent, self-determined action. In order to act, one must forget about the past, because the accomplishments of the past are intimidating and often frightening. In the world of the Greeks, one could find "the actuality of an essentially unhistorical culture [*Bildung*] and a culture [*Bildung*] which is nevertheless, or rather therefore, unspeakably rich and full of life."[44] An education that does not inspire creative thought and action, but adherence to convention and existing institutions can not be called *Bildung*, but merely training and drilling, which substitutes for action. An impoverished culture lacking great and inspiring minds, which is governed by slaves to history, tradition, metaphysics, and moral values, cannot provide the environment necessary to nurture a genius.

Adorno also criticizes a one-sided emphasis upon the conformity to traditional standards, values, and structure. *Bildung* inherits culture's double nature. On the one hand, cultural practices require adaptation and conformity, for they aim at taming, restraining, and sublimating human instincts and drives. On the other hand, culture possesses an oppositional dimension, which lies in its stand against reality and its resistance to traditional structures and norms. Culture and *Bildung* are concerned with both the conservation and the cancellation of culture. Contemporary culture emphasizes conformity and thus neglects the creative and critical potential of its products and practices. By privileging one aspect of culture over another, *Bildung* is broken in half and ceases to exist.

By following Nietzsche's and Adorno's arguments on *Bildung* and culture, their aim of creating a tension between the preservation of human faculties and the liberation from the constraints of tradition and convention becomes apparent. Both long for the cultural and intellectual preservation of tradition, yet also turn against it. Nietzsche's standard of cultural development is the Greeks, who, so Nietzsche claims, ascribed meaning to life without binding themselves to ideologies and the knowledge of facts. The educational methods which Nietzsche promotes are clearly in favor of a strong authority of the teacher, obedience, and discipline. Aphorism eight from the *Twilight*'s "Maxims and Arrows" has become a cliché for the disciplinary tone often associated with German education: "*From the military school of life.*—What does not kill me makes me stronger."[45] The aphorism clarifies the relationship between education and experience, which Adorno also stresses. Both Nietzsche and Adorno agree that *Bildung* cannot obtain divorced from the experience of life; however, Adorno questions the modern subject's ability to experience at all. According to Adorno, the half-educated individual is engaged in a continuous attempt at self-preservation without a self. Lacking the capacity for experience, the modern subject can no longer affirm its subjectivity and thus undermines the possibility for *Bildung* on the subjective level,[46] while capitalist society and the culture industry undermine it on an objective level. Experience, which requires a consciousness of continuity, is today replaced by partial, unconnected, and substitutable information.

Adorno wants to rescue some aspects of the humanistic ideals of culture and the artistic accomplishments of high modernism from commercialization and stereotyped reproduction. He accepts that the identification with the father (i.e., tradition) is a necessary first step toward detachment and the constitution of the individual. Adorno is aware of the impossibility of reaching the ideal of *Bildung*, and attaches to it little hope for the future. In this sense, Nietzsche's "military school" expresses, amidst the hopelessly commercialized and ideology-dominated culture, the extent of Adorno's optimism. At the same time, even this "optimism" is restrained, for that which does not kill can victimize by manipulation and distortion, by weaving an ever tighter net around the already existing context of delusion. Adorno was fully aware of the paradoxical nature of his call for *Bildung*. However, his attitude toward *Bildung* has elements in common with his attitude toward culture: without it society slips into barbarism. As Rath points out, *Bildung* includes a thinking against oneself.[47] For Nietzsche and Adorno the integrity of thought cannot be achieved by nostalgically conforming to tradition, but by critically reflecting on its ideological and metaphysical moments. The spiritual and intellectual strength for critical reflection comes, however, from that space that *Bildung* used to fill. It is here that the mind finds the courage to resist fusing with society and becoming an undifferentiated identity. This strategy of differentiation, by Adorno's account, is the anachronism of our time: to hold on to *Bildung* after society has taken away the basis for it. Since *Bildung* no longer exists, *Bildung* can no longer be criticized from the standpoint of *Bildung*, or in other words, from a person possessing *Bildung*. For the idea and ideal of *Bildung* to survive, there is no other possibility than to pursue the critical self-reflection of *Halbbildung*.[48]

5

Heresy of the Mind:
Essays and Aphorisms

It seems that Adorno is becoming an authority in the Federal Repub-
lic, highly respected. What a fraud. In what I have read of him, I find
nothing worthy of serious consideration, not even in his brilliant,
vastly knowledgeable writings that examine things from every possible angle and in which he assumes a vantage point of the greatest wisdom. And yet he is taken seriously. I quickly become bored with him.
Such hodgepodges of anything and everything that comes to mind are
intolerable.

—Karl Jaspers on Adorno

While reading and following the often circular motion of Adorno's thought constellations demands intellectual strength and utmost concentration, the experience of reading Nietzsche seems infinitely more pleasurable, provoking
amusement and laughter. "Those who read Nietzsche without laughing—,"
writes Gilles Deleuze, "without laughing often, richly, even hilariously—have, in
a sense, not read Nietzsche at all."[1] Here a major difference between the two
thinkers comes into play, the difference between Nietzsche's "gay" and Adorno's
"melancholy" science. While Nietzsche evokes, in Deleuze's words, the "schiz-
ophrenic laughter or revolutionary joy" of the great books, Adorno might be said
to come out on the side of those books that Deleuze sees as exhibiting the

"anguish of petty narcissism, the dread of guilt."[2] Scholars, such as Eagleton—who labels Adorno a nostalgic *haut bourgeois* intellectual with "mandarin fastidiousness" and "remorseless tunnel vision,"[3]—certainly associate Adorno with the latter of Deleuze's categories. While some critics are quick to dismiss Adorno's thought as well as his style of presentation, Adorno's writings must not be understood solely as narcissistic outpourings—certainly no text could be said to be free of narcissistic inclinations, least of all Nietzsche's—but rather as a tortured search for explanations and ways of overcoming the inhumane conditions of human existence. The dread of guilt and bad conscience hovers even over his early writings, feelings which are immensely intensified in the post-Auschwitz reflections of a man who questions the propriety of pleasure and whose concept of negativity is diametrically opposed to joyful affirmations of life.

While Nietzsche's nomad thought "continually evade[s] the codes of settled people,"[4] Adorno's critical negativity and aesthetic reflection can be said to invade these codes continually: he circles endlessly around the same issues in an attempt to shift perspectives and contexts and to mobilize subject and object positions, while at the same time penetrating these questions from different angles. While both Nietzsche and Adorno relentlessly analyze, evaluate, judge, dismiss, and criticize the conditions of life, Adorno's avoidance of affirmation and his refusal to outline positive alternatives constitute the more agonizing task. Where Nietzsche's philosophizing with a hammer appears forceful, dynamic, ironic, and frivolous, Adorno's appears labored and somber. While they both emphasize the importance of art and the realm of the aesthetic for their respective projects, Adorno sees in art and style the potential for protest and resistance, rather than the life-giving, regenerative force, the source of pleasure, and condition for life invoked by Nietzsche. Rather than celebrating with Nietzsche art's potential for renewal, Adorno emphasizes art's potential for opposition to bourgeois delusion and the dictates of capitalist society. Adorno admires the analytical, critical, destructing, that is, deconstructing Nietzsche, and the evader of codes is cherished as long as such evasion remains a critical and negative activity that does not lead to affirmative postulations. Their differences in mood and style rest upon not only differences in temperament and historical circumstance, but also upon fundamental differences in their approach to their work. Both want to demolish the status quo by relentlessly pointing out the ideologies, fantasies, perversions, and self-deceptions through which it perpetuates itself, and both operate upon similar premises in terms of their demand to twist out of metaphysics and the self-destructive dynamic of enlightenment. Both use similar forms of expression to not only verbalize their thoughts but also to perform it, thereby achieving a correlation between what is said and how it is said. However, their idiosyncratic critical labor speaks with very distinct voices.

Aside from their idiosyncratic modes of expression and their differences in mood and style, Nietzsche's and Adorno's respective evasions and invasions of the codes of civilization rely on a number of similar textual strategies and rhetorical gestures, such as irony, the use of metaphors, provocation, exaggeration, play, and playing the devil's advocate. Gillian Rose, Sabine Wilke, Rainer Hoffmann and others have pointed out in detail how Adorno also strategically deploys parallaxes, parataxis, chiasm, and tautology.[5] The discovery of the "New Nietzsche," which recognized the importance of style in and for Nietzsche's texts and their interpretation, has inspired numerous studies of the Nietzschean narratives: the topic of "Nietzsche's styles" may surely earn its place as one of the most popular fields of research in the history of Western ideas.[6] In her examination of Adorno's "search for style," Rose takes note of Adorno's engagement with Nietzsche— most evident, according to Rose, in "The Essay as Form" and in *Minima Moralia*—and remarks that in these two works Adorno simultaneously explicates his style most fully.[7] Both "The Essay as Form" and *Minima Moralia* testify to Adorno's refusal to separate "substantial issues from the development of methodology and empirical techniques."[8] According to Rose, Adorno's concern with method and style are of a different order: "Adorno's 'methods' present seminal ideas; they are not devices imposed on material in order to organise and explain it. 'Method' (and even more 'style') means for him the relation between ideas and the composition of texts. It does not mean devising procedures for applying theories."[9] Rose further argues that both Nietzsche's and Adorno's works must not be read literally but from a methodological point of view.[10] In their attempt to present an ungrounded and ungroundable philosophy, they engaged in contradictions, and in an attempt to resist popularization, they tried "to defy the norms which they opposed, and they wrote in essays or in fragments to avoid the appearance and presuppositions of the traditional philosophical systems," thereby running the risk of having their thought decontextualized, misinterpreted, and misunderstood.[11]

Nietzsche's and Adorno's preoccupation with style and modes of expression and representation suggest their intensifying concern with both method and aesthetics, a concern that spurred the interest and understanding of both style as politics and the politics of style. Nietzsche's and Adorno's preference for aphoristic and essayistic writing as the most appropriate forms of expression must be understood as the stylistic and formal consequences of their critique of ideology, including their radical skepticism, their rejection of metaphysics, and their distrust of philosophical systems. If the aphorism and essay respectively register Nietzsche's and Adorno's protest against the reduction of thought to logic and systems, they also function positively to affirm perspectivism, contradiction, multiplicity, and complexity. Essays and aphorisms provide the forum for the critique of ideology, while the aphoristic and essayistic style enacts the performative aspect of the critique of ideological substance. By resisting the notions of absolute truth, completeness, and finality in both their manner of writing and argumentation, and by including the reader into their thought processes, Nietzsche and Adorno allow their readers to witness writing as a process of becoming and to appreciate the text as a product that offers no universal, definite, and irrevocable conclusion or insight. The openness of these forms of writing mirrors the openness and freedom of movement of the reflecting mind that accepts no higher authority; unorthodox thought attempts to lay bare all ideological presupposi- tions—including its own—and requires in turn unorthodox forms of expression that resist systematization and unequivocal declarations of certainty. Hence Adorno contends that "the essay's innermost formal law is heresy."[12]

Aphorisms and essays violate the principles of formal philosophical and sci- entific discourse. They disregard the closed structure of presentation, which usu- ally includes an introduction and an exposition that reason and argue toward a foregone conclusion. Aphorisms and essays are more concerned with exploring thoughts by way of reflection than with proving a point. In his genre study of aphorisms, Franz Mauthner characterizes aphoristic writing as *sprachkünst- lerische Klärungsarbeit* (linguistically artistic work of explanation).[13] Mauthner divides the process of aphoristic creation into two parts: the conception of an idea and its elucidation. Aphoristic writing, and it can be argued by extension also Adorno's concept of essayistic writing, is therefore directly related to aphoristic thought processes; the thinker has an idea, which might be conceived intuitively and spontaneously or as the fruit of a complex thought process, and then pro- ceeds to elaborate upon this idea. In aphoristic writing the elucidation process may vary from one-sentence maxims to lengthy and complex essayistic explo- rations of a theme. Essays or essayistic explorations give thinkers the opportu- nity to wrestle with their own positions while commenting, criticizing, and reflecting upon their subject and their own standpoint. The essay is by definition an experimental form of writing. When Montaigne, to whom Adorno briefly refers in "The Essay as Form," gave his various writings on humanity the title *Essais*, he did so with the expressed purpose to represent with his title not only the incomplete and tentative nature of his own conclusions, but also to further the recognition that the act of writing itself takes on its own dynamic—a dynamic closely related to the author's experiences and prejudices and often conflicting with his intentions. In this way, the essay points beyond the author and beyond itself. Montaigne's purpose was to find ways and principles of living, for himself and for humanity as a whole. Written over a period of twenty years, the *Essais* are testimony to change and thus contain many inconsistencies and contradic- tions; Montaigne admits: "I do contradict myself now and then; but truth . . . I never contradict."[14] For Montaigne, life was not as a static subject to be appre- hended, but rather a dynamic process requiring flexible forms of representation: "I do not portray being: I portray passing."[15] Significant to the essayistic project is also Montaigne's skepticism toward what Adorno called identity thinking. Tra- ditionally, the assertion of resemblance seeks out similarities and tends to equate the dissimilar. Montaigne's account of resemblance clearly departs from this mode of thought by emphasizing difference rather than identity. Resemblance "does not make things as much alike as difference makes them unlike."[16]

Essayistic and aphoristic writing is based as much on experience as it springs from the speculative musings of the mind. Since this mode of writing is fragmentary and does not move in progressive stages, it defies notions of origin, teleology, completion, finality, and totality. Like the Adornoan essay, the aphorism rejects adherence to the formal structures of a closed exposition, such as introduction, explanation, a demonstration providing evidence and proof, and a deductive and singular conclusion. It mimics the open structure of thought, and truth is not understood as static, ahistorical knowledge to be acquired and conserved, but rather as a historically contingent phenomenon dependent upon multiple insights and numerous cultural, political, and social variables. Traditional structures of thought neither lead to absolute truth nor can they lead to truths. In a parallel fashion, the project of debunking metaphysical notions thus includes dismantling the rigid structures in which they are presented. New ways of thinking require new forms of expression. Nietzsche and Adorno emphasize the experimental and tentative nature of their thought; Adorno speaks of the "consciousness of its own fallibility and provisional character,"[17] and Nietzsche writes: "He who considers more deeply knows that, whatever his acts and judgments may be, he is always wrong.[18]

The following discussion focuses on Nietzsche's and Adorno's use of aphorisms and essays in order to show how the ideas explored in the previous chapters, including Nietzsche's and Adorno's critique of reason, metaphysics, historical consciousness, and modernity, are expressed and reflected in this particular form of writing. Although their modes of expression are for the most part motivated by their critical intentions, the importance of art—and especially music—and the influence of their aesthetic sensibilities and creative drive on the compositions of their texts should not be underestimated. In Adorno's and Nietzsche's texts it becomes clear that style and form consistently point beyond criticism to the aesthetics of presentation. Form and content coexist in an interdependent relationship, and it should not be assumed that the search for style solely concerns the appropriate expression of content alone. Rather, both content and style, in the manner of artistic material, take on their own dynamic, and, therefore, the style influences the content to the same extent that the content influences the style. In other words, the search of style is not just a one-way search for suitable expression, because the mode of expression, the dynamics of form and style, also partially determines what is being written as well. In this context "The Essay as Form" provides a productive basis for an analysis of the interactive relationship between Adorno's ideas and their textual presentation, while selected remarks by Nietzsche on the use of aphorisms facilitate an examination of this relationship in his works.

ADORNO'S THEORY OF THE ESSAY

The difficulties associated with Adorno's method and style, as well as the contradictions arising from critical theory and its (re)presentation, have all been

194 of the Mind

subject to numerous studies. Many scholars, including Wilke and Peter Bürger, point out the persistence of idealism in Adorno's aesthetic and philosophical thought. Wilke investigates Adorno's model of representation and criticizes in his theory the traditional, idealist dichotomization of form and content, the aesthetic experience and the concept, and discursive, intellectual operations and the aesthetic experience.[19] Bürger makes a similar argument when he attributes to Adorno's aesthetic theory a traditional, idealistic view of the artwork and the artist/genius.[20] Adorno's entwinement of philosophy and art and his presentation of theory in aestheticized form have also been singled out for criticism. Bubner diagnoses in Adorno's writings, most especially in the *Aesthetic Theory*, a suspension and dissolution of theory in favor of aesthetics: "Can theory become aesthetic?" Bubner asks and answers in the affirmative.[21] To the question whether it should, Bubner answers most definitely in the negative. In Bubner's view, Adorno's work testifies to this transformation of philosophy into art, of aesthetic theory into aestheticized theory. Bubner not only rejects Adorno's aesthetization of theory and his tendency to collapse the distinction between philosophy and art, but also claims that Adorno reaches the limits of aesthetic theory by postulating on the one hand the autonomy of genuine art, then undermining this autonomy on the other, by further arguing that genuine art necessarily yields an aesthetic experience that sets free art's critical potential. Bubner sees a contradiction in this predetermination of so-called autonomy, and he argues that Adorno's view of art preconceives an aesthetic experience that leaves no real freedom for truly autonomous aesthetic reflection. In Adorno, the aesthetic experience serves predetermined critical functions and provides the basis of philosophical investigation, cognition, and the theoretical formation of consciousness. In resistance to Hegel, Adorno attempts to overcome the epistemological limitations of philosophy and theory by emphasizing and incorporating into philosophy the aesthetic experience.[22] Bubner argues that this strategy leads to a self-denial of philosophy in Adorno's work. The recognition of art as a medium of knowledge and insight only opens itself to the philosophical eye, and a philosophy of art that elevates art to an autonomous status and recognizes the aesthetic experience as a mode of recognition and understanding must not deny its own function in this promotion, which Bubner compares to an elevation of the aesthetic experience to a knighthood.[23] In the end, all these complications would be avoidable, Bubner contends, if philosophy would stop pretending to be something that it is not. The attempt to transform theory into aesthetics causes confusion between theoretical semblance and works of art.[24]

The contradictions generated by Adorno's aesthetization of theory and the theoretical overdetermination of the aesthetic experience are linked to Habermas's displeasure with Adorno's and Nietzsche's totalization of the critique of enlightenment. He criticizes Adorno, Horkheimer, and Nietzsche for seeking recourse in aesthetic rather than rational criteria. However, the invocation of the aesthetic realm, an inadmissible escape route from modernity for Habermas, appears to follow the inner logic of Nietzsche's and Adorno's thought and their critiques of rationality and enlightenment in particular, for such a critique solely based upon rationality and enlightenment would indeed involve itself in a performative contradiction. Taking into account the limitations of philosophy and theoretical thought against which Adorno and Nietzsche write their texts, the aesthetic dimension they develop in their thought and in their writing appears as a legitimate extension to philosophy's quest for knowledge and understanding.

Many of the problems, traditionalisms, and contradictions traced by Adorno scholars and critics are connected to this attempt to overcome the limits of rationality, philosophical thought, and critical discourse by way of the aesthetic experience. In Adorno's endeavor to expand the boundaries of traditional philosophical discourse and its reception and to free philosophy from the limits of discursive logic, rationality, and speculation, he envisiones the philosophical text as an aesthetic entity. The underlying functions and operation of the production and reception of philosophical texts perform in a way similar to the aesthetic experience of genuine art, by inducing flashes of insight, provoking moments of recognition, and engendering expressions of the unsayable. These moments of recognition effect a deeper understanding of the riddles of being and of the conundrum we call reality. Obviously indebted to Benjamin, Adorno emphasizes the aesthetic dimension of philosophy in many of his writings, including his 1931 inaugural lecture for the University of Frankfurt, the "Theses on the Language of the Philosopher," and "The Essay as Form." In the inaugural lecture, on the topicality of philosophy (*Die Aktualität der Philosophie*), Adorno states that philosophy today must renounce all claims to totality and must divest itself from the illusion that thought and thinking can comprehend the totality of existence.[25] However, despite the necessity of relinquishing its claim to an absolute and stable truth, philosophy must continue to search for truth. Adorno conceives this search as a process of decoding signs rather than of positing facts, findings, and conclusions. Truth reveals itself through interpretation and critical reflection and in sudden flashes of recognition and insight:

> Plainly put: the idea of science (*Wissenschaft*) is research; that of philosophy is interpretation. In this remains the great, perhaps the everlasting paradox: philosophy persistently and with the claim of truth, must proceed interpretively without ever possessing a sure key to interpretation; nothing more is given to it than fleeting, disappearing traces within the riddle figures of that which exists and their astonishing entwinings.[26]

When operating within the philosophical paradox, in which one interprets and decodes without actually having recourse to a code, truth reveals itself in and as a moment of thought, in fleeting allusions, rather than concrete, unequivocal results. Philosophy cannot solve the riddle of being, but merely changes its ciphers into a text. However, Adorno asserts that the interpretation of the ciphers of being in no way implies a search for a singular meaning, for it is not the duty of philosophy to produce unequivocal interpretations. It should neither act as if an inherent meaning could be discovered, nor should it present and justify reality as meaningful. The function of solving a riddle is not to search for meaning or singular solutions behind the riddle but to illuminate such potential solutions through a flash of lightning.[27] Moreover, philosophy does not have the duty of finding an intention behind reality, but rather of constructing figures and drawing pictures that interpret "unintentional reality."[28]

Thus it may be said that philosophy and critical discourse compensate for their limitations and for the limitations of rationality through aesthetics and the aesthetic experience. In the convergence of philosophy and art, the entwinement of critical reflection and the aesthetic experience is brought to light: both "read" and interpret reality, construct figures and pictures of it, and render aspects of reality intelligible by generating flashes of insight. On the one hand, philosophy needs the aesthetic experience to complete its mission of decoding signs and constructing a text about reality, while on the other, art needs philosophy and critical reflection to extract and liberate its truth content. However, unlike philosophy, whose "artistic" material is language, artistic and musical creations are not bound to language and concepts in their attempt of express the unsayable. But artworks must nevertheless rely on language and critical reflection to mediate between subject and object, between art and the observer. Adorno's regrets regarding philosophy's reliance on concepts make his ideal of a text that does not subsume the non-identical understandable: "The cognitive utopia would be to use concepts to unseal the non-conceptual with concepts, without making it their equal."[29] The idea of gaining knowledge and understanding by putting in words the unsayable, by conceptualizing without imposing the violence of identity thinking, points toward Adorno's Benjaminian notion of the constellation/configuration. Adorno envisions philosophical interpretation not as the search for a true present meaning awaiting discovery, but rather as a search that throws a "sudden" and "momentary" light upon the question it simultaneously consumes. One finds the answers to the riddle of being by ordering and reordering the disparate elements of a question until they form a figure from which the "solution jumps out": "So philosophy has to bring its elements, which it receives from the sciences, into changing constellations, or, to say it with less astrological and scientifically more current expression, into changing trial combinations."[30]

As a central notion of Adorno's later writings, the constellation or configuration represents the ideal of nonconceptual insight and registers opposition to identity thinking, integration, subsumption, and the universal context of delusion. In the "Theses on the Language of the Philosopher," which were also written in the early thirties, Adorno uses the term to propagate what Wilke describes as one of the fundamental principles of Adorno's artistic construction of texts. The answer to the reification and staleness of traditional philosophical language is not to invent new terms and concepts, but to keep using traditional terminology, because at present new words and concepts can be constructed only through a change in the configuration of the words.[31] Based on his critique of language and concepts as instruments of power and ideology, Adorno elaborates in *Negative Dialectics* upon his claim that truth comes to light only in constellations of words and thoughts:

> By themselves, constellations represent from without what that concept has cut away within: the surplus which the concept is equally desirous and incapable of being. By gathering around the object of cognition, the concepts potentially determine the object's interior. They attain, in thinking, what was necessarily excised from thinking.[32]

Through essayistic writing, the writer takes the opportunity to construct constellations that bring to light the surplus of the non-identical excluded by conceptual thought and identity thinking. Constellations are riddles in which theoretical thought circles around the concept.[33] In a constellation, the central idea is presented and represented from ever-shifting perspectives and through figures of thought that use a combination of codes, rather than any single code. Because of their experimental and nonteleological qualities, essays, like aphorisms, allow for both this circular motion and perspectivist changes in the point of view. It is therefore not surprising that Adorno's inaugural lecture ends with a plea for the essay. Here Adorno's defense of essayistic writing as a form complementing the productivity of thought lays the groundwork for "The Essay as Form" written between 1954 and 1958. While considering the state and duty of contemporary philosophy, Adorno had already maintained in the thirties that the essay is its most appropriate form of expression. In Adorno's view, having given up its delusions of grandeur, thought has to take risks and embrace experimental modes of thinking and writing. Adorno gladly accepts the charge of essayism—supposedly an insult to "serious" philosophy—and argues that it was only in the century after Kant that the essay has gone from being a form of great philosophy to becoming "an insignificant form of aesthetics."[34] However, the erosion of certainty in "great" philosophy demands that the tradition of the "aesthetic essay," which offers limited, contoured, and nonsymbolic interpretations, be continued. Incapable of producing or understanding reality in its totality, the mind can still penetrate aspects of it. It may be possible "to explode in miniature the mass of merely existing reality."[35]

Adorno's search for alternative modes of representation and communication is informed by his critique of totality and his deep-seated skepticism toward language and concepts, as well as his rejection of reductive categories and false identities. To escape the pitfalls of the jargon of authenticity and reified language—declaring that Nietzsche was lucky that he did not live long enough to be disgusted by it—Adorno refuses to claim any logical totality for his arguments. Adorno's often abstruse and demanding style testifies to his preference of presenting ideas in their complexity rather than adjusting his discourse in order to make himself easily understood. Despite Adorno's resistance to the ideology of consumption, he nevertheless makes concessions to his readers. If it were to be consistent in its opposition to the language of consumption, which affirms power and domination, Adorno's text would have to be hermetic and resist inter-pretation.[36] However, although his complex and idiosyncratic thought critiques traditional concepts of philosophy and language, Adorno's texts do communicate and open themselves up to interpretation. In his quest to express his critique in an appropriate stylistic manner, Adorno often ignores conventional and norma-tive standards of writing. The enigmatic character and radical quality of Adorno's style might indeed explain in part the attractiveness and popularity, albeit prob-lematic and fleeting, of Adorno's texts in the sixties. Rainer Hoffmann provides a long list of some of the contradictory features of Adorno's idiosyncratic texts. He finds them to be fragmentary, idiomatic, and paradoxical-paratactic montages characterized by suspension, mobility, virtuality, interdependence, interference, convergence, and indifference.[37] The texts are oscillating between neither-nor, one as well as the other, negation and affirmation, authenticity and inauthentic-ity; in their multiplicity they exhibit at times an irritating lack of contour, an erratic use of concepts, deformations, encodings, irregularities, and intellectual obscurity as well as subtle-sublime artistry. The labyrinths of thought lead to mimetic and mediated differentiations, but also to unmediated and schematic coarseness, abstract and violent mutilation, brutal assumptions, prejudices, absolutes, and mannerist figures of speech.[38]

In his theses on the language of the philosopher, Adorno opposes the call for the comprehensibility of philosophical language, which he likens to a demand for social consumption. He sees the demand for ease of communication as being based upon the idealist belief that the signifying character of language permits language to be separated from its subject. This demand for comprehensible philosophical language, Adorno argues, is deceptive because it presupposes an intact relationship between words, concepts, and social reality. Adorno maintains that such a view of language is naive and ahistorical. He advocates instead the "truthful deployment of words according to the historical status of truth in them."[39] As Wilke points out, the philosophical basis for Adorno's critique of lan-guage and domination operates with relatively simple labels: conceptually clear and comprehensible language affirms domination, while language that is not, negates it.

Despite his tendency to proclaim his own prejudices in a way that implicitly stylizes them into objective truths, Adorno does not view his ideas as declarations of truth but rather as dynamic explorations of the mind. Adorno shares among many other traits with Nietzsche his tendency for programmatic, wholesale judg-ments. However, both thinkers always put into question and undermine their own judgments and proclamations of truths by the paradoxical, contradictory, and het-erogeneous construction of their texts and arguments. Adorno constructs his con-stellated figures of thought by restating his ideas from shifting perspectives and by enlarging upon them with a different emphasis and within a different context:

This gives an impression of confusion, but in fact amounts to a set of parallaxes, apparent displacements of an object due to changes of observation point. This is quite consistent with the idea that the object cannot be captured, and that a set of presentations may best approximate it.[40]

For Adorno, the essay allows for the creation of thought constellations, which are complex webs of ideas that interact with rather than dominate each other. In contrast to discursive logic, the ideas in an essay can be developed without regard for hierarchical order, grounding principles, or contradictions: "It neither makes deductions from a principle nor draws conclusions from coherent individual observations. It coordinates elements instead of subordinating them."[41]

By overcoming the oppressiveness of external order, the essay expresses the freedom of the mind. Unconcerned with providing objective or factual proof, but focused on reflecting upon its subject from various points of view, the essayistic form therefore resists the myths of scientific rationality and metaphysical thought. It defies notions of a beginning and an end; not origin and telos determine the structure, but the object under exploration itself:

It starts not with Adam and Eve but with what it wants to talk about; it says what occurs to it in that context and stops when it feels finished rather than when there is nothing to say. Hence it is classified as a trivial endeavor. Its concepts are not derived from a first principle, nor do they fill out to become ultimate principles.[42]

The essay's antisystematic impetus debunks notions of completeness and totality. There is no preconceived structure into which the material is fitted; rather, the structure of the essay is guided and formed by the material. Adorno claims that the idea of the essay is the result of the radical critique of systems: "In relationship to scientific procedure and its philosophical grounding as method, the essay, in accordance with its idea, draws the fullest conclusions from the critique of system."[43] The refusal to systematize thought and to subordinate and categorize its elements simultaneously expresses through style a radical critique of identity thinking. In the essay, the various elements relate to the whole in terms of a reciprocal action, for "specific moments are not to be derived from the whole, nor vice versa."[44] The essay affirms the right of the particular against universality and totality and protects the non-identical from subsumption. It "allows for the consciousness of nonidentity, without expressing it directly; it is radical in its non-radicalism, in refraining from any reduction to a principle, in its accentuation of the partial against the total, in its fragmentary character."[45]

As Rose points out, many of Adorno's titles, such as *Notes to Literature*, *Prisms*, *Impromptus*, and *In Search of Wagner*, emphasize his antitotalitarian aim and the fragmentary, preliminary, and experimental nature of his thought. The titles' choice of terms reject notions of finality, continuity, or completeness. Adorno contends that the philosophy of identity produces a false mental continuity, which conceals the breaks, disruptions, and antagonisms of thought, writ-

ing, and reality behind a logical order. However, to the essay these discontinuities are essential and should not to be hidden by structural and stylistic devices,
but, on the contrary, should be made visible. The essay always concerns itself
with "a conflict brought to a standstill."[46] By and in themselves, continuity, unity,
and harmony do not exist, are always imposed upon the subject, and are therefore an illusion silencing the inherent antagonisms of the subject matter. Uncon-
sciously and atheoretically, the essay annuls "theoretically outdated claims to
completeness and continuity in the concrete *modus operandi* of the mind as
well."[47] Essayistic writing is thus the strategic procedure deployed to eradicate
the surpassed claims of philosophy.

Adorno refers in this context to the Romantic fragment as the precursor to
his theory of the essay.[48] He understands the Romantic emphasis on self-reflection, the fragmentary, and the process of becoming as a result of epistemological
considerations, for the Romantics visualized thought processes as discontinuous
and potentially infinite: "The romantic conception of the fragment as a construction that is not complete but rather progresses onward into the infinite through
self-reflection champions this anti-idealist motive in the midst of Idealism."[49] In
the manner of Friedrich Schlegel's description of Romantic poetry as a process
of eternal becoming, Adorno perceives his essays as dynamic entities that cannot
be defined or exhausted by any theory. For this reason the essay is "the critical
form par excellence."[50] Yet the Adornoan essay goes beyond the Romantic conception of the progressive and fragmentary nature of writing by arguing that the
essay conflicts with Romantic notions of the universal and the artistic genius as
the authentic creator of the New. It not only resists the idea of universality, the
notions of a complete and completed work, and categorizations such as major
and minor works, but also disregards the metaphysics of original creation. The
thinker/writer/artist receives and creates in the audience flashes of insight, but
they appear neither as some form of original inspiration nor as a kiss from the
muse. Pronouncing the death of the autonomous subject, which has always been
an ideological construct, and asserting the impossibility of original creation,
Adorno argues that the essay's openness does not imply that it is based upon a
vague mood or feeling or philosophical and theoretical arbitrariness:

> The essay, which is always directed toward something already created, does not pre-
> sent itself as creation, nor does it covet something all-encompassing whose totality
> would resemble that of creation. Its totality, the unity of a form developed imma-
> nently, is that of something not total, a totality that does not maintain as form the the-
> sis of the identity of thought and its object that it rejects as content.[51]

Freed from the compulsion of identity, the essay resists the idea of a masterpiece
and thus allows the tension between the subject and the object to speak for itself.
In eluding official thought, the essay contains moments of "something inextin-
guishable."[52] Identity thinking and systematization are defense mechanisms that
protect thought from becoming vulnerable to diversity and prevent the subver-

sion of its claims. While identity thinking excludes the heterogeneous, antagonistic elements in the interest of self-preservation, the essay suspends the need for exclusions by rejecting the traditional notions of totality. Since the essay's structure negates systems, its unity is of a different order—not imposed, but determined by the interaction between subject and object, theory and experience.

Firstly, the essay recognizes not only the historicity of truth, its *Zeitkern*, but also the entwinement of truth and untruth. Secondly, the essay does not accept the metaphysical prejudice of separating truth from untruth or truth from history. The separation of truth from historical circumstance, which the essay form opposes, is the "old injustice done to the transitory."[53] The essay does not pretend to pronounce eternal truth, but rather truths that affirm the transitory nature of truth: "The essay, however, does not try to seek the eternal in the transient and distill it out; it tries to render that transient eternal. Its weakness bears witness to the very nonidentity it had to express."[54] Since it does not insist on the traditional notion of truth, the essay, like the aphorism, supports experimental and provocative thought. It is less concerned with results than with the process of critical reflection. Experimental thought presented in the mobile form of the essay incurs the risk of producing falsehoods. Like Nietzsche, Adorno reaffirms that truths cannot come into being without moments of untruth: "The daring, anticipatory, and not fully redeemed aspect of every essayistic detail attracts other such details as its negation; the untruth in which the essay knowingly entangles itself is the element in which its truth resides."[55] In the essay, moments of truth are propelled by moments of falsehood, and rather than becoming subdued by ideological claims to truth, this dynamic is celebrated.

In the same way that it denies grounding principles and traditional notions of truth, the essay denies a definition of its concepts. The essay makes no apologies for using concepts without removing all doubt about their usage. By refusing to define them, the essay resists reifying concepts and avoids fetishizing their relationship to language. As Bubner points out, Adorno's unwillingness to articulate and explain his argumentative basis and intellectual principles contradicts the traditional understanding of philosophical theory, which calls for rational and logical justifications and an explanation of its constitutive and operating principles.[56] The hallmark of Adorno's work, according to Bubner, is his consistent refusal to satisfy the traditional expectations of theoretical discourse. In praising Nietzsche for his departure from traditional philosophical discourse and for his radical critique of concepts, Adorno voices his regret that scientific inquiry remains bound to positivism and has not included the critique of concepts in its investigations. Whereas science and scholasticism remain committed to the definition and formulation of concepts rather than to their critical reflection, the essay "incorporates the anti-systematic impulse into its own way of proceeding and introduces concepts unceremoniously, 'immediately,' just as it receives them."[57] Adorno contends that it is a scientific superstition to believe that concepts are indeterminate until they are defined by scientists: "Science needs the notion of the concept as a *tabula rasa* to consolidate its claim to authority, its claim to be the sole power to occupy the head of the table. In actuality, all concepts are already implicitly concretized through the language in which they stand."[58] Bound to their linguistic and historic context, concepts cannot be simply defined. They have no inherent or describable meaning, for they reveal their meaning only within the framework of their constellation.

It is the intention of the essay to offer an intellectual experience and not a definitional procedure. Adorno compares this reading experience to learning a language by living in a foreign country, rather than by formal instruction. While the person living in the foreign country learns the language by experiencing it, the student learns it through grammatical explanations and definitions of meanings. The former learns the usages of concepts and words through hearing them in multiple contexts, as well as through using them on the basis of trial and error, and the essay relies, like the foreigner in a foreign country, upon the dynamic of experience and reflection. Like the foreign speaker, "the thinker does not actually think but rather makes himself into an arena for intellectual experience."[59]

In the essay, the concepts form configurations independently of a static framework; the configurations crystallize within a dynamic forcefield, leading to an intellectual encounter that evokes the aesthetic experience. The thoughts developed in the essay do "not progress in a single direction; instead the moments are interwoven as in a carpet."[60] The logic of the essay is related to the logic of art and music, for it develops according to its own precepts. Attempting to release the latent forces within it, the essay is not opposed to logic but rather gives back to language what discursive logic has taken away. Music, the most immaterial of all arts, represents most closely the utopian ideal of this nonconceptual expression. In his account of the development of the concept of absolute music, Dahlhaus asserts the "topos of Unsayability" as the central mark of modern art, literature, and music.[61] Based upon modern skepticism and the distrust of discursive language, music—because of its nonconceptual nature—takes on a privileged role in expressing the inexpressible. Dahlhaus maintains that Adorno's *Aesthetic Theory* might be the first aesthetic theory in which the term 'art' can be substituted by the word 'music'.[62] Andrew Bowie sees Adorno in the tradition of a counterdiscourse of modernity, that is, a counterdiscourse to Hegel in which the key players are Schelling, Hölderlin, and, of course, Nietzsche.[63] According to Bowie's argument, "music's resistance to wholesale interpretation and conceptual determination" explain its philosophical significance to modern thought and to Adorno, and Adorno's emphasis on music attempts to salvage "at least some aspects of subjectivity in a world increasingly dominated by mechanisms which threaten to abolish it."[64]

Without the essay, a critique of ideology would be unthinkable, because this form does not duplicate on a stylistic level what it denies in its argument. As a stylistic strategy for a radicalized critique of rationality, metaphysics, and enlightenment, the essay not only thematizes issues of representation but also embodies the very criticism it brings forth in its arguments, particularly in its openness of structure and negation of systems and identity. In its affinity to music, as well as figural and pictorial representation, the essay represents moments of resistance and protest paralleling those of autonomous art, while the process of writing essays parallels artistic composition in that the composer/writer/painter follows the logic of the material rather than imposing upon it external norms of conceptual design and order. The essay coordinates rather than subordinates and becomes readable as a dynamic forcefield of constellations. As a text, "The Essay as Form" itself practices what it preaches. Adorno explores his subject not by attempting to define it, but by circling around his topic in order to explore its different potentials. While he refers to the historical tradition of the essay, he resists establishing a consistent narrative on its origin and development. His essay on the essay is an unsystematic explication of this form's functions and potential, which insists upon illuminating the discontinuities of the topic in its style and structure. Simultaneously, this text serves as a defense of the essay against the demands of the conventions of disciplinary discourses. Behind "The Essay as Form" resides the probable intention to testify to the freedom of the spirit and to show the author's effort as a process of labor. For this reason, Adorno's text seems at times convoluted and exhibits the same tendency toward overdetermination that Bubner notes in relation to Adorno's understanding of the aesthetic experience. While at the beginning Adorno explains the essay's diminished reputation in Germany as a result of the German rigidity that has little patience with experimental and freespirited explorations, at the end he makes similar assertions, with the difference that they are now turned into negative rather than positive affirmations of the essay's potential. Ultimately, Adorno emphasizes the essay's critical dimension and its oppositional force against the orthodoxy of philosophical thought. The affirmation of the "freedom of the spirit" culminates in the assertion that the inner law of the essay is "heresy."[65]

Adorno delivers the final point of "The Essay as Form," a repudiation of the Platonic notion of an idea as "existing eternally and neither coming into being nor passing away, neither changing nor diminishing,"[66] by citing Nietzsche:

> If we affirm one single moment, we thus affirm not only ourselves but all existence. For nothing is self-sufficient, neither in us ourselves nor in things: and if our soul has trembled with happiness and sounded like a harp string just once, all eternity was needed to produce this one event—and in this single moment of affirmation all eternity was called good, redeemed, justified, and affirmed.[67]

The essay does not capitulate before or submit to the burden of what exists, and although Adorno agrees with Nietzsche's emphasis on the process of becoming, he resists—finding absurd the call to accept one's fate—the affirmation of even one single moment. To say yes to an individual moment of a false existence is to capitulate before the powers controlling human existence. Going beyond Nietzsche, Adorno asserts that the essay distrusts even Nietzsche's justification and affirmation of the single moment. There is no other way to express happiness except through negation, for the affirmation of life would be the affirmation of a life that does not live.[68]

Adorno clarifies his rejection of Nietzsche's joyful affirmations through his selection of titles, including *Minima Moralia*'s subtitle of *Reflections from Damaged Life* and the reversal of Nietzsche's *Gay Science* into the "melancholy science."[69] As Rose points out, Adorno is engaged in interventions or *Eingriffe*—the title of a collection of his essays—that must be understood within the context of the Nietzschean tradition of irony. Rose points out many of Adorno's "ironic inversions," including his transformation of Kierkegaard's *The Sickness unto Death* to "The Health unto Death," Freud's *Beyond the Pleasure Principle* to "This side of the pleasure principle," and finally Hegel's "The whole is the true" to "The whole is the false." Rose sees Adorno's *Minima Moralia* as ironic in two senses of the word: as an "'expression of meaning by use of words normally conveying the opposite meaning' and 'apparent perversity of fate or circumstance'."[70] Rose suggests that one should not at all times read Adorno literally, but as an ironist who alters ideas or phrases. She further suggests that Adorno's own tendency toward totalizations, such as the universal context of delusion, the administered society, the end of the individual, and the reification of culture also cannot be taken literally, but should rather be read as dramatizations of "these ideas, presenting them *as if* they were absolutely and literally true, in order to undermine them more effectively."[71] In other words, Rose suggests that readers must sometimes take Adorno literally and sometimes not.[72] Although Rose's assertions seem convincing, they fail to take into account the consequences of this oscillation between literal and nonliteral reading, firstly for the interpretation of Adorno's thought and, secondly, for the notion of irony itself. Adorno sees irony within the general process of societal decay. It is the modern paradox that the state of affairs which could have once been ironized by exaggeration has become reality. Irony, convicting "its object by presenting it as what it purports to be; and without passing judgement" was once an effective expression of protest, but has now "itself come into contradiction with truth.[73] Agreement and reconciliation, which are the formal a priori of irony, have become universal affirmations of the existing order, and in the age of bourgeois delusion, the medium of irony, the difference between ideology and reality, has disappeared.[74] It is no longer possible to play with, let alone laugh about the gap between ideal and reality, and Adorno—literally or not—pronounces indeed the end of irony:

> The gesture of the unthinking That's-how-it-is is the exact means by which the world dispatches each of its victims, and the transcendental agreement inherent in irony becomes ridiculous in face of the real unanimity of those it ought to attack. Pitted against the deadly seriousness of total society, which has absorbed the opposing voice, the impotent objection earlier quashed by irony, there is now only the deadly seriousness of comprehended truth.[75]

The dwindling ability, or even the incapacity, to differentiate between ideology and reality, or delusion and truth, undermines the formal basis for irony. Irony can no longer thematize the break between reality and an utopian idea of something better, and can therefore no longer serve as a reconciling force as well; the oppositional dimension of irony has been absorbed, and in the face of present reality, irony is turned into a farce unable to escape affirmation and false and imposed reconciliations. Irony no longer protests against the bourgeois context of delusion but rather participates in its perpetuation.

Adorno's own brand of irony, an irony of "deadly seriousness," makes it difficult to decide when to read him literally and when not. The nonliteral readings that Rose suggests seem possible only from a position of detachment and by distancing oneself from the text. Rose's suggestion for an occasional nonliteral reading implies that Adorno tends to exaggerate at times and that he these exaggerations, or—as Bubner argues—overdeterminations—should not to be taken at face value. Thus, intended or not, the deadly seriousness of Adorno's writing appears at times to allow the reader to avoid taking him seriously.

NIETZSCHE'S APHORISMS

As a stylistic protest, essayistic and aphoristic writing reflects the "deadly seriousness" of total society and opposes participation in the universal context of delusion. Trying to elude systems of domination, Adorno's fragmentary mode of communication is a way to circumvent the degradation of life to consumption and the principle of exchange.[76] In his introduction to *Minima Moralia*, Adorno describes his choice to write a collection of aphorisms as reflecting his wish to confront the negative and to oppose the liquidation of the particular. He characterizes this work as an attempt to approach philosophy from the point of view of subjective experience.

The aphoristic style of writing appears not only appropriate for Nietzsche's thought, but also necessary for his antisystematic and antimetaphysical critique in an antisystematic and antimetaphysical fashion. Through the aphoristic form, Nietzsche rejects on a stylistic level traditional philosophical thought, and furthers his project of the reevaluation of all values. Furthermore, the aphoristic nature of Nietzsche's thought undermines all attempts to read his work as a coherent philosophy of life. In his article on the fragment, Behler notes how this mode of writing no longer allows for a coherent reading, by which the reader brings its pronouncements under a hierarchical or dialectical order. Even if we assumed such a continuous discourse in Nietzsche's case, Behler argues, we would immediately sense that his thought was already one step ahead of such suppositions. Nietzsche's philosophy expresses itself in another language, a language no longer of the whole, but of the fragment, of plurality and of disjunction.[77]

Behler's argument that the aphoristic, fragmentary quality of Nietzsche's writing thwarts all attempts to systematize Nietzsche is well taken, although it is neither uncontested nor unproblematic. Many Nietzsche scholars, editors, and translators assert that Nietzsche's writings must be read as a coherent set of texts. To disconnect single aphorisms from a work, which decontextualizes them, results in fateful misinterpretations and misrepresentations of Nietzsche's thought. Scholars generally divide Nietzsche's writing into three phases or periods, and many point out, for example, the tight structure of Nietzsche's books, exemplified by the presence of prefaces and epilogues, the division into chapters and subchapters, and the numbering of the aphorisms. However, the fact that the books are structured does not necessarily imply that all of Nietzsche's writings can be read as an organic system, nor does this fact support the assertion that Nietzsche's work dissolves into an arbitrary assortment of fragments. As Shapiro points out, this latter conclusion is shared—despite their opposing views on Nietzsche—by both Habermas and the French exponents of the New Nietzsche: "accompanied by a simple reversal of their valorization of the discontinuous, fragmentary, and irrational," Habermas's construction of an aestheticist Nietzsche draws a parallel picture to that of the New Nietzsche.[78] While the postmoderns praise this discontinuity, Habermas reproaches Nietzsche for this supposedly irrational and aestheticist critique of enlightenment. For the postmoderns, Nietzsche's style of writing reflects the realities of the postmodern world, characterized by the death of God and the subject, the end of metaphysics, and the end of the myth of rationality and enlightenment. For Habermas, Nietzsche provides an ill-suited model for Adorno and Horkheimer's critique of enlightenment, not only because it collapses the distinction between reason and power but also because it renounces claims to truth and retains "only the rhetorical claim of the aesthetic fragment."[79]

A paradoxical, and somewhat unsatisfactory, solution to the problem of coherence and continuity of Nietzsche's work might lie in Friedrich Schlegel's ambivalence toward systems; in the *Athenaeums-Fragment* no. 52, he asserts that it is equally deadly to the mind to have a system than it is to have none and that one will have to combine both possibilities. Nietzsche himself proposes a different, but related answer when he compares aphorisms to the links of a chain. As part of a train of thought, they require the reader to assemble this chain by employing their own faculties. This assembly process demands a great deal from the reader, but, as Nietzsche claims, aphorisms are presumptuous.[80] It is worth noting that Nietzsche does not ask readers to reconstruct a chain according to the author's intention or some other a priori. While a reader's deployment of his or her own mode of assembly does, of course, not preclude him or her from constructing an idiosyncratic, wilful chain, it does preclude the option of reading Nietzsche's books as disconnected, decontextualized, and arbitrary fabrications.

Nietzsche's aphorisms include a rich variety of forms and structures, such as maxims, proverbs, warnings, provocative exclamations, ironic phrases, surprise endings, fictional dialogues, and figurative expressions.[81] Some aphorisms consist of one sentence, others are essayistic explorations and complex interpretive efforts. Nietzsche himself did not differentiate between the various subforms of aphoristic writing, and, according to Behler, Nietzsche avoided the term "fragment" because of its connection to Romanticism.[82] In the preface to the *Genealogy of Morals*, Nietzsche explains that the whole third essay constitutes the exemplary interpretation of one single aphorism. Reading aphorisms, in Nietzsche's view, is an exercise in the art of interpretation, an art that has been unlearned even by the best of modern readers, some of whom

> find difficulty with the aphoristic form: this arises from the fact that today this form is *not taken seriously enough*. An aphorism, properly stamped and molded, has not been "deciphered" when it has simply been read; rather, one has than to begin its *exegesis*, for which is required an art of exegesis.[83]

Nietzsche has the same complaint concerning aphorisms that Adorno has with regard to essays: that neither form is respected and taken seriously enough. Nietzsche's reference to the art of exegesis not only illustrates the importance he places upon the practice of interpretation, but also has implications for the notion of aphorisms as the links of a chain. While the latter contradicts claims to a decontextualized reading, the call for interpretation contradicts the postulation of an arbitrary meaning. Nietzsche's proposal that an aphorism can and should be deciphered questions the legitimacy of the Derridian and postmodern emphasis upon the indeterminacy and undecidability of Nietzsche's work. However, Nietzsche does not suggest that the reader must apprehend the "right" meaning hidden in the text, because he places his emphasis upon the process of interpretation. To interpret his writings, Nietzsche suggests the necessity of rumination: "one has almost to be a cow and in any case *not* a 'modern man'."[84] Offering his own ruminations to the reader, Nietzsche presents the Third Essay, which is preceded by a brief aphorism, as an exemplary practice of the art of exegesis. However, the aphorism supposedly interpreted in the Third Essay stands in a very general and open-ended relationship to the essay explicating the meaning of ascetic ideals. The aphorism, taken from *Zarathustra* reads: "Unconcerned, mocking, violent—thus wisdom wants us: she is a woman and always loves only a warrior."[85] Aside from yet another woman as metaphor—here truth is replaced by wisdom—and the stereotypical proclamation that women love strong and aggressive men, the aphorism is suggestive of very little of what actually follows in the Third Essay. After having read the Third Essay's explication of the meaning of the ascetic ideal as an instrument of power, it is of course possible to establish a connection between the essay and the aphorism, but it is doubtful that without awareness of Nietzsche's line of argument any reader would interpret the aphorism in terms of the relationship between the ascetic ideal and mechanisms of power and domination.

Nietzsche's interpretation of the aphorism is neither compulsory nor necessarily compelling, and it identifies his practice of exegesis as highly subjective and driven by personal and external interests rather than by factors immanent to the text. Nietzsche thus demonstrates that one aphorism has the potential for endless commentary and interpretation. An aphorism cannot be understood and apprehended once and for all, it must be reread and reinterpreted in order to explore its many potentials. Nietzsche wants to motivate his readers to think for themselves and to be critical and skeptical toward everything presented to them as truth. The reader must be willing to question and doubt everything. "*The old man*: Do you want to be the teacher of mistrust of truth, then?—*Pyrrhon*: Of mistrust such as there has never yet been on earth before, of mistrust of all and everything. It is the only path to truth."[86] Aphorisms present this distrust of claims to truth in an antisystematic manner that permits an attack from many different vantage points upon all claims, foundations, and assumptions, including those of the aphorism itself. Aphorisms undermine any attempt to affirm one single point of view.

Nietzsche characterizes his thought as a "schooling in suspicion."[87] He wants to provoke and seduce his readers into taking on the challenge of questioning all points of view. In order to do so, Nietzsche admits to wearing various masks, including the mask of evil. This element of play and performance is central to Nietzsche's thought and style, through which philosophy becomes a profoundly reflective play with ideas and an enactment of possibilities on the page. Aphorisms are the form of writing that allows for this kind of masquerade and exploration of ideas. For Behler, the issue is to leave Nietzsche's text be in its contradictions, oppositions, and tensions between science and life, art and science, Classicism and Romanticism, and purposeless and life-giving art without defusing it through schematization or reduction to principles; then Nietzsche's text shows itself to be a great game.[88]

A reading of Nietzsche's aphorisms as playful provocations assumes that his contradictory statements are integral to his texts and recognizes that Nietzsche's ironic textual strategy opens up the gap between ideology and reality. Despite his reputation as a master of irony, Nietzsche himself has—like Adorno, albeit for different reasons—a critical attitude toward irony. In his study of Nietzsche's notion of irony, Behler shows that Nietzsche seldom uses the term, and when he does, he attaches to it mostly negative connotations.[89] Nietzsche criticizes irony, according to Behler's findings, because he associates it with an attitude of practical pessimism, that is, with Socratism, scholasticism, decadence, and Romanticism. However, Behler shows the convergence between Nietzsche's ideas and practice of irony and the concepts of Romantic, tragic, and world-historical irony as well as the relationship between the mask and the classical notion of *dissimulatio*. Considering that it only seems possible to love one's fate either through utter devotion to a higher cause or through an ironic gesture cultivating a pathos of distance, it is not difficult to agree with Behler that Hegel's world-historical irony is of critical import for Nietzsche's notion of *amor fati*. According to Hegel, the individual is subjected to the will of world history, and world-historical irony constitutes itself in the disparity between the individual's interests and efforts and the cunning of reason, which turns the individual—while thinking that it is pursuing its own interests—into an instrument fulfilling not his own will but rather that of world history. In Nietzsche there exists, of course, no higher plan or power whose will must be followed, and the irony of world history lies not in the presence of a higher plan and a rational order, but in the belief in their existence, which allows individuals to submit to a nonexistent will. Nietzsche maintains that the march of history is indeed full of ironies, including the lack of a positive reception of his own work: "*amor fati* is my inmost nature. But this does not preclude my love of irony, even world-historical irony."[90] As one of the few positive statements about irony, Nietzsche's proclaimed love of irony shows his appreciation of the absurdities of life, which he prefers to encounter with laughter rather than deadly seriousness.

The importance of Nietzsche for the tradition of irony—highlighted in the writings of Thomas Mann—comes to light also in an investigation of irony as the classical phenomenon of *dissimulatio*. Wearing various masks and costumes enables Nietzsche to explore various points of view and to simultaneously make visible an ironic tension between truth and lie, ideals and reality, and the negation and affirmation of life. The aphorism is uniquely suited for this—often sarcastic—play with masks and ironies, and for this reason it consists of thought that produces thoughts; an aphorism is "a text without end for the thinker."[91] Nietzsche demands an active reader, an exploring nomad, and experimenting skeptic. There is no absolute truth to be found, but there are many ways to find truths. Although Nietzsche makes no claim to provide a particular way to gain knowledge and understanding, he does hope to speed up the development of the "free spirits" who can think critically.[92] While Adorno sees the essay as testimony to the *freedom of the spirit*, Nietzsche finds aphorisms the appropriate expression and food for thought for the *free spirits*, the ideal thinkers—that is, writers and readers—of the future. The free spirits are self-determined individuals who refuse to allow anyone or anything to dominate them. Nietzsche admits that such free spirits are a construct of his imagination, but they nonetheless represent his ideal audience, an audience that does not exist. Aphorisms inspire the free spirits, because they are for the "adventurers and circumnavigators of that inner world called 'man'."[93] Unafraid of experimentation, alienation, and distortion, the free spirits are curious perspectivists who ask: "Can *all* values not be turned round? and is good perhaps evil? and God only an invention and finesse of the devil? Is everything perhaps in the last resort false? And if we are deceived, are we not for that very reason also deceivers? *must* we not be deceivers?"[94] Truth is a matter of perspective, and because thinkers produce fictions about the world, they are guilty of deception. However, through the continuous rethinking and correction of these fictions by a fearless and truthful thinker moments of truth can be born. The aphoristic form provides the space for reconsideration and guarantees freedom from the untruthful constraints of systematic thought. It allows the thinker to examine subjects from a distance and from outside of the metaphysical structures of thought.

Similar to Adorno's shifting constellations and parallactic figures of thought, Nietzsche's aphorisms are representative of his perpectivism. Aphorisms allow for the contradictions resulting from these changing points of view without forcing the thinker to reconcile conflicting statements. Nietzsche asserts that the short and fragmentary nature of aphorisms should not lead the reader to assume that the thinker is unaware of these contradictions, or that the fragmentary form of writing characterizes undeveloped thoughts.

> *Against the censurers of brevity.*—Something said briefly can be the fruit of much long thought: but the reader who is a novice in this field, and has as yet reflected on it not at all, sees in everything said briefly something embryonic, not without censuring the author for having served him up such immature and unripened fare.

> *Against the shortsighted.*—Do you think this work must be fragmentary because I give it to you (and have to give it to you) in fragments?[95]

Nietzsche indicates that the process of gaining knowledge and understanding cannot be an effort to obtain comprehensive information or the "whole truth," and he shares Adorno's antitotalitarian impetus: the latter contends that the essay is the ideal form for the partial and the particular and expresses the concern for the nonidentical "in refraining from any reduction to a principle, in its accentuation of the partial against the total, in its fragmentary character."[96] Similar to Nietzsche's defense of fragmentary, that is, aphoristic thought and writing, Adorno argues that the "customary objection that the essay is fragmentary and contingent itself postulates that totality is given, and with it the identity of subject and object, and acts as though one were in possession of the whole."[97] Calling for the abandonment of teleological and ontological speculation, Nietzsche, like Adorno, nevertheless affirms the possibility to some form of truth—be it as truths in the plural or as truthfulness. Philosophers, according to Nietzsche, fail to recognize the contingency and mutability of the so-called truth and the historical constructedness of their own concoctions. Furthermore, "they involuntarily think of 'man' as an *aeterna veritas*, as something that remains constant in the midst of all flux, as a sure measure of things. . . . Lack of historical sense is the family failing of all philosophers."[98] In order to debunk metaphysical speculation, philosophy needs to acknowledge the processes of becoming and the dynamics of power and domination in history: "But everything has become: there are *no eternal facts*, just as there are no absolute truths. Consequently what is needed from now on is *historical philosophizing*, and with it the virtue of modesty."[99] Aphorisms emphasize the moment and take the particular into account; however, their truths transcend time and space. Once the search for the eternal in the transient has been abandoned, Adorno contends that the aim of the essay is to celebrate the transitory. The essay "does not try to seek the eternal in the transient and distill it out; it tries to render the transient eternal."[100] Nietzsche in turn claims the same for aphorisms, the form in which the transitory finds its form of eternity. "The aphorism, the apophthegm, in which I am the first master among Germans, are the forms of 'eternity'; my ambition is to say in ten sentences what everyone else says in a book—what everyone else *does not* say in a book."[101]

"Eternal"—Nietzsche puts "eternity" in quotation marks—is not the content (i.e., the argument or insight presented), but the endless possibility for reflection. Striving after a little immortality of his own, Nietzsche wants to "create things upon which time tries its teeth in vain."[102]

> *In praise of the maxim.*—A good maxim is too hard for the teeth of time and whole millennia cannot consume it, even though it serves to nourish every age: it is thus the great paradox of literature, the imperishable in the midst of change, the food that is always in season, like salt—though, unlike salt, it never loses its savour.[103]

Transcending time and space, the aphorism's fragmentary multiplicity offers the potential for constantly changing interpretations. Defying finality, the "endless melody"[104] of the aphorism is of greater value to the reader than an exhaustive discussion leaving nothing to the imagination. Never exhaustively explored nor completely fleshed out, the aphorism's presentation of thoughts can be compared to the expressive dimensions of relief figures:

> *The effectiveness of the incomplete.*—Just as figures in relief produce so strong an impression on the imagination because they are as it were on the point of stepping out of the wall but have suddenly been brought to a halt, so the relief-like, incomplete presentation of an idea, of a whole philosophy, is sometimes more effective than its exhaustive realization: more is left for the beholder to do, he is impelled to continue working on that which appears before him so strongly etched in light and shadow, to think it through to the end, and to overcome even that constraint which has hitherto prevented it from stepping forth fully formed.[105]

Nietzsche praises the styles of writing, "in which the fixed form is constantly being broken up, displaced, transposed back into indefiniteness, so that it signifies one thing and at the same time another."[106]

For Adorno, Nietzsche's suspension of certainty reflects the true nature of philosophy. In rebelling against the imposition of principles, rules, and orders, aphoristic writing makes visible the limitations of factual and instrumentalized truths of science and systematic philosophy. Because of their denial of completeness and finality, aphorisms can serve to emphasize philosophy's difference from both factuality and fictionality. It constitutes the form that can rescue philosophy from the prison house of dogma, ideology, and scholasticism and appropriately express its suspended nature, because philosophy "is nothing but the expression of its inexpressibility. In this respect it is a true sister of music. There is scarcely a way to put the suspension into words, which may have caused the philosophers—except for Nietzsche, perhaps—to gloss it over."[107]

Aphorisms and essays offer Nietzsche and Adorno a way out of traditional philosophical discourse—although they are both certainly aware of a tradition of aphoristic and essayistic writing. It is important, however, to remember that despite their overwhelming reliance on and shared estimation of aphorisms and essays as form, both Nietzsche and Adorno relied upon many styles. Adorno wrote numerous essays, and even his *Negative Dialectics* and his monumental theory of the aesthetic can be read and understood as essayistic writing—as gigantic essays—for they adhere to the basis principles outlined in the essay about the essay. Exhibiting shifts in styles and genres, the Nietzschean narratives exemplify "a battery of narrative styles and forms"[108] and are notoriously difficult to classify.[109]

Stylistic pluralism is one significant facet of Nietzsche's perspectivism and Adorno's constellation. Alexander Nehamas's study of Nietzsche's life as literature establishes a relationship between Nietzsche's styles, his perspectivism, and his rejection of the philosophical tradition. Nehamas rejects the notion that Nietzsche's search for styles reflect his effort to find a single "adequate means of expression" and argues that Nietzsche's stylistic pluralism is another facet of his perspectivism and "one of his essential weapons in his effort to distinguish himself from the philosophical tradition."[110] The same motivation underlies Adorno's practice and his efforts to criticize and subvert traditional philosophy by reestablishing a connection between philosophy and social reality. However, like Nietzsche, who insists upon expounding a philosophy of life, Adorno refuses to give practical instructions or final answers to the questions posed. The provisionary truths of their writings provide insights into the untruth of all truth and the uncertainty of all certainties.[111]

"Why I Write Such Good Books"

> Ultimately, nobody can get more out of things, including books, than
> he already knows. For what one lacks access to from experience one
> will have no ear. . . . Whoever thought he had understood something
> of me, had made up something out of me after his own image—not
> uncommonly an antithesis to me.
>
> —Nietzsche, "Why I write such good books"

While it would be difficult to argue that Adorno created an antithesis to Nietzsche out of Nietzsche, one could argue with some justification that he created a
Nietzsche according to his own image. In Adorno's writing, Nietzsche functions
primarily as a critic of ideology, and Adorno eclectically cites Nietzsche's works
to invent a Nietzsche who suits his own purposes. To speak in general terms,
Adorno devoted his life's work to uncovering ideology, and in this he perceives
a genuine kinship to Nietzsche, who relentlessly laid bare the ideological underpinnings of Christianity, bourgeois society, metaphysics, rationality, and
unmasked the ideologies informing all areas of society and social interaction,
including educational institutions and modern art. For Adorno, ideology is not
merely false consciousness, or as the dictionary defines it, "the body of ideas
reflecting the social needs and aspirations of the individual, group, class, or cul-

ture."[1] Although ideology is certainly based upon and shaped by the needs and ambitions of a culture, it does not become ideology because these needs and aspirations interfere with the discovery of truth in form of wishful thinking and the dogmatic adherence to beliefs. Ideas become ideology and weave themselves into a universal context of delusion when they pretend not to be ideology and instead claim to be truth or an objective statement or reflection of reality. It is not false consciousness as such, but the denial of the social, historical, and cultural constructedness of ideas, values, and norms and the concealment of their multiple functions in the service of exercising power that constitute ideology. His insight into the processes of ideology formation and utilization place Nietzsche ahead of his time. For this reason Adorno regards him as one of the most important figures of philosophy. Nietzsche not only uncovered and argued against patterns of false consciousness, but also recognized the human-all-too-human desire to perpetuate these patterns, norms, and values which serve to validate human behavior. He expended a great amount of intellectual energy analyzing these patterns of thought and behavior and their multiple and changing functions. Furthermore, he thematized the human tendency to "forget" that conventions are conventions and that as a result fiction becomes stylized into truth.

At the very basis of the critique of ideology stands a radicalized critique of rationality, and this critical questioning of rationality causes Nietzsche and Adorno to engage in what Habermas calls a performative contradiction. Indeed, the critique of rationality is a paradoxical enterprise, for by questioning rationality, criticism puts into question its own foundation. As a rational activity, criticism cannot—if it wishes to generate reasonable discourses and remain within the parameters of communicability—deny its own rational presuppositions and preconditions and its involvement in the creation and perpetuation of the myths of rationality. However, for Nietzsche and Adorno, the point is not to avoid such paradoxes and contradictions or to deny their own complicity with the ideologies of rationality, but rather to problematize them, to question and undermine their own activity, authority, and claim to legitimation. Undermining the foundations of criticism can be conceptualized more productively in terms of a deliberate *demonstrative* contradiction necessitated by the very operation of a radical critique of ideology rather than in terms of an ill-fated *performative* contradiction attacking the foundations of Western tradition. Although Habermas is correct in his assessment of a contradiction in the performance of Nietzsche's and Adorno's criticism, the term *performative contradiction*—while emphasizing the performance aspect—de-emphasizes the demonstrative quality of and the critical impetus behind this self-reflective performance. Since rationality functions as a tool of ideology and power within the context of delusion and since—having reached its limits—it reverts to myth, a fundamental critique of ideology would not be possible without interrogating the ideological functions of rationality itself. This debasement of rationality informs the framework for Nietzsche's and Adorno's thought and constitutes the very core of their radicalization of modern self-reflection. It also motivates their turn toward the aesthetic realm in order to expand the limitations of recognition and understanding imposed by rationality and rational discourse—without, however, falling back onto myth, irrationality, superstition, beliefs, and wishful thinking.

Accompanying the critique of rationality is the recognition of the death of the autonomous, rational subject. As Nietzsche points out in a pre-Freudian fashion, the individual can no longer be conceptualized as the self-identical, self-conscious, and rationally acting agent of his own consciousness, but rather as a fragmented, "civilized" being tormented by its instincts and desires. Driven by the dictates of social, cultural, and institutional conventions, this divided self is not propelled and motivated to action by reason as such, but is capable of utilizing rationality to its own end. Nietzsche's and Adorno's thought diverges from traditional enlightenment philosophy and the idea of universal reason and postulates instead rationality as an instrument pressed into the service of the will to self-preservation and to power. Certainly, rationality underlies human achievements, but it is no longer seen as the foundation for human action. Refuting the glorification of reason as the ennobling human faculty, rationality becomes, by Nietzsche's and Adorno's account, an instrument and a means to an end.

While Adorno speaks of the human drive toward self-preservation, Nietzsche takes it a step further by positing the will to power. Although for the most part the will to self-preservation underlies the will to power, no claim to a universal validity of this connection is made. As Nietzsche points out, human beings rather will nothingness than will nothing, and therefore, in some cases, the immediate interest of the self might be sacrificed in the interest of the exercise of power. Nietzsche demonstrates this sacrifice through the example of the ascetic priest, who renounces his life-affirming instincts and drives, but who also with this perverted renunciation nullifies neither the will to power nor the experience of pleasure. On the contrary, the self-renunciation and the negation of life employed in the service of the decadent, degenerative, and reactive will to power is a sign of degenerating life attempting to preserve itself. It brings with it a sadistic kind of self-gratification, the kind of satisfaction and pleasure derived from control, domination, and from offering a cure for the ailments of humanity. Socrates, the ascetic priest, and Wagner are the most prominent examples of those pretending to be healers of humanity, offering, respectively, rational discourse, self-sacrificing morality, and decadent art as a cure—a cure, however, that only hastens the decline of culture. Although Nietzsche establishes a hierarchy of forces by separating the will to power in terms of the active, aristocratic drive and the reactive, decadent drive, these two drives are ultimately inseparable. As Deleuze convincingly argues, the two forces cannot in any fundamental sense be divided, because active forces become reactive and reactive forces have the capacity to become active. According to Nietzsche, the life-negating forces of the ascetic are, paradoxically, reactive forces in the service of life: "*the ascetic ideal springs from the protective instinct of a degenerating life* which tries by all means to sustain itself and to fight for its existence."[2] An apparent enemy and denier of life, the ascetic priest is "among the greatest *conserving* and yes-creating forces of life."[3] He is capable of utilizing and changing the direction—and thus the quality—of the self-negating forces, such as bad conscience and *ressentiment*. Therefore, the oscillation between action and reaction, meanings and values must remain always ambivalent, and, as Deleuze argues, an evaluation of active and reactive forces entails the interpretation of the degree of their development in relation to negation and affirmation.[4]

Although not directly concerned with an interpretation of Nietzsche's notion of the will to power, much of Adorno's work—especially the *Dialectic*'s "Excursus" and *Minima Moralia*—testifies to a basic agreement with Nietzsche's psychological insight into the functioning of the will to power and with Deleuze's assessment of the entwinement of action and reaction, of the aristocratic and decadent forces. The entwinement and interaction of these oppositional forces within the individual embody the duplicity and ambiguity of modernity. The intensified struggle with the forces of action and reaction, as well as myth and enlightenment, is the hallmark of the modern individual sitting, in Nietzsche's words, between two chairs and saying Yes and No in the same breath. Exemplary for the history of enlightenment, the self-sacrificing, cunning subject, Odysseus, acts out both reactive and active forces: attesting to the will to self-mastery, the active forces strive for emancipation from the forces of nature and myth; however, while striving for enlightenment and liberation, the active forces become irrevocably entangled with reactive forces, and the will to liberate the self from nature turns into the domination of nature and the self. Rationality is instrumentalized—at the cost of the repression of instincts and desire and the deferral of pleasure in the hope of future reward—in order to further the individual's ambitions. As both Adorno and Nietzsche point out, the principle of exchange pervades human action and the interaction with nature, others, and the self. The individual pays the price for the sacrifices made in the interest of furthering his or her goals, for these self-renunciating sacrifices lead to the denial of the inner nature and toward the further fragmentation of the already damaged subject. Instrumentalized rationality and its tools, including logic, dialectics, and systems, are the means to advance and justify the end. Philosophical systems, religion, metaphysics, and the other shadows of God legitimize claims to power, and they furthermore alleviate existential fears by providing the illusion of normativity and order.

Nietzsche and Adorno are not only concerned with uncovering fictions, ideologies, and the reversions to myth within the history of civilization, but also face the question of *how* this disclosure should and can take place. If the history of civilization is not a rational, progressive march towards enlightenment or toward some goal—be it a classless society, a state directed by God's will, or the realization of freedom or the world spirit—then it can neither be portrayed nor understood by progressive or linear narratives presenting definite beginnings and ends. A historical narrative reflecting the historical entwinement of myth and reason must make visible the breaks and discontinuities in the continuous process of becoming and in the continuous struggle between forces. These historical counternarratives must question not only the origins and functions of the historical developments themselves, but also their ideological functions as representations and interpretations of history. Both the *Dialectic* and the Nietzschean notion of genealogy present such experimental counternarratives to traditional histories, and they attempt to escape the construction of ideology by making clear that they do not offer representations of history or the revelation of truth, but alternative interpretations. Habermas and Rath point out some of the many parallel lines of argumentation between the *Genealogy* and the *Dialectic*. However, the similarities do not end with the arguments presented by these works, but also encompass the theoretical framework and the self-reflective mode behind the construction of these narratives. As manifestation of the free spirit or the sovereign mind, neither the *Genealogy* nor the *Dialectic* is concerned with accounting for historical facts and figures, but with interpreting the functions, utilizations, and transformations of values, norms, structures of thought, institutions, and systems. The *Genealogy* and the *Dialectic* present narratives that identify themselves as interpretations, and both reach back to myth in order to deconstruct the master narratives of Western civilization. Like the *Dialectic*, the *Genealogy* demonstrates the entwinement of myth and enlightenment, not just as a claim and argument but also in its narrative construction. However, genealogy's critical impetus should not be understood as merely mirroring the argument—the entwinement of myth and reason—on the level of presentation or style, for by undermining traditional methods of apprehending and writing history, Nietzsche's and Adorno's genealogical explorations go beyond enacting their central theses. Their reinterpretation of myth, values, and conventions, breaks open and undercuts the power of both myth and enlightenment without, however, falling back into myth or negating entirely their intention to enlighten. Both narratives make their own reliance upon mythological structures and themes and their complicity with enlightenment visible. By confronting rationality—the very foundation of thought and criticism—with myth, they thematize their involvement in the perpetuation of the myths of enlightenment in an attempt to escape the ideologization of their own thought.

    This self-reflective mode of thought evident in the contradictions, paradoxes, repetitions, endless variations of themes and issues, the questioning of norms and perceptions, and the constant attempt at undermining their own presuppositions testify to a profound intellectual kinship between Nietzsche and Adorno—a kinship that, on the surface, appears strained because of various dividing factors, including Adorno's Marxism, the importance of sociological and economic considerations to Adorno's thought, and Adorno's negativity. However, their shared concern with a critique of ideology and the formal and stylistic aspects of criticism brings them not only to formulate similar lines of

argumentation but also to experiment with similar forms and styles appropriate
to the expression of their arguments. Their role as cultural diagnosticians, their
shared interest in art in general and music in particular, and their concern with
form and style create the basis for the centrality of art to their social criticism.
Art and cultural developments are not only the central focus of Nietzsche's and
Adorno's works, but also occupy a key position in the reflections leading to the
formulation of their ideas. Thus, their preoccupation with form and style is not a
concern with the cosmetics of representation, but the manifestation of the drive
toward an antifoundational and antisystematic questioning of existing values,
judgments, and conditions. In their Wagner critiques, Adorno and Nietzsche exe-
cute the exemplary fusion of the critique of art and ideology. Wagner functions
as the quintessential type of the modern artist, while their discussions of his
music dramas demonstrate the failures and ambiguities of modern art. Their writings on the Wagner phenomenon presents a form of criticism that deciphers the
aesthetics of ideology and the ideology of the aesthetic.

Recently, Wagner's great-grandson Gottfried Wagner, the black sheep of the
Wagner family and the Bayreuth circle, followed the Nietzschean-Adornoan tradition of an ideological-critical approach to Wagner's work. Understanding Wagner as a cultural and ideological phenomenon, Gottfried Wagner finds Nietzsche
to be the most brilliant and perceptive critic of Wagner and his circle.[5] He claims
that there exists a long tradition of anti-Semitism and authoritarianism in the
Wagner family—from Wagner, Cosima Wagner, Winifred Wagner to his uncle,
Wieland, and his father Wolfgang Wagner—and insists that it stands in direct
connection with National Socialism. Furthermore, he argues that his great-grand-
father's anti-Semitism cannot be separated from his music dramas, and he con-
tests the widely held view that Wagner's anti-Semitic outbursts were aberrations
of his essayistic work divorced from his art. Gottfried Wagner decries the public
relations manipulations of Bayreuth, and the Bayreuth circle's attempt to repress
public knowledge not only of the Wagner family's involvement with National
Socialism, but also of the extent to which there exists, in Gottfried Wagner's
view, a direct ideological line from Wagner's anti-Semitism to the Holocaust.
Gottfried Wagner condemns the silence with which the Wagner circle and part of
the cultural establishment met critical investigations of Wagner's racism. He
approvingly mentions the work of Hartmut Zelinsky, Paul Lawrence Rose, and
Marc Weiner and encourages further investigations into the subject of Wagner
and anti-Semitism.[6] Gottfried Wagner's view confirms the validity of Adorno's
early approach to Wagner and the attempt to explore the roots of fascism in and
through Wagner. That Adorno later deviated from this path might be seen in the
context of what Gottfried Wagner calls the pseudo-leftist drift of Bayreuth in the
sixties, when Wagner became fashionable within a larger segment of the German
cultural establishment, including leftist intellectual circles. Marc Weiner's recent
work has filled a gap in the reception of Wagner by providing a detailed analysis of the anti-Semitic images and themes of Wagner's music dramas. It is hoped

that this trend in the reception and critique of Wagner will continue and that Nietzsche's and Adorno's critiques of Wagner will receive further recognition as pioneering attempts to gain an understanding of the ideological disaster in the cultural history of Germany.

There are—as Bolz's essay on Nietzsche's traces in Adorno's *Aesthetic Theory* points out—many similarities in Nietzsche's and Adorno's notions of subjectivity, the artist, and aesthetic truth. These notions are central to Nietzsche's and Adorno's thought and have important implications for their critique of ideology and for the attempt to realize a self-critical ideology critique. The recourse to a critique of ideology through the aesthetic and the emphasis upon the conjunction of ideology critique and aesthetic theory constitute—as an extension of Nietzsche's and Adorno's critique of metaphysics and the refusal to accept reason as the supreme grounding of thought—an important aspect of their social criticism. While the truth content of art retains the promise of expressing potential truths, the creative and creating artist, the critical thinker, and the reflecting and self-reflecting philosopher extracting the truth content of aesthetic phenomena retain the promise of the autonomous subject amidst the ever-widening web of cultural decay, commodification, social distortion, political ineptitude, and institutional ossification.

It is evident from many of Adorno's remarks about Nietzsche that he feels a certain solidarity with him. He admires the solitary, dignified, and polite philosopher who wanders through the mountains of the Engardin and lives as modestly and as independently as possible. He respects Nietzsche for his intellectual vigor and his profound insights without, however, absorbing them uncritically. Pütz maintains that for Adorno, Nietzsche serves as a witness to or critic of an idea or experience, but never as a guarantor of a hypothesis or axiom. Adorno, according to Pütz, does not refer to or cite Nietzsche at the beginning of a reflection or a line of argumentation, but almost always at its conclusion, and this placement marks Nietzsche as a philosopher of the end and perhaps of a new beginning.[7] Extending Pütz's claim, an examination of Adorno's references to Nietzsche suggests that arguments and thoughts from Nietzsche's works are eclectically chosen to support specific ideas, as additional justifications or defenses against potential rebuttals. Adorno's reception of Nietzsche is multifaceted, but brought to a point, Nietzsche can be said to provide for Adorno momentary flashes of insight. Adorno transforms these flashes of insight to serve his own purposes, thereby giving rise to the problem that Nietzsche mentions in "Why I write such good books." On the one hand, Nietzsche contributes flashes of insight to Adorno's writing, and on the other hand, these insights undergo an eclectic appropriation in Adorno's texts. Taking on the function to confirm or discredit ideas and to provide moments of truth, Nietzsche's thoughts are, to a certain degree, decontextualized. Although Nietzsche perceives himself as the writer of good books, his mode of writing not only creates good books but also opens up the possibility for endless appropriation and misappropriation from all sides of the political and ideological spectrum. As far as Adorno's references to Nietzsche are concerned, it can never be a question of whether or not he interprets Nietzsche correctly or even adequately; the issue is how Nietzschean thoughts are interpreted and utilized, and what potential Adorno sees in them for the formulation of his own critical theory. There is no question, however, that the Nietzschean insights have a profound impact upon Adorno's work. They generate provocations and interruptions and thus intervene in Adorno's texts as decontextualized frames of reference in the disparate constellations of thought. Although Adorno creates on the one hand a Nietzsche to serve his own purposes, his appropriation of Nietzsche's thought is on the other never complete. There always remains a non-identical residue that will not be subsumed by Adorno's text, and, consequently, Adorno's reception of Nietzsche oscillates between the assimilation of Nietzsche's insights and the nonviolent, antisystematic, and antitotalitarian inclusion of the non-identical.

By emphasizing Nietzsche's negativity and de-emphasizing the affirmative Nietzsche, Adorno brings the dialectic of negation and affirmation in Nietzsche's thought to a standstill. In *Minima Moralia*, he sharply criticizes the Nietzschean notions of *amor fati*, the *Übermensch*, and the affirmation of life, but pays little attention to the affirmative aspects of Nietzsche in the rest of his *oeuvre*. His affinity to Nietzsche is underscored by the rather cynical condemnation of mass society and mass culture: while Nietzsche decries the mentality of the slaves and the modern structures and institutions coercing the "herds" to conform to and internalize the norms and conventions of society, Adorno laments human alienation and estrangement from the nature, community, and the self and the loss of individual autonomy due to individual and collective ego weakness. Adorno dismisses Nietzsche's utopian construction of a master mentality and postulates— in what many see as a rhetorical gesture—the total loss of individual agency. In the administered world tied to the universal context of delusion and manipulated by the culture industry, conformity replaces consciousness and the individual lacks consciousness of his or her own unfreedom. While Nietzsche perceives an "aristocratic" remainder, a potential for self-determination, Adorno delineates the total defeat of self-reflectivity. Ironically, in his very denial of the Nietzschean affirmations and the constructive potentialities expressed in Nietzsche's thought, Adorno mobilizes Nietzsche precisely for the project of radicalized self-reflection. Not only is Nietzsche rescued by Adorno from those rebuking him as a prefascist thinker, but Adorno simultaneously rescues himself from his own pessimism and from falling prey to his own totalizing postulations. Nietzsche's voice resists and refuses to conform; his is the voice of sanity amidst the madness of commodification; his is the voice of difference amidst the pressure for homogeneity, and his is the ironic voice of self-debasement amidst the arrogance, pseudo-harmonization, and self-satisfaction of modern culture. Thus, despite the projection of Nietzsche as a model of critical negativity, Nietzsche paradoxically acts in the end as a figure of self-affirmation and hope.

While Adorno's texts uncover multiple potentials and certain aspects of Nietzsche, they certainly fail to give the whole picture, and Adorno seems particularly interested neither in interpreting Nietzsche's work in its entirety nor in presenting a well-rounded image of Nietzsche. Adorno's interest lies in the productive continuation of the Nietzschean paradoxes, contradictions, and disparate insights. Nietzsche plays an important role in the expansion of critical theory from a narrowly Marxist to a broadly based, interdisciplinary framework. The discussion between Adorno and other Frankfurt School theorists about Nietzsche on the 153rd anniversary of the French Revolution testifies to Adorno's defense of Nietzsche as a philosopher making significant contributions to the critique of Marxism. It should also be kept in mind that the agenda of the Frankfurt School only began to gain depth and breadth when Horkheimer took over the directorship in 1930. While the early projects of the Frankfurt School under Carl Grünberg focused on economic developments and Marxist research into the possibilities for revolutionary change, the institute under Horkheimer came to an expanded understanding of social philosophy and its fields of research. Horkheimer wanted not only to unite the efforts of researchers from various fields but also to widen the Marxist focus upon economic circumstances by insisting that social phenomena cannot be deduced exclusively from material existence.[8] His interest lay in exploring "the interconnection between the economic life of society, the psychic development of the individual and transformations in the realm of culture . . . including not only the so-called spiritual contents of science, art and religion, but also law, ethics, fashion, public opinion, sport, amusement, life style etc."[9] In linking the economic, psychic, and cultural spheres, Horkheimer rejected dogmatic Marxism's insistence upon the primacy of economic conditions and dismantled the traditional Marxist relegation of culture to the less influential superstructure of society. In this reconstruction of the Marxist project, Adorno became one of Horkheimer's most prominent and valuable allies, and his appearance on the theoretical scene at the institute further solidified Horkheimer's program. Adorno also avoids reducing social and cultural phenomena to economic conditions and maps out a more complex web of human interaction. Adorno's interest in art and his view of aesthetic theory as an extension of social criticism and ideology critique firmly established the realm of culture as a primary field of research within the formulation of critical theory. A further departure from Marxist orthodoxy is, of course, Adorno's inclusion of Nietzsche in his work. In Nietzsche, Adorno finds a model for the expansion of aesthetic theory into social and cultural criticism, and it would seem that this inclusion, more than any single line of argumentation, constitutes Nietzsche's extraordinary significance for the formulation of a self-reflective critical theory. To ascertain the extent to which Nietzsche can provide a constructive critique of Marxism calls for a detailed examination; the conclusion of this study can only be the more general assertion that the dialogue with Nietzsche and the incorporation of Nietzschean insights into critical theory rescues Adorno from Marxist dogmatism and from the orthodox tendencies within his own thought.

What becomes visible in Adorno is a Nietzsche who might not always be right, but whose thought offers in its contradictions and ambiguities the possibility to extract moments of truth. These truths are, of course, not eternally or universally valid truths, but revelations of the moment, and Adorno's references to Nietzsche appear to be presentations of these genuine insights rather than a sustained effort at coming to terms with Nietzsche's works. Jaspers maintains that the essence of Nietzsche lies not so much in a particular thought or idea but in "the communication of movement."[10] The same holds true for Adorno's Nietzsche reception: its continued relevance lies not only in the reception or appropriation of particular ideas, but also in the entwinement of diverse traditions and ideas, the communication of movement between Nietzschean and Marxist, Freudian, Hegelian, and Kantian thought, and the dialogue with Nietzsche in the attempt to arrive at a better understanding of the social and cultural transformations of our times.

NOTES

INTRODUCTION

1. Gillian Rose, *The Melancholy Science* (New York: Columbia University Press, 1978), 3.

2. Theodor W. Adorno and Max Horkheimer, *Dialectic of Enlightenment*, trans. John Cumming (New York: Continuum, 1993), xvi. Hereafter cited as *DE*.

3. *DE* 44.

4. Max Horkheimer, *Kritische Theorie—Eine Dokumentation*, vol. 2, ed. Alfred Schmidt (Frankfurt: Fischer, 1968), 274.

5. Cf. Peter Pütz, "Nietzsche im Lichte der kritischen Theorie," *Nietzsche-Studien* 3 (1974): 178.

6. Theodor W. Adorno, *Minima Moralia: Reflections from Damaged Life*, trans. E. F. N. Jepfcott (London and New York: Verso, 1978), 74. Hereafter cited as *MM*.

7. *MM* 74.

8. *MM* 74.

9. Theodor W. Adorno, *Prisms*, trans. Samuel and Shierry Weber (Cambridge, Mass.: MIT Press, 1981), 65. Adorno's comment refers to Oswald Spengler as a writer who imitates Nietzsche's tone but, unlike Nietzsche, sanctions the existing conditions.

10. Theodor W. Adorno, "Commitment," *Notes to Literature*, trans. Shierry Weber Nicholsen, vol. 2 (New York: Columbia University Press, 1992), 88.

11. Rose, *Melancholy Science*, 11.

12. Ibid.

13. Walter Benjamin, *Briefe*, vol. 2, ed. Gershom Scholem and Theodor W. Adorno (Frankfurt: Suhrkamp, 1966) 554.

14. Concerning Thomas Mann's Nietzsche reception, see: Renate Werner, "'Cultur der Oberfläche'. Zur Rezeption der Artisten-Metaphysik im frühen Werk Heinrich und Thomas Manns," *Nietzsche und die deutsche Literatur*, ed. Bruno Hillebrand, vol. 2 (Tübingen: Max Niemeyer Verlag, 1978), 82–121; Peter Pütz, "Thomas Mann und Nietzsche," *Nietzsche und die deutsche Literatur*, 121–55; and Inge and Walter Jens, "Betrachtungen eines Unpolitischen: Thomas Mann und Friedrich Nietzsche," *Nietzsche und die deutsche Literatur*, 155–60. Also see Peter Pütz, *Kunst und Künstlerexistenz bei Nietzsche und Thomas Mann* (Bonn: Bouvier Verlag, 1975).

15. Thomas Mann, *Gesammelte Werke in dreizehn Bänden*, vol. 11 (Frankfurt: Fischer, 1974), 109.

16. Thomas Mann, *Die Entstehung des Doktor Faustus: Roman eines Romans* (Frankfurt: Fischer, 1984), 31–33.

17. Theodor W. Adorno, "Aus Sils Maria," *Ohne Leitbild: Parva Aesthetica* (Frankfurt: Suhrkamp, 1967).

18. Adorno, "Sils," 49.

19. Ibid., 48.

20. Ibid.

21. Ibid., 50.

22. Ibid.

23. Jacques Derrida, *Spurs: Nietzsche's Styles*, trans. Barbara Harlow (Chicago and London: The University of Chicago Press, 1979), 139.

24. Adorno, "Sils," 51.

25. Max Horkheimer, *Gesammelte Schriften*, vol. 12, ed. Gunzelin Schmid Noerr (Frankfurt: Fischer, 1985), 570.

26. Ibid., 12:568.

27. Ibid., 12:567.

28. Friedrich Nietzsche, *Ecce Homo*, trans. and ed. Walter Kaufmann (New York: Vintage Books, 1989), 225.

29. Karol Sauerland, *Einführung in die Ästhetik Adornos* (Berlin: de Gruyter, 1979), 106.

30. Max Scheler, *Ressentiment*, ed. Lewis A. Coser, trans. William W. Holdheim (New York: Free Press of Glencoe, 1961).

31. Martin Heidegger, *Nietzsche*, ed. David Farrell Krell (San Francisco: Harper-Collins, 1991).

32. Theodor Adorno, *Jargon der Eigentlichkeit* (Frankfurt: Suhrkamp, 1964), 12.

33. Karl Jaspers, *Reason and Existence*, trans. W. Earle (London: Routledge & Kegan Paul, 1956), 30.

34. Ibid., 31.

35. Ibid., 32.

36. *MM* 155.

37. Martin Jay, *The Dialectical Imagination* (Boston: Little, Brown and Company, 1973), 67.

38. Rolf Wiggershaus, *Die Frankfurter Schule* (Munich: Deutscher Taschenbuch Vertag, 1988), 110.

39. *MM* 91.

40. *MM* 74.

41. Jürgen Habermas, *The Philosophical Discourse of Modernity: Twelve Lectures*, trans. Frederick Lawrence (Cambridge, Mass.: MIT Press, 1987), 129. Hereafter cited as *PDM*.

42. Theodor W. Adorno, "Ohne Leitbild: Anstelle einer Vorrede," *Ohne Leitbild: Parva Aesthetica*, 13.

43. *PDM* 15.

44. Norbert Rath, "Zur Nietzsche-Rezeption Horkheimers and Adornos," *Vierzig Jahre Flaschenpost: 'Dialektik der Aufklärung' 1947 bis 1987*, ed. W. van Reijen and Gunzelin Schmid Noerr (Frankfurt: Fischer, 1987), 77.

45. Friedrich Nietzsche, *On the Genealogy of Morals*, trans. Walter Kaufmann (New York: Vintage Books, 1989), 77. Hereafter cited as *GM*.

46. Wiggershaus, *Frankfurter Schule*, 12.

47. Reinhart Maurer, "Nietzsche und die kritische Theorie," *Nietzsche-Studien* 10 (1981/82): 35.

48. Rüdiger Sünner, *Ästhetische Szientismuskritik: zum Verhältnis von Kunst und Wissenschaft bei Nietzsche and Adorno* (Frankfurt: Peter Lang, 1986), 33.

49. Sünner, *Szientismuskritik*, 101–2.

50. Bernd Bräutigam, *Reflexion des Schönen—Schöne Reflexion Überlegungen zur Prosa ästhetischer Theorie: Hamann, Nietzsche, Adorno* (Bonn: Bouvier Verlag, 1975), 246–62.

51. Norbert W. Bolz, "Nietzsches Spur in der Ästhetischen Theorie," *Materialien zur ästhetischen Theorie Th. W. Adornos: Konstruktion der Moderne*, ed. Lindner and Lüdke (Frankfurt: Suhrkamp, 1980), 391.

52. Rudolf Reuber, *Aesthetische Lebensformen bei Nietzsche* (Munich: Fink, 1989).

CHAPTER 1. THE *BILDUNGSROMAN* OF REASON

1. Immanuel Kant, "What is Enlightenment?" *Philosophical Writings*, trans. Lewis White Beck, ed. Ernst Behler, foreword by René Wellek (New York: Continuum, 1991), 263.

2. Matei Calinescu, *Five Faces of Modernity* (Durham, N.C.: Duke University Press, 1987), 41–2.

3. *DE* 118.

4. *DE* xiii.

5. *DE* xvi.

6. *DE* xiv.

7. *DE* 19.

8. *DE* 4.

9. Theodor W. Adorno, *Negative Dialectics*, trans. E. B. Ashton (New York: Continuum, 1987) 373. Hereafter cited as *ND*.

10. *DE* 7.

11. *DE* 6.

12. Friedrich Nietzsche, *Beyond Good and Evil*, trans. Walter Kaufmann (New York: Vintage Books, 1989), 15. Hereafter cited as *BGE*.

13. *BGE* 16.

14. *BGE* 29.

15. *BGE* 29.

16. *DE* 6.

17. *DE* 7.

18. *DE* 6.

19. *DE* 30.

20. *DE* 4.

21. *DE* 4.

22. *BGE* 30.

23. *BGE* 28.

24. *BGE* 28.

25. *DE* 21.

26. *DE* 18.

27. *DE* 6.

28. *DE* 4.

29. *GM* 84.

30. *GM* 84.

31. *GM* 84.

32. *GM* 85.

33. *GM* 88.

34. Theodor W. Adorno, *Eingriffe: Neun kritische Modelle* (Frankfurt: Suhrkamp, 1963), 132. Translation Matthew Pollard.

35. For constructive criticism of the totalizing tendency, see for example: Helga Geyer-Ryan, "Von der *Dialektik der Aufklärung* zur Dialektik der *Odyssee*," *Die Aktualität der 'Dialektik der Aufklärung,'* ed. Harry Kunneman and Hent de Vries (Frankfurt, New York: Campus Verlag, 1989), 114–27; Helga Geyer-Ryan and Helmut Lethen, "Von der Dialektik der Gewalt zur *Dialektik der Aufklärung*," *Vierzig Jahre Flaschenpost*, 41–71; Norbert Bolz, "Das Selbst und sein Preis," *Vierzig Jahre Flaschenpost*, 111–28; Martin Seel, "Plädoyer für die zweite Moderne," *Die Aktualität der 'Dialektik der Aufklärung,'* 36–66; Heidrun Hesse, *Vernunft und Selbstbehauptung: Kritische Theorie als Kritik der neuzeitlichen Rationalität* (Frankfurt: Fischer, 1984).

36. Albrecht Wellmer, *Zur Kritik von Moderne und Postmoderne. Vernunftkritik nach Adorno* (Frankfurt: Suhrkamp, 1985), 147.

37. Axel Honneth, *Kritik der Macht: Reflexionsstufen einer kritischen Gesellschaftstheorie* (Frankfurt: Suhrkamp, 1985), 9, 70.

38. Herbert Schnädelbach, "Die Aktualität der *Dialektik der Aufklärung*," *Die Aktualität der 'Dialektik der Aufklärung,'* 27.

39. Schnädelbach, *Die Aktualität der 'Dialektik der Aufklärung,'* 27.

40. *PDM* 83.

41. *PDM* 84.

42. *PDM* 85.

43. *PDM* 86.

44. *PDM* 94.

45. *PDM* 86.

46. *PDM* 87.

47. *PDM* 92.

48. *PDM* 92.

49. *PDM* 94.

50. *PDM* 94.

51. *PDM* 84.

52. *PDM* 95.

53. *PDM* 95.

54. *PDM* 96.

55. *PDM* 106.

56. *PDM* 106.

57. *PDM* 106.

58. *PDM* 106.

59. *PDM* 120 and 128.

60. *PDM* 107.

61. *PDM* 112.

62. *PDM* 112–13.

63. *PDM* 113.

64. *PDM* 113.

65. *PDM* 128–29.

66. *PDM* 119.

67. *PDM* 130.

68. *PDM* 129.

69. Ernst Behler, *Irony and the Discourse of Modernity* (Seattle and London: University of Washington Press, 1990), 19–20.

70. Jürgen Habermas, "Modernity—An Incomplete Project," *The Anti-Aesthetic* (Port Townsend, Wash.: Bay Press, 1983), 5.

71. Behler, *Irony*, 16.

72. Habermas, "Modernity," 14.

73. Ernst Behler, *Derrida—Nietzsche Nietzsche—Derrida* (Paderborn, Germany: Schöning, 1988), 162.

74. Friedrich Nietzsche, *Twilight of the Idols*, trans. R. J. Hollingdale (New York: Penguin Books, 1990), 40. Hereafter cited as *TI*.

75. Since Adorno has been established as the primary author of this chapter of the *Dialectic*, the discussion will attribute "Excursus I" to Adorno and not speculate about Horkheimer's contribution.

76. *DE* 44.

77. *DE* 44.

78. *DE* 44.

79. *DE* 44; see *Kritische Studienausgabe*, vol. 11, ed. G. Colli and M. Montinaro (Berlin: de Gruyter, 1988), 570. Hereafter cited as *KSA*.

80. Henning Ottmann, "Nietzsches Stellung zur antiken und modernen Aufklärung," *Nietzsche und die philosophische Tradition*, ed. Josef Simon (Würzburg: Königshausen und Neumann, 1985), 9.

81. Ottmann, "Nietzsches Stellung," 11.

82. *BGE* 11–12.

83. *BGE* 12.

84. Ottmann, "Nietzsches Stellung," 25.

85. Friedrich Nietzsche, "Nachgelassene Fragmente 1884–1885," *KSA*, 11:570.

86. *KSA*, 11:295. The translation is my own.

87. *DE* 44; *KSA*, 11:570.

88. *DE* 38.

89. *DE* 38.

90. *DE* xvi.

91. Theodor Adorno, "Resignation," *Telos* 35 (Spring 1975): 168.

92. *DE* 24.

93. *DE* 24.

94. Gunzelin Schmid Noerr, "Unterirdische Geschichte und Gegenwart in der *Dialektik der Aufklärung*," *Die Aktualität der 'Dialektik der Aufklärung,'* 67–87.

95. For the debate on the uniqueness of the destruction of Jewry in Nazi Germany, see the edition *Historikerstreit* (Munich: Piper Verlag, 1987), which contains contribu-

tions of leading historians and philosophers in response to the debate that ensued after Habermas's critique of Andreas Hillgruber and Ernst Nolte.

96. Friedrich Nietzsche, *The Birth of Tragedy*, trans. Walter Kaufmann (New York: Random House, 1967), 94. Hereafter cited as *BT*.

97. Friedrich Nietzsche, *The Gay Science*, trans. Walter Kaufmann (New York: Random House, 1974), 38. Hereafter cited as *GS*.

98. *BT* 95–96.

99. *BT* 96.

100. *BT* 97.

101. *BT* 96.

102. *BT* 96.

103. *TI* 39–40.

104. *TI* 41.

105. *TI* 42.

106. *TI* 105.

107. *TI* 44.

108. *TI* 44.

109. *BT* 83–84.

110. *BT* 84.

111. David Couzens Hoy, "Critical Theory and Critical History," *Critical Theory*, ed. David Couzens Hoy and Thomas McCarthy (Oxford and Cambridge: Blackwell Publishers, 1994), 124.

CHAPTER 2. WRITING HISTORY

1. *DE* ix.

2. *DE* ix.

3. Cf. *GS*, aphorism 7 of book 1 and *GM*, preface.

4. *GS* 81.

5. *GS* 81.

6. Eric Blondel, "The Question of Genealogy," *Nietzsche, Genealogy, Morality: Essays on Nietzsche's "Genealogy of Morals,"* ed. Richard Schacht (Berkeley: University of California Press, 1994), 309.

7. Friedrich Nietzsche, *On the Advantage and Disadvantage of History for Life*, trans. Peter Preuss (Indianapolis: Hackett, 1980). Hereafter cited as *ADH*.

8. *ADH* 14.

9. *ADH* 14.

10. *ADH* 17.

11. *ADH* 21.

12. *ADH* 21.

13. *ADH* 22.

14. *ADH* 22.

15. *ADH* 18–19.

16. *GM* 162.

17. *GM* 162.

18. *GM* 20.

19. *TI* 66.

20. *TI* 66.

21. *GM* 77.

22. *GM* 77.

23. *GM* 77.

24. *GM* 78.

25. *GM* 80–81.

26. *GM* 28.

27. Benjamin Sax, "Foucault, Nietzsche, History: Two Modes of the Genealogical Method," *History of European Ideas*, vol. 11 (1989): 776.

28. Sax, "Foucault," 776–77.

29. Daniel W. Conway, "Genealogy and Critical Method," *Nietzsche, Genealogy, Morality: Essays on Nietzsche's "On the Genealogy of Morals,"* ed. Richard Schacht (Berkeley: University of California Press, 1994), 325.

30. Conway, "Genealogy," 324.

31. Cf. Gary Shapiro, "Translating, Repeating, Naming: Foucault, Derrida, and *The Genealogy of Morals*," *Nietzsche as Postmodernist*, ed. Clayton Koelb (Albany: State University of New York Press, 1990), 41.

32. Sax, "Foucault," 778.

33. Ibid., 779.

34. Ibid., 780.

35. Shapiro, "Translating," 41.

36. Ibid.

37. Michel Foucault, *Discipline and Punish*, trans. Alan Sheridan (New York: Vintage Books, 1979), 23.

38. Michel Foucault, "Nietzsche, Genealogy, History," *Language, Counter-Memory, Practice*, trans. Donald F. Bouchard and Sherry Simon (Ithaca, N.Y.: Cornell University Press, 1977), 139.

39. Ibid., 154.

40. Ibid.

41. Ibid., 139.

42. *GM* 21.

43. Foucault, "Nietzsche," 139.

44. Ibid., 140.

45. Ibid., 142.

46. Ibid., 154.

47. Ibid., 153.

48. Ibid., 160.

49. *BGE* 48.

50. *BGE* 47.

51. *BGE* 48.

52. *BGE* 48.

53. Michel Foucault, "Discourse on Language," *The Archaeology of Knowledge*, trans. A. M. Sheridan Smith (New York: Pantheon Books, 1972), 216.

54. Sax, "Foucault," 772.

55. Ibid.

56. Ibid., 773.

57. *PDM* 248.

58. *PDM* 249.

59. "Structuralism and Poststructuralism: An Interview with Michel Foucault," *Telos* 55 (Spring 1983): 205.

60. Ibid., 200.

61. Hoy and McCarthy, *Critical Theory*, 146.

62. "Structuralism and Poststructuralism," 206.

63. *PDM* 249.

64. *PDM* 265.

65. *PDM* 125.

66. *PDM* 126.

67. Shapiro, "Translating," 40.

68. Ibid., 41.

69. Allan Megill, *Prophets of Extremity* (Berkeley: University of California Press, 1985), 235.

70. Foucault, "Nietzsche," 147.

71. Cited from a 1977 interview with Foucault in Megill, *Prophets of Extremity*, 234.

72. *GM* 18.

73. *GM* 20.

74. Foucault, "Nietzsche," 143.

75. *GM* 20.

76. Cf. *GM* 20.

77. *DE* ix.

78. *DE* 97; 99.

79. *DE* 101.

80. *DE* 43.

81. *DE* 45.

82. *DE* 46.

83. *DE* 45.

84. *DE* 54.

85. *DE* 50.

86. *DE* 51. In *Beyond the Pleasure Principle*, Freud describes this compulsive mechanism of attempting to gain control over a situation through repetition and the repetitious enactment of a supplemental action in terms of a child's game. Substituting his mother for a spool, the little boy plays "fort—da" with the spool in an effort to better endure his mother's periodic absences.

87. *GM* 97.

88. *GM* 116.

89. *GM* 118.

90. *GM* 120.

91. *GM* 126.

92. *DE* 48–49.

93. *DE* 56.

94. *TI* 33.

95. *DE* 49.

96. *DE* 57.

97. *DE* 57.

98. *DE* 57.

99. *DE* 53.

100. Theodor W. Adorno, *Stichworte: Kritische Modelle 2* (Frankfurt: Suhrkamp, 1969), 48. The translation is my own.

101. *GM* 70.

102. *GM* 70.

103. *GM* 70.

104. *GM* 70.

105. *GM* 70.

106. *GM* 70–71.

107. The German text reads: ". . . daß er als Verfallener ihnen nicht verfällt."

108. *DE* 77.

109. *DE* 30.

110. *DE* 59–60.

111. *DE* 34.

112. *DE* 35.

113. *DE* 36.

114. *BGE* 161.

115. *BGE* 160.

116. *BGE* 161.

117. *BGE* 161.

118. *BGE* 161.

119. *BGE* 161.

120. *DE* 44.

121. *ND* 320.

CHAPTER 3. THE CRITIQUE OF METAPHYSICS

1. *ND* 404.

2. Theodor W. Adorno, *Against Epistomology: A Metacritique; Studies in Husserl and the Phenomenological Antinomies* (Oxford: Blackwell, 1982), 17.

3. Adorno, *Stichworte*, 154.

4. Theodor Adorno, *Aesthetic Theory*, trans. Robert Hullot-Kentor (Minneapolis: University of Minnesota Press, 1997), 3. Hereafter cited as *AT*.

5. Adorno, *Metacritique*, 17.

6. *ND* 371.

7. Adorno, *Metacritique*, 371.

8. *MM* 226.

9. Nietzsche, *Human, All Too Human*, trans. R. J. Hollingdale (Cambridge: Cambridge University Press, 1986), 80. Hereafter cited as *HAH*.

10. *HAH* 80.

11. *MM* 226.

12. *MM* 226.

13. Adorno, *Metacritique*, 18.

14. Ibid.

15. *TI* 45.

16. *TI* 45.

17. *TI* 45.

18. *TI* 46.

19. *TI* 46.

20. *TI* 46.

21. *TI* 46.

22. *TI* 47.

23. *TI* 47.

24. *TI* 46.

25. *TI* 47; also see Adorno, *Metacritique*, 19.

26. Adorno, *Metacritique*, 19.

27. Nietzsche, "Ueber Wahrheit und Lüge im aussermoralischen Sinne," *KSA*, 1:880.

28. Peter Dews, "Adorno, Poststructuralism and the Critique of Identity," *The Problems of Modernity: Adorno and Benjamin*, ed. Andrew Benjamin (London and New York: Routledge, 1989), 12.

29. *ND* 169.

30. Nietzsche, "On Truth and Lie in an Extra-Moral Sense," *The Portable Nietzsche*, trans. Walter Kaufmann (New York: Viking Press, 1954), 45–46. Hereafter cited as *TL*.

31. *TL* 46.

32. *TL* 46.

33. *TL* 46.

34. Adorno, *Metacritique*, 10.

35. *ND* 5.

36. *ND* 5–6.

37. *ND* 5.

38. *ND* 4.

39. Walter Benjamin, *Ursprung des deutschen Trauerspiels* (Frankfurt: Suhrkamp), 16.

40. Susan Buck-Morss, *The Origin of Negative Dialectics: Theodor W. Adorno, Walter Benjamin, and the Frankfurt Institute* (New York: The Free Press, 1977), 95.

41. Ibid., 92.

42. Ibid., 93.

43. Adorno, *Prisms*, 231.

44. Anke Thysen, *Negative Dialektik und Erfahrung: Zur Rationalität des Nichtidentischen bei Adorno* (Frankfurt: Suhrkamp, 1989), 194–95.

45. This translation is taken from Allan McGill, *Prophets of Extremity*, 52–53. For original see *KSA*, 1:888–89.

46. *MM* 126–27.

47. *GS* 171.

48. *GS* 171.

49. *GS* 171.

50. *HAH* 12.

51. *DE* 30.

52. Theodor Adorno, *Hegel: Three Studies*, trans. Shierry Weber Nicholsen (Cambridge, Mass.: MIT Press, 1993), 76.

53. *HAH* 16.

54. *MM* 50.

55. *ND* 20.

56. *ND* 22.

57. Cf. Theodor Adorno, "Elements of Anti-Semitism: The Limits of Enlightenment," *Dialectic of Enlightenment*, 168–208.

58. *ND* 23.

59. Adorno, *Jargon der Eigentlichkeit*, 74.

60. Adorno, *Metacritique*, 28.

61. Ibid.

62. Cf. Habermas, *Erkenntnis und Interesse* (Frankfurt: Suhrkamp, 1973) and *The Philosophical Discourse of Modernity*; Reinhard Maurer, "Nietzsche und die Kritische Theorie"; also various contributions to the *Adorno-Konferenz 1983*, almost all of which attempt to disassociate Adorno from Nietzsche.

63. *TL* 47.

64. *TL* 47.

65. Adorno, *Stichworte*, 16–17.

66. Ibid.

67. Adorno, *Hegel*, 35.

68. *HAH* 13.

69. *ND* 169.

70. Adorno, *Eingriffe*, 162.

71. Ibid., 160.

72. Ibid., 159.

73. Ibid., 171.

74. *GS* 169.

75. *GS* 169.

76. *GS* 171.

77. *BGE* 9.

78. *BGE* 10.

79. *BGE* 12.

80. *BGE* 12.

81. *GS* 38.

82. *GS* 38.

83. For an illuminating discussion of Nietzsche's view of deception, truth, and irony, see Ernst Behler, "Nietzsches Auffassung der Ironie," *Nietzsche-Studien* 4 (1975): 1–35.

84. Derrida, *Spurs: Nietzsche's Styles*, 119.

85. Adorno, *Ohne Leitbild*, 13.

86. *GM* 25.

87. *MM* 81.

88. *MM* 97.

89. *MM* 25.

90. *MM* 123.

91. *GS* 74.

92. *MM* 15.

93. *MM* 15.

94. *MM* 15.

95. Pütz, "Nietzsche," 179.

96. *DE* 118.

97. Adorno, *Hegel*, 47.

98. Ibid.

99. *MM* 96.

100. *MM* 96–97.

101. *MM* 97.

102. *MM* 97.

103. *MM* 97.

104. *MM* 98.

105. *MM* 98.

106. *MM* 98.

107. *MM* 98.

108. *MM* 98.

109. *MM* 98.

110. Adorno, *Prisms*, 65.

111. *MM* 98.

112. *MM* 98.

113. Adorno was personally acquainted, for example, with the Austrian writer Ingeborg Bachmann. Although her works are part of today's German literary canon of classical modernity, he never mentions them. He disliked the philosopher Hannah Arendt, although the intense personal aversion was mutual. Arendt found Adorno to be one of the most "repulsive human being[s] I know"; she resented the fact that Adorno had changed his Jewish name, Wiesengrund, to his mother's maiden name and held him responsible for Walter Benjamin's despondency in exile. See Hannah Arendt and Karl Jaspers, *Correspondence 1926–1969*, ed. Lotte Kohler and Hans Saner, trans. Robert and Rita Kimber (New York: Harcourt Brace Jovanovich, 1992), 634; and Wolfgang Heuer, *Hannah Arendt* (Reinbeck: Rowohlt, 1987) 25, 32.

114. Histories of the Frankfurt School—see Martin Jay's *Dialectical Imagination* and Rolf Tiedemann's *Die Frankfurter Schule*—mention several women who collaborated on various projects, but the fact remains that none attained a position of prominence within the school. Monika Plessner's *Die Argonauten auf Long Island* provides further evidence for the contention that women played supporting roles. In Plessner's book there is, for instance, much talk about Gretel Adorno's cooking, but no serious mention of her work at the School and for her husband.

115. *BGE* 88.

116. *EH* 266.

117. Linda Singer, "Nietzschean Mythologies: The Inversion of Value and the War against Women," *Soundings* 66.3 (Fall 1983): 282.

118. *BGE* 163.

119. *EH* 266.

120. It should be noted, however, that Nietzsche did encourage his sister Elisabeth to read and study, and that he was in favor of granting women the right to attend the university. See Curt Paul Janz, *Friedrich Nietzsche: Biographie* (Munich: Hanser, 1978) and H. F. Peters, *Zarathustra's Sister: The Case of Elisabeth and Friedrich Nietzsche* (New York: Crown, 1977).

121. Friedrich Nietzsche, *Thus Spoke Zarathustra*, in *The Portable Nietzsche*, trans. Walter Kaufmann (New York: Viking Press, 1954), 178.

122. Nietzsche, *Zarathustra*, 179.

123. *BGE* 1.

124. *BGE* 163.

125. Peter Burgard, ed., *Nietzsche and the Feminine* (Charlottesville and London: University Press of Virginia, 1995), 5. This volume contains a thorough bibliography of works addressing the question of Nietzsche and the feminine.

126. Derrida, *Spurs: Nietzsche's Styles*, 51.

127. Ibid., 37.

128. Burgard, *Nietzsche and the Feminine*, 3.

129. Cf. Adrian Del Caro, "The Pseudoman in Nietzsche, or the Threat of the Neuter," *New German Critique* 50 (Spring/Summer 1990): 149. Although Del Caro's article constitutes a pertinent critique of Derrida's project in *Spurs*, it contains also highly problematic lines of argumentation. Falling back onto essentialism, Del Caro criticizes Derrida for denying that "essential differences can ever be known" (149). Instead, Del Caro advocates a problematic "synthesis," a combination of the truths of *essential* woman and *essential* man.

130. Rosi Braidotti, "The Ethics of Sexual Difference: The Case of Foucault and Irigaray," *Australian Feminist Studies* 3 (1986): 2.

131. Keith Ansell-Pearson, *An Introduction to Nietzsche as Political Thinker* (Cambridge: Cambridge University Press, 1994), 188–89.

132. Ansell-Pearson, *An Introduction*, 189.

133. Robert Holub, "Nietzsche and the Women's Question," *German Quarterly* 18.1 (Winter 1995): 68. This is a review of Peter Burgard's and Paul Patton's editions on Nietzsche.

134. Holub, "Nietzsche and the Women's Question," 69.

135. Ibid., 71.

136. Christine Kulke, "Die Kritik der instrumentellen Rationalität—ein männlicher Mythos," *Die Aktualität der 'Dialektik der Aufklärung,'* 146–47.

137. Geyer-Ryan and Lethen, *Vierzig Jahre Flaschenpost*, 43.

138. Burgard, *Nietzsche and the Feminine*, 29.

139. Ibid.

140. Ibid.

141. Ibid., 29–30.

142. Luce Irigaray, "Ecce Mulier? Fragments," *Nietzsche and the Feminine*, 316–31.

143. Kelly Oliver, *Womanizing Nietzsche: Philosophy's Relation to the Feminine* (London: Routledge, 1995).

144. Ibid., xcii.

145. Claudia Crawford, *To Nietzsche: Dionysus, I love you! Ariadne* (Albany: State University of New York Press, 1995).

146. Burgard, *Nietzsche and the Feminine*, 2.

147. Holub, "Nietzsche and the Women's Question," 71.

148. Heide Schlüpmann, "Zur Frage der Nietzsche-Rezeption in der Frauenbewegung gestern und heute," *Nietzsche heute: die Rezeption seines Werkes nach 1968* (Bern and Stuttgart: Franke Verlag, 1988), 178.

149. *GS* 126.

150. *GS* 126.

151. *MM* 95.

152. *MM* 95.

153. *MM* 96.

154. *MM* 96.

155. *MM* 96. 'Femininity' is used by the translators for 'das Weib'; Adorno's text reads: "das Weib selber ist bereits der Effekt der Peitsche."

156. *MM* 96.

157. *MM* 92.

158. *MM* 92.

159. *MM* 92–93.

160. The subversive dimension of gender performance refers to Judith Butler, *Gender Trouble: Feminism and the Subversion of Identity* (New York: Routledge, 1990) and *Bodies That Matter: On the Discursive Limits of "Sex"* (New York: Routledge, 1993).

161. *MM* 93.

162. *MM* 93.

163. *MM* 32.

164. *MM* 32.

165. *MM* 90.

166. *MM* 90.

167. *MM* 90.

168. *MM* 91.

169. *MM* 91.

170. *MM* 91.

171. *MM* 91.

172. *DE* 70.

173. *DE* 71.

174. Klaus Theweleit, *Male Fantasies*, 2 vols., trans. Erica Carter and Chris Turner in collaboration with Stephen Conway (Minneapolis: University of Minnesota Press, 1989); Jacques Le Rider, *Modernity and the Crisis of Identity: Culture and Society in Fin-de-Siècle Vienna* (New York: Continuum Publishing Company, 1993); Bernd Widdig, *Männerbünde und Massen: Zur Krise männlicher Identität in der Literatur der Moderne* (Opladen, Germany: Westdeutscher Verlag, 1992).

175. *DE* 72.

176. *DE* 73.

177. *DE* 74.

178. Friedrich Nietzsche, *Nietzsche contra Wagner*, in *The Portable Nietzsche*, 419.

179. Andreas Huyssen, *After the Great Divide* (Bloomington: Indiana University Press, 1986), 53.

180. Ibid., 51.

181. Friedrich Nietzsche, *The Case of Wagner*, trans. Walter Kaufmann (New York: Random House, 1967), 185. Hereafter cited as *CW*.

182. *CW* 182–83.

183. *CW* 184.

184. Huyssen, *After the Great Divide*, 48.

185. Ibid., 53.

CHAPTER 4. WAGNER'S AESTHETICS AS THE ORIGIN OF TOTALITARIANISM

1. Theodor W. Adorno, "Selbstanzeige des Essaybuches *Versuch über Wagner*," *Gesammelte Schriften*, vol. 13 (Frankfurt: Suhrkamp, 1971), 504. The translation is my own since none is available.

2. Adorno, "Selbstanzeige," 504; translation by Matthew Pollard.

3. Ibid.

4. For a brief discussion of Nietzsche's attack upon Bayreuth on ideological and aesthetic grounds and on the counteroffensive by the Wagnerians, see Massima Ferrari Zumbini, *Nietzsche-Studien* 19 (1990): 246–91.

5. Andreas Huyssen, "Adorno in Reverse: From Hollywood to Richard Wagner," *New German Critique* 29 (Spring/Summer 1983): 13.

6. Ibid.

7. Mazzino Montinari, "Nietzsche—Wagner im Sommer 1878," *Nietzsche Studien* 14 (1985): 13–21.

8. Friedrich Nietzsche, *KSA*, 15:133–34. The translation is my own.

9. Martin Gregor-Dellin, *Richard Wagner* (Munich: Deutscher Taschenbuch Verlag, 1980) and Curt Paul Janz, *Friedrich Nietzsche: Biography*, vol. 1 (Munich: Deutscher Taschenbuch Verlag, 1981).

10. Marc A. Weiner, *Richard Wagner and the Anti-Semitic Imagination* (Lincoln and London: University of Nebraska Press, 1995), 338.

11. Friedrich Nietzsche, *Sämtliche Briefe: Kritische Studienausgabe in 8 Bänden*, vol. 3 (Berlin: de Gruyter, 1986), 365. Hereafter cited as *SB*.

12. Peter Wapnewski, "Nietzsche und Wagner Stationen einer Beziehung," *Nietsche-Studien* 18 (1989): 421.

13. Thomas Baumeister, "Stationen von Nietzsches Wagnerrezeption und Wagnerkritik," *Nietzsche-Studien* 16 (1987): 289.

14. *BT* 22.

15. *BT* 22–23.

16. *BT* 24.

17. *BT* 142.

18. *KSA*, 7:764. Translation is my own.

19. *KSA*, 7:765. Translation is my own.

20. *KSA*, 7:768. Translation is my own.

21. *KSA*, 7:759. Translation is my own.

22. Mazzino Montinari, *Nietzsche lesen* (Berlin: de Gruyter, 1982), 45.

23. *KSA*, 8, 531. Translation by Matthew Pollard.

24. *KSA*, 12:160.

25. *KSA*, 12:256.

26. Friedrich Nietzsche, "Nietzsche Contra Wagner," *The Portable Nietzsche*, trans. Walter Kaufmann (New York: Viking Press, 1968), 676. Hereafter cited as *NcW*.

27. *NcW* 676.

28. Dieter Borchmeyer, "Wagner and Nietzsche," *Wagner Handbook* (Cambridge, Mass.: Harvard University Press, 1992).

29. *EH* 284.

30. *EH* 286.

31. *KSA*, 15:158.

32. *CW* 155.

33. *CW* 188.

34. *CW* 169; 184.

35. *CW* 156.

36. *TI* 117.

37. Ernst Behler, "Sokrates und die griechische Tragödie," in *Nietzsche Studien* 18 (1989): 156. The translation is my own.

38. Walter Kaufmann, *Nietzsche: Philosopher, Psychologist, Antichrist* (Princeton and London: Princeton University Press, 1974), 398.

39. Ibid., 401.

40. Ibid., 400.

41. *BT* 106.

42. *TI* 44.

43. *CW* 155.

44. Silke-Maria Weineck, "Loss of Outline: Decadence as the Crisis of Negation," *Pacific Coast Philology* 29.1, September (1994): 37.

45. Erwin Koppen, *Dekadenter Wagnerismus* (Berlin: de Gruyter, 1973), 323.

46. Dieter Borchmeyer, "Nietzsches Begriff der Decadence," *Die Modernisierung des Ich: Studien zur Subjektkonstitution in der Vor und Frühmoderne*, ed. Manfred Pfister (Passau: Wissenschaftsverlag, 1989), 88.

47. *BT* 33.

48. *BT* 83–84.

49. *BT* 83.

50. *BT* 83.

51. Wolfdietrich Rasch, *Die literarische Décadence um 1900* (Munich: Beck, 1986), 25.

52. Rasch, *Die literarische Décadence*, 35.

53. Ibid.

54. *KSA*, 11:476.

55. Ibid.

56. *EH* 248.

57. *EH* 248.

58. *EH* 248.

59. Paul Bourget, *Essais de Psychologie Contemporaine*, vol. 1 (Paris: Plon, 1901), 20. The translation is taken from Weineck's "Loss of Outline," 45.

60. *CW* 170.

61. Kaufmann, *Nietzsche*, 73.

62. *CW* 170.

63. Borchmeyer, "Nietzsches Begriff," 88.

64. *BGE* 196–97.

65. *NcW* 672–73.

66. *NcW* 673.

67. Rasch, *Die literarische Décadence*, 19.

68. *EH* 224.

69. Weineck, "Loss of Outline," 37.

70. *CW* 169.

71. *TI* 92.

72. *TI* 93.

73. *TI* 92.

74. *GM* 163.

75. *CW* 166.

76. *CW* 166.

77. *KSA*, 13:294.

78. *KSA*, 13:246–47.

79. *KSA*, 13:247. The translation is my own.

80. *KSA*, 13:247.

81. *KSB*, 7:177. The translation is my own.

82. *HAH* 107.

83. *EH* 250.

84. *EH* 250.

85. *TI* 33.

86. Terry Eagleton, *The Ideology of the Aesthetic* (Oxford: Blackwell, 1990), 359.

87. Ibid., 358–59.

88. Ibid., 358.

89. Ibid., 358–60.

90. Ibid., 360.

91. Huyssen, "Adorno in Reverse," 29.

92. *MM* 43.

93. Huyssen, "Adorno in Reverse," 11.

94. Walter Benjamin, "Das Kunstwerk im Zeitalter seiner technischen Reproduzierbarkeit," *Illuminationen* (Frankfurt: Suhrkamp, 1977), 167.

95. Theodor W. Adorno, "Culture Industry," *Dialectic of Enlightenment*, trans. John Cumming (New York: Continuum, 1993), 121. Hereafter cited as "Culture."

96. Adorno, "Culture," 121.

97. Letter of March 18, 1938 to Walter Benjamin, *Aesthetics and Politics*, ed. Ronald Taylor (London: New Left Books, 1977), 123. For an illuminating discussion of the Adorno-Benjamin debate, see Sabine Wilke, "'Torn Halves of an Integral Freedom': Adorno's and Benjamin's Reading of Mass Culture," *The Aesthetics of the Critical Theorists* (Lewiston, N.Y.: Edwin Mellen Press, 1990), 124–51.

98. *MM* 44.

99. *ND* 367.

100. Huyssen, "Adorno in Reverse," 26.

101. Ibid., 30.

102. Peter Osborne, "Adorno and Modernism," *The Problems of Modernity: Adorno and Benjamin*, 26.

103. Ibid.

104. *AT* 243.

105. See the discussion of Albrecht Wellmer in "Wahrheit, Schein, Versöhnung: Adornos ästhetische Rettung der Modernität," *Adorno Konferenz 1983*, ed. Ludwig von Friedeburg und Jürgen Habermas (Frankfurt: Suhrkamp, 1983).

106. *AT* 127.

107. Andrew Bowie, "Music, Language and Modernity," *The Problems of Modernity*, 80.

108. Rüdiger Bubner, "Kann Theorie ästhetisch werden? Zum Hauptmotiv der Philosophie Adornos," *Materialien zur ästhetischen Theorie Theodor W. Adornos, Konstruktionen der Moderne*, ed. Burkhard Lindner und W. Martin Lüdke (Frankfurt: Suhrkamp, 1980), 129. The translations are my own.

109. Bubner, "Kann Theorie . . . ," 130. The translation is my own.

110. Hans Robert Jauß, "Negativität und ästhetische Erfahrung: Adornos ästhetische Theorie in der Retrospektive," *Materialien zur ästhetischen Theorie Theodor W. Adornos: Konstruktionen der Moderne*, 146.

111. *AT* 13.

112. *AT* 346.

113. *AT* 15.

114. *AT* 14.

115. *AT* 13.

116. *AT* 14.

117. *AT* 13.

118. *AT* 13.

119. Adorno, "Commitment," 413.

120. Ibid., 77.

121. Theodor W. Adorno, *Introduction to the Sociology of Music*, trans. E. B. Ashton (New York: Seabury Press, 1972), 211.

122. Theodor W. Adorno, *Philosophy of Modern Music*, trans. Anne G. Mitchell and Wesley V. Bloomster (New York: Seabury Press, 1973), 42–43.

123. Ibid., 37.

124. *AT* 15.

125. *AT* 157–58.

126. Lambert Zuidervaart, *Adorno's Aesthetic Theory: The Redemption of Illusion* (Cambridge: MIT Press, 1991), 93.

127. For an excellent discussion of Adorno's critique of surrealism, see Buck-Morss's *The Origin of Negative Dialectics*.

128. Ibid., 129.

129. Martin Jay, *Adorno* (Cambridge: Harvard University Press, 1984), 141.

130. Ibid., 144.

131. *AT* 21.

132. *AT* 6.

133. *DE* xvi.

134. Theodor W. Adorno, "The Schema of Mass Culture," *The Culture Industry: Selected Essays on Mass Culture*, ed. J. M. Bernstein (London: Routledge, 1991), 56.

135. Adorno, "Culture," 121.

136. Ibid., 161.

137. Ibid., 131.

138. Ibid., 144.

139. Ibid.

140. Ibid., 134.

141. Ibid., 136.

142. Ibid., 166–67.

143. Ibid., 145.

144. Ibid., 139.

145. Ibid., 154.

146. Ibid., 125–26.

147. Ibid., 126.

148. Ibid., 125.

149. Adorno, *Introduction to the Sociology of Music*, 209.

150. Jay, *Adorno*, 142.

151. Ibid.

152. Adorno, "Culture," 157.

153. Ibid., 157–58.

154. Theodor W. Adorno, "On the Fetish Character in Music and the Regression of Listening," *The Culture Industry: Selected Essays on Mass Culture*, 36. Hereafter cited as "Fetish."

155. Ibid., 40.

156. Ibid., 41.

157. Ibid.

158. Ibid.

159. Ibid., 48.

160. Ibid., 49.

161. Ibid., 39.

162. Ibid.

163. Ibid., 41.

164. Huyssen, "Adorno in Reverse," 15.

165. Ibid.

166. Ibid.

167. Theodor W. Adorno, *In Search of Wagner*, trans. Rodney Livingstone (London: NLB, 1981), 47–48. Hereafter cited as *SW*.

168. Adorno,"Notiz über Wagner," *Gesammelte Werke*, vol. 18 (Frankfurt: Suhrkamp, 1984), 204–9.

169. Adorno, "Wagners Aktualität," *Gesammelte Werke*, 16:543–64.

170. Adorno, "Wagner und Bayreuth," *Gesammelte Werke*, 18:210–25.

171. Adorno, "Nachschrift zu einer Wagner-Diskussion," *Gesammelte Werke*, 16:665–70.

172. Adorno, "Nachschrift," 668–69.

173. Adorno, "Aktualität," 544.

174. Ibid., 546.

175. Ibid., 545.

176. Adorno, "Notiz über Wagner," 208.

177. Adorno, "Wagner, Nietzsche, and Hitler," *Gesammelte Werke*, 19:406.

178. Adorno, "Wagner, Nietzsche, and Hitler," 406. Here Adorno refers implicitly to his *Studies of the Authoritarian Character*. When he claims that Wagner's character traits "gain a significance by far transcending the biographical occasion in the light of present-day socio-psychological knowledge," it can be assumed that he also refers to the findings of this study.

179. Ibid.

180. Ibid., 407.

181. Adorno's argument closely resembles Sander L. Gilman's work on the psychology of anti-Semitism and Jewish self-hatred: Sander Gilman, *Jewish Self-Hatred: Anti-Semitism and the Hidden Language of the Jews* (Baltimore: Johns Hopkins University Press, 1986).

182. Adorno, "Wagner, Nietzsche, and Hitler," 407.

183. Ibid., 409.

184. Ibid., 410.

185. Ibid.

186. Ibid.

187. Ibid., 411.

188. Cf. Carl Dahlhaus, "Soziologische Dechiffrierung von Musik. Zu Theodor W. Adornos Wagner-Kritik," *International Review of the Aesthetics and Sociology of Music* 1 (1970): 137–46; Rainer Cadenbach, "Theodor W. Adornos *Versuch über Wagner*," *Zu Richard Wagner*, ed. Helmut Loos and Günther Massenkeit (Bonn: Bouvier, 1984), 145–59.

189. Jay, *Adorno*, 132.

190. Fredric Jameson, *Marxism and Form* (Princeton: Princeton University Press, 1971), 4.

191. Adorno, "Nachschrift," 666.

192. *SW* 15.

193. *SW* 16.

194. *SW* 16.

195. *SW* 21.

196. *SW* 24.

197. *SW* 25.

198. Thomas Mann, "The Sorrows and Grandeur of Richard Wagner," *Pro and Contra Wagner* (Chicago: University of Chicago Press, 1985), 103.

199. *SW* 30.

200. *SW* 29.

201. *SW* 103.

202. *SW* 104.

203. *SW* 45.

204. *CW* 173.

205. *CW* 173.

206. *SW* 35.

207 *CW* 172–73.

208. *SW* 30.

209. *SW* 30.

210. *SW* 31.

211. *SW* 35.

212. *SW* 30.

213. *NcW* 676.

214. *SW* 22.

215. *SW* 31.

216. *SW* 31.

217. *CW* 14.

218. *CW* 167.

219. *NcW* 670.

220. *SW* 14.

221. *GM* 102.

222. Sarah Kofman, "Wagner's Ascetic Ideal According to Nietzsche," *Nietzsche, Genealogy, Morality*, ed. Richard Schacht (Berkeley: University of California Press, 1994), 201.

223. *GM* 97.

224. *GM* 100.

225. *GM* 101.

226. *GM* 103.

227. *GM* 154.

228. *SW* 145.

229. *SW* 146.

230. *SW* 17.

231. *NcW* 676.

232. *CW* 180.

233. *SW* 102.

234. *SW* 100.

235. *CW* 27.

236. *NcW* 681.

237. *SW* 49.

238. *SW* 38.

239. *SW* 49.

240. *SW* 107.

241. *CW* 178.

242. *SW* 124.

243. *SW* 132.

244. *MM* 50.

245. *SW* 107.

246. *CW* 167.

247. *CW* 162.

248. *SW* 91.

249. *SW* 91.

250. *SW* 49.

251. *SW* 37.

252. *CW* 177.

253. *SW* 42.

254. *SW* 42.

255. *SW* 34.

256. *SW* 31.

257. *SW* 31.

258. *SW* 85.

259. *SW* 108.

260. *SW* 83.

261. *SW* 83.

262. *SW* 84.

263. Letter to Carl Fuchs, *SB*, 8:554.

264. *CW* 157.

265. *CW* 157.

266. *NcW* 666–67.

267. *CW* 169.

268. *MM* 154.

269. *CW* 191.

270. *CW* 191.

271. *CW* 192.

272. *CW* 192.

273. *SW* 143.

274. *SW* 44.

275. Adorno, "Selbstanzeige," 507.

276. *CW* 165–66.

277. Adorno, "Culture," 143.

278. *SW* 107.

279. *MM* 16.

EXCURSUS

1. Wilhelm von Humboldt, *Gesammelte Schriften*, vol. 1 (Berlin: Königlich Preussische Akademie der Wissenschaften, 1903–36), 106.

2. Cf. E. D. Hirsch Jr., *Cultural Literacy: What every American Needs to Know* (Boston: Houghton Mifflin, 1987); Alan Bloom, *The Closing of the American Mind: How Higher Education Has Failed Democracy and Impoverished the Souls of Today's Students* (New York: Simon 1987); William J. Bennett, *Our Children and Our Country: Improving America's Schools and Affirming the Common Culture* (New York: Simon & Schuster, 1988); and Robert von Hallberg, *Canons* (Chicago: University of Chicago Press, 1984).

3. Marc Weiner, "Editor's Column," *German Quarterly* 69.5 (Fall 1996): v–ix.

4. Theodor Adorno, "Theorie der Halbbildung," *Gesellschaftstheorie und Kulturkritik* (Frankfurt: Suhrkamp, 1975), 81.

5. Berndt Herrmann, *Theodor W. Adorno: Seine Gesellschaftstheorie als ungeschriebene Erziehungslehre* (Bonn: Bouvier Verlag, 1978), 12.

6. Theodor Adorno, "Erziehung nach Auschwitz," *Erziehung zur Mündigkeit* (Frankfurt: Suhrkamp, 1971), 88.

7. Theodor Adorno, "Erziehung—wozu?" *Erziehung zur Mündigkeit* (Frankfurt: Suhrkamp, 1971), 107.

8. *ADH* 24. Interestingly enough, both Hollingdale and Preuss translate *Bildung* with the term "culture." The German reads "Unsere moderne Bildung ist . . . gar keine wirkliche Bildung, es bleibt in ihr bei dem Bildungs-Gedanken, bei dem Bildungs-Gefühl." Friedrich Nietzsche, "Vom Nutzen und Nachteil der Historie fuer das Leben," *Unzeitgemaesse Betrachtungen II, KSA*, 1:273.

9. Timothy F. Murphy, *Nietzsche as Educator* (Lanham, Md.: University Press of America, 1984), 1.

10. Friedrich Nietzsche, "Über die Zukunft der Bildungsanstalten," *KSA*, 1:667.

11. Adorno, "Halbbildung," 81.

12. Adorno, "Erziehung—wozu?" 112.

13. Adorno, "Halbbildung," 70.

14. Ibid., 71.

15. *DE* 215.

16. Adorno, "Halbbildung," 81.

17. Ibid., 73.

18. *ND* 366.

19. *ND* 367.

20. Martin Jay, "Hierarchy and the Humanities: The Radical Implications of a Conservative Idea," *Telos* 62 (Winter 1984–85): 131.

21. *ND* 367.

22. Adorno, "Halbbildung," 77.

23. Ibid., 74.

24. *NL* 248.

25. Nietzsche, "Schopenhauer as Educator," *Untimely Meditations*, transl. R. J. Hollingdale (Cambridge: Cambridge University Press, 1983), 169.

26. Gerhard Schmidt, "Nietzsches Bildungskritik," *Zur Aktualität Nietzsches*, ed. M. Djuric and J. Simon (Würzbug, Germany: Königshausen & Neumann, 1984), 9.

27. *ADH* 41

28. Nietzsche, "Schopenhauer," 165.

29. Nietzsche, "Bildungsanstalten," 667.

30. Ibid., 647.

31. Ibid.

32. Ibid., 698.

33. Nietzsche, "Schopenhauer," 136.

34. Cf. Martin Vogel, *Nietzsche und Wagner: Ein deutsches Lesebuch* (Bonn: Verlag für systematische Musikwissenschaft, 1984).

35. *EH* 281.

36. *EH* 280.

37. Nietzsche, "Schopenhauer," 138–39.

38. Ibid., 184.

39. Ibid., 185.

40. Ibid., 175.

41. Ibid., 170.

42. Ibid.

43. Ibid., 192.

44. *ADH* 46.

45. *TI* 33.

46. Adorno, "Halbbildung," 88.

47. Norbert Rath, *Adornos Kritische Theorie* (Paderborn, Germany: Schöningh, 1982), 134.

48. Adorno, "Halbbildung," 94.

CHAPTER 5. HERESY OF THE MIND

1. Gilles Deleuze, "Nomad Thought," *The New Nietzsche*, ed. David B. Allison (Cambridge, Mass.: MIT Press, 1985), 147.

2. Ibid.

3. Eagleton, *The Ideology of the Aesthetic*, 363.

4. Deleuze, "Nomad Thought," 149.

5. Cf. Rose, *Melancholy Science*; Sabine Wilke, *Zur Dialektik von Exposition und Darstellung: Ansätze zu einer Kritik der Arbeiten Martin Heideggers, Theodor W. Adornos und Jacques Derrridas* (New York: Peter Lang, 1988); and Rainer Hoffmann, *Figuren des Scheins: Studien zum Sprachbild und zur Denkform Theodor W. Adornos* (Bonn: Bouvier, 1984).

6. Some of the most widely discussed works about Nietzsche's styles include: Derrida, *Spurs: Nietzsche's Styles*; Alexander Nehamas, *Nietzsche: Life as Literature* (Cambridge, Mass.: Harvard University Press, 1985); Gary Shapiro, *Nietzschean Narratives* (Bloomington: Indiana University Press, 1989); Bernd Magnus, Stanley Stewart, and Jean-Pierre Mileur, *Nietzsche's Case: Philosophy as/and Literature* (New York: Routledge, 1993); earlier studies include: Sarah Kofman, *Nietzsche et la métaphor* (Paris: Payot, 1972); Paul de Man, *Allegories of Reading: Figural Language in Rousseau, Nietzsche, Rilke, and Proust* (New Haven and London: Yale University Press, 1979).

7. Rose, *Melancholy Science*, 11.

8. Ibid.

9. Ibid.

10. Ibid., 19.

11. Ibid.

12. Theodor W. Adorno, "The Essay as Form," *Notes to Literature*, vol. 1 (New York: Columbia University Press, 1991), 23.

13. Franz Mauthner, "Der Aphorismus als literarische Gattung," *Der Aphorismus*, ed. Gerhard Neumann (Darmstadt, Germany: Wissenschaftliche Buchgesellschaft, 1976), 47.

14. Montaigne, *Selections from the Essays*, trans. and ed. Donald M. Frame (Arlington Heights, Ill.: AHM Publishing Corporation, 1973), v.

15. Montaigne, "Essays," v.

16. Ibid., vi.

17. Adorno, "Essay," 16.

18. *HAH* 182.

19. Wilke, *Zur Dialektik*, 125.

20. Peter Bürger, *Zur Kritik der idealistischen Ästhetik* (Frankfurt: Suhrkamp, 1983), 129–35.

21. Bubner, "Kann Theorie . . . ," 108–37.

22. Ibid., 133.

23. Ibid.

24. Ibid.

25. Adorno, "The Actuality of Philosophy," trans. Benjamin Snow, *Telos* 31 (Spring 1977): 120–32. Hereafter cited as "Actuality."

26. Ibid., 126.

27. Ibid.

28. Ibid., 127.

29. *ND* 10.

30. Adorno, "Actuality," 127.

31. Adorno, "Thesen über die Sprache des Philosophen," *Philosophische Frühschriften*, Gesammelte Werke, ed. Rolf Tiedemann (Frankfurt: Suhrkamp, 1973), 1:131.

32. *ND* 162.

33. *ND* 163.

34. Adorno, "Actuality," 133.

35. Ibid.

36. Cf. Wilke's discussion, 132.

37. Hoffmann, *Figuren*, 265.

38. Ibid.

39. Adorno, "Thesen," 368. The translation is my own.

40. Rose, *Melancholy Science*, 12–13.

41. Adorno, "Essay," 22.

42. Ibid., 4.

43. Ibid., 9.

44. Ibid., 14.

45. Ibid., 9.

46. Ibid., 16.

47. Ibid.

48. For examinations of Adorno's *Aesthetic Theory* as a continuation of early Romanticism, see Bubner, "Adornos Negative Dialektik," *Adorno-Konferenz 1983*, 35–40; Bubner, "Kann Theorie . . . ," 108–37; and Jochen Hörisch, "Herrscherwort, Geld und geltenden Sätze. Adornos Aktualisierung der Frühromantik und ihre Affinität zur poststrukturalistischen Kritik des Subjekts," *Materialien*, 397–414.

49. Adorno, "Essay," 16.

50. Ibid., 18.

51. Ibid., 17.

52. Ibid.

53. Ibid., 10.

54. Ibid., 11.

55. Ibid., 19.

56. Bubner, "Kann Theorie . . . ," 108–9.

57. Adorno, "Essay," 12.

58. Ibid.

59. Ibid., 13.

60. Ibid.

61. Carl Dahlhaus, *Die Idee der absoluten Musik* (Munich and Kassel: Barenreiter, Deutscher Taschenbuch Verlag, 1978), 145.

62. Carl Dahlhaus and Michael Zimmermann ed., *Musik zur Sprache gebracht* (Munich and Kassel: Barenreiter, Deutscher Taschenbuch Verlag, 1984), 130.

63. Bowie, "Music, Language, and Modernity," 67–85.

64. Ibid., 80–81.

65. Adorno, "Essay," 23.

66. Ibid.

67 Ibid.

68. *MM* 19.

69. *MM* 15.

70. Rose, *Melancholy Science*, 16.

71. Ibid., 26.

72. Ibid., 17.

73. *MM* 210.

74. "Disappeared" is actually not an entirely correct translation, for Adorno uses the unusual German word "geschwunden" instead of "verschwunden"; "ist geschwunden" could indicate disappeared, but also diminished, decreased.

75. *MM* 211–12.

76. Ernst Behler, "Das Fragment," *Prosa Kunst ohne Erzählen*, ed. Klaus Weissenberger (Tübingen, Germany: Niemeyer Verlag, 1985), 142.

77. Behler, "Fragment," 142.

78. Shapiro, *Nietzschean Narratives*, 7.

79. Jürgen Habermas, "Critical Theory and Modernity," *New German Critique* 26 (Spring/Summer 1982): 22.

80. Nietzsche, *KSA* 8:361.

81. For a thorough discussion of aphorisms as a genre, see Gerhard Neumann, ed., *Der Aphorismus. Zur Geschichte, zu den Formen und Möglichkeiten einer literarischen Gattung* (Darmstadt, Germany: Wissenschaftliche Buchgesellschaft, 1979).

82. Behler, "Fragment," 142.

83. *GM* 23.

84. *GM* 23.

85. *GM* 97.

86. *HAH* 362.

87. *HAH* 5.

88. Ernst Behler, "Nietzsche und die romantische Metapher von der Kunst als Spiel," *Echoes and Influences of German Romanticism*, ed. Michael S. Batts et al. (New York: Peter Lang, 1986), 28.

89. Ernst Behler, "Nietzsche's Auffassung der Ironie," *Nietzsche-Studien* 4 (1975): 3.

90. *EH* 324.

91. *HAH* 263.

92. *HAH* 6.

93. *HAH* 10.

94. *HAH* 7.

95. *HAH* 243.

96. Adorno, "Essay," 9.

97. Ibid., 11.

98. *HAH* 12–13.

99. *HAH* 13.

100. Adorno, "Essay," 11.

101. *TI* 115.

102. *TI* 115.

103. *HAH* 250.

104. *HAH* 110.

105. *HAH* 92.

106. *HAH* 238.

107. *ND* 109.

108. Shapiro, *Nietzschean Narratives*, 2.

109. This is especially true of *Zarathustra*, a work that contains aphorisms but is certainly not aphoristic. Due to its prophetic annunciations and the postulation of questionable utopian constructs, it is not surprising that Adorno virtually ignores this work.

110. Alexander Nehamas, *Nietzsche: Life as Literature*, 20.

111. Pütz, "Nietzsche," 186.

CONCLUSION

1. *The American Heritage Dictionary of the English Language*, ed. William Morris (Boston: Houghton Mifflin, 1979).

2. *GM* 120.

3. *GM* 121.

4. Gilles Deleuze, "Active and Reactive," *The New Nietzsche*, 99.

5. Gottfried Wagner, *Wer nicht mit dem Wolf heult: Autobiographische Aufzeichnungen eines Wagner-Urenkels* (Cologne: Kiepenheuer & Witsch, 1997), 269–70.

6. Cf. Hartmut Zelinsky, *Richard Wagner: ein deutsches Thema: eine Dokumentation zur Wirkungsgeschichte Richard Wagners 1876–1976* (Frankfurt: Zweitausendeins, 1976); Paul Lawrence Rose, *Wagner: Race and Revolution* (New Haven and London: Yale University Press, 1992); and Marc Weiner, *Richard Wagner and the Anti-Semitic Imagination*. In the context of Wagner's anti-Semitism mention should be made also of Jacob Katz, *The Darker Side of Genius: Richard Wagner's Anti-Semitism* (Hanover and London: Brandeis University Press/University Press of New England, 1986) and Leon Stein, *The Racial Thinking of Richard Wagner* (New York: Philosophical Library, 1950).

7. Pütz, "Nietzsche," 179.

8. David Held, *Introduction to Critical Theory* (Berkeley and Los Angeles: University of California Press, 1980), 33.

9. Held, *Introduction to Critical Theory*, 33.

10. Karl Jaspers, *Nietzsche and Christianity* (Chicago: Regnery, 1961), 99.

SELECTED BIBLIOGRAPHY

Adorno, Theodor W. "The Actuality of Philosophy." Trans. Benjamin Snow. *Telos* 31 (Spring 1977): 120–32.

―――. *Against Epistomology: A Metacritique; Studies in Husserl and the Phenomenological Antinomies*. Oxford: Blackwell, 1982.

―――. *Aesthetic Theory*. Trans. Robert Hullot-Kentor. Minneapolis: University of Minnesota Press, 1997.

―――. "Commitment." *Notes to Literature*. Vol. 2. Trans. Shierry Weber Nicholsen. New York: Columbia University Press, 1992. 76–94.

―――. *Eingriffe: Neun kritische Modelle*. Frankfurt: Suhrkamp, 1963.

―――. *Erziehung zur Mündigkeit*. Frankfurt: Suhrkamp, 1971.

―――. "The Essay as Form." *Notes to Literature*. Vol. 1. New York: Columbia University Press, 1991. 3–23.

―――. *Hegel: Three Studies*. Trans. Shierry Weber Nicholsen. Cambridge, Mass.: MIT Press, 1993.

―――. *In Search of Wagner*. Trans. Rodney Livingstone. London: New Left Books, 1981.

————. *Introduction to the Sociology of Music*. Trans. E.B. Ashton. New York: Seabury Press, 1972.

————. *Jargon der Eigentlichkeit*. Frankfurt: Suhrkamp, 1964.

————. *Kierkegaard*. Frankfurt: Suhrkamp, 1986.

————. *Kritik: Kleine Schriften zur Gesellschaft*. Frankfurt: Suhrkamp, 1971.

————. *Minima Moralia: Reflections from Damaged Life*. Trans. E. F. N. Jepfcott. London and New York: Verso. 1978.

————. "Nachschrift zu einer Wagner-Diskussion." *Gesammelte Werke*. Vol. 16. Frankfurt: Suhrkamp, 1984. 665–70.

————. *Negative Dialectics*. Trans. E. B. Ashton. New York: Continuum, 1987.

————. "Notiz über Wagner." *Gesammelte Werke*. Vol. 18. Frankfurt: Suhrkamp, 1984. 204–9.

————. *Ohne Leitbild: Parva Aesthetica*. Frankfurt: Suhrkamp, 1967.

————. *Philosophy of Modern Music*. Trans. Anne G. Mitchell and Wesley V. Bloomster. New York: Seabury Press, 1973.

————. *Prisms*. Trans. Samuel and Shierry Weber. Cambridge, Mass.: MIT Press, 1981.

————. "Resignation." *Telos* 35 (Spring 1978): 165–68.

————. "The Schema of Mass Culture." *The Culture Industry: Selected Essays on Mass Culture*. Ed. J. M. Bernstein. London: Routledge, 1991. 53–84.

————. "Selbstanzeige des Essaybuches *Versuch über Wagner*." *Gesammelte Schriften*. Vol. 13. Frankfurt: Suhrkamp, 1971.

————. *Stichworte Kritische Modelle 2*. Frankfurt: Suhrkamp, 1969.

————. "Theorie der Halbbildung." *Gesellschaftstheorie und Kulturkritik*. Frankfurt: Suhrkamp, 1975.

————. "Thesen über die Sprache des Philosophen." *Philosophische Frühschriften*. *Gesammelte Werke*, vol. 1. Ed. Rolf Tiedemann. Frankfurt: Suhrkamp, 1973. 366–71.

————. "Wagners Aktualität." *Gesammelte Werke*. Vol. 16. Frankfurt: Suhrkamp, 1984. 543–64.

————. "Wagner, Nietzsche, and Hitler." *Gesammelte Werke*. Vol. 19. Frankfurt: Suhrkamp, 1984. 404–12.

————. "Wagner und Bayreuth." *Gesammelte Werke*. Vol. 18. Frankfurt: Suhrkamp, 1984. 210–25.

————. *Zur Metakritik der Erkenntnistheorie*. Frankfurt: Suhrkamp, 1981.

———— and Max Horkheimer. *Dialectic of Enlightenment*. Trans. John Cumming. New York: Continuum, 1993.

Allison, David. B, ed. *The New Nietzsche*. Cambridge, Mass.: MIT Press, 1988.

Ansell-Pearson, Keith. *An Introduction to Nietzsche as Political Thinker*. Cambridge: Cambridge University Press, 1994.

Anonymous, *Historikerstreit*. Munich: Piper Verlag, 1987.

Arendt, Hannah and Karl Jaspers. *Correspondence 1926–1969*. Trans. Robert and Rita Kimber. Ed. Lotte Kohler and Hans Saner. New York: Harcourt Brace Jovanovich, 1992.

Baumeister, Thomas. "Stationen von Nietzsches Wagnerrezeption und Wagnerkritik." *Nietzsche-Studien* 16 (1987): 288–309.

Behler, Diana. "Nietzsche's View of Woman in Classical Greece." *Nietzsche-Studien* 18 (1989): 359–76.

Behler, Ernst. "Das Fragment." *Prosa Kunst ohne Erzählen*. Ed. Klaus Weissenberger. Tübingen: Niemeyer, 1985. 125–43.

————. *Irony and the Discourse of Modernity*. Seattle: University of Washington Press, 1990.

————. "Nietzsches Auffassung der Ironie." *Nietzsche-Studien* 4 (1975): 1–35.

————. *Nietzsche—Derrida Derrida—Nietzsche*. Paderborn, Germany: Schöningh, 1988.

————. "Nietzsche und die romantische Metapher von der Kunst als Spiel." *Echoes and Influences of German Romanticism*. Ed. Michael S. Batts. New York: Peter Lang Verlag, 1986. 11–28.

————. "Socrates und die griechische Komödie." *Nietzsche-Studien* 18 (1989): 141–57.

Benhabib, Seyla. *Critique, Norm, and Utopia: A Study of the Foundations of Critical Theory*. New York: Columbia University Press, 1986.

Benjamin, Walter. *Briefe*. Ed. Gershom Scholem and Theodor W. Adorno. Frankfurt: Suhrkamp, 1966.

————. "Das Kunstwerk im Zeitalter seiner technischen Reproduzierbarkeit." *Illuminationen*. Frankfurt: Suhrkamp, 1977. 136–69.

————. *Ursprung des deutschen Trauerspiels*. Frankfurt: Suhrkamp, 1978.

Bennett, William J. *Our Children and Our Country: Improving America's Schools and Affirming the Common Culture*. New York: Simon & Schuster, 1988.

Blondel, Eric. *The Body and Culture*. Trans. Seán Hand. Stanford: Stanford University Press, 1991.

266 Selected Bibliography

──────. "The Question of Genealogy." *Nietzsche, Genealogy, Morality: Essays on Nietzsche's "On the Genealogy of Morals."* Ed. Richard Schacht. Berkeley: University of California Press, 1994. 306–17.

Bloom, Alan. *The Closing of the American Mind: How Higher Education Has Failed Democracy and Impoverished the Souls of Today's Students.* New York: Simon & Schuster, 1987.

Bohrer, Karl Heinz, ed. *Mythos und Moderne.* Frankfurt: Suhrkamp, 1983.

Bolz, Norbert W. "Nietzsches Spur in der Ästhetischen Theorie." *Materialien zur ästhetischen Theorie Th. W. Adornos: Konstruktion der Moderne.* Ed. Burkhardt Lindner and W. Martin Lüdke. Frankfurt: Suhrkamp, 1980. 369–96.

──────. "Das Selbst und sein Preis." *Vierzig Jahre Flaschenpost: 'Dialektik der Aufklärung' 1947 bis 1987.* Ed. W. van Reijen und Gunzelin Scmid Noerr. Frankfurt: Fischer, 1987. 111–26.

Borchmeyer, Dieter. "Nietzsches Begriff der Decadence." *Die Modernisierung des Ich: Studien zur Subjektkonstitution in der Vor und Frühmoderne.* Ed. Manfred Pfister. Passau, Germany: Wissenschaftsverlag, 1989. 84–95.

──────. "Wagner and Nietzsche." *Wagner Handbook.* Cambridge, Mass.: Harvard University Press, 1992. 327–42.

Bourget, Paul. *Essais de Psychologie Contemporaine.* Vol. 1. Paris: Plon, 1901.

Bowie, Andrew. "Music, Language and Modernity." *The Problems of Modernity.* Ed. Andrew Benjamin. London and New York: Routledge, 1991. 67–85.

Braidotti, Rosi. "The Ethics of Sexual Difference: The Case of Foucault and Irigaray." *Australian Feminist Studies* 3 (1986): 2–15.

Bräutigam, Bernd. *Reflexion des Schönen—Schöne Reflexion: Überlegungen zur Prosa ästhetischer Theorie—Hamann, Nietzsche, Adorno.* Bonn: Bouvier Verlag, 1975.

Bubner, Rüdiger. "Adornos Negative Dialektik." *Adorno-Konferenz 1983.* Ed. Ludwig von Friedeburg and Jürgen Habermas. Frankfurt: Suhrkamp, 1983. 35–40.

──────. "Kann Theorie ästhetisch werden?" *Materialien zur ästhetischen Theorie Th. W. Adornos: Konstruktion der Moderne.* Ed. B. Lindner and W.M. Lüdke. Frankfurt: Suhrkamp, 1979. 108–37.

Buck-Morss, Susan. *The Origin of Negative Dialectics: Theodor W. Adorno, Walter Benjamin, and the Frankfurt Institute.* New York: The Free Press, 1977.

Burgard, Peter, ed. *Nietzsche and the Feminine.* Charlottesville and London: University Press of Virginia, 1995.

Bürger, Peter. "Decline of the Modern Age." *Telos* 62 (1984/85): 117–30.

──────. "Das Vermittlungsproblem in der Kunstsoziologie Adornos." *Materialien zur ästhetischen Theorie Th. W. Adornos: Konstruktion der Moderne.* Ed. B. Lindner and W. M. Lüdke. Frankfurt: Suhrkamp, 1979. 169–84.

———. *Zur Kritik der idealistischen Ästhetik*. Frankfurt: Suhrkamp, 1983.

Butler, Judith. *Bodies That Matter: On the Discursive Limits of "Sex."* New York: Routledge, 1993.

———. *Gender Trouble: Feminism and the Subversion of Identity*. New York: Routledge, 1990.

Cadenbach, Rainer. "Theodor W. Adornos *Versuch über Wagner.*" *Zu Richard Wagner*. Ed. Helmut Loos and Günther Massenkeit. Bonn: Bouvier, 1984. 145–59.

Calinescu, Matei. *Five Faces of Modernity*. Durham, N.C.: Duke University Press, 1987.

Colli, Giorgio. *Distanz und Pathos. Einleitung zu Nietzsches Werken*. Frankfurt: Europäische Verlagsanstalt, 1982.

Conway, Daniel W. "Genealogy and Critical Method." Nietzsche, Genealogy, Morality: Essays on Nietzsche's *"On the Genealogy of Morals."* Ed. Richard Schacht. Berkeley: University of California Press, 1994. 318–33.

Crawford, Claudia. "She?" *Sub-stance* 29 (1981): 83–96.

———. *To Nietzsche: Dionysus, I love you! Ariadne*. Albany: State University of New York Press, 1995.

Dahlhaus, Carl. *Die Idee der absoluten Musik*. Munich and Kassel: Barenreiter, Deutscher Taschenbuch Verlag, 1978.

———. "Soziologische Dechiffrierung von Musik. Zu Theodor W. Adornos Wagner-Kritik." *International Review of the Aesthetics and Sociology of Music* 1 (1970): 137–46.

Dahlhaus, Carl, and Michael Zimmermann, eds. *Musik zur Sprache gebracht*. Munich and Kassel: Barenreiter, Deutscher Taschenbuch Verlag, 1984.

Del Caro, Adrian. "The Pseudoman in Nietzsche, or the Threat of the Neuter." *New German Critique* 50 (Spring/Summer 1990): 135–56.

Deleuze, Gilles. "Nomad Thought." *The New Nietzsche*. Ed. David B. Allison. Cambridge: MIT Press, 1985. 142–49.

Derrida, Jacques. *Spurs: Nietzsche's Styles*. Chicago: University of Chicago Press, 1978.

Dews, Peter. "Adorno, Poststructuralism and the Critique of Identity." *The Problems of Modernity: Adorno and Benjamin*. Ed. Andrew Benjamin. London: Routledge, 1989. 1–22.

Diethe, Carol. "Nietzsche and the Woman Question." *History of European Ideas* 11 (1989): 865–75.

Doane, Mary Ann. "Veiling Over Desire: Close-ups of the Woman." *Feminism and Psychoanalysis*. Ed. Richard Feldstein and Judith Roof. Ithaca, N.Y.: Cornell University Press, 1989. 105–41.

Eagleton, Terry. *The Ideology of the Aesthetic*. Oxford: Blackwell, 1990.

Foucault, Michel. *Discipline and Punish*. Trans. Alan Sheridan. New York: Vintage Books, 1979.

————. "Discourse on Language." *The Archaeology of Knowledge*. Trans. A. M. Sheridan Smith. New York: Pantheon Books, 1972. 215–37.

————. *Language, Counter-Memory, Practice*. Trans. Donald F. Bouchard and Sherry Simon. Ithaca, N.Y.: Cornell University Press, 1977.

————. *Madness and Civilization*. Trans. Richard Howard. New York: Vintage Books, 1979.

————. Interview with Gérad Raulet. "Structuralism and Poststructuralism: an Interview with Michel Foucault." *Telos* 55 (Spring 1983): 63–69.

Funke, Monika. *Ideologiekritik und ihre Ideologie bei Nietzsche*. Stuttgart: Frommann Verlag, 1974.

Früchtl, Josef. *Memesis: Konstellation eines Zentralbegriff bei Adorno*. Würzburg, Germany: Königshausen & Neumann, 1986.

Geyer-Ryan, Helga. "Von der Dialektik der Aufklärung zur Dialektik der *Odyssee*." *Die Aktualität der 'Dialektik der Aufklärung.'* Ed. Harry Kunneman and Hent de Vries. Frankfurt, New York: Campus Verlag, 1989. 114–27.

Geyer-Ryan, Helga, and Helmut Lethen. "Von der Dialektik der Gewalt zur *Dialektik der Aufklärung*." *Vierzig Jahre Flaschenpost: 'Dialektik der Aufklärung' 1947 bis 1987*. Ed. W. van Reijen and Gunzelin Schmid Noerr. Frankfurt: Fischer, 1987. 41–71.

Gregor-Dellin, Martin. *Richard Wagner*. Munich: Deutscher Taschenbuch Verlag, 1980.

Grimm, Ruediger. *Nietzsche's Theory of Knowledge*. Berlin: de Gruyter, 1977.

Habermas, Jürgen. *Erkenntnis und Interesse*. Frankfurt: Suhrkamp, 1973.

————, ed. *Friedrich Nietzsche: Erkenntnistheoretische Schriften*. Frankfurt: Suhrkamp, 1968.

————. "Modernity—An Incomplete Project." *The Anti-Aesthetic*. Port Townsend, Wash.: Bay Press, 1983. 3–15.

————. *The Philosophical Discourse of Modernity: Twelve Lectures*. Trans. Frederick Lawrence. Cambridge, Mass.: MIT Press, 1987.

Hallberg von, Robert. *Canons*. Chicago: University of Chicago Press, 1984.

Heidegger, Martin. *Nietzsche*. Trans. David Farrell Krell et al. 4 vols. San Francisco: Harper & Row, 1979–85.

Held, David. *Introduction to Critical Theory*. Berkeley and Los Angeles: University of California Press, 1980.

Herrmann, Bernd. *Theodor W. Adorno: Seine Gesellschaftstheorie als ungeschriebene Erziehungslehre.* Bonn: Bouvier Verlag, 1978.

Hesse, Heidrun. *Vernunft und Selbstbehauptung Kritische Theorie als Kritik der neuzeitlichen Rationalität.* Frankfurt: Fischer, 1984.

Heuer, Wolfgang. *Hannah Arendt.* Reinbeck: Rowohlt, 1987.

Hillebrand, Bruno, ed. *Nietzsche und die deutsche Literatur.* 2 vols. Tübingen, Germany: Max Niemeyer Verlag, 1978.

Hirsch, Jr., E. D. *Cultural Literacy: What every American Needs to Know.* Boston: Houghton Mifflin, 1987.

Hoffmann, Rainer. *Figuren des Scheins Studien zum Sprachbild und zur Denkform Theodor W. Adornos.* Bonn: Bouvier Verlag, 1984.

Holub, Robert. "Nietzsche and the Women's Question." *German Quarterly* 68.1 (Winter 1995): 67–71.

Honneth, Axel. *Kritik der Macht: Reflexionsstufen einer kritischen Gesellschaftstheorie.* Frankfurt: Suhrkamp, 1985.

Hörisch, Jochen. "Herrscherwort, Geld und geltende Sätze. Adornos Aktualisierung der Frühromantik und ihre Affinität zur poststrukturalistischen Kritik des Subjekts." *Materialien zur ästhetischen Theorie Th. W. Adornos: Konstruktion der Moderne.* Ed. Burkhardt Lindner und W. Martin Lüdke. Frankfurt: Suhrkamp, 1980. 397–414.

Horkheimer, Max. *Gesammelte Schriften.* Vol. 12. Ed. Gunzelin Schmid Noerr. Frankfurt: Fischer, 1985.

———. *Kritische Theorie—Eine Dokumentation.* Vol. 2. Ed. Alfred Schmidt. Frankfurt: Fischer, 1968.

Hoy, David Couzens "Critical Theory and Critical History." *Critical Theory.* Ed. David Couzens Hoy and Thomas McCarthy. Oxford: Blackwell Publishers, 1994. 101–43.

Humboldt, Wilhelm von. *Gesammelte Schriften.* Vol. 1. Berlin: Königlich Preussische Akademie der Wissenschaften, 1903.

Huyssen, Andreas. "Adorno in Reverse: From Hollywood to Richard Wagner." *New German Critique* 29 (Spring/Summer 1983): 8–38.

———. *After the Great Divide.* Bloomington: Indiana University Press, 1986.

———. "Critical Theory and Modernity: Introduction." *New German Critique* 26 (1982): 3–11.

Irigaray, Luce. "Ecce Mulier? Fragments." *Nietzsche and the Feminine.* Ed. Peter J. Burgard. Charlottesville: University Press of Virginia, 1994. 316–31.

———. *Marine Lover of Friedrich Nietzsche.* Trans. Gillian C. Gill. New York: Columbia University Press, 1991.

Jameson, Frederic. *Marxism and Form*. Princeton: Princeton University Press, 1971.

Janz, Curt Paul. *Friedrich Nietzsche: Biography*. Munich: Hanser, 1978.

Jaspers, Karl. *Nietzsche and Christianity*. Chicago: Regnery, 1961.

———. *Reason and Existenz*. Trans. W. Earle. London: Routledge & Kegan Paul, 1956.

Jauß, Hans Robert. "Der literarische Prozeß des Modernismus von Rousseau bis Adorno." *Adorno-Konferenz 1983*. Ed. Ludwig von Friedeburg and Jürgen Habermas. Frankfurt: Suhrkamp, 1983. 95–130.

———. "Negativität und ästhetische Erfahrung. Adornos ästhetische Theorie in der Retrospektive." *Materialien zur ästhetischen Theorie Th. W. Adornos: Konstruktion der Moderne*. Ed. B. Lindner and W. M. Lüdke. Frankfurt: Suhrkamp, 1980. 138–68.

Jay, Martin. *Adorno*. Cambridge: Harvard University Press, 1986.

———. *The Dialectical Imagination*. Boston: Little, Brown and Company, 1973.

———. "Hierarchy and the Humanities: The Radical Implications of a Conservative Idea." *Telos* 62 (1984–85): 131–44.

Jens, Walter and Inge. "Betrachtungen eines unpolitischen: Thomas Mann und Friedrich Nietzsche." *Nietzsche und die deutsche Literatur*. Vol. 2. Ed. Bruno Hillebrand. Tübingen, Germany: Niemeyer, 1978. 155–59.

Kant, Immanuel. "What Is Enlightenment?" *Philosophical Writings*. Trans. Lewis White Beck. Ed. Ernst Behler. New York: Continuum, 1991. 263–69.

Katz, Jacob. *The Darker Side of Genius: Richard Wagner's Anti-Semitism*. Hanover and London: Brandeis University Press/University Press of New England, 1986.

Kaufmann, Walter. *Nietzsche: Philosopher, Psychologist, Antichrist*. Princeton and London: Princeton University Press, 1974.

Kaulbach, Friedrich. "Ästhetische und philosophische Erkenntnis beim frühen Nietzsche." *Zur Aktualität Nietzsches*. Würzburg, Germany: Königshausen & Neumann, 1984. 63–98.

Kimmerle, Gerd. *Die Aporie der Wahrheit: Anmerkungen zu Nietzsches 'Genealogie der Moral.'* Tübingen, Germany: Konkursbuchverlag, 1984.

Kittler, Friedrich. "Wie man abschafft, wovon man spricht: Der Autor von 'Ecce homo'." *Literaturmagazin* 12. Ed. Born, Manthey and Schmidt. Reinbeck, Germany: Rowohlt, 1980. 153–75.

Kofman, Sarah. *Nietzsche et la métaphor*. Paris: Payot, 1972.

———. "Wagner's Ascetic Ideal According to Nietzsche." *Nietzsche, Genealogy, Morality*. Ed. Richard Schacht. Berkeley: University of California Press, 1994. 193–213.

Koppen, Erwin. *Dekadenter Wagnerismus*. Berlin: de Gruyter, 1973.

Krahl, Hans-Jürgen. "The Political Contradictions in Adorno's Critical Theory." *Telos* 21 (1974): 164–67.

Kulke, Christine. "Die Kritik der instrumentellen Rationalität—ein männlicher Mythos." *Die Aktualität der 'Dialektik der Aufklärung.'* Ed. Harry Kunneman and Hent de Vries. Frankfurt, New York: Campus Verlag, 1989. 128–49.

Kunnas, Tarmo. *Politik als Prostitution des Geistes.* Munich: Edition Wissenschaft & Literatur, 1982.

Le Rider, Jacques. *Modernity and Crisis of Identity: Culture and Society in Fin-de-Siècle Vienna.* New York: Continuum, 1993.

Lyotard, Jean-François. "Adorno as the Devil." *Telos* 19 (1974): 127–37.

———. *The Postmodern Condition: A Report on Knowledge.* Trans. Geoff Bennington and Brian Massumi. Minneapolis: University of Minnesota Press, 1979.

Magnus, Bernd, Stanley Stewart, and Jean-Pierre Mileur. *Nietzsche's Case: Philosophy as/and Literature.* New York: Routledge, 1993.

de Man, Paul. *Allegories of Reading: Figural Language in Rousseau, Nietzsche, Rilke, and Proust.* New Haven and London: Yale University Press, 1979.

Mann, Thomas. *Die Entstehung des Doktor Faustus: Roman eines Romans.* Frankfurt: Fischer, 1984.

———. *Gesammelte Werke in dreizehn Bänden.* Vol. 11. Frankfurt: Fischer, 1974.

———. *Pro and Contra Wagner.* Chicago: University of Chicago Press, 1985.

Maurer, Reinhart. "Nietzsche und die kritische Theorie." *Nietzsche-Studien* 10 (1981/82): 34–58.

Mauthner, Franz. "Der Aphorismus als literarische Gattung." *Der Aphorismus.* Ed. Gerhard Neumann. Darmstadt, Germany: Wissenschaftliche Buchgesellschaft, 1976. 42–51.

Megill, Allan. *Prophets of Extremity.* Berkeley: University of California Press, 1985.

Merten, Ralph. *Adorno: Individuum und Geschichte.* Essen, Germany: Verlag die blaue Eule, 1985.

Mirbach, Thomas. *Kritik der Herrschaft: Zum Verhältnis von Geschichtsphilosophie, Ideologiekritik und Methodenreflexion in der Gesellschaftstheorie Adornos.* Frankfurt: Campus, 1979.

de Montaigne, Michel Eyquem. *Selections from the Essays.* Trans. and ed. Donald M. Frame. Arlington Heights, Ill.: AHM Publishing Corporation, 1973.

Montinari, Mazzino. *Nietzsche lesen.* Berlin: de Gruyter, 1982.

———. "Nietzsche—Wagner im Sommer 1878." *Nietzsche-Studien* 14 (1985): 13–21.

Mörchen, Hermann. *Macht und Herrschaft im Denken von Heidegger und Adorno.* Stuttgart: Klett-Cotta, 1980.

Murphy, Timothy F. *Nietzsche as Educator.* Lanham, Md.: University Press of America, 1984.

Naeher, Jürgen. *Die Negative Dialektik Adornos.* Opladen, Germany: Leske und Budrich, 1984.

Nehamas, Alexander. *Nietzsche: Life as Literature.* Cambridge, Mass.: Harvard University Press, 1985.

Neumann, Gerhard, ed. *Der Aphorismus. Zur Geschichte, zu den Formen und Möglichkeiten einer literarischen Gattung.* Darmstadt, Germany: Wissenschaftliche Buchgesellschaft, 1979.

Nietzsche, Friedrich. *Beyond Good and Evil.* Trans. Walter Kaufmann. New York: Vintage Books, 1989.

———. *The Birth of Tragedy.* Trans. Walter Kaufmann. New York: Random House, 1967.

———. *The Case of Wagner.* Trans. Walter Kaufmann. New York: Random House, 1967.

———. *Ecce Homo.* Trans. and ed. Walter Kaufmann. New York: Vintage Books, 1989.

———. *The Gay Science.* Trans. Walter Kaufmann. New York: Random House, 1974.

———. *Human, All Too Human.* Trans. R. J. Hollingdale. Cambridge: Cambridge University Press, 1986.

———. *Kritische Studienausgabe.* 15 vols. Ed. Giorgio Colli and Mazzino Montinari. Berlin: Deutscher Taschenbuch Verlag/de Gruyter, 1988.

———. *Nietzsche contra Wagner.* In *The Portable Nietzsche.* Trans. Walter Kaufmann. New York: Viking Press, 1954. 661–83.

———. *On the Advantage and Disadvantage of History for Life.* Trans. Peter Preuss. Indianapolis: Hackett, 1980.

———. *On the Genealogy of Morals.* Trans. Walter Kaufmann. New York: Vintage Books, 1989.

———. "On Truth and Lie in an Extra-Moral Sense." In *The Portable Nietzsche.* Trans. Walter Kaufmann. New York: Viking Press, 1954.

———. *Sämtliche Briefe: Kritische Studienausgabe in 8 Bänden.* Vol. 3. Berlin: de Gruyter, 1986.

———. *Thus Spoke Zarathustra.* In *The Portable Nietzsche.* Trans. Walter Kaufmann. New York: Viking Press, 1954. 103–439.

———. *Twilight of the Idols.* Trans. R. J. Hollingdale. New York: Penguin Books, 1990.

Oliver, Kelly. *Womanizing Nietzsche: Philosophy's Relation to the Feminine.* London: Routledge, 1995.

Osborne, Peter. "Adorno and Modernism." *The Problems of Modernity: Adorno and Benjamin.* Ed. Andrew Benjamin. London and New York: Routledge, 1991. 23–48.

Ottmann, Henning. "Nietzsches Stellung zur antiken und modernen Aufklärung." *Nietzsche und die philosophische Tradition.* Ed. Josef Simon. Würzburg, Germany: Könighausen & Neumann, 1985. 9–33.

Pecora, Vincent P. "Nietzsche, Genealogy, Critical Theory." *New German Critique* 53 (Spring/Summer 1991): 104–30.

Peters, H. F. *Zarathustra's Sister: The Case of Elisabeth and Friedrich Nietzsche.* New York: Crown, 1977.

Plessner, Monika. *Die Argonauten auf Long Island.* Berlin: Rowohlt, 1995.

Poster, Mark. "What Does Wotan Want?" *New German Critique* 53 (Spring/Summer 1991): 131–48.

Pütz, Peter. *Kunst und Künstlerexistenz bei Nietzsche und Thomas Mann.* Bonn: Bouvier Verlag, 1975.

———. "Nietzsche im Lichte der kritischen Theorie." *Nietzsche-Studien* 3 (1974): 175–91.

———. "Thomas Mann und Nietzsche." *Nietzsche und die deutsche Literatur.* Vol. 2. Ed. Bruno Hillebrand. Tübingen, Germany: Niemeyer, 1978. 128–54.

Rasch, Wolfdietrich. *Die literarische Décadence um 1900.* Munich: Beck, 1986.

Rath, Norbert. *Adornos Kritische Theorie.* Paderborn, Germany: Schöning, 1982.

———. "Zur Nietzsche-Rezeption Horkheimers und Adornos." *40 Jahre Flaschenpost: 'Dialektik der Aufklärung' 1947 bis 1987.* Ed. W. van Reijen und Gunzelin Schmid Noerr. Frankfurt: Fischer, 1987. 73–110.

Reuber, Rudolf. *Aesthetische Lebensformen bei Nietzsche.* Munich: Fink, 1989.

Rose, Gillian. *The Melancholy Science.* New York: Columbia University Press, 1978.

Rose, Paul Lawrence. *Wagner: Race and Revolution.* New Haven and London: Yale University Press, 1992.

Sauerland, Karol. *Einführung in die Ästhetik Adornos.* Berlin: de Gruyter, 1979.

Sax, Benjamin. "Foucault, Nietzsche, History: Two Modes of the Genealogical Method." *History of European Ideas* 11 (1989): 769–80.

Scheler, Max. *Ressentiment.* Trans. William W. Holdheim. Ed. Lewis A. Coser. New York: Free Press of Glencoe, 1961.

Schlüpmann, Heide. *Friedrich Nietzsches ästhetische Opposition.* Stuttgart: Metzler, 1977.

——. "Zur Frage der Nietzsche-Rezeption in der Frauenbewegung gestern und heute." *Nietzsche heute: die Rezeption seines Werkes nach 1968.* Ed. Sigrid Bauschinger, Susan Cocalis, and Sara Lennox. Bern and Stuttgart: Franke Verlag, 1988. 176–83.

Schmid Noerr, Gunzelin. "Unterirdische Geschichte und Gegenwart in der *Dialektik der Aufklärung.*" *Die Aktualität der 'Dialektik der Aufklärung.'* Ed. Harry Kunneman and Hent de Vries. Frankfurt, New York: Campus Verlag, 1989. 67–87.

Schmidt, Gerhard. "Nietzsches Bildungskritik." *Zur Aktualität Nietzsches.* Ed. M. Djuric and Josef Simon. Würzburg, Germany: Königshausen & Neumann, 1984. 3–13.

——. "Nietzsche und Sokrates." *Nietzsche kontrovers.* Vol. 4. Ed. R. Berlinger and Wiebke Schrader. Würzburg, Germany: Königshausen & Neumann, 1984. 7–33.

Schmucker, Joseph F. *Adorno—Logik des Zerfalls.* Stuttgart: Frommann-Holzboog, 1977.

Schnädelbach, Herbert. "Die Aktualität der Dialektik der Aufklärung." *Die Aktualität der 'Dialektik der Aufklärung.'* Ed. Harry Kunneman and Hent de Vries. Frankfurt: Campus Verlag, 1989. 15–35.

Seel, Martin. "Plädoyer für die zweite Moderne." *Die Aktualität der 'Dialektik der Aufklärung.'* Ed. Harry Kunneman and Hent de Vries. Frankfurt, New York: Campus Verlag, 1989. 36–66.

Shapiro, Gary. *Nietzschean Narratives.* Bloomington: Indiana University Press, 1989.

——. "Translating, Repeating, Naming: Foucault, Derrida, and *The Genealogy of Morals.*" *Nietzsche as Postmodernist.* Ed. Clayton Koelb. Albany: State University of New York Press, 1990. 37–56.

Singer, Linda. "Nietzschean Mythologies: The Inversion of Value and the War against Women." *Soundings* 66.3 (Fall 1983): 281–95.

Stein, Leon. *The Racial Thinking of Richard Wagner.* New York: Philosophical Library, 1950.

Strong, Tracy B. *Friedrich Nietzsche and the Politics of Transfiguration.* Berkeley: University of California Press, 1988.

Sünner, Rüdiger. *Ästhetische Szientismuskritik: Zum Verhältnis von Kunst und Wissenschaft bei Nietzsche und Adorno.* Frankfurt: Lang Verlag, 1986.

Taureck, Berhard H. F. *Nietzsche und der Faschismus.* Hamburg: Junius, 1989.

Taylor, Ronald, ed. *Aesthetics and Politics.* London: New Left Books, 1977.

Theweleit, Klaus. *Male Fantasies.* 2 vols. Trans. Erica Carter and Chris Turner in collaboration with Stephen Conway. Minneapolis: University of Minnesota Press, 1989.

Thysen, Anke. *Negative Dialektik und Erfahrung: Zur Rationalität des Nichtidentischen bei Adorno.* Frankfurt: Suhrkamp, 1989.

Wagner, Gottfried. *Wer nicht mit dem Wolf heult: Autobiographische Aufzeichnungen eines Wagner-Urenkels.* Cologne: Kiepenheuer & Witsch, 1997.

Wapnewski, Peter. "Nietzsche und Wagner Stationen einer Beziehung." *Nietsche-Studien* 18 (1989): 401–23.

Weineck, Silke-Maria Weineck. "Loss of Outline: Decadence as the Crisis of Negation." *Pacific Coast Philology* 29.1 (September 1994): 37–50.

Weiner, Marc A. "Editor's Column." *German Quarterly* 69.5 (Fall 1996): v–ix.

———. *Richard Wagner and the Anti-Semitic Imagination.* Lincoln and London: University of Nebraska Press, 1995.

Wellmer, Albrecht. "Wahrheit, Schein, Versöhnung. Adornos ästhetische Rettung der Modernität." *Adorno Konferenz 1983.* Ed. Ludwig von Friedeburg und Jürgen Habermas. Frankfurt: Suhrkamp, 1983. 138–76.

———. *Zur Dialektik von Moderne und Postmoderne.* Frankfurt: Suhrkamp, 1985.

Werner, Renate. "'Cultur der Oberfläche'. Zur Rezeption der Artistenmetaphysik im frühen Werk Heinrich und Thomas Manns." *Nietzsche und die deutsche Literatur.* Vol. 2. Ed. Bruno Hillebrand. Tübingen: Niemeyer Verlag, 1978. 82–127.

White, Alan. *Within Nietzsche's Labyrinth.* New York & London: Routledge, 1990.

Widdig, Bernd. *Männerbünde und Massen: Zur Krise männlicher Identität in der Literatur der Moderne.* Opladen, Germany: Westdeutscher Verlag, 1992.

Wiggershaus, Rolf. *Die Frankfurter Schule.* Munich: Deutscher Taschenbuch Verlag, 1988.

———. *Theodor W. Adorno.* Munich: Verlag C. H. Beck, 1987.

Wilke, Sabine. "'Torn Halves of an Integral Freedom': Adorno's and Benjamin's Reading of Mass Culture." *The Aesthetics of the Critical Theorists.* Lewiston, N.Y.: Edwin Mellen Press, 1990. 124–51.

———. *Zur Dialektik von Exposition und Darstellung: Ansätze zu einer Kritik der Arbeiten Martin Heideggers, Theodor W. Adornos und Jacques Derrida.* New York: Peter Lang, 1988.

Zelinsky, Hartmut. *Richard Wagner: ein deutsches Thema: eine Dokumentation zur Wirkungsgeschichte Richard Wagners 1876–1976.* Frankfurt: Zweitausendeins, 1976.

Zenck, Martin. *Kunst als begriffslose Erkenntnis.* Munich: Fink Verlag, 1977.

Zuidervaart, Lambert. *Adorno's Aesthetic Theory: The Redemption of Illusion.* Cambridge, Mass.: MIT Press, 1991.

Zumbini, Massimo Ferrari. "Nietzsche in Bayreuth: Nietzsches Herausforderung, die Wagnerianer und die Gegenoffensive." *Nietzsche-Studien* 19 (1990): 246–91.

INDEX

Adorno, Gretel, 3, 240 n114
Adorno, Theodor, *Aesthetic Theory*, 16,
80, 139, 140, 156, 194, 212; "Aus Sils
Maria," 6; "Education after
Auschwitz," 176; *Eingriffe*, 204; *Essay
as Form*, 5, 191, 192, 195, 197, 203;
"Odysseus or Myth and
Enlightenment," 39, 47, 67, 69, 70;
"Excursus II," 5, 69; *Hegel: Three
Studies*, 89; *In Search of Wagner*, 117,
135, 136, 152, 153, 156, 157, 159,
168, 199; *Introduction to the Sociology
of Music*, 148; *Jargon of Authenticity*,
10; "Juliette or Enightenment and
Morality," 3; *Kierkegaard*, 11;
"Melancholy Science," 15; *Minima
Moralia*, 3, 5, 29, 96, 98, 105, 136,
138, 150, 165, 166, 191, 204, 216,
220; "Nachschrift zu einer Wagner-
Diskussion," 152, 158, 159; *Negative
Dialectics*, 79, 135, 138, 197, 212;
Notes to Literature, 103, 141; "Notiz

über Wagner," 151, 152, 153; "On the
Fetish Character in Music and the
Regression of Listening," 148;
Philosophy of Modern Music, 142;
Prisms, 199; "A Portrait of Walter
Benjamin," 86; *Stichworte*, 80;
"Theory of Pseudo-Education," 175;
"Theses on the Language of the
Philosophyer," 195, 196; Adornos'
review of *Wagner, Nietzsche, and
Hitler*, 154; "Wagners Aktualität," 152,
153; "Wagner und Bayreuth," 152;
Adorno's canon of modern art, 103,
143; Adorno's musical canon, 143;
Contradictions, 4; critique of
Nietzsche, 98; in search of Wagner,
151–171; integrity of, 57
Adorno/Horkheimer, *Dialectic of
Enlightenment*, 2, 5, 6, 12, 14, 15, 18,
23, 25, 26, 28, 29, 31, 31, 32, 34, 35,
36, 39, 40, 41, 42, 43, 47, 49, 50, 54,
58, 66, 67, 68, 69, 77, 78, 98, 105,

self-criticism, 15, 26
self-destruction, 52, 70, 134
self-legitimation, 88
self-negation, 72, 76
self-preservation, 12, 26, 30, 34, 68, 70,
71, 72, 73, 76, 88, 89, 90, 96, 112,
201, 215; in Bildung, 181
self-renunciation, 71
self-sacrifice, 101, 112
Shapiro, Gary, 59, 60, 206
Sils, Maria, 6, 7, 8
siren, 74, 75, 76
socialism, failure of, 9
Socrates, 29, 46, 47, 52, 54, 122, 126,
127, 128, 183, 215; as archetype of
theoretical man, 44, 45
Socratism, 5, 43–47, 126, 129, 209
Spengler, Oswald, 224 n9
Stalinism, 43
Stirner, Max, 108
Stravinsky, Igor, 143
Stücker, Helene, 108
style, 5, 18, 67, 68, 126, 135; Adorno's,
19, 97, 190; and affirmation, 203; and
art, 190; and criticism, 191, 192–212,
217; and ideology, 211; and method,
191; and music, 160; and philosophy,
20, 195, 200, 211; as performance,
191; and power, 198; and truth, 193,
198, 210; and women, 104, 105, 107;
clarity of, 198; narcissism, 190;
Nietzsche's, 19, 104, 105, 107, 191;
politics of 191
subjectivity, 11, 69, 70, 170, 202, 215
Sünner, Rüdiger, 16
symptomatology, 54, 55; of morality, 69
systems, 90, 92, 93, 139, 200; antisystematic, 50, 62, 201, 205, 208; critique of,
10, 12, 14, 15, 27, 89, 96, 170, 199,
218; language of, 91; of thought, 89;
philosophical, 90, 216; rejection of, 5,
42

Taylor, Charles, 21
teleology, 5, 23
theatre, gendering of, 114, 115
theoretical type, 44, 45, 47

theory, aestheticization of, 194
Theweleit, Klaus, 113
Thysen, Anke, 87
Tillich, Paul, 11
totalitarianism, 30, 135, 137; antitotalitarian, 50, 67, 68, 79, 210; antitotalitarian-
ism in style, 199; critique of, 12; in
Wagner, 19; totalitarian ideologies and
Wagner, 163, 164
totality, 199, 200, 210; critique of, 197; in
Wagner, 163, 164, 165, 166
truth, 62, 80, 94, 95, 96, 97, 102, 193,
195, 208, 209, 210, 222; absolute
claims to, 92; and concepts, 92; and
error, 41, 45, 92, 95, 96, 201; and
illusion, 80, 94; and ideology, 93,
205; and language, 92; and legitimation, 92–97, 101, 103; and untruth,
41, 201, 209; and woman, 103, 104;
as relational phenomenon, 84; claims
to, 24, 33, 35, 47, 51, 57, 58, 61, 63,
97, 145; construction of, 214; correspondence theory, 92; consensus, 94;
desire for, 13, 14, 41, 44; discovery
of, 95, 96; historical nature of, 86,
87, 92; historicity of, 49, 93, 201,
210; in art, 143, 150; life-affirming,
95; positivistic claims to, 87; self-
destruction of, 93, 94; truthfulness,
57; truths, 93, 94, 193; will to, 46,
95, 96; wisdom, 207

Übermensch, 11, 16, 27, 155, 156, 178,
220
universal context of delusion, 204, 214,
220
utopian thought, 14, 23, 25, 27, 38; rejection, of 5, 42

values, 12, 13, 14, 26, 34, 57, 95, 209; as
interpretation, 77; functions of, 18, 52,
217; origins of, 55, 56; reevaluation of,
50, 54; spheres of, 35, 36, 38, 58
Verblendungszusammenhang, 80; *see also*
universal context of delusion; bourgeois context of delusion
Vogel, Martin, 183